MAGDA NACHMAN
AN ARTIST
IN EXILE

MODERN

BIOGRAPHIES

MAGDA NACHMAN
AN ARTIST
IN EXILE

———

LINA BERNSTEIN

BOSTON
2020

Library of Congress Cataloging-in-Publication Data

Names: Bernstein, Lina, 1949- author.
Title: Magda Nachman : an artist in exile / Lina Bernstein.
Description: Boston : Academic Studies Press, 2020. | Series: Modern biographies | Includes bibliographical references.
Identifiers: LCCN 2020000573 (print) | LCCN 2020000574 (ebook) | ISBN 9781644692677 (hardback) | ISBN 9781644692684 (paperback) | ISBN 9781644692691 (adobe pdf)
Subjects: LCSH: Nachman, Magda, 1889-1951. | Artists--Russia--Biography. | Expatriate artists--India--Biography.
Classification: LCC N6999.N23 B47 2020 (print) | LCC N6999.N23 (ebook) | DDC 709.2 [B]--dc23

LC record available at https://lccn.loc.gov/2020000573
LC ebook record available at https://lccn.loc.gov/2020000574

ISBN 9781644692974 hardback
ISBN 9781644692981 paperback
ISBN 9781644692998 ebook PDF
ISBN 9781644693001 ePub

Cover design by Ivan Grave
Book design by PHi Business Solutions Ltd.

Published by Academic Studies Press
1577 Beacon Street
Brookline, MA 02446, USA

press@academicstudiespress.com
www.academicstudiespress.com

For David

Contents

Illustrations

Acknowledgments

Throughout my research adventures and writing, I have been helped by a number of individuals and organizations. I am eternally grateful to Viktoria Schweitzer for presenting me with her transcriptions of Magda Nachman's and Julia Obolenskaya's letters and for telling me that one could not read those two young women's correspondence without wanting to know more about them.

It is also a pleasure to thank my group of fellow biographers, who read and commented on my manuscript in its various iterations, providing constructive criticism and warm encouragement: Mary Dearborn, Eric Laursen, David Perkins, and Mary and Robert Bagg. I wish also to thank two other enthusiastic readers, Annette Aronowicz and Alla Zeide.

I am grateful to Larisa Alekseeva—author of *Tsvet vinograda*, a book about Julia Obolenskaya and Konstantin Kandaurov—for many interesting conversations about our protagonists and for introducing me to the collections of the State Literary Museum in Moscow.

Lyudmila Maksimovskaya took me to Ust-Dolyssy, one of Magda Nachman's places of refuge during the Russian Civil War, and supplied me with copies of the newspaper *Molot*.

I am grateful to Ole Birk Laursen for generously sharing with me his knowledge of anarchist archival depositories and supplying me with some important archival documents.

Magda's extended family—in Sweden, England, Wales, Switzerland, and Russia, from Moscow to Siberia—generously shared with me their reminiscences, family correspondence, artworks by Magda, and photographs, without which the story of their great aunt Magda Nachman would have been even more incomplete than it unfortunately is. In particular, I would like to thank Theo Lehner, Sophie Seifalian, Margret Price, Natalia Mikaberidze, Oksana Selivanova, and Aleksei Knorre.

I thank Primavera Boman-Behram for permission to work in and make use of written and photographic documents from the Hilder Holger archive.

Margit Franz shared with me her knowledge of the interwar culture of Bombay and its European refugees.

I thank Kenneth Robbins, a connoisseur of Indian culture, for introducing me to Carmel Berkson, a remarkable individual and sculptor who lived in Mumbai for forty years and who in turn put me in touch with Carmen Kagal, through whom I met several museum curators in Mumbai and some owners of portraits by Magda Nachman.

Jeroo Chavda, daughter of the artist and Magda's friend Shiavax Chavda, was my faithful *cicerone* at art shows and around Mumbai.

A number of generous owners of Magda's artworks in India shared their reminiscences with me and allowed me to photograph paintings belonging to them: Shireen Sabavala, Hira and Adrean Steven, Saryu Doshi, Roshan Cooper, Maya and Ayesha Malhotra, Shared Patel, and Darryl and Brian D'Monte. I am also grateful to other owners of Magda's artworks from around the world who found me on the internet and sent me reproductions of pictures belonging to them: Jacqueline Hale (USA), Noam Mualem Yosef (Israel), John Burns (UK), and Ann Woodhall and Louis Price (UK).

I am grateful to Franklin & Marshall College for travel grants supporting my research in Russia and India. And I offer thanks to Oindrila Raychaudhuri, the archivist of Mumbai's Tata Institute of Fundamental Research.

At Academic Studies Press, Angela Brintlinger has been an exacting and inspiring editor, and Ekaterina Yanduganova has been unstinting in her encouragement.

I am especially thankful to my dear friend and colleague Lena Nekludova, who accompanied me on my journey to Ust-Dolyssy and coauthored three papers with me related to this biography. She was also my constant sounding board, improving my writing with her probing questions and sharp ear for wrong notes.

I owe the biggest debt of all to David Kramer—my most discerning reader, harshest and most unsparing critic, unfailing supporter—who made the crooked straight and the rough places plain. To him this book is dedicated.

Preface

I know that my account of Magda Nachman's life will be patchy. There are many gaps in the record. When Czesław Miłosz tells us, "Obviously, all biographies are false," he reminds us that in our choice of what to include and what to leave out, in what is known and what is unknown, in what we choose to emphasize, never mind how we choose to interpret, we fail to achieve the whole truth. Miłosz goes on to say that "the value of biographies, then, is solely that they allow one to re-create the era in which a given life was lived." Solely? That is surely not always the case. The subjects of some biographies tower above their time. However, in the case of Magda Nachman, I cannot but agree all too heartily with Miłosz. A reticent, quiet, sensitive character, she seldom appears in the center of events that were raging about her, and it is precisely that absence from the limelight that makes her a fitting subject around which to re-create the era in which she lived. Evidence of her participation in the fateful developments of her time survives in letters, official documents, and a few paintings. But even those meager surviving traces of her life harbor a vivid testimony, an imprint on her epoch.

The project of writing the life of Magda Nachman came to me by happenstance. It was the gift of my friend and colleague Viktoria Schweitzer, who, while collecting archival material for her book on the great Russian poet Marina Tsvetaeva, gathered documents from cross-referenced archival folders—just in case, you never know—for some possible future use. Viktoria was among the first scholars engaged in Tsvetaeva's resurrection. And while resurrecting the poet, she resurrected the poet's milieu—her friends, relatives, acquaintances, and chance personages who had been pulled into her orbit. Magda Nachman is one of those personages; she moved on the periphery of Tsvetaeva's world, yet Magda's name is indissolubly linked to that of the great Russian poet by her well-known oil portrait of Tsvetaeva. Magda painted it in 1913 at the Crimean dacha of the poet Maximilian Voloshin, into which—as luck would have it—Magda and her friend the artist Julia Obolenskaya had wandered in search of a place to spend the summer.

Viktoria transcribed a correspondence between Magda and Julia covering the years of the artists' apprenticeship and the beginning of their professional lives. This period, from 1908 to 1921, coincided with World War I, the two Russian Revolutions, and the Russian Civil War. There was no reason to include more than a few excerpts from those letters in the book on Tsvetaeva that Viktoria was writing. That book was published in 1988, and the correspondence was filed away for a future project. In 2010, realizing that she would not have time for the book she had envisioned on the artistic and literary circle of Koktebel, Viktoria suggested that I might be interested in taking it on. She gave me her transcripts and threw in a copy of a talk given in the 1920s by Julia Obolenskaya in memory of her teacher Léon Bakst, who taught both Julia and Magda at the Zvantseva Art Academy, which flourished in St. Petersburg from 1906 until the 1917 revolution.[1]

This book is in part a tribute to the vision and courage of Julia Obolenskaya, Magda's closest friend and chief correspondent, who saved hundreds of letters written to her and also her own letters, many of them returned to her for safekeeping by her correspondents as they were leaving Russia. Through the time of the revolutions and the Russian Civil War, Bakst's students from the Zvantseva Art Academy, scattered all over the country, continued to correspond with one another. These young men and women bore witness in their letters to the historical events that swirled around them. When the dust settled in the late 1920s and the Soviet regime had firmly established itself, many of the letters that Obolenskaya had saved would have been considered incriminating simply because they offered an objective description of recent events. For this reason, personal statements describing those years are rare, for in the 1930s, the consequences of such material being discovered by the secret police—whether under the name GPU, OGPU, GUGB, or NKVD—were severe. Julia exercised a certain degree of self-preservation by blacking out a line here or discarding half a page there, but for the most part, she preserved her correspondence as it had been written. (She likely destroyed all letters arriving from émigrés: in the archival collection there are no letters that she received from her friends abroad, although there is internal evidence that such letters had indeed been received.)

Some of the letters that Julia saved were written by important cultural figures, such as the poets Maximilian Voloshin and Vladislav Khodasevich,

---

1   Since then, Obolenskaya's talk has been published. See Iuliia Obolenskaia, "V shkole Zvantsovoi pod rukovodstvom L. Baksta i M. Dobuzhinskogo" (edited and with a commentary by Lina Bernstein and Elena Nekludova), *Toronto Slavic Quarterly* 37 (2011): 209–242.

while other letters and diary entries provide descriptions of such individuals. But many of Julia's correspondents were simply her school friends, summer acquaintances, and relatives. The preservation of such cultural artifacts in the face of destructive political forces had become for her a moral imperative.

Before she was evacuated from Moscow at the beginning of World War II, Julia gathered the most valuable letters, sewed them into a large canvas sack, and deposited them at the Tretyakov Gallery. The remainder—hundreds of letters, several notebooks containing diaries, pictures, and photographs—were left in her room of the communal apartment and were salvaged after her death in 1945 and deposited in the State Literature Museum, where they were stored in a closet for many years, of interest to no one and in danger of being eaten by mice or thrown out with the trash. Their survival is a tribute to Obolenskaya and to the devoted archivists who recognized their value and preserved them. Thanks to the almost miraculous survival of this treasure, we have a small window into how some private lives were affected by momentous events.

When I received Viktoria's transcripts of the Nachman–Obolenskaya correspondence, I understood that sooner or later, I would be traveling to Russian archives to verify all the letters and collect more material. I would also have to visit the places from which the letters were written: St. Petersburg, Julia's and Magda's birthplace; Moscow, where they both lived and worked; villages in the Russian countryside, to which Magda had fled during the civil war; and of course Koktebel, on the Crimean peninsula, which was the center of the literary and artistic circle that Viktoria had been planning to write about.

But before even thinking about traveling, I thought I would see what I could find on the internet from the comfort of home. The search words "Magda Nachman" predictably yielded many web pages related to Marina Tsvetaeva, all of which repeated the same two pieces of information: The first was the association of Magda's name with her portrait of Tsvetaeva. The second, which I will discuss later, was what Magda Nachman wrote to Julia Obolenskaya on the death of Tsvetaeva's daughter Irina, words much quoted and discussed, sometimes with opprobrium against Magda.

But there was more. I learned that in 1933, Magda painted a portrait of Vladimir Nabokov, apparently now lost, a surviving photograph of which appears on the dust jacket of *Glory*, the 1971 translation of Nabokov's novel *Podvig*, published in Paris in 1932. In 1933, the year of the portrait, Nabokov was living in Berlin. Where, when, how did Magda meet Nabokov? Viktoria had heard from someone who had known someone who had heard from someone else that at some point, Magda had left Russia for Berlin. Magda Nachman was not Viktoria's main research subject, and she did not pursue the snippets of information about Magda coming her way. Nabokov's portrait suggested that by 1933, Magda had left Russia and had arrived—settled?—in Berlin. When did she leave and under what circumstances?

The mountain of questions grew with each new discovery. Another snippet recalled by Viktoria had to do with Magda marrying an Indian national called Acharya who had come to Russia to take part in the Second or Third Congress of the Third Communist International. That Magda had indeed married the prominent Indian nationalist Mandayam Parthasarathi Tirumal (M. P. T.) Acharya I inferred from reading on the internet that Acharya had left Russia in 1922 "with his Russian wife." I read as well that Acharya had died in Bombay. So Berlin or no Berlin, Magda seems to have married Acharya, left Russia, and perhaps at some point emigrated with him to India. Thinking I might be able to find evidence of Magda in India through possible connections with other European refugees in India, I asked an Indian colleague whether she knew of any such refugees during the 1930s and 1940s. She mentioned the renowned Viennese expressionist dancer Hilde Holger, who had fled to Bombay in 1939.

Hilde Holger became a name to conjure with. She would lead me to London and Bombay. I would learn that Hilde had settled in Bombay in 1939 and that Magda Nachman, who had arrived there a few years earlier, had become her close friend and collaborator.

Thus it was that from my internet portal I was hearing tidings of Magda from Russia, Germany, and India. It appeared that she had had the misfortune to occupy a front-row seat at the Russian Revolution and Civil War, the rise of Nazism, and the bloody strife surrounding Indian independence. I was impressed that Magda, driven by fate across the globe, had held fast to her artistic ideals, becoming by the end of her life an admired and respected artist. Yet after her death, she vanished almost without a trace. What a life! Where did it all go? What can be reconstructed? What resurrected?

I knew then that I would be writing not a study of the Koktebel literary circle, but a biography of the artist Magda Nachman. I began contacting archives, museums, and newspaper depositories that might have more information on Magda's origins, whereabouts, and works in Russia and Western Europe. I also decided to look into the India connection. A bit of googling showed me that Magda's husband, Acharya, is a fairly well known figure in Indian history. He even has a Wikipedia page, though it gives a rather meager biographical sketch. I read that little was known about his life after 1922—that would be about when he and Magda left Russia—but that he arrived in Bombay, perhaps in 1935, perhaps in 1948. Could I trace Magda to India? Acharya ended up in India, but I could not find any mention of Magda in connection with him.

The only other name I had to work with, Hilde Holger, produced plenty of hits: encyclopedia articles, biographies, and an "official website." At the Hilde Holger home page, I opened the menu item "Archive | Art Collection" and typed "Magda Nachman" into the search box. Lo and behold! a drawing materialized labeled "Bombay–Hilde by Magda Nachman" (figure 1).

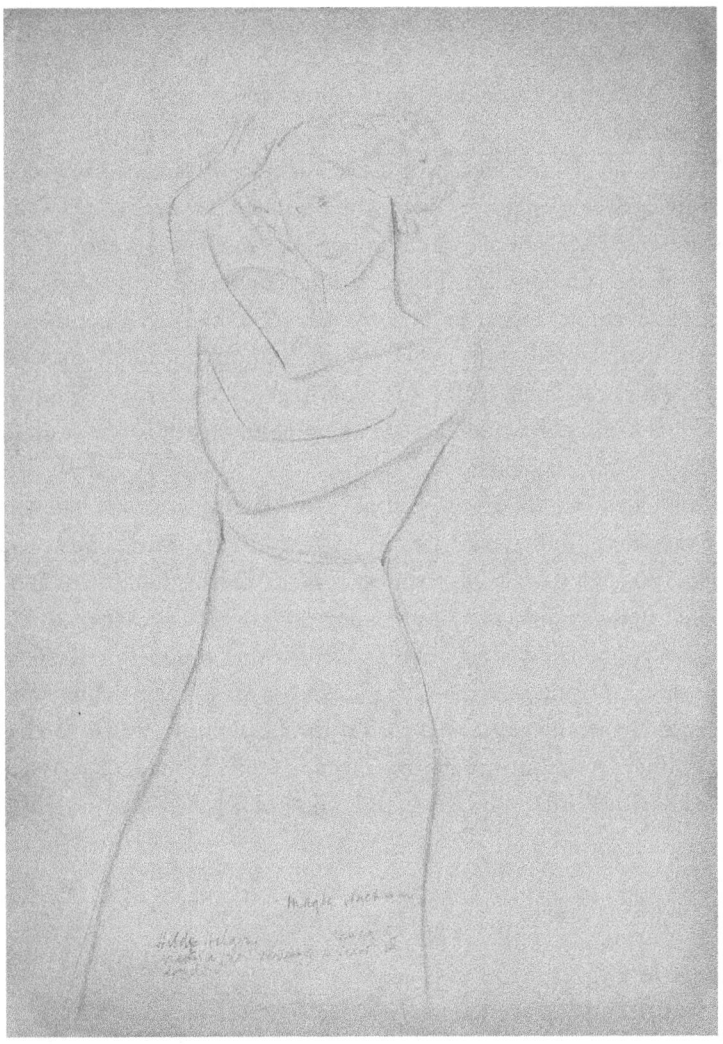

Figure 1. Magda Nachman. *Hilde Holger* (*Hilde Holger Archive © 2001 Primavera Boman-Behram*).

I gazed on the image with wild surmise. Then I wrote to the "contact" address on the website, and received a reply from the keeper of the archive, who turned out to be none other than Hilde Holger's daughter, Primavera Boman-Behram. Prim, as I was soon calling her, lived in London, whither her mother had immigrated in 1948 with her husband, the well-known homeo-pathic physician Ardeshir Kavasji Boman-Behram, whom she had married in 1940. Prim's archive, which resides in her London townhouse, richly docu-ments her mother's professional life, including her Indian years. Prim sent me scans of numerous documents pertaining to that period, and Magda's name appeared frequently. I now knew for certain that Magda had emigrated from Berlin to Bombay, and I could see that I would sooner or later be going to India in search of her.

Magda's flight from Berlin to India was also confirmed somewhat later by her great-niece, Sophie Seifalian, who also lives in London. She found me on the internet in the course of genealogical research on her family, for I had given some talks and published some articles connected with Magda, and our names had begun to appear in tandem. When Sophie's letter appeared in my "inbox," my first impulse was to hop on the next plane for London. On more sober reflection, I telephoned. I was soon treated to a cache of family photo-graphs, oral history, documents—including obituaries of Magda from Indian newspapers—and an invitation to visit.

Sophie's cousin Theo, who had been the family historian, had collected quite a number of Indian publications on Magda. He sent me copies of a por-tion of his collection of letters and photographs, hastily duplicated. Tragically, Theo died that summer, and I now unfortunately have no access to his fam-ily archive. Nonetheless, from Prim and from other relatives of Magda's I had learned much. I could now map Magda Nachman's life and thereby my book devoted to it. I would retrace Magda's path of exile from Russia to Germany and from there to India. I now knew that sometime in the 1930s, Magda had followed her husband to Bombay. And I followed her there.

CHAPTER 1

The Great Little Lady of the Bombay Art World

Magda Nachman died on February 12, 1951, at the age of sixty-one, in Bombay. Here is a portion of an obituary that appeared in a Bombay newspaper two days later:

> Fate struck a cruel blow to the art world on Monday last. The large gathering of artists and art-lovers, who had thronged the hall of the Institute of Foreign Languages to witness the opening of the exhibition of the paintings of the versatile artist Magda Nachman, were in for a melancholy surprise. Magda Nachman, it was announced, had passed away a few hours before the opening of the exhibition.[1]

From this obituary, published in the Bombay *Free Press Bulletin*, and others carried by many Indian newspapers, one may infer that Magda Nachman had achieved considerable acclaim, respect, and love from Bombay artists, the museum-going public, and many friends in whose reminiscences she comes alive as a warm, modest, and sensitive person. One of the obituaries called her "the great little lady of the Bombay art world." The journal *Aesthetics* devoted half of its January–March 1951 issue to articles on Magda solicited from several Indians and Europeans living in Bombay. The writers included the editor of the journal, R. C. Gupta; the dancer Hilde Holger; the lama Anagarika Govinda; the artist Li Gotami; a correspondent of the *Jewish Advocate*, Miss H. Kohn; the Czech writer in India Vilem Haas; the art critic Hermann Goetz; the British cultural affairs officer Wayne M. Hartwell; Major C. E. Dust; Mrs. Gertrude Murray Correa; and the writer Irene Pohrille.[2] In a private letter to Hilde

---

1 *Free Press Bulletin*, February 14, 1951.
2 *Aesthetics* 5, no. 1 (1951): 2–18. This journal, published by the Bombay Youths' Art and Culture Circle, promoted modern Indian artists and published illustrated essays on the newest developments in world art. Within the same covers one could find pictures by M. F. Hussain,

Holger, Charles Petras, an expatriate Austro-Hungarian journalist and founder of the Institute of Foreign Languages (IFL) in Bombay, a meeting place for the cultures of India and the West,[3] informed his friend of Magda's death:

> Please read now the other side of this letter and don't be shocked. ... On 12.2.51 Magda Nachman died two hours before the opening of her exhibition at the IFL in Bombay, so that Oscar Brown[4] had to open it as a Memorial Exhibition. Over 500 people came & within an hour they sold paintings for 6000.—The newspapers were carrying headlines about her & it. It is said that Bombay had never seen as brilliant a gathering as the one that night. Yes, a bit late ... isn't it?

A bit late indeed. Magda had spent all her adult artistic life on the run, facing hunger, poverty, and obscurity. In India, her last refuge, she became a successful artist and a mentor to a group of young modern painters.

She had been hospitalized a month before the opening of the exhibition, which had been organized by her friends to raise money for her medical care. St. George's Hospital, where she died, was a public hospital for the poor, with overcrowded rooms, dirt, and stench. Still, Magda likely received better treatment than other inmates because she was "white," a decided advantage in 1951, when the British had only recently left.

India! What an unlikely place for a girl from St. Petersburg to end up. It is easy to imagine Russian émigrés after the 1917 Revolution and the Civil War fleeing to Constantinople, Prague, Riga, Berlin, and Paris; or European Jews escaping to Palestine, South America, or the United States. But India was an uncommon destination for those pushed around by the events of that time. Fearing professional competition and social burden, the British were notoriously stingy with their visas, and the few that they issued went generally to the young and capable. British policy restricted entry into India even by persons

---

Jamini Roy, and K. H. Ara, and works by Picasso, Braque, and Matisse as well as works by Chinese and Japanese artists.

3   In 1946, Petras opened an international center, called the Institute of Foreign Languages, in Bombay, which he later expanded to New Delhi (1950). He arranged performances, cultural radio programs, and exhibitions, which included Magda's solo shows, two of which were posthumous: one in Bombay in 1951 (mentioned above), and one in Delhi the following year. Petras promoted Indian modern art and exhibited many contemporary up-and-coming Indian artists (for example, S. H. Raza).

4   Oscar Brown was the chief presidency magistrate of Bombay.

who were not found politically undesirable and whose friends or relatives already in India were ready to render support. The numbers are chilling: from January 1938 to February 1939, the government of India, having decided that not more than 150 foreigners would be allowed to compete for employment in India, issued 269 entry visas to Jewish refugees, among them 128 women and sixteen children.[5] Petras, Holger, and Nachman were among the lucky few. Others included the Czech editor, screenwriter, and avant-garde film critic Willy Haas and his friend the composer and musicologist Walter Kaufmann, like Haas also from Bohemia, who in 1936 created the signature tune for All-India Radio. Several Austrian artists and art collectors made it to Bombay and subsequently became a major force in promoting and supporting Indian modern art.

≋ ≋ ≋

I flew to Mumbai at the end of January 2014, arriving late at night. A driver from the Kings International Hotel, a smallish man, strong and assured in his movements, met me at the airport. Carrying my suitcase, he walked ahead of me toward the car, turning his head every few seconds to keep an eye on me, repeating "Come, come"—a mantra that soon became familiar to me as the standard call of a guide to his charge as he leads you through a crowd, or when you are crossing a road together, or when he is just taking you somewhere: "Come, come."

I wanted to see Mumbai as the Bombay it was in Magda's time, 1936 to 1951. The city's population explosion came later. In the mid 1930s, a building boom turned the city into a huge construction site that saw the erection of modern Art Deco buildings on land reclaimed from the Arabian Sea. And because there were few zoning regulations, the city became a hodgepodge of the spacious and elegant alongside congestion, filth, and squalor.

Poverty, but not destitution, must have been familiar to Magda. Bazaars, workers' quarters, and the city streets on which tradesmen hawked their wares offered her the models for the city's poor who populate her works. In her time, the city must have been a much friendlier place than it appeared to me in 2014, without the incessant honking and enveloping pollution from the endlessly congested traffic. There were instead light horse-drawn carriages, private and for hire, along with omnibuses and rattling trams. And there was interesting

---

5   See Joachim Oesterheld, "British Policy towards German-Speaking Emigrants in India, 1939–1945," in *Jewish Exile in India, 1933–1945,* ed. Anil Bhatti and Johannes H. Voigt (New Delhi: MANOHAR in association with Max Mueller Bhavan, 1999), 26.

architecture: earlier colonial Gothic Revival and newly erected Art Deco apartment and office buildings, and palatial movie theaters, all enfolding sunny spots of greenery.

I had come here to walk by Magda's side, and those walks began on my first morning in Mumbai.

That first night, as we pulled into the courtyard of the Kings International Hotel, I did not know that the ocean was near. I did not see it, nor did I smell it. But when I looked out my window in the morning, I saw the ocean sprawled before me in all its gray glory. I went out, and as I was crossing the sand, I met two small children, who bravely came up to me, said, "Good morning," and shook hands, their chaperone, apparently a proud father, encouraging them to speak English. He told me that the beach was called Juhu. The name pierced my heart, for I had learned from Primavera that Hilde Holger had danced here, on this very spot, in the 1940s, in a dress designed by Magda. And it was here that Hilde took her dance students, here that magnificent pictures of her choreography had been taken (figures 2 and 3).

The beach lay in front of me, beautiful and relatively clean, a light mist hovering above the water. Just a few people were strolling or jogging along the

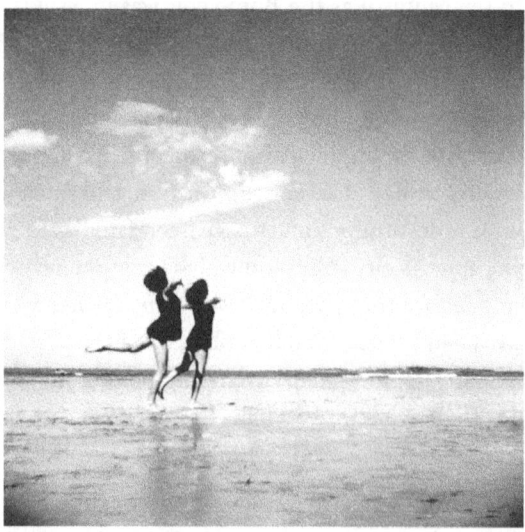

Figure 2. Students of Hilde Holger on Juhu beach (*Hilde Holger Archive © 2001 Primavera Boman-Behram*).

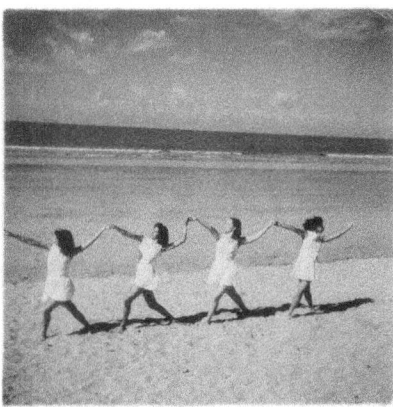

Figure 3. Students of Hilde Holger dancing on Juhu beach (*Hilde Holger Archive © 2001 Primavera Boman-Behram, London, UK*).

shore at this early hour. Some braved the murky water. A beggar went from group to group pointing to his mouth. Beach photographers looking for customers were already at work. As I walked along, vivid images of girls and young women dancing at the water's edge arose before my eyes, for this is where I had seen Hilde Holger and her pupils in old photographs.

I would later learn that farther south, closer to Hilde's dance school and home, the waterfront lacked the expanse and sense of freedom offered by Juhu beach.

Hilde became Magda's intimate friend. Born Hilde Sofer in 1905 into a Jewish family in Vienna, she had pursued a successful career as an expressionist dancer under the stage name Hilde Holger. In 1926, she opened the New School for Movement Arts, which became one of the most important dance academies in Vienna. All this came to an end in March 1938, when Austria was annexed to Germany. As a Jew, she was henceforth forbidden to perform or teach. Hilde assumed that by the end of the summer, she would be able to resume her artistic activities. Yet the situation became only worse. A friend convinced her to flee, and on June 6, 1939, he put her on a train out of Vienna, having booked a berth for her on a ship headed for Bombay. Her family perished in the Holocaust.

Viennese-born Hilde and Russian-born Magda, dancer and painter, assimilated Jew and half-Jewish Lutheran, became collaborators in Bombay. Magda had been bilingual since childhood: Russian and German were spoken at home, and she had studied French and English at school and was fluent in both. Later, she added Italian. I suppose that they spoke German together. In 1941, Hilde opened a dance studio in Bombay, which she called *School for Art and Modern Movement*. Magda designed costumes and stage sets for Hilde's productions, painted portraits of Hilde and her little daughter, Primavera, and made many sketches of Hilde's young student-dancers.

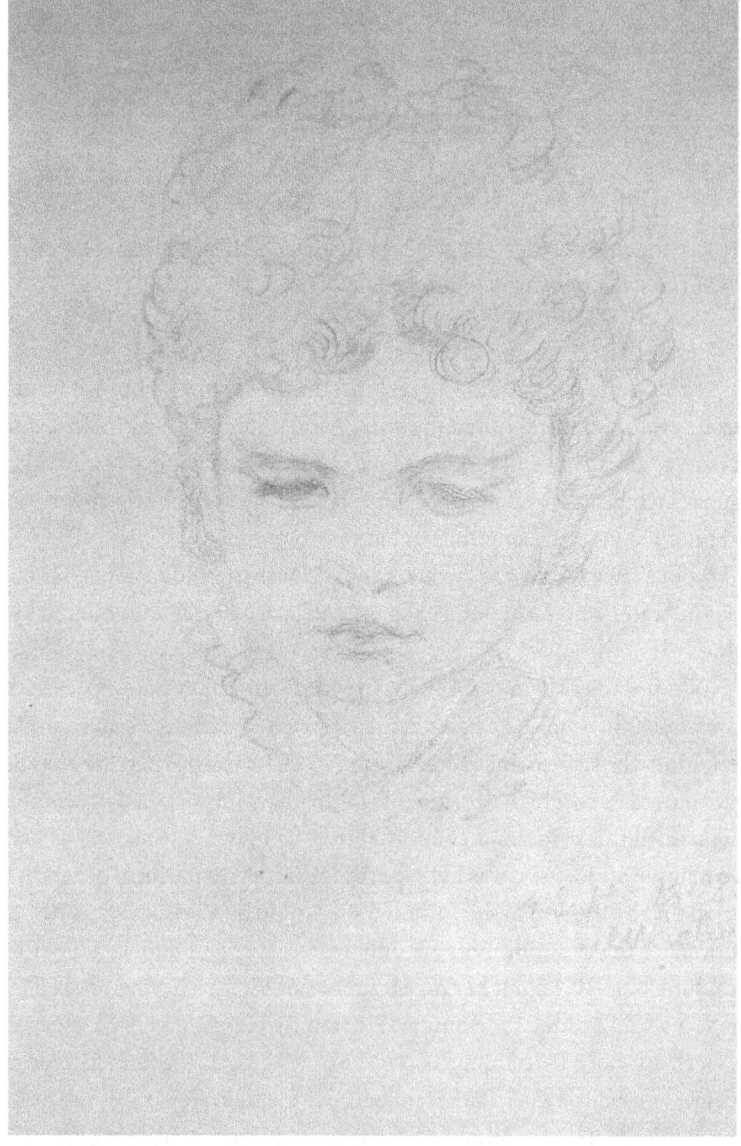

Figure 4. Magda Nachman. *Primavera R. Boman-Behram* (*Hilde Holger Archive © 2001 Primavera Boman-Behram*).

Nergesh Tejani, a former student of Hilde's, wrote to me about Hilde and Magda:

> I will never forget Magda Nachman. Hilde had dressed me up in a buffoon's costume [designed by Magda], and Magda loved it and painted me in it. Magda was short, heavyset, with a short neck and solid trunk-like legs with thick, maybe swollen, ankles. I think she was graying when I knew her. Her husband was a slight, very thin, dark man with dark-rimmed glasses who roamed around the apartment clad only in a towel around his waist. I seem to remember him addressing her as though he was constantly annoyed. Perhaps it was the lack of privacy with the models traipsing in and out. There were also many cats going in and out of the house. Magda and her husband—I think his name was Acharya—had a myriad cats who used to tickle me while I sat for the portrait at their home somewhere beyond Marine Drive—close to the water. She used to get really upset if I moved, even if the cats were tormenting me.

In Hilde's studio, Magda met other painters who would come to make sketches of the students, among them Shiavax Chavda, who had been a student of Bakst's student Vladimir Polunin, a scene painter for the Ballets Russes in London. What an improbable connection with Magda, who had studied with Léon Bakst, a Ballets Russes designer, in St. Petersburg! Chavda was at the time a rising young artist of the Bombay school who was to become one of the most prominent Indian painters of his generation. His name appears together with Magda's and Hilde's on the studio's ballet programs.

What strange good fortune was it that had brought me on my first morning in India to Juhu beach, where both women had left their footprints? I took it as a good omen.

CHAPTER 2

In Magda's Footsteps

I had arranged accommodation in Mumbai with the help of an acquaintance in New York. Here I would spend most of the next six weeks.

Six weeks. It was only the first day, and already I felt that time was running out. So I began calling for appointments as soon as my landlady left me to my own devices. In preparing for this journey, I had made a long list of persons and places to visit, and I felt that there was not a minute to lose. I would try to set up my first meeting for nine o'clock the next morning. Fortunately, I was not left completely to my own devices, for when I asked Suresh, the servant who worked in the apartment, to bring my breakfast between 7:30 and 8:00 because I would like to be out in time for a nine o'clock meeting, he said, "Nine? Hmm, why don't you make it for 10:30 or 11:00? That would be like nine o'clock in Indian time."

One of the people on my list was Maya Malhotra, who, I knew, as a young girl had sat for Magda in 1950. When I called her mobile, she was at a noisy party. We could hardly hear each other, and so she just shouted, "Come to Bombay Gymkhana at noon." "What? Where?" "Oh, ask anyone, they'll know." "They," of course, did know. Bombay Gymkhana is a social club. Almost every middle-class person belongs to a club here, and the names of the clubs are common currency.

If I wanted to follow in Magda's Bombay footsteps, I would have to find out where she had lived. I knew from a letter that Acharya had written from Bombay to Magda in Zurich in April 1936 that he was living at the time in the Fort area of the city. And I knew from Acharya's letter to Magda's niece Klara in 1951, after Magda's death, that the Acharyas had been living in Malabar Hill, at 63C Walkeshwar Road. I knew nothing of their whereabouts in the intervening years. I set out to meet Maya half hoping that she would recall something about Magda's studio where her portrait was painted.

Maya told me that her parents had wanted all three of their children to be painted by Magda. As I would discover, Magda was in demand as a portrait painter for well-to-do families, mostly among the Parsi community. Of the three children, only Maya's portrait was completed (figure 5), for Magda died the following year.

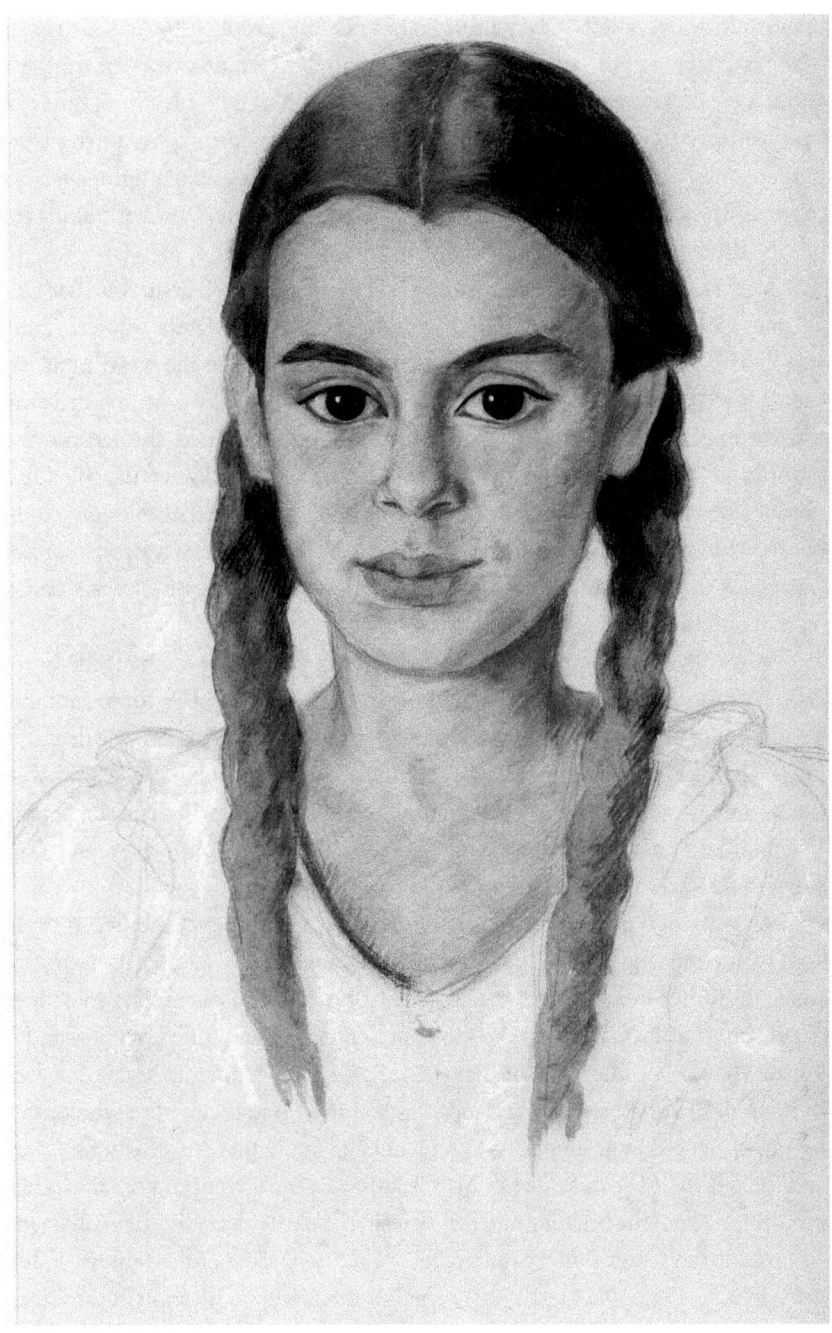

Figure 5. Magda Nachman. *Portrait of Maya Malhotra* (pastel, 10.5″ × 18″; *courtesy of Ayesha Malhotra, Calgary, Canada*).

As Maya recalled—sixty-four years after the event—she was driven to Magda's Malabar Hill apartment by the family chauffeur every morning for about a week. (From other models, I learned that Magda took a long time and many sittings to finish her work. If Maya's memory is correct, her portrait was perhaps unusual in the brevity of its execution.) She recalled a light, spacious room, a studio in a third-floor apartment, with large windows overlooking the ocean. There was a circular garden downstairs.

Maya kept repeating that it was a good address, a good area, Malabar Hill, although she also remembered her parents saying that Magda was very poor and married to a communist. I asked Maya to take me to the apartment. We took a taxi and arrived at the building that she recalled by a winding driveway leading uphill. The cluster of apartment buildings to which she led me was number 64 Walkeshwar Road. But from Acharya's letter, I knew that the house number was 63, on the opposite side of the street, the side that overlooked the ocean, which, if Maya's memory of windows overlooking the ocean was correct, was a plus for that being the address of Magda's apartment. But it was number 64 that had the winding driveway.

Was Maya's memory awry? Had the house numbers been changed? In any case, Maya most likely wouldn't have known the house number, for in Mumbai, buildings are not identified by their numbers but by their names and surrounding landmarks. In giving directions, Mumbaikars—or Bombayites as they were then—never mention the building number. Rather, they will say, for example, "My building's name is 'Swallow'; it is next to a bank and opposite an old banyan tree on such-and-such street."

As we stood contemplating number 64, Maya suddenly recalled that she knew someone who lived in that building. She stared at the building as if she were weighing in her memory whether that person really lived here. She must have decided in the affirmative, for she took out her mobile and called her husband to ask for a telephone number. She dialed, spoke for a few moments, and up we went to the fourth floor. Her acquaintances, as it turned out, owned the whole compound of structures at number 64 and had been living there for thirty-five years, and indeed the husband, now in his seventies, had grown up there. They knew everything about the building and everyone in it, but they knew nothing of Magda.

A few days later, I met Shireen Sabavala, the widow of the famous Indian artist Jehangir Sabavala (1922–2011), and the apartment question became even more confused. Like Maya, she had sat for Magda in her studio on Walkeshwar, which she remembered as a room in a small and scantily furnished shack on the ocean side of the road, with piles of newspapers lying around. Magda painted

Shireen's portrait in 1942 or 1943, when Shireen was about twenty-five years old. She repeated several times that Magda and Acharya had been very poor, very poor. Someone must have let them stay in that "outer house." Now, "shack" and "outer house" do not comport with Maya's description of an airy third-floor apartment. Having concluded that Maya had confused the apartment of her acquaintances at 64 with Magda's apartment at 63, I now wondered whether the Acharyas had first lived in the "shack" at number 63 and later moved into an apartment in a larger building in the same compound. Thus Maya, who had visited Magda's studio eight years after Shireen Sabavala, might have been in a different apartment at number 63. In any case, I now knew that the Acharyas had lived in Malabar Hill at least since the early 1940s.

But it turned out that Magda and Acharya had settled in Malabar Hill even earlier. While looking through the Bombay Art Society catalogue for 1937, I found Magda's address—56 Ridge Rd., Malabar Hill, Bombay 6—and several months later, I received photographic confirmation from London: Sophie Seifalian sent me a card written by her grandmother to her mother, Magda's niece, with the Acharyas' new Malabar Hill address. With the card came also a photograph (figure 6): Magda standing in front of her apartment. On the

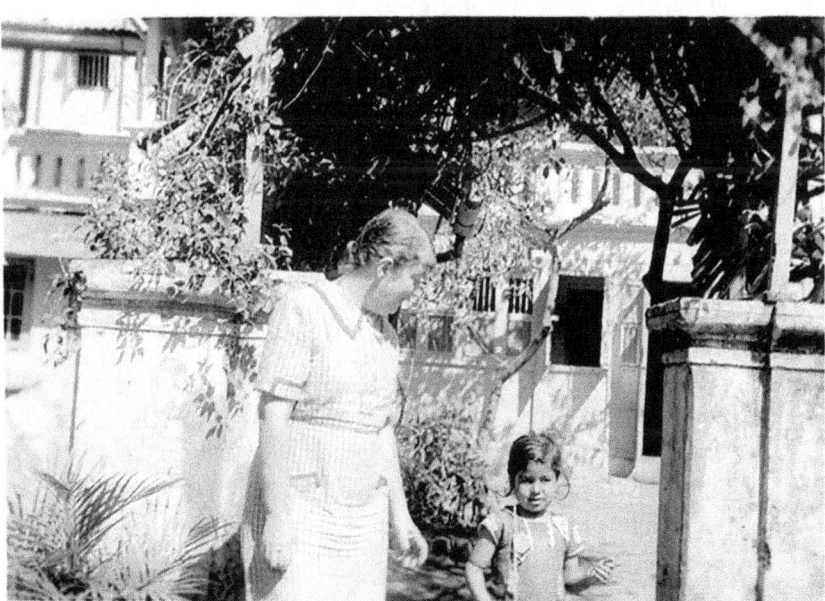

Figure 6. Photograph of Magda at the entrance of her home in Bombay (*courtesy of Sophie Seifalian*).

back of the photo Magda had written in German, "Behind me is the door and a window of my apartment. In front of the yard entrance. I let my hair grow to look neater. It was taken in January." So, Malabar Hill had become home for the Acharyas almost immediately after their arrival in Bombay.

Magda, whom Shireen described as "a very small sweet lady with a charming face," took a long time to paint Shireen's portrait, for which she had posed in a red sari. Shireen recalled that Magda would hold her brush in a peculiar way, with a crooked thumb. "Perhaps arthritis," she said. She visited the Walkeshwar studio many times. When the portrait was done, her grandmother refused to pay the hundred-rupee fee. Shireen has no idea what happened to it. What a pity! When I met her, she was in her late nineties, still very beautiful and graceful, and still teaching yoga. Shireen died in 2017, at age 100.

She showed me a portrait of her late husband painted by Magda in 1942. Both of them knew Magda well and thought highly of her. It seems that Magda, though quiet and gentle, commanded respect. Aesthetically, her work was quite different from that of the crowd of young artists with whom Jehangir Sabavala ran. Nevertheless, it seemed that everyone took her seriously and admired her work. Pensively, Shireen said, "Although not a beauty, Magda had a good face and thoughtful eyes. Very thoughtful eyes."

Maya had brought me to Magda's neighborhood, but not, as it turned out, quite to the correct building, as I would soon verify. And she also put me in contact with people who could show me the area. Malabar Hill is one of the oldest Mumbai peninsulas. Many high-rises that have sprung up long after Magda's time now suffocate the quaint, smaller buildings on Walkeshwar road. Some bungalows, as they are called, still nestle on the sides of Malabar Hill, exquisite in their architecture and entwined with greenery. This is the area of the sacred Parsi forest, with its central "Tower of Silence," where the devout Parsis used to expose their dead to the vultures. (There are no more vultures. They have died out from eating the carcasses of cattle that had been medicated with the anti-inflammatory drug diclofenac. The tower is indeed silent.)

At the top of the hill an old Hindu temple stands on the edge of a sacred pool. Both pool and temple predate the city of Bombay. The governor's mansion, surrounded by a forest, occupies a good part of the peninsula. The forests here are prehistoric jungles, though now much diminished. Here is how Magda saw her neighborhood (figure 7), and even this black-and-white reproduction of a painting whose whereabouts remain a mystery captures the flood of light and color that I was seeing.

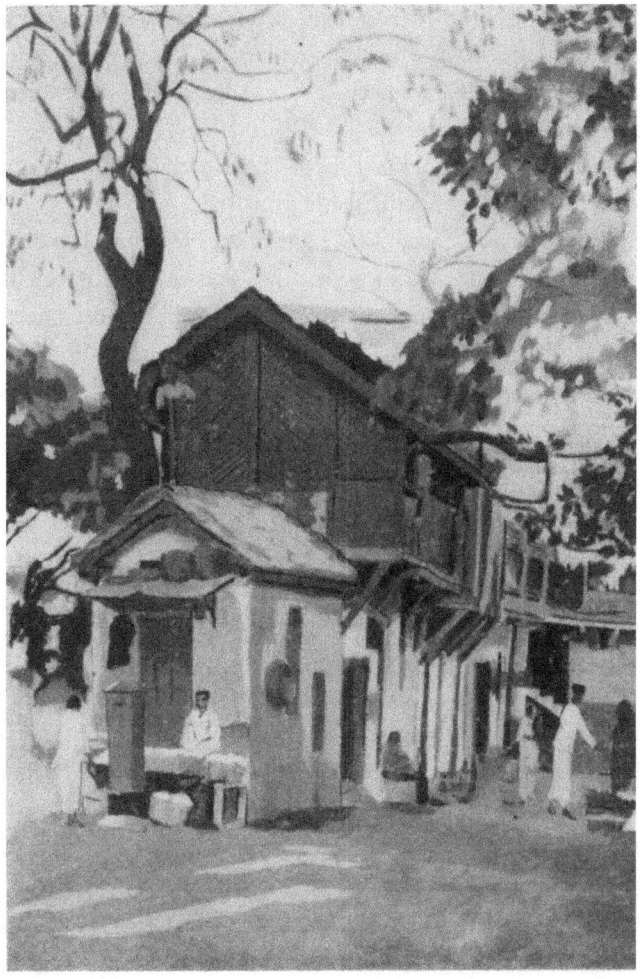

Figure 7. Magda Nachman. *A Street in Bombay* (*Bombay Art Society catalog, 1937*).

I was eventually able to verify that Magda did not live in compound 64. Maya must have confused her sittings in Magda's studio with visits to her acquaintances across the road. But another artist, Krishnaji Howlaji Ara (1914–1985), had in fact lived at number 64, occupying a small room on the ground floor, as our host, the owner of the building, pointed out to me. Ara was from a low caste. The son of a chauffeur, he received little formal schooling and supported himself by cleaning cars, painting in his spare time. Several persons played a pivotal role in the life of this major Indian modernist, propelling his artistic career, and Magda was one of them. She was twenty-five years older than Ara, but just as poor. They lived across the road from each other, and became friends. Magda even gave drawing lessons to the young artist.[1] Later, when I saw portraits by Ara, I was struck by his sitters' eyes—they reminded me so much of portraits by Magda.

That they in fact did live across the road from each other, at number 64 and number 63, was verified by a remarkable eyewitness account. A few days after my visit to Walkeshwar 64, I went to see one of the oldest painters now living in Mumbai, Akbar Padamsee. I was told that Mr. Padamsee had been ailing, and indeed, in the depths of his bright living room, he sat behind a small table in a wheelchair as if he were a maharaja seated on a dais receiving supplicants. A few guests were sitting in a semicircle in front of him at some distance. It was clear that our interview would occupy but a segment in his evening of visits. I asked him whether he had known Magda Nachman.

> You say she died in 1951? I am too young to remember Magda Nachman. I left for Paris in 1950 or maybe in 1951. And I was just a boy, very young. The Bombay Art Society was there,[2] and they had exhibitions. Husain showed there, and Raza, and Souza. And there was this man, Schlesinger, he was Jewish, came from Germany. He came to the Bombay Art Society exhibition, and Husain noticed the foreigner and decided to approach him. Schlesinger said to Husain, "you are painters, but you do not know what art is." "What is art, then?" asked Husain. And Schlesinger replied, "Egon von Schiele is art. Come to my house. I will show you what art is." Schlesinger showed him his art books. Husain had known nothing about such art. All the painters then began to use his house as a library. Then Raza went to talk to Schlesinger. He looked at Oskar Kokoschka, and saw that a landscape can be painted from the top.

---

1   See Margit Franz, "Jewish Represeter of the Indian Soul," in *Jews and the Indian National Project*, ed. Kenneth X. Robbins and Marvin Tokayer (New Dehli: Niyogi Books, 2015), 182.

2   The Society began its work in 1888 as an organization promoting art of the Bombay community, professionals and amateurs alike. By Magda's time it had become a more professional organization with a selection committee for exhibits, awards for best works, and sales to the general public. In 1939 it acquired a permanent hall for lectures, discussions, small art shows, and its yearly exhibition (the space was taken away for the duration of the war). The society also organized shows in Pune (Poona) in which Magda participated as well. See *Bombay Art Society: Diamond Jubilee, 1888–1948* (Bombay: Bombay Art Society Diamond Jubilee Committee, 1949). The book is wonderfully illustrated by Bombay artists.

"Yes," I inserted, "Raza's *View of Bombay from Malabar Hill* is a view from above, as if painted from Ara's studio window."

"Ah, Ara," mused Mr. Padamsee:

> I would go to his studio very often. At an exhibition, I once plucked up my courage and came up to him, I was probably around 17 and he was already a well-known artist. But I wanted to talk to him, and he invited me to his studio. ... Oh. ... Oh ... wait a moment. ... Of course I knew Magda Nachman! She lived opposite Ara's studio. I went one day to see Ara, and he said that Magda had been complaining bitterly about the Bombay Art Society. They had rejected her work. Ara then said that Magda would be coming. And then she arrived. She was a stout sort of woman, short, not beautiful at all, not beautiful, but very forceful, very forceful. Now my memory is coming. She ran in with a piece of paper in her fist and shouted, "They rejected me! They rejected me! Who are *they* to reject me? What do *they* know about art? They rejected my work!" she was standing there ... terrible. Then Ara introduced us, and she took me to the window to point out her studio. I saw her, I talked to her. Now I remember.

I learned that the main building of the compound number 63 had been rebuilt following an explosion in a ground-floor restaurant in the 1990s. Instead of erecting a new high-rise, the owner restored the smallish building exactly as it had been before the blast. And there I saw the round wall of the old garden that Maya had mentioned in her recollections.

I walked all over Malabar Hill, stopping at Hindu and Jain temples, which Magda, too, must have known. Even now, this area is different from the rest of the city. The feeling of a neighborhood and sense of belonging are noticeable in the children playing around the hilltop pool and young women coming up from the pool with their laundry baskets.

Magda and Ara recorded their neighborhood and its people in paint: the houses, the ocean, and the hard life of the poor their constant companions. Although Malabar was a good address, as Maya insisted, many residents were leaving the city during the war years, and landlords were eager to lease, even at reduced rates (thus even the struggling Ara could afford a room here). As one of the neighbors recalled from her childhood, some "foreigners" lived in a shack in the compound at 63 Walkeshwar, and the neighborhood children were not allowed to disturb them. (That must have been Magda the foreigner!) All who offered their reminiscences about the Acharyas' abode saw their memories clearly before their eyes and tried hard to describe those images. If only I could have captured what they were seeing! I wonder where the picture of withered trees shown in figure 8 was painted. There are trees like this one in the court-yard of Magda's bungalow.

The artists whom Mr. Padamsee mentioned in his recollection banded together in Bombay in the late 1930s, and by the end of the following decade, they had formed the Progressive Artists' Group. In many newspaper reports, Magda's name is surrounded by the names of those younger artists. Though she painted in a style very different from theirs, she exhibited together with them.

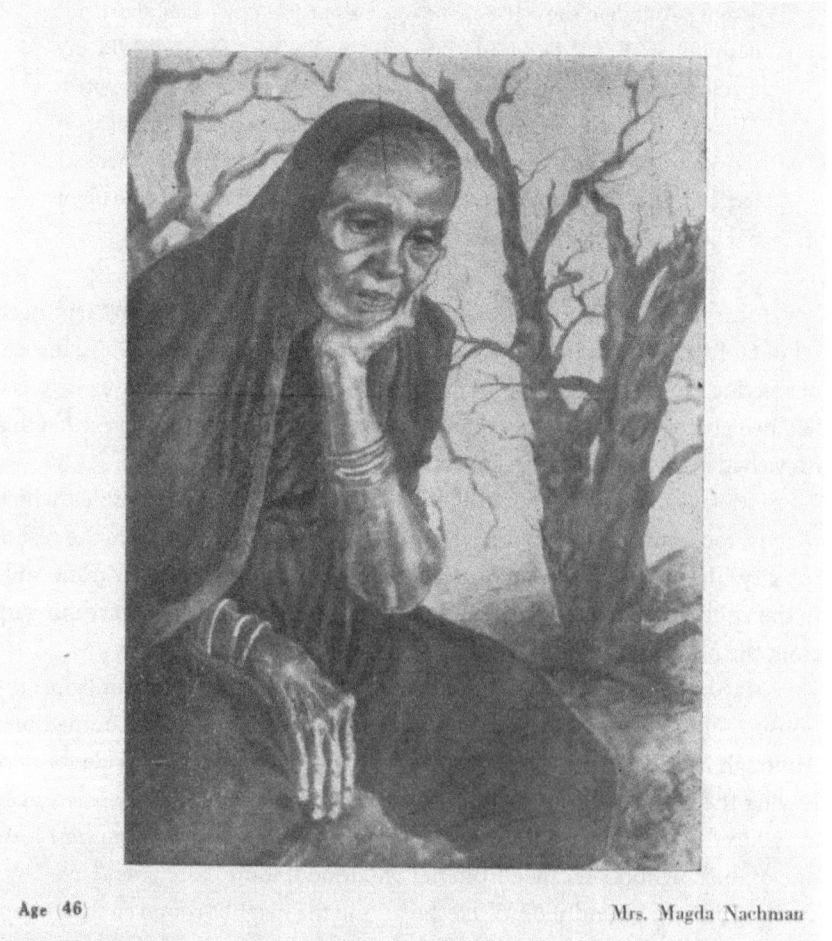

Age (46)   Mrs. Magda Nachman

Figure 8. Magda Nachman. *Age* (*Bombay Art Society catalog, 1947*).

The painter Francis Newton ("F. N.") Souza was their leader. The art historian Partha Mitter has described these Bombay artists' formative years:

> They were initiated into international modernism by three figures from Vienna who were resident in the city in the 1940s: Walter Langhammer, Rudi von Leyden, and Emmanuel Schlesinger, who helped wean these artists away from the provincial modernism of Britain.[3]

Another art historian, Yashodhara Dalmia, in her book *The Making of Modern Indian Art: The Progressives*, confirms Mitter's assertion: "In a twist of destiny, the war émigrés from Europe who landed in Bombay proved to be deeply involved with the arts and became central to its development in India in its formative years." She names the same three men, who were not only patrons of art and the Progressive Artists' Group; they also introduced a European art sensibility that was radically different from the Royal Academy of Arts style taught in art colleges in India.[4]

The Progressive Bombay Artists came from various class backgrounds, from high to low, and represented a variety of religions, ethnicities, and languages. Not numerous but a vibrant group, they exhibited remarkable creativity and daring. And they began to attract the attention of the city's establishment. One of their promoters and supporters was Kekoo Gandhy, later a founder of the preeminent gallery of modern art in Bombay, the Chemould Art Gallery. Sadly for me, Mr. Gandhy and his wife, Shared, who knew everyone and everything in Indian modern art, died a year before my trip to Mumbai. I met their daughters in their parents' "bungalow," a palazzo in Bandra, in northern Mumbai. Here I saw a painting by Walter Langhammer. Subsequently, I saw several paintings by Langhammer as well as some works by another teacher and supporter of the Progressives, A. R. von Leyden. Not themselves great artists, they nevertheless brought new ideas to their eager students, showed them fine examples of modern European art, and encouraged their experiments.

In his autobiographical notes, Kekoo Gandhy writes, "Among the European painters who came to India during the War was Walter Langhammer, an Austrian. ... The year must have been 1936."

---

3   Partha Mitter, *The Triumph of Modernism: Indian Artists and the Avant-garde 1922–1947* (London: Reaktion Books, 2007), 227.

4   Yashodhara Dalmia, *The Making of Modern Indian Art: The Progressives* (New Delhi: Oxford University Press, 2001), 59.

In fact, Langhammer left Vienna for Bombay only in 1938. Magda had arrived in Bombay earlier, sometime in 1936, and very soon began exhibiting with the Bombay Art Society. Established in 1888, the society was famous for its annual exhibitions, whose openings were anticipated as celebratory social events and inaugurated by high-ranking officials. Mr. Gandhy continued thus:

> Langhammer fell in love with the light and color of India and all the young artists. Here, he would often say, he saw a future in the modern art movement; he felt it was all over [in] Europe. So people like Ara, Raza, Husain, Souza, and Raiba, the great names of the Indian Progressive Art Movement, became his students. Every Sunday, it was open house at his studio on Nepean Sea Road.
>
> He would tell them what makes a good painting. He would share his experiences of Europe and tell them about events in the art world, seen at first hand. They found a windfall in this readymade teacher. And he had so much love and affection for them. It was not just the artists alone—the people around them too were responsible, in a way, for the birth of the Progressives. There were factors like the excitement over the prospect of impending Independence, the feeling that now Indian artists would not have to go through Westminster, that India would have its own embassies in different parts of the world, and that we would be able to make our own connections. ...
>
> Apart from Langhammer, there was Dr. E. Schlesinger and Rudi von Leyden, both German. Rudi ... had a younger brother, A. R. Leyden, a sculptor who styled himself as a painter after Langhammer and was called "little Langhammer." They had arrived before Langhammer because their father foresaw the arrival of Hitler by two or three years. They were all warm and outgoing people, generous too ... the unexpected arrival of all these Europeans—most of them Jews fleeing from Austria—really started the Progressive movement off. ... With Langhammer came a lot of professionals, doctors ... a sort of mini-influx of Jews. They valued art and provided patronage. ... They had a great enthusiasm for Indian artists—who else was interested?—and they pioneered buying.[5]

---

5   Kekoo Gandhy, "The beginnings of the art movement," http://www.india-seminar.com/2003/528/528%20kekoo%20gandhy.htm. A parallel development can be noticed in American art during the war years. Writing about American art coming into its own in the WWII period, Mary Dearborn remarks, "The infusion of ideas and energy that the wartime émigrés brought to the American art scene was a potent tool in the mix" (Mary Dearborn, *Mistress of Modernism: The Life of Peggy Guggenheim* [Boston: Houghton Mifflin, 2004], 242).

Kekoo Gandhy became a member of the artistic milieu which Magda had joined on her arrival in Bombay. He knew Magda well and loved her; even his daughter Shireen, who had not been interested much in her parents' stories about old Bombay, said that she remembered a period when her father all of a sudden began talking about Magda long after Magda's death and was talking about her to anyone who would listen, or even if they would not. One of the Mumbai art collectors, and an art historian herself, Saryu Doshi, told me that it was Kekoo Gandhy who suggested that she buy a painting by Magda from his own collection (figure 9).

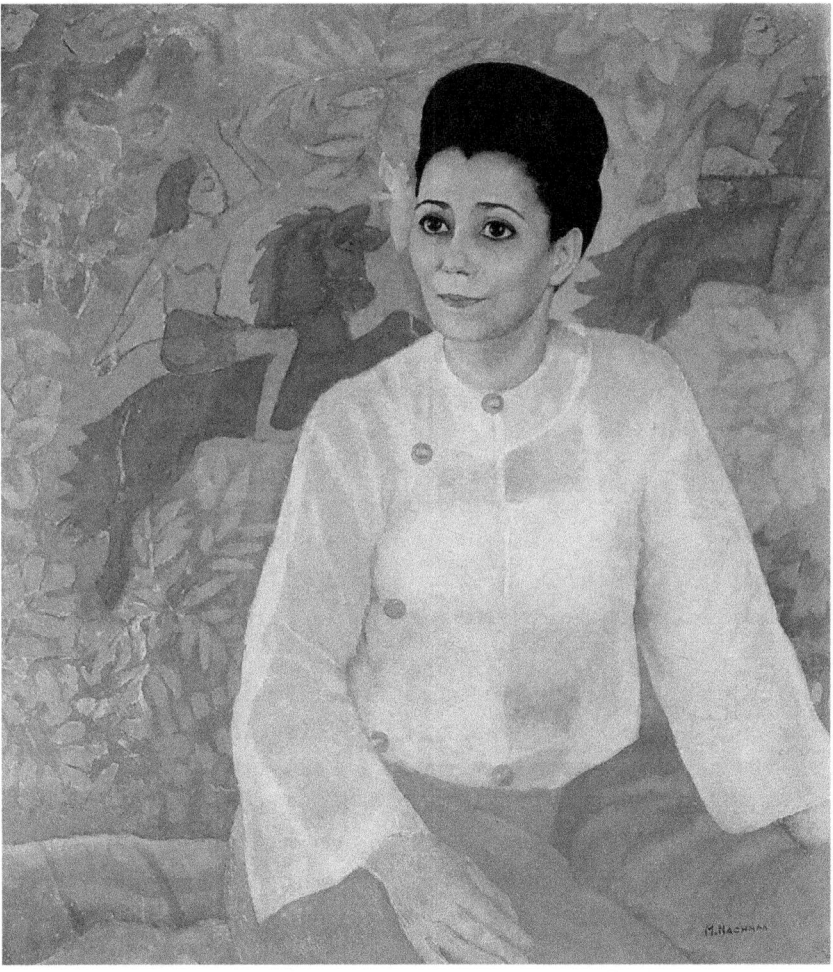

Figure 9. Magda Nachman. *Portrait of a Burmese Lady* (*courtesy of Saryu Doshi*).

CHAPTER 3

Once There Was and Once There Was Not

In India, Magda once remarked to a friend about her life in St. Petersburg, "Maybe it is still going on, on some distant planet, but I have left it forever." Indeed, how did a girl born into the Russian capital's upper middle class grow up to become the "great little lady of the Bombay art world"?

The daughter of a German-Lutheran mother and a Jewish father, Magda Matilda Elizabeth Nachman was born on July 20, 1889, in Pavlovsk, a suburb of St. Petersburg, into a comfortable home at a time of intense cultural activity and the appearance of new artistic movements in literature, art, theater, ballet, and music as well as a time of social ferment, political instability, and changing social norms. Magda grew up in the capital of the empire in a family that could afford to educate her and provide her access to the city's cultural life. Years later, in Bombay, Magda remembered with nostalgia her parents' silver wedding anniversary in 1900:

> [The celebration] was grand with big dinner party, theatricals, etc. My
> mother was smart in silvery grey silk and silver flowers in her hair. I was
> a small creature and had to play the role of an elf. And I still remember a
> silver basket full of marvelous orchids which my parents got as a present.

In Bombay, at the time she recalled this past event, Magda exclaimed, "But how far outside their orderly and prosperous life I am now!"[1]

Her father, Maximilian Nachman, born in 1843 or 1844, left Riga in 1864 to matriculate at the law faculty of St. Petersburg University. He graduated in 1868, and in 1870, on defending his thesis, was awarded a diploma and the title "candidate in jurisprudence." In 1875, he married Klara Emilia Maria von Roeder. Klara's surname suggests an origin in the minor German nobility, of

---

1   Quoted by H. Kohn in "Memories of Magda Nachman," *Aesthetics* 5, no. 1 (1951): 15.

which there was a substantial population in the Russian capital, many of whom had come from Riga or one of the other Hanseatic cities that had been absorbed into the Russian Empire in 1710 following Russia's victory over Sweden in the Great Northern War. By the time Magda was born—the sixth of seven children—her father had become a successful lawyer. Years later, in 1950, in the *Illustrated Weekly of India*, Lama Anagarika Govinda, Magda's close friend and an admirer of her art, published a tribute to her, including a very brief biographical sketch. He noted that her father had been a legal adviser to the Imperial German Embassy—information that could have come only from Magda herself. Maximilian was also employed in St. Petersburg by the Nobel Brothers Petroleum Company as a legal consultant and was a shareholder in the company.[2]

Although marriages between Jews and Russian Orthodox were forbidden in Imperial Russia, there was no such prohibition between Jews and Lutherans, provided that the children were brought up Christian. It is likely that all seven children of Maximilian and Klara were baptized in the Lutheran faith, although I have obtained baptismal certificates for only three of them. Those three, including Magda's, were issued by the Evangelical Lutheran Church of Saint Catherine in St. Petersburg. On all three, Maximilian is identified as a person "of the Jewish faith." Yet there is no hint of Jewish identity in Magda's letters or in the letters of her friends and relatives. Magda's baptismal papers name as her godparents a professor's wife, Matilda Kholson (née Schoendorf), and a lawyer, Arthur von Lieven (the von Lievens belonged to one of the oldest Baltic German families, and many of them were employed in the imperial bureaucracy and military service). The godparents of other Nachman children were also well-positioned members of the Russian–German professional class. When they grew up and married, Magda's siblings chose mostly those of German background as husbands and wives.

It is not only the fact that Maximilian married a gentile that suggests that Judaism was not a significant presence in the family of the Riga Nachmans. Archival documents show that a number of Maximilian's siblings converted to Christianity. Why was Maximilian not among them? Conversion would have opened many doors for him that remained closed even under Alexander II's liberalizing reforms. Perhaps it was out of reverence for his parents or other

---

2 This information on Maximilian comes from Magda's great-grandniece Natalia Mikaberidze. The Nobel Brothers Petroleum Company was an oil-producing company that had its origins in a refinery founded by Robert and Ludvig Nobel in Baku, Azerbaijan, in 1876. In 1879, it was turned into a shareholding company with headquarters in St. Petersburg. Their younger brother Alfred is known as the inventor of dynamite and the founder of the Nobel Prize.

family members of their generation. Maximilian's father, Israel (Julius), was a merchant of high standing at some point. (The gradation within the merchant estate depended on overall wealth of the merchant and could fluctuate with the ups and downs of the market.) A sizable number of Riga Nachmans belonged to the professional or merchant estate, and some were active in the city's Jewish community.

Russian Jews were subject to a number of restrictions as to where they could reside, what occupations they could pursue, and what kind of education they could receive. However, several factors allowed Maximilian to settle in St. Petersburg and obtain a law degree. As a member of a well-to-do family in Riga, a more Westernized and therefore more liberal part of the Russian Empire, he was able to complete classical high school (such schools, called gymnasia, as a rule provided an excellent education for their university-bound students). By the time of his matriculation at the law faculty of St. Petersburg University, Alexander's reforms granted Jewish graduates the right to reside in the city. That right would disappear by the end of the century, after Alexander's assassination in 1881 and the accession to the throne of his son, Alexander III. But those like Maximilian who had obtained the right of residency retained it even under the new tsar.

It is noteworthy that in her letters to friends written between 1908 and 1921, Magda mentions her mother, her siblings, her nieces and nephews, but not a word about her father. Of course, Maximilian was a professional man in an age when fathers were often aloof from family life, and his daughter might not have seen much of him. He may have died before 1908.

The Nachmans' street addresses reflect their prosperity and social standing. For a long time, they lived at Moika 11, a street off Nevsky Prospect, the main Petersburg thoroughfare. And later, they lived on Kirochnaya Street (its name derives from the German word for church, *Kirche*; the Evangelical Lutheran Church of St. Anna, one of the city's oldest and most opulent Lutheran churches, stands on the corner). Still later, they moved to Bolshaya Dvoryanskaya, to a new building with an elevator, which was needed by Magda's invalid younger brother. This was Magda's last address in St. Petersburg, and in a letter she lamented the move, because it took her farther from the city center.

Photographs of Magda, her parents, and her siblings from that time were taken in fashionable ateliers in Petersburg and abroad, and they exude a sense of well-being. A picture of Magda and her younger brother Walter—wearing a dress, as was common at that time—holding a basket of flowers was taken by H. Rentz and F. Schrader, photographers who, as the reverse of the photograph boasts, had won medals and received praise from the tsar himself (figure 10).

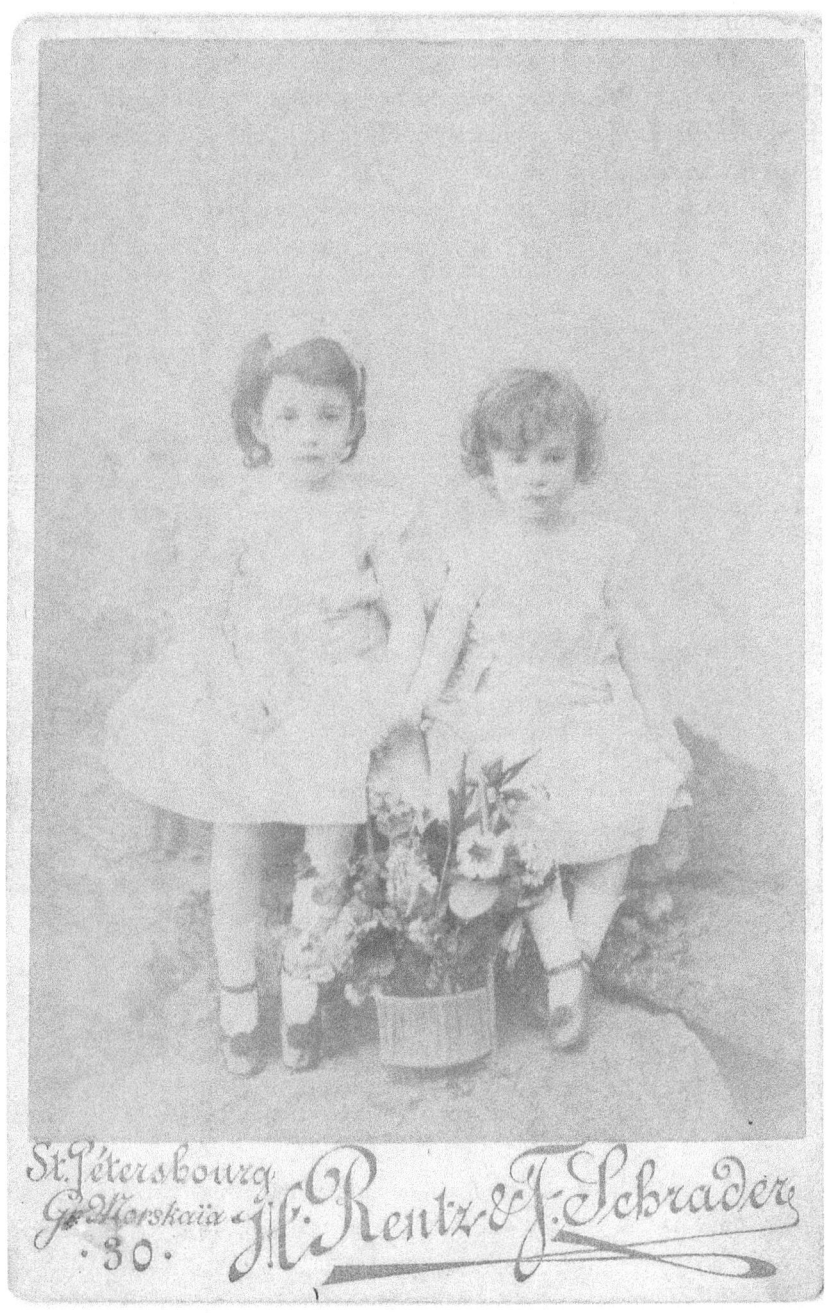

Figure 10. Photograph of Magda and her younger brother Walter (*courtesy of Sophie Seifalian*).

Figure 11 shows Magda's father, Maximilian, as a young man, in a portrait by Alfred Lorens, one of the oldest and most famous portrait and landscape photographers of Petersburg, who opened a studio on Nevsky Prospect in 1855, where he produced photographic views of the city, its famous environs, and its residents of all walks of life.[3]

A later photograph of Maximilian and Klara was taken in Munich while they were vacationing (figure 12). To me, they look like a kind and prosperous couple.

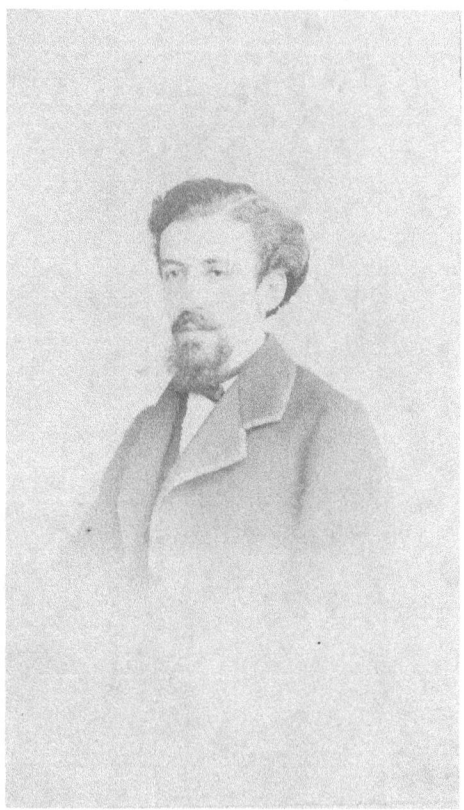

Figure 11. Magda's father Maximilian Maximilianovich Nachman (*courtesy of Sophie Seifalian*).

---

3   Lorens was one of the first professional photographers whose works had commercial success; he also was an inventor and promoter of photographic equipment, then in its infancy, and was the first to introduce cameras into the Russian army.

Figure 12. Maximilian and Klara Nachman, Magda's parents (*courtesy of Sophie Seifalian*).

There is also a photograph of Magda's two older sisters Erna and Adele, wearing enormous hats with a garden of artificial flowers on top, taken in Nice (figure 13).

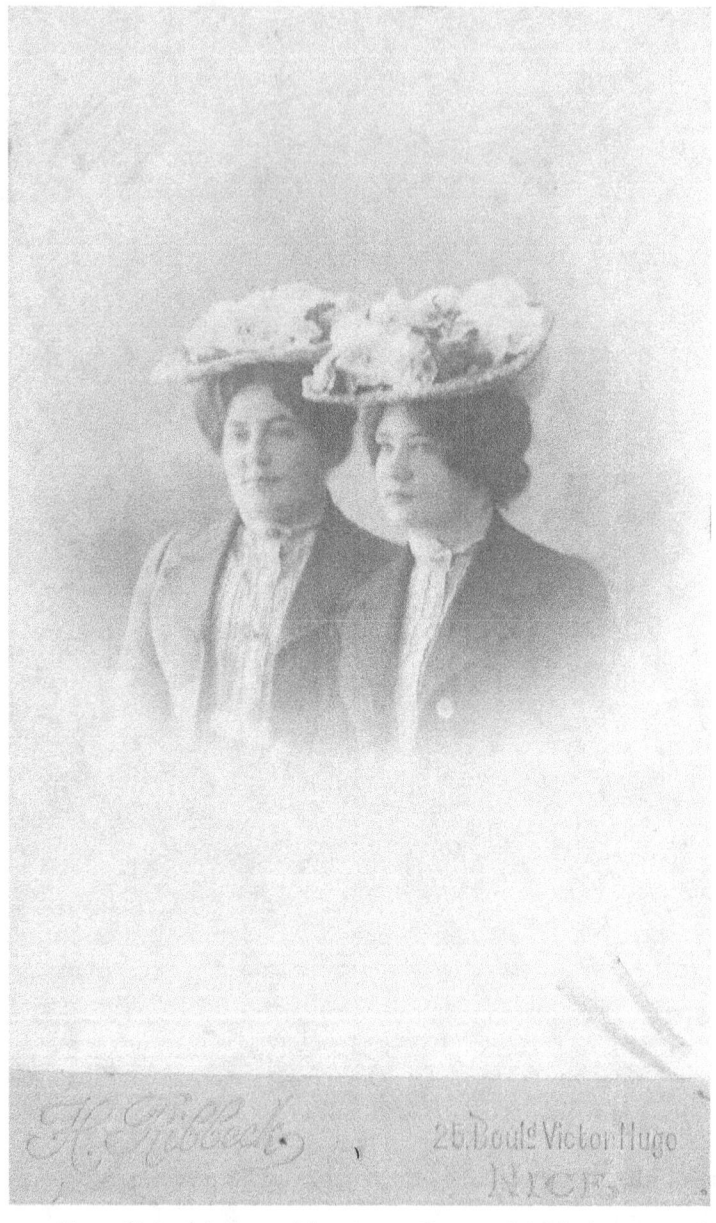

Figure 13. Two of Magda's three older sisters, Erna and Adele (*courtesy of Sophie Seifalian*).

Like other of the Nachman children, Magda attended the Saint Anna Gymnasium, known as the "Annenschule," established in 1736 to educate the children of German families residing in St. Petersburg. From Magda's diploma, we know what subjects she took: Russian literature, German, French, English, history, geography, mathematics, physics, natural history, singing, home arts, and stenography. She passed all her exams with high marks and graduated in 1906 with the award of a silver medal, which qualified her to work as a private tutor or governess without further certification or to teach at a progymnasium (a school that prepared pupils for gymnasium after primary school).

Magda's older sisters married shortly after leaving high school, as did many young women of their generation and social class. The eldest sister, Eleanor, took singing lessons for a while even after her marriage. The next sister, Erna, was qualified as a governess, but she married shortly after she left school. And the third sister, Adele, together with her Prussian husband, opened a language school in Lausanne, Switzerland.

Magda, the youngest sister, was the only woman in her family who made an independent professional career. From 1907 to 1917, an influential Russian feminist organization, the League for Women's Equal Rights, was advocating for women's education and social equality. Societal norms were changing, and women were entering professions (especially in teaching and medicine). St. Petersburg offered someone of Magda's station professional opportunities.

Magda's talents were many. She could have become a translator from German, French, English, and even Italian (she would later do translations on occasion). She was an expert stenographer. She was enthralled by history and even submitted an application to audit courses at the history–philology faculty at St. Petersburg University (women could not enroll as regular students, but her high school diploma allowed her to enroll as an auditor).

But Magda's greatest interests and talents were artistic, and so she began attending art classes at the Mutual Aid Society of Russian Artists[4] even before completing her high school exams. There she met other aspiring artists, some of whom became her closest friends, among them Julia Obolenskaya, Natalia Grekova, and, a bit later, Varya Klimovich-Toper. They formed a tightly knit group, calling themselves "our quartet," and they remained together for many years, until outside circumstances separated them (figure 14). All four would become students of the great artist and teacher Léon Bakst.

---

4   The Society was founded by St. Petersburg artists in 1871 and continued its work until 1918. Its goals were to support needy artists, organize exhibitions, and offer art classes.

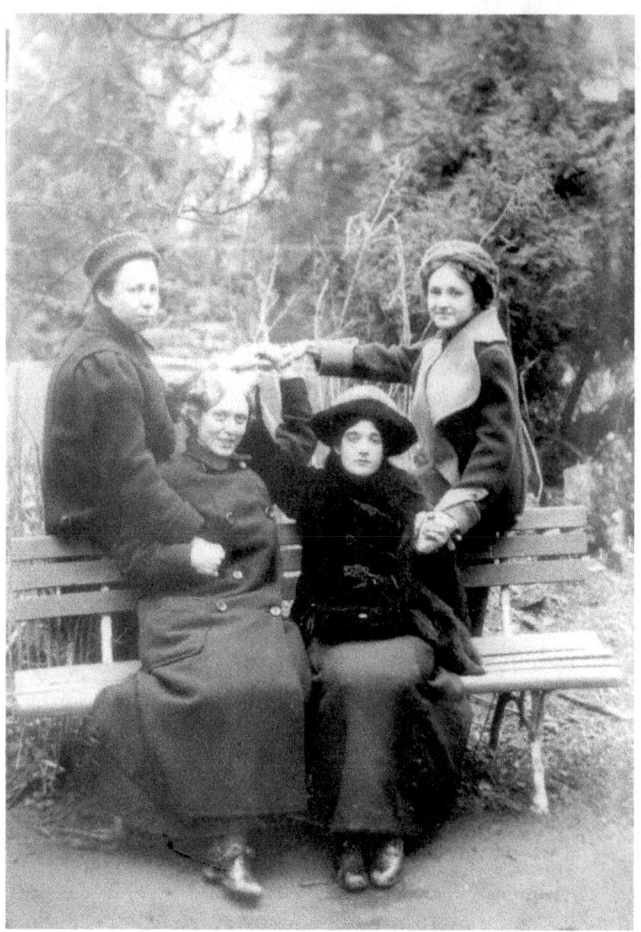

Figure 14. The "quartet": (left to right) Natalia Grekova, Varya Klimovich-Toper, Magda Nachman, Julia Obolenskaya (*courtesy of RGALI, Moscow*).

It was the spring of Magda's seventeenth year. And it was the spring of Russian Modernism, a time of rapid developments in artistic taste, dress, philosophy and literature, music, dance, politics, even hairstyles.

CHAPTER 4

The School and the Teacher

The spring of the twentieth century is catching us in uncharted waters of artistic currents. Much has thawed under the sun's hot rays; much has been destroyed. The warm air is enshrouded in fog and teeming with new life, with sparkling fragile wings. They may be destined to live but a day. ... New directions, new schools are growing with amazing speed.

—Léon Bakst

At the beginning of the twentieth century, art education in St. Petersburg was dominated by the conservative pedagogical methods employed at the Imperial Academy of Arts. Exhibitions of student works, according to the prominent art critic Alexander Rostislavov, produced "a strange impression ... [they lacked] the true, original artistry." After visiting a show in the Baron Stieglitz School, that critic wrote:

> It is strange that a student art exhibition should leave the impression that the true goal of the school is not art but the development of such respectable qualities as assiduity, diligence, and precision.[1]

Even the once progressive splinter group the Wanderers—realist artists whose work was inspired by social concerns and moral responsibility both in the subject matter of their paintings and in the way art was disseminated—who themselves had left the Academy in the 1860s in protest of its conservatism, had become ossified, and some of its members had become teachers at the Academy.

Aside from the Imperial Academy, there were numerous private art academies in the capital, but most of them hired their teachers from among the graduates of the Academy, who simply perpetuated its methodology. Later, in 1926,

---

1   A. Rostislavov, "Trudoliubie vmesto khudozhestva" (Diligence instead of Art), *Mir Iskusstva* 1 (1901): 50. All translations in this book are by the author unless otherwise indicated.

this is how Magda's closest friend and colleague, Julia Obolenskaya, described art education in St. Petersburg in the first decade of the twentieth century:

> By that time, the Academy of Arts had lost its prestige. And the teachers, who had been themselves trained in the Academy, dissuaded students from entering it. They brought the same haphazardness to their teaching that they had inherited from the Academy. Their instruction consisted in pointing out some particular errors in drawing and in supplying small recipes in painting, which were different for each teacher. Young people stumbled in the dark, despaired, and tried different schools.[2]

Such was the situation at the Mutual Aid Society of Russian Artists in 1907, where Magda and Julia had been taking classes since their high school graduation the previous year. As Julia notes in her memoirs, certain teachers were better than others, and so a group of students (including Julia, Magda, and Natalia Grekova) petitioned the administration to allow them to study with only those teachers. The administration refused. In protest, Magda and a group of other like-minded students decided to leave the Mutual Aid Society at the end of the 1907 spring term and invite one of the better teachers, Dmitry Kardovsky,[3] to conduct classes that they would fund themselves. Calling their endeavor the New School, they rented a space and planned on opening after the summer recess.

But when autumn arrived, the remodeling of the space had not been completed, and so there was some delay in the opening of the New School. Julia, Magda, and Natalia decided to use this delay to investigate other opportunities. They began attending classes at the Zvantseva Art Academy, which had opened in 1906 and for which, at the time, they had not considered themselves sufficiently developed artistically. They were in awe of the principal instructor, Léon Bakst (1866–1924), who a decade earlier had been a founding member of the powerful and influential association of artists Mir Iskusstva (World of Art). The three young women were so taken with Bakst and his academy that they were unhappy when later that fall, the New School finally opened and they were obliged by their previous agreement to return. But the unhappiness of the young women was so palpable that after a month, their friends released them from their obligation, and they happily transferred to Zvantseva.

---

2   Obolenskaia, "V shkole Zvantsovoi," 211.
3   Dmitry Kardovsky (1866–1943)—Russian artist, illustrator, and stage designer.

Thus in the fall of 1907, Magda, together with Julia Obolenskaya and Natalia Grekova, began her artistic career at the Zvantseva Art Academy. They found a congenial atmosphere among other young artists, some of whom would become close friends. They also found a teacher, Bakst, who became a pivotal figure in their development as artists.

The founder of the academy, Elizaveta Nikolaevna Zvantseva (1864–1921), was an art educator and herself an artist, who had studied at several Russian and French art academies. She attended the Moscow School of Painting, Sculpture, and Architecture (1885–1888) and then the Imperial Academy of Arts, in St. Petersburg, where she was a student of the preeminent realist painter Ilya Repin, a member of the Wanderers group. Strong, willful, and at the same time mild and kind, Zvantseva attracted Repin by her charm and independence. He fell in love with her, and in 1889, while visiting her estate Tartaley near Nizhny Novgorod, he painted five portraits of her.[4] Repin pleaded with her, sent numerous letters, and suffered:

> How I love you! Good God, God, I never imagined that my feeling toward you would grow to such a passion. I am beginning to be afraid for myself. … Indeed, not once in my life, never, no one did I love so transgressively, with such self-abandonment. … Even art has receded somewhere and you, you are in my mind and in my heart every second. Your image is everywhere.

The letter is signed "your slave."[5] Zvantseva did not reciprocate his love, although she remained his devoted friend. (Zvantseva never married, and later—at least from 1906—established a relationship with a woman, Elena Karmin, with whom she spent the rest of her life.)

In 1897, Zvantseva left the Imperial Academy and traveled with a friend, the artist Konstantin Somov (1869–1939), to Paris, where she attended classes at the Académie Colarossi and at the Académie Julian, schools that boasted liberal training, in opposition to the conservative École des Beaux Arts. Not only did Zvantseva have the experience of a more progressive method of art instruction, she was also able to see some of the art created by graduates of the studios she attended, such as Pierre Bonnard and Édouard Vuillard. Unlike

---

4   Only one of the portraits survives and is now in the Helsinki Ateneum Art Museum.

5   Ilya Repin, a letter of January 28, 1889, in "Pis'ma I. E. Repina E. N. Zvantsevoi," in *Mir iskusstv. Almanakh*, vol. 4, ed. E. Terkel' (St. Petersburg: Dmitrii Bulanin, 2001), 667.

many Russian artists and the Russian public, she was therefore well acquainted with Impressionism and Post-Impressionism. Her own artistic tastes had begun to shift slowly from the realist work of the Wanderers (even in 1898, Somov called her "My dear Wanderess") to more abstract approaches.

A number of women artists who came from abroad at this time to study in Paris would return to their home countries and open art studios or schools. Zvantseva returned to Moscow in 1899 and opened her own art academy. But her school failed to thrive, and in 1906 she closed the academy, and at the urging of Somov, who suggested that "there was a strong need for a good school in Petersburg,"[6] moved herself and her academy to the capital. Somov suggested that she invite as teachers his close friends and colleagues Bakst and Mstislav Dobuzhinsky (1875–1957). Zvantseva took this advice as well, and both Bakst and Dobuzhinsky accepted her offer. Bakst, in fact, had long been thinking about how to reform art education, and he enthusiastically took on the artistic direction of the academy. As he wrote that autumn in a letter to his wife, "The instruction system has been changed according to my plan. We shall see what will come of it."[7]

The teachers at Zvantseva's academy—Bakst, Dobuzhinsky, and later Kuzma Petrov-Vodkin (1878–1939)—occupy an important place in the history of art. From its inception in 1898, Somov, Bakst, and Dobuzhinsky had belonged to Mir Iskusstva, an association of artists and art and literary critics who expressed their views in a journal of the same name, whose editor-in-chief was Sergei Diaghilev, later famous as the founder and artistic director of the Ballets Russes in Paris. The founding members of the association aspired to supersede the tired academism through greater experimentation, motivated in part by the artistic ferment in Western Europe, and like their colleagues they were frustrated that in contrast to Russian literature, Russian art was almost unknown in the West. In 1898, to remedy the situation, Diaghilev took an exhibition of works by Russian and Finnish artists from St. Petersburg to Munich, Düsseldorf, Cologne, and Berlin. And again, in 1906, he brought the exhibition *Two Centuries of Russian Painting and Sculpture* from St. Petersburg to the Salon d'Automne in Paris, and from there to Berlin and Venice. More importantly, *Mir Iskusstva* was prominent in introducing Western art to Russia, hastening the end of Russian provincialism and putting St. Petersburg on the map as a center of contemporary art. In an 1899 exhibition

---

6   Letter to E. N. Zvantseva, August 14, 1906, http://konstantinsomov.ru/let_4/.
7   Letter of November 29, 1906, quoted in Irina Pruzhan, *Lev Samoilovich Bakst* (Leningrad: Iskusstvo, 1975), 120.

in St. Petersburg, Diaghilev included works by forty-two European artists, among them the Swiss symbolist Arnold Böcklin, the American proponent of "art for art's sake" James McNeill Whistler, and the French impressionist Edgar Degas.

The journal *Mir Iskusstva* aimed to promote and defend the ideas of contemporary European art and new tendencies in Russian art by publishing articles on current trends and particular artists, expansive theoretical essays by Diaghilev in support of artistic experimentation, and high-quality reproductions of works by contemporary European and Russian artists. Its readers could learn about and see reproductions of paintings by such figures as Cézanne, Degas, and Matisse, whose works and even names might have been previously inaccessible to those unable to travel abroad. It introduced its readers to Japanese art, which had become very popular in Europe but was just making its appearance in Russia.[8] The journal also discussed many aspects of Russian art, both old and new. Its literary section presented Russian symbolist writers, poets, and theoreticians. Highly critical of the previous generation of writers and artists who had insisted on the supremacy of social engagement in artistic pursuits, they argued that art should develop organically without any constraints from the outside, social or otherwise. The journal was published in what the miriskusniki—as the artists associated with *Mir Iskusstva* were known—called Style Moderne, a local adaptation of Art Nouveau, the Viennese Secession, and German Jugendstil, as exemplified in a 1902 magazine cover by Bakst (figure 15).

Magda's artistic sensibility developed under the influence of her teachers and in reaction to a host of competing movements that were raging around her. As Bakst put it, "The spring of the twentieth century is catching us in uncharted waters of artistic currents." He navigated his students through those currents, sharing with them his views on what was valuable in contemporary art and how they might find a place for themselves within it, taking them far away from both Russian academism and Style Moderne.

By the time Zvantseva opened her art academy, only two years after the closing of *Mir Iskusstva*, Bakst had moved beyond his experimentation in Style Moderne. Though still in his early forties, he was already an important artist, known as a master of the psychological portrait and an outstanding draftsman and stage designer. Yet Bakst was still searching for his unique place as an artist,

---

8   See *China and Japan in the Russian Imagination, 1685–1922: To the Ends of the Orient* (New York: Routledge, 133), in which Susanna Soojung Lim writes: "A crucial figure who introduced Japanese art to the Russian cultural elite was Sergei Kitayev (1864–1927). A naval officer who made regular trips to Japan, Kitayev amassed a remarkable collection of Japanese paintings and prints, which he displayed in an exhibition at the St. Petersburg Academy of Art in 1896."

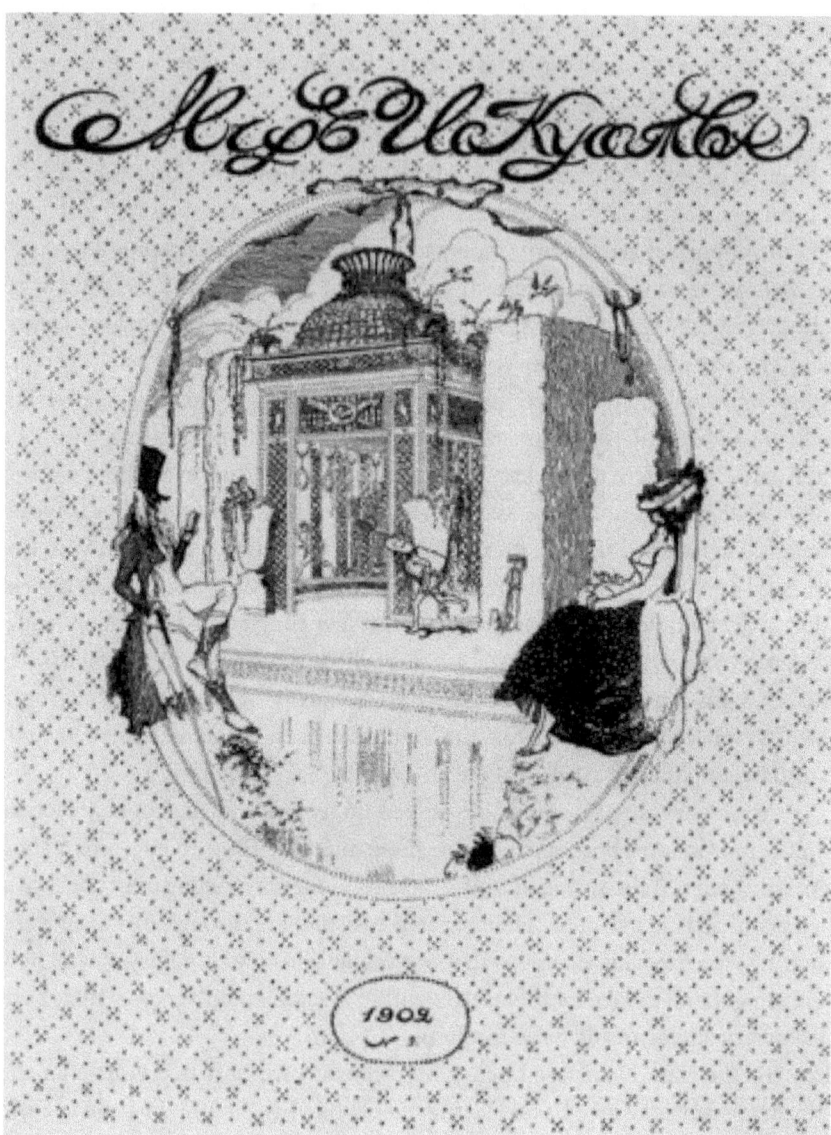

Figure 15. Cover of *Mir Iskusstva*, issue no. 2 of 1902. Drawing by Léon Bakst.

constantly changing his style and genres. The artist and memoirist Alexander Benois, another miriskusnik, wrote of him:

> Bakst has "golden hands," amazing technique, a great deal of taste, fiery enthusiasm toward art, but he does not know what to do with himself.

Bakst rushes about frantically and spreads himself thin, and meanwhile years are passing, and it is positively vexing that he does not wish to come to terms with himself, does not wish to understand the boundaries of his highly outstanding gifts.[9]

What Benois saw as weaknesses in Bakst the artist—a searching nature, an unwillingness to stick with and develop a unique style and genre, and a readiness to engage passionately with new ideas and experiments—were enormous strengths for Bakst the teacher, and ultimately for his own growth as an artist.[10] Bakst based his pedagogical principles on the theoretical work of Vyacheslav Ivanov (1866–1949), Symbolist poet and philosopher, Russian promoter of Nietzsche, and literary critic, who exerted a profound influence on Russian Symbolism. Some of the miriskusniki participated in gatherings at Ivanov's "tower" apartment, which was in the same building as Zvantseva's academy, on the floor above the academy's space (figure 16).

The Tower was one of the most important centers of Symbolist culture at the time; the first person Magda and Julia saw at the new academy, even before meeting their teacher Bakst, and whom they mistook for him at first, was one of the most important Silver Age poets, Mikhail Kuzmin, who on his way to the Tower had been paying a visit to Zvantseva. Such was the proximity of the Zvantseva art students to one of the capital's most important cultural hotspots.[11] Years later, after emigration, Dobuzhinsky recalled that

some students, following Bakst's and my own example, also were visitors of the hospitable "tower." And the school beneath the "tower" was becoming not only a school, but a small incubator, a sort of fellowship in whose exclusive atmosphere many future artists were maturing.[12]

Bakst took Vyacheslav Ivanov's idea of a cultural "sobornost" (spiritual community) as a basis for forming an artistic school as an association of like-minded individuals united by a common goal. Taking the term from Russian Orthodox

---

9   Aleksandr Benua, "L. S. Bakst. E. E. Lansere," in *Istoriia russkoi zhivopisi v XIX veke*. Moscow: "Respublika," 1999, 410–413.

10   Bakst retained a passion for learning all his life. In 1921, in a review of a Paris exhibition of Russian painters, a reviewer, G. Lukomsky, wrote that the artist's works demonstrated his "never-ending thirst to explore, to learn, and to work." See G. K. Lukomskii, "Mir iskusstva," *Zhar-Ptitsa* 1 (1921): 17.

11   Obolenskaia, "V shkole Zvantsovoi," 209–242.

12   M. V. Dobuzhinskii, *Vospominaniia* (Moscow: Nauka, 1987), 271.

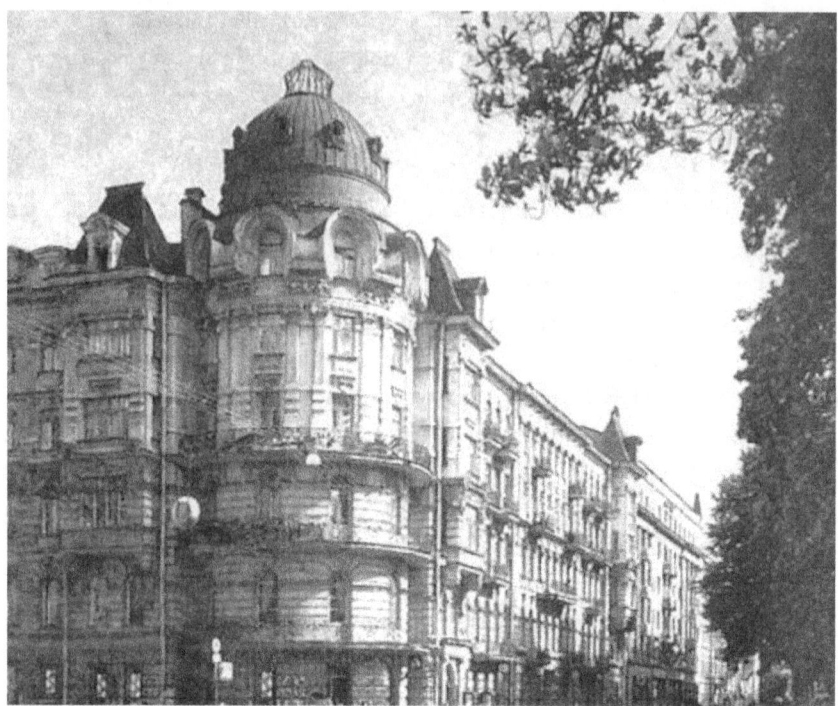

Figure 16. The "Tower": home of Vyacheslav Ivanov's apartment and the Zvantseva Academy.

religious philosophy, Ivanov imbued it with a wider meaning, relating it to the expression of common values drawn from a common source:

> Sobornost is a state of connectivity in which the connected individuals achieve the full flowering and definition of their individuality, their unique and inherent essence, their perfect creative freedom, that makes each individual manifest as a new word necessary for all. In each was the Word made flesh and it dwells in all, and in each it sounds differently, but the word of each finds its resonance in all, and all are in freely given mutual consent, because all are a single Word.[13]

Bakst developed his own views on current artistic developments in his major theoretical article "Puti classitsizma v iskusstve" ("The ways of classicism in art"). He wrote that among the enemies of art,

---

13 Viacheslav Ivanov, "Legion i Sobornost'," in *Sobranie sochinenii v 4 tomakh*, vol. 3: *Stat'i* (Brussels: Foyer Oriental Chrétien, 1979), 261.

the last, the most formidable, of art in general and of a school in particular, is certainly the individualism that was solemnly declared a quarter century ago as the guarantor of the legitimacy of an artist's existence.[14]

According to Bakst, European art that had flourished from the thirteenth century to the end of the eighteenth had been born out of a common aspiration and common striving of all the representatives of the artistic schools and movements, from apprentices to masters, toward a common understanding of what constitutes true art—each school building on the achievements of its forerunners. But true art had come to an end and sunk into degradation in the nineteenth century. Classical art had become ossified in the hands of academic epigones.

The goal of Bakst's teaching was to create a unified artistic school, like those of antiquity and the Renaissance, in which ideas and their technical implementation would be worked out in an atmosphere of common endeavor that would nevertheless also allow the free development of each individual's contribution to the common vision. Julia, paraphrasing her teacher, called the atmosphere Bakst created a "breath of life":

> The subliminal mood was wonderful. To be never alone, not cut off from the whole, to be a part of the whole, to carry out one's task in a common endeavor, to look at the world with such big eyes, the eyes of the whole school, and at the same time to remain oneself, certainly in contrast to all other schools, which were subjugated by their teacher or by an idea—all this created a solid foundation under our feet, so firm that surely we shall never again experience the like.[15]

Bakst saw in their common endeavor a way toward a truly modern Russian art, which at the moment was in its infancy. He believed that contemporary artists should not look to the past for their models; they needed to work out new ideals of beauty as well as the forms in which those ideals could be expressed. Thus, copying old masters—the main academic teaching method—was forbidden in Bakst's classes. As Julia wrote:

> Discussion of Rembrandt and other old masters was supposed to have for us only a certain general educational significance: indeed, there could

---

14 Leon Bakst, "Puti klassitsizma v iskusstve" (part 1), *Apollon* 2 (1909): 72.
15 Obolenskaia, "V shkole Zvantsovoi," 231.

have been no direct continuity between the art of their completed cultural epoch and the trials of us young savages.[16]

Contemporary artists must develop a fresh, even naive, eye and begin to paint without preconceptions and restrictions, like children who have not yet been "taught" by the examples of their elders; like primitive peoples (including Russian peasants) who have not come into contact with European artistic traditions and are unafraid of bright colors and primitive lines; like the artists of antiquity, who were present at the birth of European art. Bakst's school aimed to develop such an unspoiled, naive vision. In her memoirs, Julia wrote:

> already in a month of instruction, namely under Bakst, our opened eyes saw keenly and clearly, and we walked as though in a daze from the surging joy of a new way of seeing.[17]

As a teacher, Bakst would generously share his own fascinations with his students. The captivating quality of his instruction, noted by many of them, was drawn from his own passionate study of the art of ancient Greece and Egypt; that of Asia, in particular the Japanese command of line; and his own desire to experiment with the mutual influence of colors.

Following the Japanese masters, Bakst insisted on the supremacy of line, which imparts rhythm to a work of art and informs its content. In a picture Magda painted in India (figure 17), decades after her school days, the quality of line taught by Bakst is evident.

When they arrived at the Zvantseva academy, the three friends at once noticed a painting by a fellow student, Nadezhda Lermontova, who soon joined their circle. It was a female nude, completed the previous summer following a year of study under Bakst, painted entirely in shades of green. Dobuzhinsky, who taught drawing at the school, disparaged it as a "green samovar," not quite seeing what Lermontova was aiming at. That the painting was monochromatic, and green at that, was clearly throwing down the gauntlet before the canons of academic art. The first shock that Magda and her friends experienced on seeing Lermontova's nude gave way to a desire to experiment, to put colors in conversation with each other or even to provoke an argument among them through unexpected combinations. This desire grew even stronger when Lermontova's

---

16   Ibid., 218–219.
17   Ibid., 216.

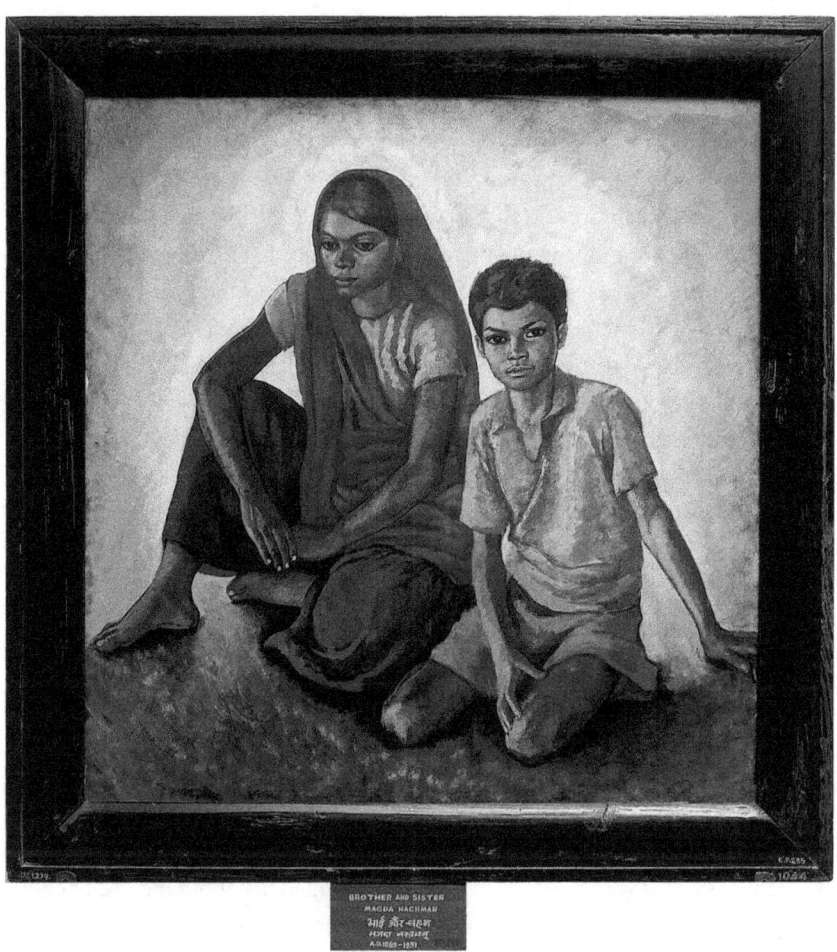

Figure 17. Magda Nachman. *Brother and Sister (courtesy of the Baroda Museum and Picture Gallery, Vadodara, India).*

painting was singled out by Bakst as the best among the students' summer efforts. The new students tried to emulate Lermontova but without much success: they were unable to break with their prior artistic training and preconceptions. They would achieve freedom in the use of color only after a long struggle to produce compositions using just two or three colors, usually with broad brush strokes on very coarse canvas—a typical Bakst assignment.

In class, Bakst would choose one student's work, assemble all the others around it, and critique it without mincing words, pointing out all the shortcomings and infelicities in tone and line, color relationships, composition, and every imaginable detail, thus working out a common understanding of their common goals. However, he suggested no general recipes for how to overcome the difficulties that he had exposed; solving the painting's artistic problems was left to the student. In one assignment, the students had been instructed to paint a model who was lying partly on green fabric, partly on red. Commenting on Julia's work, Bakst announced that it was less a civilized argument among colors than an all-out brawl. Julia wrote in her memoirs about her struggle to produce a better result. Finally, in a dream, she realized that the red and green of the fabric had to be reflected in the tones of the model's flesh. In the morning she applied her discovery to her study. It was that painting of Julia's that Bakst chose for the students' show. He now allowed Julia to use cool red paints, which earlier had been forbidden her because she would turn to them whenever she couldn't find the correct color ("Bakst often imposed such penances on students," she wrote).[18]

Julia's failure to produce a satisfactory painting and then her triumph in finding what she was looking for served as a lesson to all the students. As Julia writes, "that was a turning point in the work of the whole class. Successful works began to appear one after another."[19]

Julia remarks that "at school, Magda showed herself very strikingly ... she stood out in the sharpness of her colors. ... We were taken by the world of color—bright, resounding, contrasting; by the life of this color in its development, in its collisions with other colors; we were taken with simple and important outlines of things and people with their irreproducible typical characteristics of each thing." But often, "small, quiet, and meek" Magda—as Julia described her—was under the teacher's fire as with polite bemusement he grilled her about her use of color: "What is it, hallucination?—Cholera?—Even worse! Plague!"[20]

Despite his criticism of Magda's work, Bakst acquired at least one of her paintings, one that had been chosen for the students' exhibition in 1910 and was marked "property of Bakst" in the catalogue. Following one of Bakst's critiques of his work, his best known student, Marc Chagall, perhaps wounded by his teacher's sharp words, disappeared from the academy for a time, but then thought better of it and returned. Another student, P. V. Andreev, described these sessions of direct criticism with loving warmth:

> It is impossible to convey Bakst's wit. In his usual kind manner, the entire truth would be spoken, without delicacy, but also without even a shadow

---

18 Ibid., 216.
19 Ibid., 215.
20 Ibid., 223, 225.

of rudeness or cheekiness. Sometimes his comments hit painfully but somehow they were always fatherly and good-natured.[21]

Julia notes that Bakst's committed students, the core of the academy, never felt offended. On the contrary, his criticism gave them energy and a desire to persevere. Casual students would not stay long.

Little by little, each student worked out an individual way of painting in the framework of a common vision that allowed a great freedom in the handling of colors, which nevertheless had to be true to the essence of the subject. For his review of the students' show in 1910, Bakst summarized his instruction thus:

> I would say that in four years at school, a single work has been produced by a common hand in spite of the variety of styles arising from the natural individual characteristics of each student. This work has been perfected, being animated by a single motivation, by a single aim understood by all the students. I tried not so much to teach as to awaken a desire to search, at the same time assiduously guarding the searching young eye from falsity and banality.[22]

Bakst himself was a student at his own school. During that time, the style of his portraits began slowly to change. As his biographer noted, "His drawing had become more economical and more general; the line acquired a particular plasticity and clarity." This is especially evident in later portraits "that are done with a bare line, without chiaroscuro."[23] Bakst himself was learning from the Japanese masters, just as he insisted his students should do. In 1909, he stopped working in graphic arts, the practice of which was forbidden at the school. Something happened in his own oil painting that surprised even him: "I have climbed at last into the brightest range of tones; perhaps this is a new phase that has come naturally."[24] In a letter to the miriskusnik artist Ostroumova-Lebedeva, he repeated, "I am drowned in colors; I don't want even to hear about the graphic arts."[25] Thus did Bakst note in himself the developments he had been encouraging in his students.

---

21 P. V. Andreev, "Moi vospominaniia o Bakste," in Pruzhan, *Lev Samoilovich Bakst*, 122.

22 Lev Bakst, "Vystavka v redaktsii Apollona," *Apollon* 8 (1910): 44–45.

23 Pruzhan, *Lev Samoilovich Bakst*, 92.

24 Léon Bakst, letter to A. Benois, September 1909, in Pruzhan, *Lev Samoilovich Bakst*, 135.

25 Léon Bakst, letter to Ostroumova-Lebedeva, November 12, 1910, in Pruzhan, *Lev Samoilovich Bakst*, 135.

In the hands of another teacher, Bakst's pedagogical principles, yoking together such seemingly contradictory demands as common endeavor and originality, a high level of technical skill, and eschewal of imitation, might have led to chaos or perhaps developed only one aspect of his students' talents. Bakst's success attests to his pedagogical genius. Thus in her essay commemorating Bakst, his student Sofia Dymshits-Tolstaya remarked, "On my path as a student and as an independent artist I have met many teachers, but I never saw one equal to Bakst."[26] Despite their disagreements, Chagall wrote in his autobiography that his "fate was decided by the school of Bakst and Dobuzhinsky. Bakst changed my life. I shall never forget that man."[27]

Bakst's own enthusiasm for art was contagious; his demand that his students work six hours a day and produce a daily study in summer was carried out without question. Such sustained work had become for many of them an essential ingredient of their lives. Here is an extract from a 1911 letter from Magda to Julia:

> Today I finished my first [summer] study. I feel that the path will be right—only the path, although its constituent parts have no value. ... To paint and to live are one and the same as much as form and content are one and the same. That's why one loves form, concentrating in it all the dear fluidity of life.[28]

At the end of the 1908–1909 academic year, Bakst considered his students ready to prepare for a public exhibition. On May 9, 1909, one of their classmates, Alexander Ziloti, wrote to Julia, "Bakst said that in spring 1910 he wants to mount an exhibition of our work and show several of his own paintings as well."[29] In a letter to Julia, Magda was skeptical: "As to the news, I think it is too early for us all to exhibit."[30] But Julia replied, "Why do you consider *cher maître*'s plan with such disdain; I immediately took it seriously."[31] The show was mounted in the exhibition space of the arts journal *Apollon*[32] and opened

---

26 Sofia Dymshits-Tolstaya, Russian Museum, manuscript division, f. 100, no 249, 8.

27 Quoted in Jackie Wullschlager, *Chagall: A Biography* (New York: Alfred A. Knopf, 2008), 114.

28 June 10, 1911, RGALI, f. 2080, op. 1, no. 45, 45–48.

29 RGALI: f. 2080, op. 1, no. 28.

30 June 8, 1909, RGALI: f. 2080, op. 1, no. 45, 18–19.

31 June 15, 1909, RGALI: f. 2080, op. 1, no. 7, 3–4/op.

32 *Apollon* was published in St. Petersburg from 1909 to 1917. It published works of Symbolist poets (Alexander Blok, Mikhail Kuzmin) and Acmeists (Mandelstam, Akhmatova,

on April 20, 1910. In the spirit of collectivism, the students did not sign their paintings, which were identified only by numbers. However, we know the creators of many of the works because Magda made a sketch of the exhibition, in which she depicted herself spying on the few visitors, including two art critics—Alexander Rostislavov, wearing a pince-nez, and Adrian Prakhov, opera hat in hand (figure 18).[33] Even from this meager caricature one can see that the main

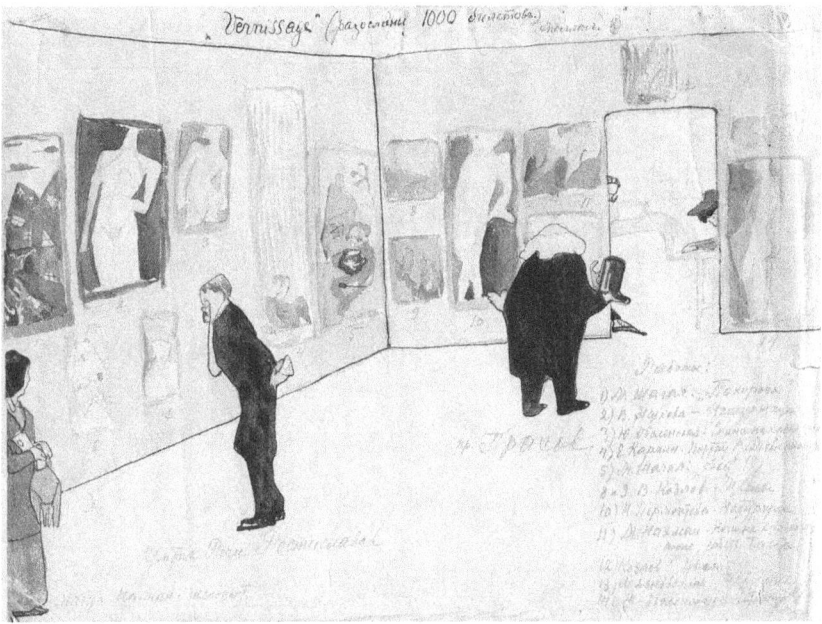

Figure 18. Magda Nachman. Drawing of the Zvantseva academy student exhibition. The first picture on the left, numbered 1, is Mark Chagall's painting *The Jewish Funeral*; number 5, on the left wall, is his *Dinner*. Magda's figure study is number 11, just above Prakhov's head; next to it, number 10, is Nadezhda Lermontova's *Model*. Obolenskaya's *Model* is number 14. Other exhibitors included in the sketch are V. Zhukova, E. Karmin, V. Kozlov, and Myaskovskaya (?). The words at the top of the sketch read, "Vernissage [opening day]" (1000 tickets sent out) (*Courtesy of RGALI, Moscow*).

Gumilev), critical surveys of European and Russian art along with high-quality reproductions, and surveys of contemporary music. The first covers of the journal were drawn by Bakst and, later, by Dobuzhinsky.

33 Sketch of the 1910 students' show by Magda Nachman, RGALI, f. 2080, op. 1, no. 106. At a later time someone added a note at the lower right of the sketch identifying the paintings and artists.

interest of the student-artists was the relationship of colors, their dialogues and contretemps. Magda's drawing is the only record of the academy's show. At the same time, Magda sketched caricatures of the participants. With a few strokes outlining the figures, she made them fully recognizable (figures 19–22).

By the time the student exhibition opened, at the very end of the season, Bakst had left for Paris to continue his work on the sets and costumes for a ballet adaptation of Rimsky-Korsakov's *Scheherazade*, which was premiered

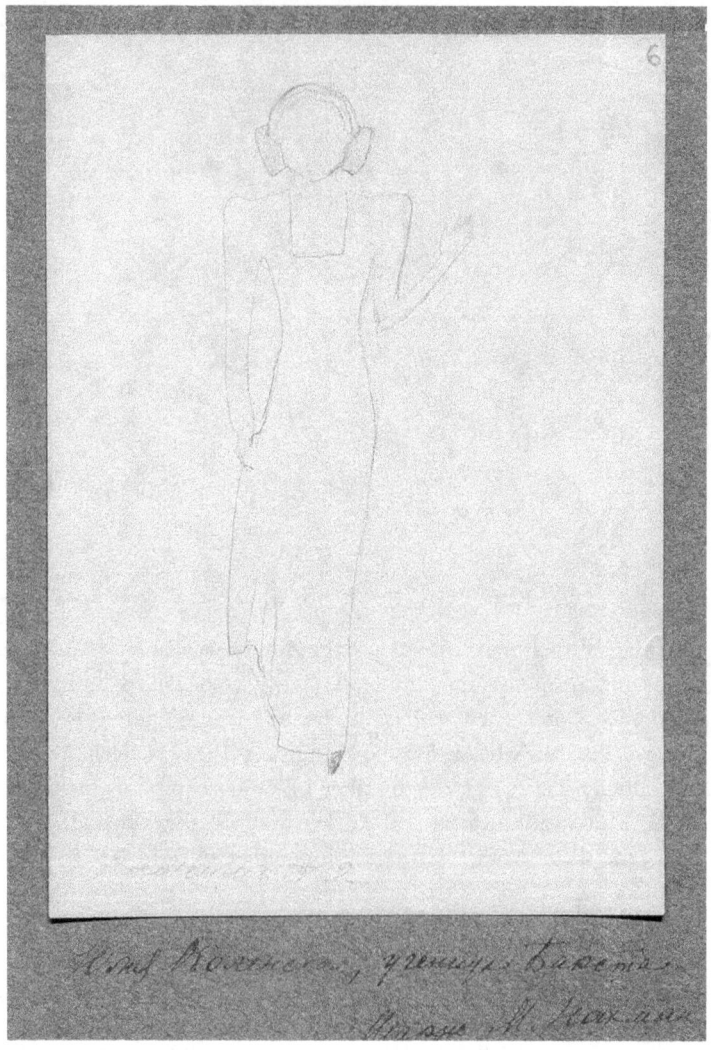

Figure 19. Magda Nachman. Sketch of Julia Obolenskaya (*courtesy of RGALI, Moscow*).

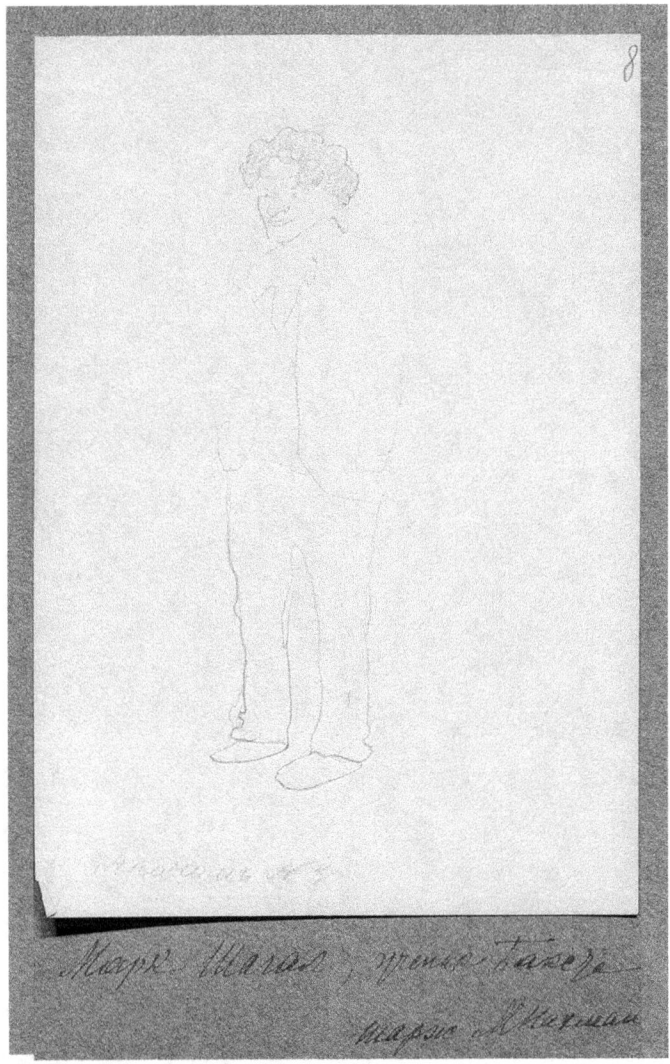

Figure 20. Magda Nachman. Sketch of Marc Chagall (*courtesy of RGALI, Moscow*).

on June 4, 1910, by Sergei Diaghilev's Ballets Russes at the Opéra Granier. The student exhibition did not attract much attention, although four reviews were published, including a highly critical, indeed hostile, piece by Repin. As Julia reported, Repin, storming through the show, railed against the young artists, calling them incompetent daubers. He had apparently found a pretext for venting his spleen against the experimentation and new directions of modernism

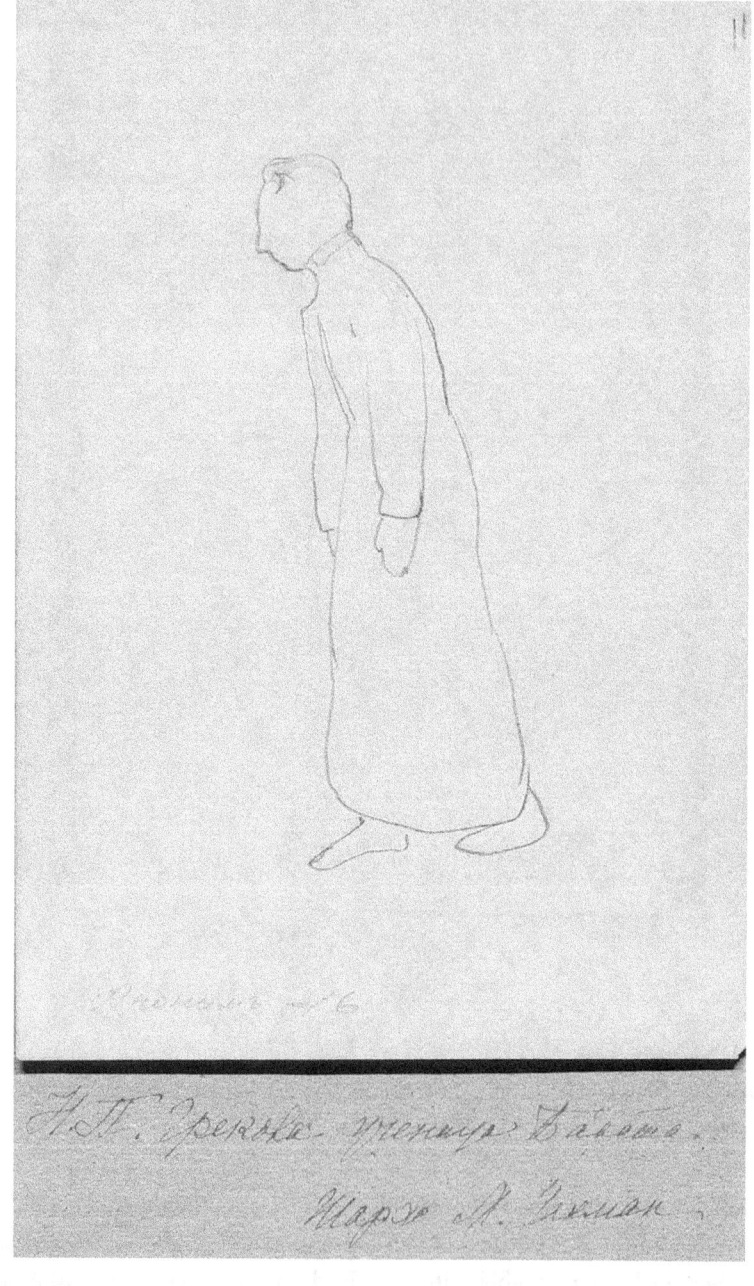

Figure 21. Magda Nachman. Sketch of Natalia Grekova (*courtesy of RGALI, Moscow*).

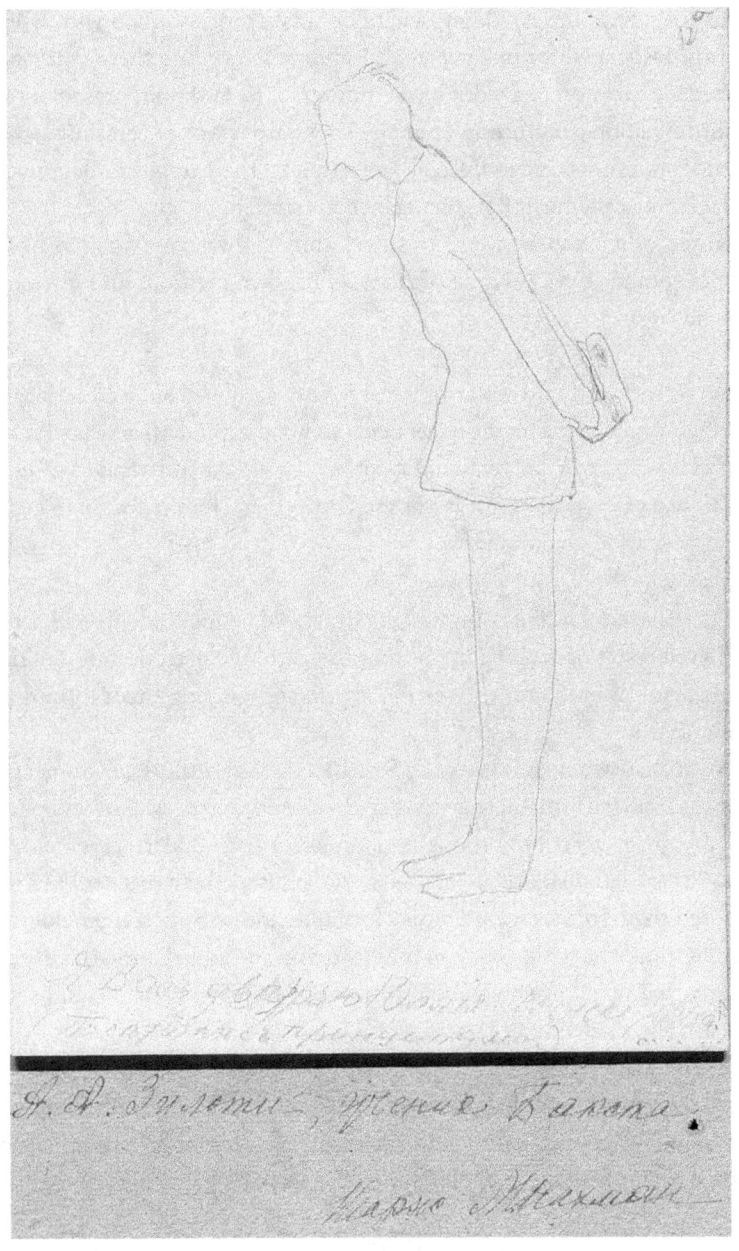

Figure 22. Magda Nachman. Sketch of Alexander Ziloti (*courtesy of RGALI, Moscow*).

and its critique of the Academy, where he was a professor and with which he had been associated for many years.[34] Repin failed to find there what for him was the sine qua non of a work of art: mimesis, the faithful representation and realistic reflection of nature and people. Those aspects were certainly lacking in the students' works. Indeed, Repin's reaction to the exhibition demonstrated how far from academism Bakst had taken his students.

Three other reviews were positive, among them one written by Bakst himself (quoted above) as an evaluation of his own methods and its results, in which he wrote:

> in recent years, a hysterical form that has been acquired by an art seeking [new forms] is the most eloquent indicator of the fact that contemporary art is suffocating and thrashing about, not knowing how to find itself, its legitimate expression, just as a fish suffocates that is thrown from its natural element onto the sand.[35]

He believed that the communality practiced by his students had achieved the desired result of keeping them from the path of barren negation of the old and mechanical imitation of Western artists and guiding them toward a new organic style.

The other two reviews were by Rostislavov (a caricature of whom appears in Magda's sketch), in the newspaper *Rech*, and Sergei Makovsky, poet, art critic, organizer of art exhibitions, and publisher and editor in chief of *Apollon*. Makovsky congratulated the students and praised their teachers for having prevented them from relying on easy formulas and parroting their elders; "the opposite from what we see, say, in the Academy," he added.[36] He was especially taken by their experiments in color, "rigorous taste" in drawing, and sense of shape artfully rendered on canvas.

The students were not hurt by Repin's vitriol; on the contrary, his strong negative reaction reinforced their view of his realist art, which they regarded as passé. As to Makovsky, although his journal had become an important forum for discussion of a variety of modern trends in poetry, art, music, and theater,

---

34 Repin's article "V adu u pifona" appeared in *Birzhevye vedomosti* on May 15, 1910. His second attack against Bakst's students and all those connected with the World of Art, Il'ia Repin, "O Aleksandre Benua, Obere i drugikh …," was published in *Birzhevye vedomosti*, November 19, 1911.

35 Bakst, "Vystavka v redaktsii Apollona," *Apollon* 3, no. 8 (1910): 45.

36 Sergei Makovskii, "Vystavka v redaktsii Apollona," *Apollon* 3, no. 8 (1910): 44.

in his tastes and inclinations, the publisher of *Apollon* was a devotee of the Style Moderne. The students lampooned Makovsky's aestheticism in an unpublished parody of *Apollon*, which they called *Daphne*, in honor of the nymph of Greek mythology who fled Apollo's clutches. They believed that both critics had failed to understand what their teacher was after. Thus Julia wrote:

> It occurs to no one that under Bakst's guidance, the young people had been brought up on principles that were completely contrary to the foundations of Mir Iskusstva, its retrospectivism contrasted to the naive savage eye; its stylization to the immediacy of a child's drawing; its graphicality to a wild, bright "porridge" of paint; and finally, its individualism to a conscious collectivism.[37]

After one has read Julia's description of the principles and aspirations that Bakst's teaching had instilled in his students, it is natural to ask why they kept apart from such modernist groups as the Futurists, "Jack of Diamonds," and "Donkey's Tail," all of which became vocal and visible in the 1910s. After all, Bakst had encouraged his students to be "daring, simple, rude, primitive. The art of the future demands a lapidary style because it cannot stand the exquisite—it is fed up with it."[38] We can compare his words with any number of avant-garde art manifestos and pronouncements, for example with the poet Benedikt Livshits's description of the exhibition in 1912 of the radical group of artists known as the Donkey's Tail: "everything has become mixed up in the maddening whirlwind of the anatomized solar spectrum, in the primordial chaos of colors, which restored to the human eye a savage acuity of vision."[39] These words are almost the same as Julia's. They call for a return to the freedom of color and to an unspoiled, raw, primitive vision.

It was by now a good half-century since the rise of the Impressionists in France, and the idea of a new way of seeing had become a commonplace in writing on art. And once artists began "seeing differently," the whole world began to open its eyes and follow them in seeing what before had been insensible to sight. In every artistic capital, groups of artists could be found who asserted the supremacy of their particular way of seeing, all competing for attention and wall space in exhibition halls.

---

37 Obolenskaia, "V shkole Zvantsovoi," 209.
38 Bakst, "Puti klassitsizma v iskusstve" (part 2), Apollon 3 (1909): 61.
39 Benedikt Livshits, *Polutoraglazyi strelets* (Leningrad: Sovetskii pisatel', 1989), 372.

But the vision that Bakst imparted to his students was very different from the credo of the more assertive avatars of the Russian avant-garde. Perhaps his biggest quarrel was with an abstract art that disdained the natural world. Moreover, Bakst, always elegantly dressed, with refined manners, could not approve the happenings staged by the avant-gardists—with their painted faces, masks, and provocative dress. Nor had he any sympathy with the images of herrings and pigs that had come down from shop signboards onto the Futurists' canvases and the newspaper advertisements superimposed on a defaced Mona Lisa in the work of such avant-gardists as Mikhail Larionov, Ilya Mashkov, and Kazimir Malevich. Bakst insisted that the goals of art should be much loftier than merely to shock the public, which he considered nothing more than rank snobbery. Nor did he believe in the call for a cataclysmic destruction of the old in order that a path might be cleared for the new—in his eyes, a crude desire for self-assertion that had nothing to do with artistic integrity. Although he advocated a clear break with tradition, he did not see a clean slate as a precondition for new growth. And he did not call for throwing the old idols "overboard from the ship of modernity," as the futurists, though largely posturing, had loudly announced in their manifesto. The old did not stand in the way of the new, Bakst argued; rather, it was the substrate from under which the new would emerge:

> I repeat, the life-giving font of health will emerge not following a cataclysm, not from under a freshly destroyed edifice; it has been imperceptibly growing through the dense underbrush, and only in places does the bright green color reveal the source of freshness, hidden in its depth.[40]

In 1914, in an article titled "On the Art of Today," Bakst wrote:

> There are two dominant movements in art at the moment. One is slavishly retrospective and the other, hostile to the former, is futuristic, with its sights set far ahead. ... The former movement pulls us back to our predecessors, to the art of the deceased, to the illumined canons, while the latter destroys everything old and builds the foundation for the art of the future that will be judged by our great-grandchildren. But where is our own art, where is the new art, where are the contemporary joy and delight in an art that really expresses our life and not that of our grandfathers or our great-grandchildren?[41]

---

40 Lev Bakst, "Puti klassitsizma v iskusstve" (part 2), *Apollon* 3 (1909): 51.
41 Lev Bakst, "Ob iskusstve segodniashnego dnia," *Stolitsa i usad'ba* 8 (1914): 18–19.

Even from Paris in 1924, Bakst, according to Dobuzhinsky's memoir, "furiously scolded the Futurists."[42]

At the Zvantseva art academy, Bakst endeavored to work out a collective understanding of a "new art" that would speak to contemporary "joy and delight" and educate artists who would create the art of their own day. The students responded to their teacher's challenge, and the artistic convictions worked out in Bakst's classes remained with them for life. They rejected the excessive aestheticism of the Style Moderne and detested the experiments of the Futurists, in which they saw an arbitrariness and pale imitation of Western models, in contrast to their earnest search for organic art. Even in 1919, in a letter to Julia, Magda wrote, "The Imaginists should be flogged without mercy—this is my covenant. In a way, they are even more loathsome than the Futurists."[43] (The Russian Imaginists borrowed their name from Ezra Pound's Imagist group—although they had little else in common with those English and American poets. Imaginism was the last short-lived Russian avant-garde movement in literature and art; it appeared in reaction to Futurism in 1919 and died out around 1925.)

After his departure in 1910, Bakst would never live in Russia again. In 1912, he returned to St. Petersburg, only to be banished by the authorities as a Jew who had no right to live in the capital.[44] He was ordered to leave within forty-eight hours, and only an appeal to the tsar by his friends allowed him to extend his stay to two weeks.[45] During that fortnight, he found time to visit his students at the academy and reassure them that their new teacher, Kuzma Petrov-Vodkin, was leading them in the right direction. Bakst had recommended Petrov-Vodkin as his successor, whose experiments with color he approved and whom he considered congenial to his artistic sensibility and approach to teaching. Although the relationship between Petrov-Vodkin and the students was stormy at times, those who remained with him learned a great deal. The economy of color and open perspective characteristic of Petrov-Vodkin's work can be seen in Magda's 1916 painting *Peasant Woman* (figure 23).[46] This is

---

42 Dobuzhinskii, *Vospominaniia*, 297.

43 June 17, 1919, RGALI, f. 2080, op. 45, no. 7, 129–130.

44 Bakst was born Leyb-Chaim Israilevich Rosenberg. He took the name Bakst, a modification of his mother's maiden name Bakster, for professional reasons, considering, rightly, that "Rosenberg" was too obviously Jewish a name for commercial success.

45 Bakst's final visit to Russia was in February 1914. He planned to return in the fall of that year, but the outbreak of World War I made such a trip impossible.

46 This painting belongs to the State Fine Arts Museum of Tatarstan, in Kazan, Russia, where it was exhibited in 1920.

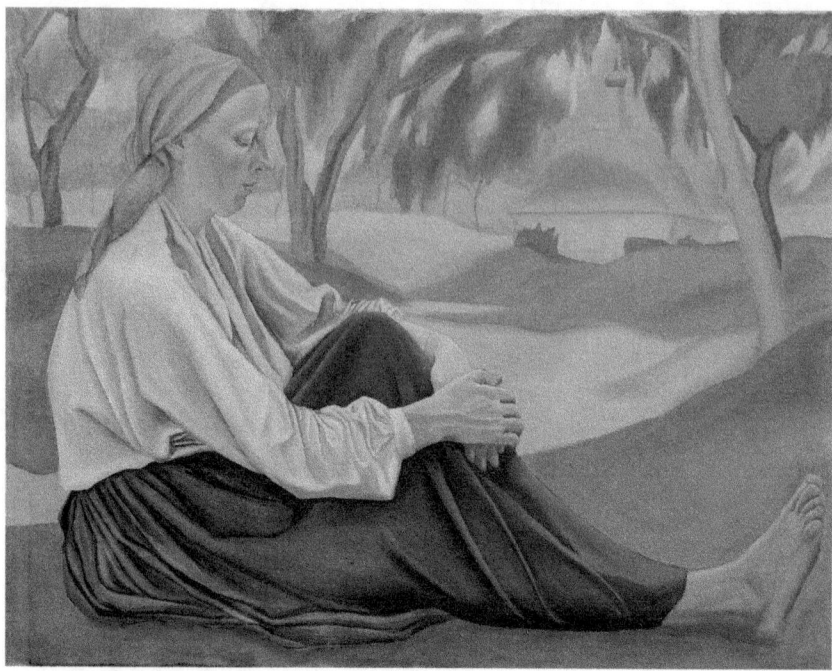

Figure 23. Magda Nachman. *Peasant Woman*, ca. 1916.

one of only a handful of her pictures executed during her Russian years whose whereabouts are known. None of Magda's works produced before 1910 appear to have survived.

CHAPTER 5

The Constellation Leo

Léon Bakst's students formed a tightly knit group of friends, which, in honor of their teacher, Julia called the "Constellation Leo."[1] Figure 24 reproduces a photograph of eight Zvantseva students. As Julia recalled:

> Just as we worked all together, we would leave school together and roam about the city in search of interesting signboards or handmade toys whose primitivism attracted us. Right at the exit, the horse-drawn tram that took the members of the State Duma to the Tauride Palace would be waiting for us [figure 25]. It was always empty, and so the conductor held its departure until we appeared. We noisily occupied both top and bottom, and on passing the State Duma, we performed "God Save the Tsar" in a minor key, under the direction of Ziloti, which sounded incredibly ominous.
>
> We went to the suburbs in search of painterly impressions ... attended exhibitions, symphony concerts, theater performances, lectures, poetry readings, and peppered our talk with quotations from *Balaganchik* [Alexander Blok's play *The Fairground Puppet Booth*] and *Seti* [the Russian Symbolist Mikhail Kuzmin's first collection of poetry].[2]

As one of the Zvantseva students, Sofia Dymshits-Tolstaya, wrote in her memoirs, "The students left the school not only with theoretical knowledge but with an expansive culture in the broad sense of the word."[3] This group of art students partook freely of the cultural riches that were available in St. Petersburg. Ziloti, whose father was a prominent Russian pianist and conductor, was a reliable source of tickets and passes for the most sought-after performances. Here is

---

1   Letter to Magda Nachman, July 9, 1909, RGALI, f. 2080, op. 45, ed. khr. 7, 5–6.
2   Obolenskaia, "V shkole Zvantsovoi," 232. Alexander Ziloti (1887–1950, Paris)—artist, photographer, art theorist. Studied at Zvantseva Academy. His mother and Bakst's wife were sisters, daughters of Pavel Tretyakov, the famous Russian Maecenas and founder of Moscow's Tretyakov Gallery. On his father's side, Ziloti was related to Sergei Rachmaninoff.
3   Sofia Dymshits-Tolstaya. Russian Museum, manuscript division, f. 100, no. 249.

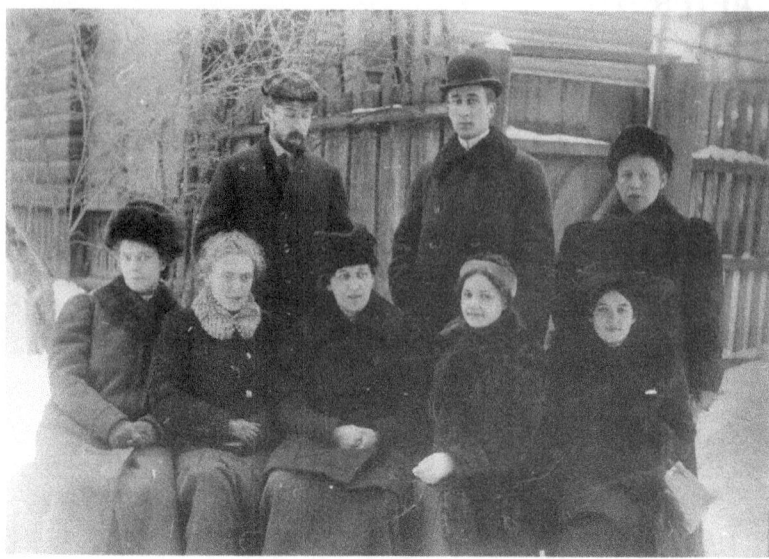

Figure 24. Students of Zvantseva art academy. Seated from left to right: Maria Pets, Varya Klimovich-Toper, Nadezhda Lermontova, Julia Obolenskaya, Magda Nachman. Standing from left to right: Nikolai Tyrsa, Aleksander Ziloti, Natalia Grekova. Not later than 1910 (*courtesy of RGALI, Moscow*).

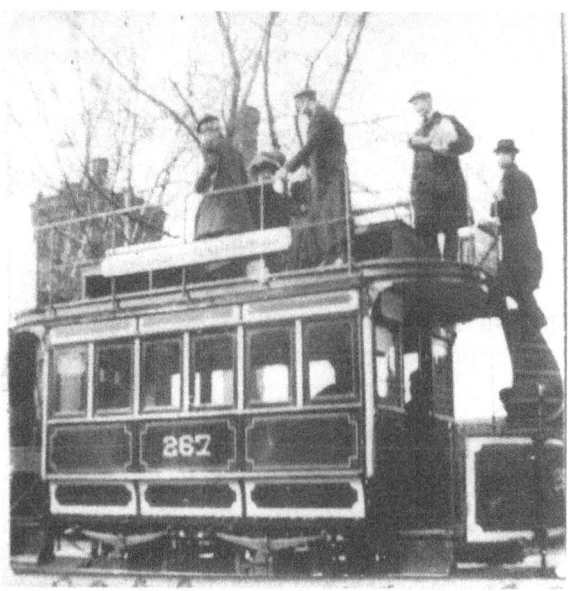

Figure 25. Horse-drawn tram on its way to the Tauride Palace, St. Petersburg (*courtesy of RGALI, Moscow*).

his note to Julia with which he sent complimentary tickets to Isadora Duncan's recital that he had managed to sweet-talk from the dancer herself:

> I am unwell, which is why I was not in "class" yesterday and also why I cannot go out this evening. Not wishing, however, that my rushing about and elo-quence before Duncan in service of her fans should be for naught and that her most exalted condescension, that is, that with her very own hands she pre-sented me with loge tickets from her side pocket, should be without effect, I am sending them along, that is, five passes, and ask you to invite Natalia Petrovna [Grekova] and Nadezhda Vladimirovna [Lermontova]. Perhaps Nikolai Andreevich [Tyrsa] or Varvara Petrovna [Klimovich-Toper] will go—in short, I leave this decision to you; in any case, if you, Magda Maxi-milianovna, and Kozlov go, there will be two additional tickets.[4]

Ziloti often finished his letters, as he did this one, with "Long live the school of Bakst!"

The following day, he sent Julia five tickets for a concert of music by Bach and Maurice Ravel: "Probably Magda Maximilianovna and Natalia Petrovna would like to go. Then ask Lermontova and Kozlov."[5] And when Pablo Casals arrived in St. Petersburg to perform, it was Ziloti who met him at the station, and of course he supplied his friends with tickets:

> In the morning I am going to meet Casals. Regards to Magda Maximilianovna—tell her that after that I will begin thinking so highly of myself that the two of you will find it even more difficult to keep me in line.[6]

Lermontova's portrait of Casals was done around that time, when the cellist was a frequent visitor in Petersburg and often stayed with the Zilotis.

But these young artists weren't just writing about concert tickets and going to the theater. In their correspondence, the friends would discuss the theories of aesthetics propounded by Nietzsche, Ruskin, and Oscar Wilde, and give their thoughts on the Russian, German, French, and English literature that they were reading. They read widely and often in the original: Shakespeare, Montaigne,

---

4   April 13, 1909, RGALI, f. 2080, op. 1, no. 28.
5   April 14, 1909, ibid.
6   January 4, 1910, ibid.

Goethe, Stefan George, Flaubert, George Sand, and Maeterlinck. They read the Greek philosophers (Plato, Aristotle), the Neoplatonic philosopher Plotinus, Rabindranath Tagore, and Russian symbolist poetry (Ivanov, Blok, Kuzmin). Bakst's students also studied Gaston Maspero's[7] books on Egyptian history, religion, art, and archeology. Their teacher's interest in those subjects was contagious. Writing to Julia, Ziloti asked:

> How is your Maspero coming along? I reread my notes and am starting on Sennacherib.[8] When I am done with him and with the rest of the book, I will read two more books also by him, *Les contes populaires de l'Egypte ancienne* [1906] and *Causeries d'Egypte* [1907], and then I will read the first one again. These two books are not too long (they are the same ones that Magda Maximilianovna bought for herself).[9]

Magda was apparently building up her library. (Later, at the time of her poverty and hunger during the Russian Civil War, she would sell some of her books to keep herself afloat.)

Recalling these friends in 1926, Julia wrote that she could not remember a single quarrel or misunderstanding,

> except perhaps some amusing principled arguments in the Hermitage between Tyrsa and Ziloti. There was no envy over someone's success: achievement of one was a cause for celebration for all.

Lermontova, a bit older than the rest, was accepted as the most talented and accomplished artist among them.

Their involvement in each other's lives was so intense that missing even a few days of school and common activities was hard, and parting in summer was a bitter sorrow. One day in spring, Grekova, sick at home with a cold, wrote Julia a note: "How are you all now? I really don't know how I will manage without you all in summer."[10] And then later, from her summer retreat, "How I miss your company, my friends! Often, I feel lonely. Indeed, I think that work would have gone better if we had been all together."[11]

---

7   Gaston Camille Charles Maspero (1846–1916), French Egyptologist.
8   King of Assyria from 705 to 681 BCE.
9   July 5, 1909, RGALI, f. 2080, op. 1, no. 28, 15–16op.
10 April 16, 1912, RGALI, f. 2080, op. 1, no. 24, 5–6, written from Pavlovsk (near St. Petersburg).
11 June 1, 1912, RGALI, f. 2080, op. 1, no. 24, 9–12.

St. Petersburg is an inhospitable city for painters. Summers are short and often rainy. Damp and foggy winters set in early, and the daylight diminishes to barely six hours at the winter solstice under cloudy skies, so that very often even in daytime, the city is enveloped in twilight. As Gogol put it in his tale "Nevsky Prospect":

> A strange phenomenon, isn't it? A Petersburg artist! An artist in the land
> of snows! An artist in the land of the Finns, where everything is wet, flat,
> unvarying, pale, gray, foggy!"

Magda once complained to Julia—recalling her Petersburg imprisonment during the long winter—"I lament the abnormality of our artistic life—eight months sitting indoors!"[12] And in those winters, she dreamed about the summer, when it would be possible to escape from the city and paint out of doors. A postcard that Magda painted and sent from Petersburg to Julia at her summer retreat depicts a monochromatic, misty cityscape contrasted with a southern landscape full of color and sunlight (figure 26). The title is "View from my window on a rainy Petersburg day."[13]

Every May, once school closed for vacation, the Zvantseva students would swiftly leave the city for dachas in Finland, Crimea, or the Caucasus, or travel to relatives or friends at estates in the provinces near Perm, Saratov, Vladimir, or Nizhny Novgorod, as the addresses on the envelopes of their correspondence attest. Dispersed to different summer places, members of the "Constellation Leo" continued their winter conversations in their letters, reporting on work in progress, discussing what they were reading, sharing news and gossip about friends, and pining for their teacher and the familiar rhythm of their classes. Bakst's watchful eye hovered over them in their imaginations even in summer and spurred them onward.

The summer letters of these young artists from 1908 to 1917 follow their growth from teenaged apprentices into confident and dedicated painters, and later, in the hard times of the Bolshevik Revolution and the Russian Civil War, their letters show them trying courageously to establish themselves as artists, or rather trying to survive as artists at a time when mere survival was a challenge.[14]

---

12   August 18, 1915, RGALI, f. 2080, op. 1, no. 45, 90–91.
13   May 22, 1912, RGALI, f. 2080, op. 1, no. 45, 59.
14   For a substantial portion of surviving correspondence between Nachman, Obolenskaya, and Grekova from 1916 to 1919 see *Nashe nasledie* 121 (2017): 61–77, and *Nashe nasledie* 122 (2017): 2–27. The correspondence is edited, introduced, and annotated by L. Bernstein and E. Nekludova.

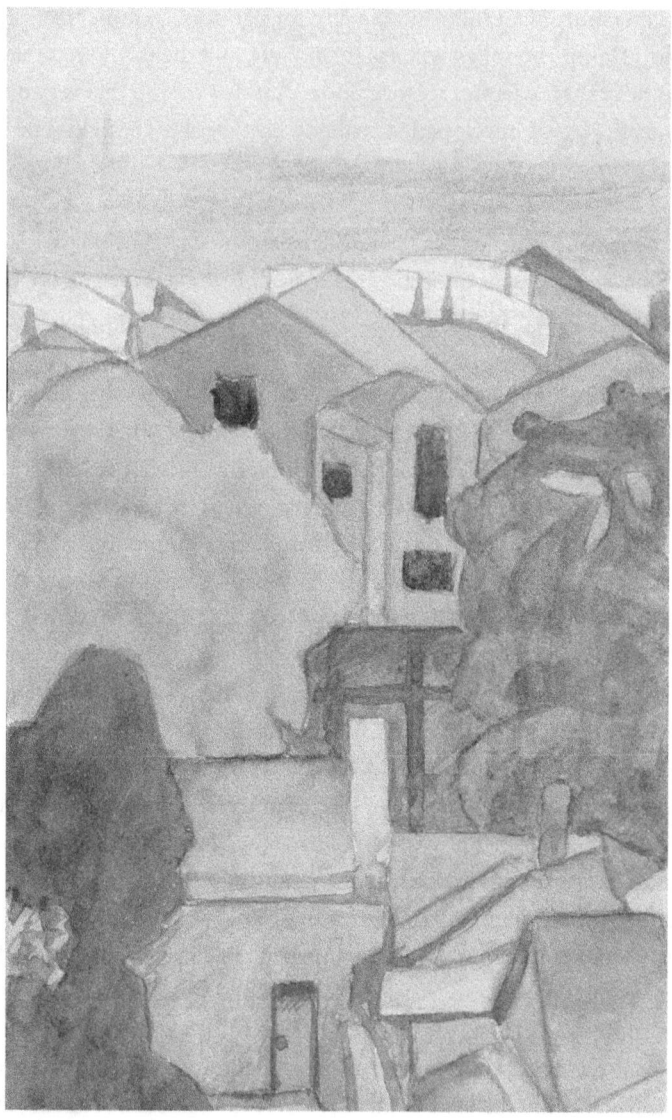

Figure 26. Magda Nachman. *View from My Window on a Rainy Petersburg Day* (*courtesy of RGALI, Moscow*).

After their first year at Zvantseva, 1907–1908, Magda spent the summer in the popular Finnish resort town of Ollila,[15] which then was under Russian rule. She stayed with the family of her older sister Eleanor, who was married to James

15 In 1948, Ollila was renamed Solnechnoe and at present is again a part of Russia.

Schmidt, curator of the Hermitage picture galleries, and there she tutored her niece and nephews. In her first letter of that summer to Julia, the beginning of what would become a years-long correspondence, Magda touched on common themes shared by all:

> A bit more than a week has passed from the last day spent in the studio, but it seems to me that I have not been working for at least two months. ... I have painted only three studies. ... You know, Bakst gave me a very difficult problem; the relationships have led me to despair. I conjure Bakst's spirit, but it does not appear.
>
> Also, I do not read much; I am bored by Ruskin. I read [Alexander Blok's] *The King on the Square* and *The Stranger*. I like *The King on the Square* better than *The Stranger*, but it has some echoes of the present that interfere.
>
> I almost forgot the main thing: *Intentions* by Oscar Wilde made a huge impression on me; it touches on so many questions about which I have been thinking for quite a while. Wilde clarified for me many of my own thoughts. For example, Wilde's views on the relationship of nature to art simply overpowered me. I would love to talk with you about this book. What is your opinion of it?
>
> Today I could not work at all because it was snowing. It was strange to see the green of the trees looking through the whiteness of the snow: a sickly impression.[16]

Bakst is invisibly present, and their obligation to fulfill his assignments is a serious concern. Thus, for example, Magda wrote to Julia: "When I recall Bakst's words, they seem a mockery to me: 'A series of portraits.'"[17] And Ziloti confided to Julia:

> This year, Finland outrages me less because my "assignment" is to paint "en plein air" and I will make my sisters sit for me one after the other. How is one to paint air, bright and fine, in terms of relationships, very difficult.

16 May 24, 1908, RGALI, f. 2080, op. 1, no. 45, 9–10op. For the contemporary Russian edition of *Intentions*, see Oscar Wilde, *Zamysly*, trans. A. Mintslova (St. Petersburg: Grif, 1906). Since 1900, works by Oscar Wilde had been steadily translated into Russian, and an eight-volume collection came out between 1905 and 1908 from the V. M. Sablin publishing house. However, these translations were frequently of inferior quality. Magda read Wilde in the original English.

17 June 8, 1909, RGALI, f. 2080, op. 1, no. 45, 18–19.

When you come right down to it, fate has wronged us painters—a pianist can work away indoors, and has only to open the piano—but we have to dirty ourselves, wash brushes, wipe our palette, and fend off the mosquitoes, but only in principle, because your whole face gets swollen from the stings in any case.[18]

And here is Julia, berating herself for her poor painterly results, writing to Magda about some new symbolist poems sent to her by one of their classmates:

In general, my correspondence is going more successfully than painting: there are seven letters (not counting "secular" ones), and 6¼ studies; and the letters are all so good, and the studies are awful. Yes, also [Evgenia] Maximovna [Kaplan][19] sent me another book: *Ostrov*, with Kuzmin's Akathists [Eastern Orthodox Lenten hymns]; but I had not expected such from him. The great bard Vyacheslav Ivanov wrote such a solemn ode that really I have difficulty quoting from it. The theme is contemporary: the siege of Troy, it seems. However, it's difficult to vouch for that.[20]

Even Bakst, whom they held in the highest esteem, did not escape their irony and criticism. Thus Magda wrote to Jula from Ollila, "Alas! I've seen the creations of our patrons at the Building Exhibition. Our redhead [Bakst] did not distinguish himself, Dobuzhinsky is better."[21] The summer in Ollila had hardly begun when Magda began pining for winter and the regularity of classes. As she wrote to Julia:

If you only knew how often I recall the sweet wintertime, the work, and our conversations, and everything and everyone. And I count the days that pass, and they pass so slowly, long and light, and it seems they will pass like this without end, serene, light, boring, and the fall will never arrive. And here I am already in the second week in Ollila. In the evenings, a violin plays out of tune and a gramophone drones, the vacationers are shouting, the children are crying. What else is worthy of mention?

… I paint very little. … Bakst will hang me in the fall.

---

18 May 19, 1909, RGALI, f. 2080, op. 1, no. 28.
19 E. M. Kaplan, another student at Zvantseva's academy.
20 June 15, 1909, RGALI, f. 2080. op 1, no. 7, 3–4op.
21 July 29, 1908, RGALI, f. 2080, op 1, no. 45, 13, 14.

... One consolation is books. I've read Flaubert's *Salammbô*. The whole book is steeped in ancient fire, bloody cruelty. Everything is monstrous and beautiful, mysterious Salammbô, the cult of the gods, the splendor of Carthage, hordes of semi-fantastic barbarians in the desert. Only to my taste, there are many unnecessary arcane details.

As for [Oscar Wilde's] *Intentions*, I don't know how I will be able to part with it. The more often I read it, the more I find it striking and beautiful. I liked best the first essay, "The Decay of Lying."[22]

Not satisfied with the Russian translations of Wilde, Magda took it upon herself in this letter to relate to Julia, who did not know English, his theory of art as propounded in *Intentions*, translating long passages for her. The essay with which she was especially taken—"The Decay of Lying"—was in tune with her own thoughts on the relationship between art and nature. With trust and enthusiasm, she championed Wilde's defense of "lying art," for according to Wilde, it is aesthetics alone that is able to "make life lovely and wonderful, fill it with new forms, and give it progress, and variety and change."

The letters betray their writers' temperaments and characters. Compare Magda's dreamy and philosophically inclined disposition with Julia's sunny and more sociable demeanor:

My dear Magda Maximilianovna,

Yesterday I received your letter and rejoiced. I live frivolously—that is all I can say. And I cannot do otherwise when a truly disgusting worm is eating at me. So as not to be tiresome—I look at things more lightly than perhaps is warranted. I began painting only three days ago; I have three lame studies; Bakst has poisoned me. It has become very difficult to work, my critical instinct has developed into something painful, although I am beginning to hope again that sooner or later I will overcome my failings. Not now, of course, but at least let it happen after I'm done with school. If only he would help.[23]

How different is Magda's reply:

I count the passing hours, days, and am happy that autumn is near, less than a month and a half till September! ... I dream about the studio every

---

22   May 8, 1908, RGALI, f. 2080, op. 1, no. 45, 3–8.
23   July 14, 1908, RGALI, f. 2080, op. 1, no. 7, 1–2op.

night, and recently I even dreamed that I was taking an exam on art history from Somov.[24]

In general, I love my dreams: I wake up, and it's so terribly sad that everything was only a dream, that these tiresome days and tiresome cares are the reality.

You are right. One should live a lighter, more superficial life, not torturing oneself. Self-torture leads nowhere; it becomes only more painful and more difficult to live.[25]

Magda's letters go beyond a desire for news, gossip, or an exchange of ideas. They betray a young person's struggle to find herself and her place in the world, in part by embracing ideals, in part by rejecting what is distasteful. With a youthful all-or-nothing intensity, she disparages the vacationers and rejects their superficial preoccupations, the banality of their conversations, the vulgarity of their amateur theatricals.

A recurring theme of Magda's ruminations is the nature of time. Her complaint in a letter of 1908, "My plans for the future are demolished every year, and every year I plan anew," would become a leitmotif in a few years, when her future was taken out of her hands by the tumultuous events precipitated by the Russian Revolutions. In this 1908 letter to Julia, while seriously ill, she confronts the issue of present and future time:

One should not think of the future, one should live in the present, in every minute, in every moment, so that there is one eternal present without the past and without the future, you know, to find the eternal present of the Indian sages who knew that time does not exist; and we can never get rid of the deception of eternal change, and that's why we understand nothing, why we don't know whether life is valuable or worthless. Forgive these strange thoughts that are now occurring to me. To get away from time, from human life, and feel the eternal living silence, always, not just in glimpses. Only in this way can one find the secret eternal kingdom.[26]

Such thinking would occupy an important place in Magda's later letters written in the Russian countryside during the difficult period of the Russian Civil War. In those letters, she would return to the question of the nature of

---

24 Andrei Ivanovich Somov (1830–1909)—art historian and curator of the Hermitage collections, father of the painter Konstantin Somov.

25 July 17, 1908, RGALI, f. 2080, op. 1, no. 45, 1–2.

26 July 29, 1908, RGALI, f. 2080, op. 1, no. 45, 13–14.

time and the purposes to which one might put one's life, determining to devote herself to a life as an artist.

Since Magda was ill in the summer of 1908, she was compelled to spend most of her time indoors. Her illness appears to have been serious. She wrote about death:

> And so I am thinking about death and dream about the fall. … It is painfully bitter to me that the entire summer has been spent in vain. I have accomplished nothing, much of life vanished along with my illness. You should understand why I am thinking God knows what about what is possible and impossible, don't condemn me for spending my time in this way.
>
> Why do you think that I do not love the earth; I love it, only in a different way from how you love it. I even feel sometimes that I am closer to it than to the human race. As far back as I can remember myself, I recall this feeling of unity with the foreknowing life of the earth and the heavens, with the life of trees and stones and the trembling air. At times, there awakens in me such a clear, momentary realization and understanding of this life. A wondrous feeling that I can neither express nor explain. Most of all it resembles an unaccountable enormous joy.
>
> The time for my move to town is getting closer and closer; I will soon begin counting the hours. Soon I will see everyone, and the winter will begin—it is so good that it's almost inconceivable.[27]

In the letters of that first summer, all the correspondents addressed each other formally with name and patronymic. By the following year, some of them had dropped the patronymics in letters to some, but not all, of their friends. Julia, Magda, and Natalia Grekova began addressing each other by their first names and dropped the formal pronoun *vy* in favor of the informal *ty*. The formal form of address persisted between them and their male friends and the somewhat older Lermontova. Informality signified greater intimacy, but their common cause and an awareness of being Bakst's students and adherents—of belonging to the Constellation Leo—established deep friendships among all of them.

After the exhibition of the students' works in the spring of 1910, a group of them joined the painter Alexander Blaznov on a journey to Ovruch—a town in the Zhitomir region (today in Ukraine)—to decorate the newly restored ancient church with frescoes. At that time, no one knew that Bakst would not return to Russia in the fall and that Petrov-Vodkin, who joined the group in

---

27 August 10, 1908, RGALI, f. 2080, op. 1, no. 45, 15–17.

Ovruch for a short time, would become their new teacher. In October, when Petrov-Vodkin assumed the artistic direction of Zvantseva Academy, not all the students remained to study with him, and Constellation Leo suffered a schism. Letters full of invective and accusations of treason were sent by those who thought that Petrov-Vodkin would subvert Bakst's teachings. Ziloti, Tyrsa, Chagall, and Lermontova, among others, left the academy. The "quartet"—Magda Nachman, Julia Obolenskaya, Natalia Grekova, and Varya Klimovich-Toper—remained and became even closer. With time, the two groups made up, but something, perhaps the "togetherness" on which Bakst had insisted, had been lost.

At first, those remaining did not perceive a significant departure from Bakst's teaching principles in their new teacher. They continued experimenting with colors. However, from what can be gleaned from letters and memoirs, as well as from Magda's picture *Peasant Woman* (figure 23), it soon became clear that Petrov-Vodkin was taking them in a direction of more abstract properties of color and a clearer separation among them. Vibrant hues and delicate tones were replaced by adding more white to their palette, and interest in vibrant color was replaced by an interest in the plastic capabilities of individual paints. As Julia wrote:

> A radical break occurred in the approach to form and design. The place of a characteristic silhouette was taken by a characteristic volumetric form. The construction of objects, the transition of their constituent parts from one into another and general monumental aspects were carefully studied. Huge monumental figures were created: ultramarine, bright red, vermilion. Painting seemed to exist without regard to the demands of nature, architecture, the size of the canvas—a self-contained manifestation, like "moon," for example.[28]

In her reminiscences about Bakst, Julia noted that she would write more extensively on Petrov-Vodkin, though to my knowledge, she never did. Magda's sketch of the students' 1910 exhibition may be the only evidence of their early experiments with color under the direction of Bakst, whose colorific sensibility shines bright in the later works of such of his students as Nikolai Tyrsa and Nadezhda Lermontova, who never studied with Petrov-Vodkin. The same is evident in Magda's surviving works from the late 1930s in which the vibrancy of her colors—perhaps typical of her youthful experiments so vividly described by Julia—returns.

Magda remained at the academy until the spring of 1913, when the time had finally come, she felt, to end her formal education. In her letters from that period, she wrote about the joyous craft of a painter that was to be her life's work.

---

28 Obolenskaia, "V shkole Zvantsovoi," 239.

CHAPTER 6

Koktebel

Julia and Magda spent the summer of 1913 in Crimea to escape the stifling Petersburg summer and to paint. They had been in Crimea in the summers of 1910 and 1911, staying in Miskhor, at the southern tip of the peninsula. This time, whether by happenstance or design, they ended up in a village in eastern Crimea, at the dacha of the poet and artist Maximilian Voloshin (1877–1932). The name of the village, Koktebel,[1] has become a synonym for Voloshin's dacha and a word of incantation in Russian cultural history. In Voloshin's time, it was the center of an active literary and artistic community, and today, it is a museum. The dacha was presided over by Voloshin and his mother, Elena Ottobaldovna, whom friends and guests called "Pra," the Russian equivalent of the German *ur*, which denominated her a sort of primordial "ur-mother." Their hospitality and generosity, their desire to promote artistic endeavors and to nourish artistic talent great or small, and their endless curiosity about people and their creative pursuits attracted poets, writers, painters, musicians, singers, dancers—in short, anyone with a creative impulse and artistic inclination. "One of Max's callings in life," wrote the poet Marina Tsvetaeva in a tribute to Voloshin, "was to put people together, to create encounters and alter fates."[2] The list of guests who visited the dacha in the 1910s and 1920s, whether for a few days or a few months, is long and includes cultural luminaries as well as those, like Magda and Julia, who were still finding their way.

Julia and her family (her mother and her mother's common-law husband; Julia's father died in 1906) left St. Petersburg in the middle of May. They traveled first to Feodosia, the principal town of eastern Crimea, which was less popular than the western side of the peninsula with its lush spas, but it was becoming known as a mecca for artists and other bohemians. Perhaps Julia had already heard about Voloshin's dacha—she certainly knew that Voloshin was an important Symbolist poet—or perhaps she learned about it from the local newspapers, as suggested in a preface to her 1913 summer diary entries, written

---

1   Pronounced more or less *cock-tuh-byell*.
2   Marina Tsvetaeva, "Zhivoe o zhivom (Voloshin)," in *Sochinenia. Proza*, vol. 2 (Moscow: Khudozhestvennaia literatura, 1980), 212.

in 1933, the year after Voloshin's death, in which she describes how they learned about Koktebel and the intriguing goings-on at Voloshin's dacha:

> In May 1913, my family and I ... left for Crimea as usual. We wanted to try new places but we had not thought of going to Koktebel. We were driven there by a pouring rain and by the unbelievably silly sketches in the local newspapers about Koktebel customs, which produced in the reader impressions contrary to the intentions of their authors.
>
> We were met by Elena Ottobaldovna Voloshina, who wore morocco boots and baggy trousers, had a gray mane, eagle's profile, and piercing eyes. "The rooms are no good"—she declared abruptly—"No conveniences. The beds are worse than useless. Nothing's good. However, you decide for yourselves. If you want—stay, if not then not." We stayed.[3]

Julia wrote to Magda, who was still in Petersburg, a few days after her arrival in Koktebel. That letter, now lost, must have been sent on or about May 16, because Magda's reply, in which she writes, "I have just received your letter," was posted in Petersburg on May 20 and stamped by the Feodosia post office three days later. Here is Magda's letter:

> My dear friend, I have just received your letter, and it filled me with joy, despite all the horrors that you are talking about. Yesterday I suddenly felt that it's the end of winter—that I am leaving. I felt it while walking along the embankment during the white night,[4] a bit stifling, and hopeless in the St. Petersburg fashion. The nights are white, the days are blinding, it smells of urban summer.
>
> I do nothing of consequence: I have been scurrying about with relatives. I have sent one abroad. The last one leaves today. All the time I have a feeling of an ending. Soon there will be a feeling of a beginning, and I rejoice in it. This constant seeing-off of first one, then another somehow tired me out. I think I'll take the room next to you, why should I live alone—the natives would eat me alive. ...
>
> How strange it is to think that soon I will again be heading into the depths of black nights, and through the window will come the smell of flowering grain. Give my regards to Max and ask him about the verb "bombilate." Do you remember: "... and it bombilates"?

---

3 Iuliia Obolenskaia, "Iz dnevnika 1913," http://www.maxvoloshin.ru/all_21/.
4 May 19, 1913, by the Julian calendar in use in Russia before 1918 (old style), is equivalent to June 1 in today's Gregorian calendar (new style). On that day, there would have been daylight from about 4:00 a.m. to 10:00 p.m., with twilight for the remaining six hours.

It's good that he has a good library, even better if you are allowed to read his books. ...

So, my friend, in a week we'll see each other!

Greetings to your mother and F. K. Are you suntanned yet or not?

Your Magda.

I infer from Magda referring to Voloshin as "Max" that Julia must have written in her letter that that was how his friends addressed the great Maximilian Alexandrovich Kirienko-Voloshin—we saw this above in Marina Tsvetaeva's tribute. It would have been unthinkable to either of them to address Voloshin to his face as anything other than Maximilian Alexandrovich, and indeed, that is how Julia addressed him in all her subsequent letters to him, and he in return addressed her as Julia Leonidovna. The reference to "and it bombilates" is to Voloshin's 1907 poem "Thunderstorm," in which the obscure Russian word *tutnet*, or bombilates, appears. Magda's offhand reminder to Julia of their having once puzzled over a poem shows that to these young women, modern poetry was familiar territory.

Julia followed up her letter to Magda with a postcard, dated May 17:

> *Crimea. Koktebel. View of dachas from the North. Profile of Pushkin.*
>
> Having sent you a rather menacing letter about the amenities, I am sending you in the way of rehabilitation of Koktebel a picture of it, so you will know where you are headed. We live at the very edge of the sea. Nearby are volcanic mountains. Address: Crimea, Koktebel near Feodosia, dacha of Mrs. Voloshin.[5]

The "profile of Pushkin" pictured on the card was part of a natural formation near Koktebel that in 1912, following a rockslide, was transformed into a profile that was now said to look more like Maximilian Voloshin. And after an earthquake in 1927, it apparently became an even better likeness.

Whether Magda received the rehabilitating postcard before she finished and posted her reply to Julia's letter or after, it is clear that she was delighted at the prospect of heading south to join her friend. By the end of May, she was in Koktebel, and on June 6, she sent the postcard pictured here to her sister Adele in Switzerland (figure 27):

> Dear Delia, I am sending you one of the scenic views of Koktebel. A small cove, which begins here, is called by one of the locals the egg cove, because, he says, these stones are toads sitting on their eggs. Farther along, the shore is even more rocky and impassable. Today I wandered among these stones. Magda

---

5   RGALI, f. 2080, op. 1, no. 7, 13/ob.

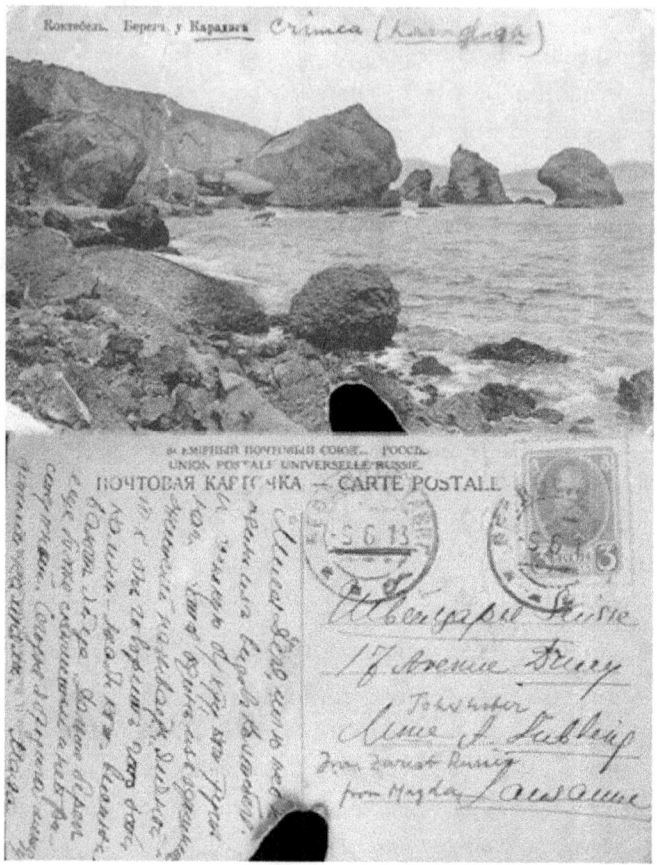

Figure 27. Postcard sent by Magda from Koktebel to her sister Adele in Switzerland. The caption on the top reads, "Koktebel. The Shore by Kara Dag."

The village of Koktebel lies about ten miles down the coast from Feodosia. In his poems dedicated to his beloved Cimmeria—the ancient name of the surrounding steppes and mountains—which he inhabits with long-dead gods and heroes, Voloshin describes the harsh and beautiful landscape of eastern Crimea. Here the mountain Kara Dag, a volcanic rock formation, runs abruptly into the sea. The name of the mountain in the Crimean Tatar language means "Black Mountain," while "Koktebel" means "Land of the Blue Hills." In Voloshin's time, the narrow shore was covered with sparkling semi-precious pebbles deposited there by the sea. Here were the beaches that the dacha inhabitants scandalized with nudity, which provoked the outcry in the newspapers mentioned by Julia.

That summer, Magda met and befriended Maximilian Voloshin; Marina Tsvetaeva and her husband, Sergei Efron; and Sergei's older sisters Vera and Lilya, all of whom would play an important role in her life.

Not every paying guest would be invited into the company of Voloshin and his friends. In the preface to her diary mentioned above, Julia remarked that although she met Voloshin shortly after her arrival at the dacha, at first "there was no real closeness" either with him or with the large group of friends who occupied other rooms at the dacha and called themselves *obormoty*— approximately "the rascals." That group, which, as Julia noted, had given her the cold shoulder, included the Tsvetaeva–Efron family, the aspiring poet Maya Cuvilliers, the legal scholar Mikhail Feldstein and his artist wife Eva, and the actor Vladimir Sokolov.[6] But soon after Magda's arrival, following the appearance of two older artists, Konstantin Bogaevsky, from Feodosia, and the Muscovite Konstantin Kandaurov, whom Voloshin introduced to Julia as "Moscow's Diaghilev," Magda and Julia were welcomed into the inner circle. Himself an artist and organizer of art exhibitions, Kandaurov noticed the young women assiduously at work on their painting. Through their acquaintance with Kandaurov, Magda and Julia were invited to poetry readings under the stars on the roof above Voloshin's studio, to excursions to the mountains Kara Dag and Syuyuryu-Kai, to outdoor painting expeditions, to nighttime sailing, to barefoot dances on the grass according to the system of Dalcroze eurhythmics (figure 28), to informal plays and charades—in a word, they had been accepted into the life of the dacha. And they both read aloud their own poetry before this august company. (Some of Julia's poems of that summer have survived; Magda's have not.) Both drew unsigned portraits of the same people in the same album (so that now it is nearly impossible to tell who did what). They exchanged their dresses for baggy trousers. And Magda acquired a nickname—"Your Quietness." Another nickname for Magda, which I found a few times in letters to her or about her, was "The Executioner." Why executioner? Was it a role she played in one of the theatricals? I would like to think that she was given this name for her hypersensitivity, remarked by many, and her firm principles.

---

6   Maya (Maria Pavlovna Cuvilliers, Princess Kudasheva during her first marriage, 1895–1985)—poet, translator, later wife of the French writer Romain Rolland. Mikhail Feldstein (1884–1938, arrested and executed), a legal scholar. His wife Eva Feldstein (Levi) (1886–1964)—a painter. Vladimir Sokolov (1889–1962)—an actor at a Moscow theater, moved to Hollywood after the revolution. Vladimir Alexandrovich Rogozinsky (1882–1951), an architect from Feodosia, was also there.

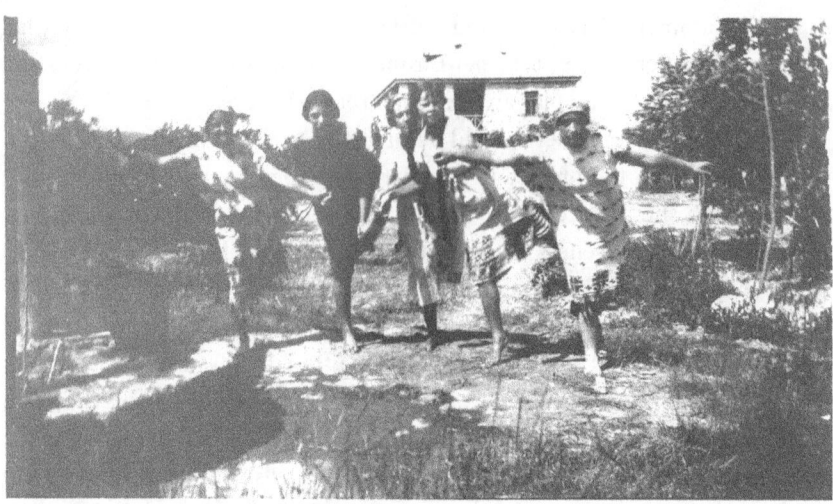

Figure 28. Barefoot dancers, Koktebel, 1913. Julia is on the left; Magda is on the right (*courtesy of RGALI, Moscow*).

The relationships and friendships begun that summer in Koktebel continued for both women for many years. Perhaps it was Magda's acquaintanceship with Voloshin, and later her friendship with his first wife, the artist Margarita Sabashnikova, who was a serious follower of Rudolf Steiner, that marked the beginning of Magda's interest in Steiner's philosophical and spiritual theories. Magda began a serious study of Steiner's work and at times participated in regular study sessions with Sabashnikova.[7] Her interest in Steiner's ideas is also reflected in letters written long after her Koktebel days.

It was during that summer that Magda painted Marina Tsvetaeva's portrait, the only oil portrait of the poet made during her lifetime. A few months later, she presented the finished painting to Marina and her husband. In her diary, Julia wrote this about Tsvetaeva's portrait:

> Her Quietness also finished her portrait. It is good and only the flatness
> of the orange folds upsets me: it is not clear what their role in the com-
> position is. But had she instilled in them a clear expression of the striving

---

7   Margarita Sabashnikova (1882, Moscow–1973, Stuttgart)—painter, memoirist, friend and
     follower of Rudolf Steiner (1861–1925), the founder of anthroposophy.

toward vertical line, their role would have been clear. ... Another mistake it seems to me is the color of the background: it is too close to the color of the face.[8]

I cannot agree with Julia's assessment. The softness of the background only emphasizes the strength of the character. The viewer's attention is drawn to Tsvetaeva's face by the contrast between the colors of the background and the subject's bright cobalt-blue dress, which in my view emphasize the color of her skin, lips, and eyes. The asymmetry of the pose is a strong expression of the poet's character: the round lyricism of the left shoulder contrasts with the straight line of the right shoulder and arm that support the figure. Although there is a soft cushion or chairback behind her, Tsvetaeva is not reclining on it. She enters the picture at an angle: an unusual and fleeting pose. And she does not look at the viewer. Rather, her eyes are looking within herself. It is a portrait of a strong, independent, and lonely person who does not rely on anything or anyone but herself. Magda caught the essence of her sitter. But readers may judge for themselves (figure 29).

Among Magda's surviving works of that summer is a pencil portrait of Sergei Efron, a study for a later large-scale portrait. Magda also painted a portrait of Pra (figure 30), about which the actor Vladimir Sokolov wrote something like the following English translation when the company held a couplet-writing contest:

Pra by her portrait looks askance,
And swallows Magda with a glance.[9]

It is a truth universally acknowledged that unhappy threesomes are unhappy for the obvious reason. For Julia, the summer of 1913 was momentous: she fell in love with Konstantin Kandaurov,[10] and he reciprocated with equal ardor. Twenty-four years her senior and married, Kandaurov was also deeply attached to his wife, Anna. Julia's complex relationship with

---

8   Julia Obolenskaya's diary, GLM, manuscript division, f. 348, op. 1., no. 1, 76–76op. At the time of this writing, the portrait is in a private collection in Russia.

9   Ibid., 52, entry for August 7.

10 For a detailed account of the relationship between Kandaurov and Obolenskaya, see Larisa Alekseeva, *Tsvet vinograda. Iuliia Obolenskaia. Konstantin Kandaurov* (Moscow: AST, 2017). Alekseeva reconstructs the relationship between Obolenskaya and Kandaurov based on their correspondence and Obolenskaya's diary.

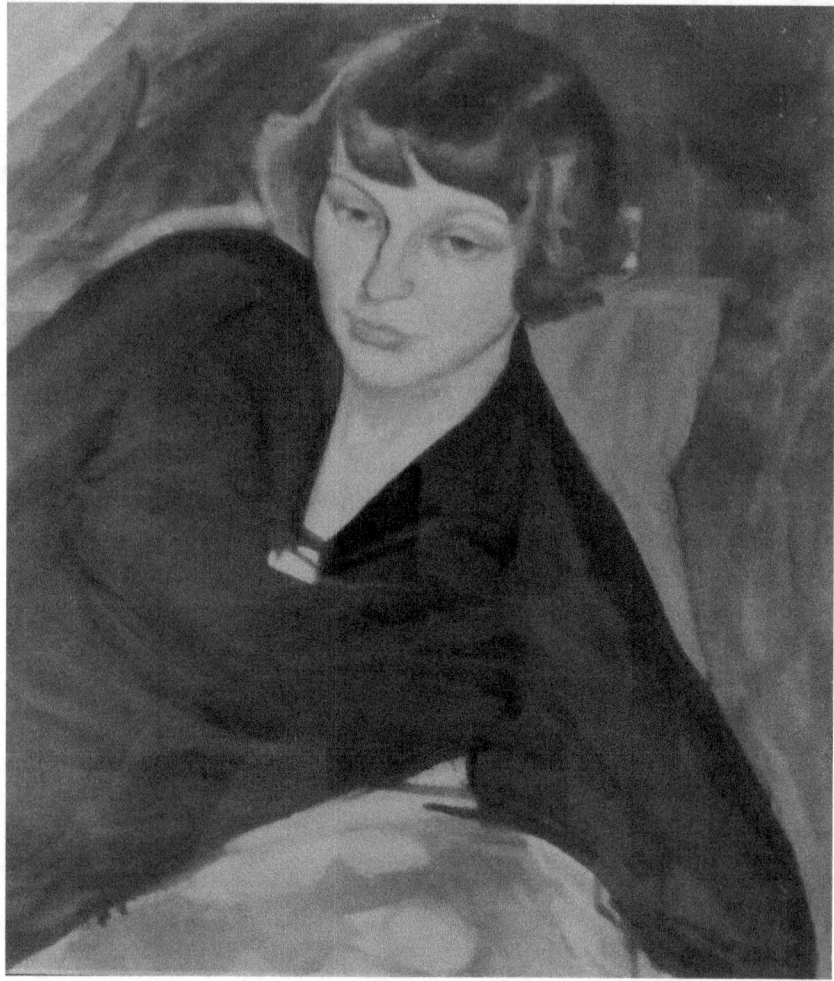

Figure 29. Magda Nachman. Portrait of Marina Tsvetaeva, 1913.

Kandaurov lasted until his death, in 1930. Over the following few years, she would return to Koktebel in the summer to be with him, and Kandaurov visited Julia occasionally in Petersburg. Magda, partly on account of her health (she was told by her doctor not to settle too close to the sea), partly, perhaps, because she was shy ("Her Quietness") and found the Koktebel crowd somewhat overwhelming, would establish her Crimean summer quarters at a remove from Koktebel, visiting Voloshin's dacha only occasionally. The exchange of letters between Magda and Julia in a few subsequent Crimean summers offers a glimpse of everyday life at the dacha, with commentary on

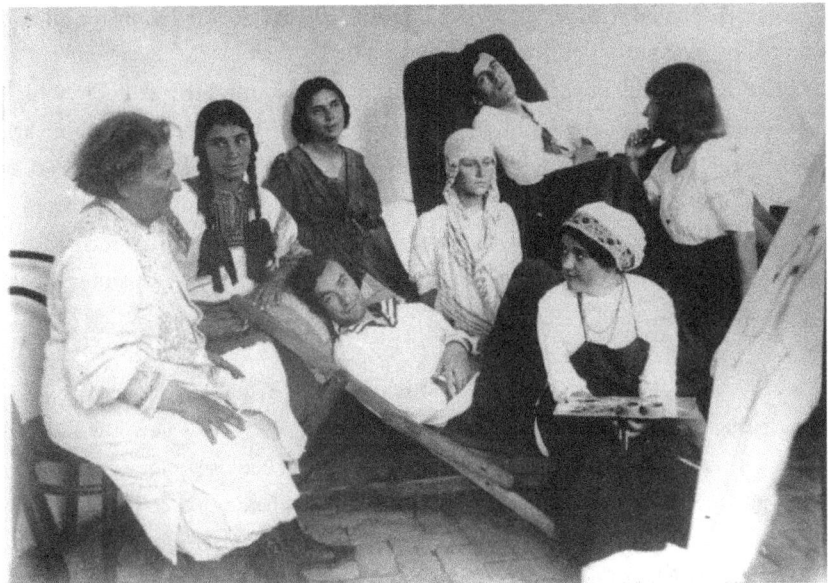

Figure 30. Photograph showing Magda painting a portrait of Pra, Koktebel, 1913 (*courtesy of RGALI, Moscow*). Sergei Efron, reclining at the upper right, appears in the same pose in Magda's 1916 portrait of him (figure 31).

the tumultuous relationships among its inhabitants, especially between Julia, Kandaurov, and Anna. Magda was Julia's confidant, and she supported her friend in her affair.

In the fall of 1914, Kandaurov began planning an "Art Exhibition 1915" that would display the work of artists representing the diverse current trends in Russian art. Although he was no admirer of the Futurists, he was not going to exclude them from his show. But he especially wanted to showcase the group of young women artists to which Julia belonged—students of Bakst and Petrov-Vodkin—whose art he admired and whose works, according to his plan, would occupy the center of the exhibition. "The women-artists," he wrote, "will be the best."[11] Knowing that there were pranksters and provocateurs among the Futurists, Kandaurov made a particular effort to enforce decorum. He wrote to Julia, "with regard to the exhibition, I had to maneuver quite a bit among painfully ambitious painters. They have many eccentricities and considerable intolerance for each other."[12] And a few days later, "There will be a great deal

---

11   March 5, 1915, GTG, manuscript division, f. 5., no. 420., 1.
12   January 10, 1915, ibid., no. 364, 2.

of noise. A scandal with Mayakovsky is brewing, but I decided to be tough and won't allow any pranks at the show."[13]

But Kandaurov miscalculated. He had not understood the extent to which the Futurists' provocative and extravagant behavior was integral to their art. They were experimenting with an art form that later in the twentieth century acquired the names "happening" and "performance art." This is how the philologist and Moscow Maecenas Andrei Akimovich Shemshurin described the scene just before the exhibition's opening in a letter to the realist painter Vasily Dmitrievich Polenov:

> There are again several shows in Moscow. ... I'd better tell you what is going on at Kandaurov's exhibition. It's called 1915. This is how it was. Larionov[14] suggested they should organize a prank because no one needs pictures anymore. The participants agreed, but it had not been decided what in particular to carry out. This conversation took place in the morning, after which they dispersed.
>
> When they gathered the next day, they saw that Larionov had painted his self-portrait. The work was done directly on the wall. Because there was a fan on the wall, it became part of the composition. Aside from the fan, Larionov glued pieces of cardboard from a hatbox, fragments of a map, stretched some ropes and wrapped strips of cardboard, and so on. He called all this Rayonism. Those taking part gasped when they saw it. Of course, not with indignation but with awe over the originality of the contrivance. It became clear to all that the public would talk only about Larionov. Then they decided somehow to minimize his originality. And so Lentulov[15] hauled a shirt, a galosh, and a piece of soap; hung it all on the wall, daubed something around it, and called it a portrait of Burlyuk.[16]

---

13 March 5, 1915, ibid., no. 434, 1. Vladimir Mayakovsky (1893–1930)—one of the major Russian Futurist poets. He began as a painter and continued to illustrate his own literary works.

14 Mikhail Larionov (1881–1964, Fontenay-aux-Roses, France)—Russian avant-garde painter, a founding member of two avant-garde groups, Bubnovy valet (Jack of Diamonds, 1909–1911) and Osliny khvost (Donkey's Tail, 1912–1913), creator of Rayonism (together with his wife, the avant-garde painter Natalia Goncharova; the term comes from the idea of painting based on rays of light). In 1915, Larionov moved to Paris and worked for Diaghilev's Ballets Russes.

15 Aristarkh Lentulov (1882–1943)—avant-garde painter and stage designer; a founding member of the Jack of Diamonds.

16 David Burlyuk (1882, Riabushky [Ukraine]–1967, Long Island, New York)—inspirational force behind Russian Futurism, Futurist painter and poet, publicist, book illustrator.

They say this picture has been sold already. Mayakovsky provided his self-portrait. He glued half of his top hat, a glove, a book of poetry, a deck of cards, fragments of *The Russian Word*, and painted the gaps between these things.

Malevich and Morgunov[17] displayed their coat of arms, because their pictures are in Petrograd.[18] There is something daubed on the coat of arms, and a real spoon is attached. Under the coat of arms there is a caption: "we are Februarists (on such and such day of February we became free of reason)." With those creations Larionov's prank was annihilated. Vasya Kamensky[19] thought up the most original one: He brought a mouse trap with a live mouse, a frying pan, and a mortar, or so it seems, and something else from the kitchen.[20]

Kamensky walked with his mousetrap—his "movable exhibit"—around the exhibition halls, and Kandaurov tried to pacify the women who had arrived for the opening and were terrified at the sight.

The newspapers were not slow to publish reviews of the exhibition. The critics looked at the works produced by the Futurists and others of the avant-garde and saw nothing but scraps of newspapers and posters, fragments of sticks and rope—random objects that did not coalesce into something recognizable. Here, for example, is how the critic Yakov Tugenhold described Mikhail Larionov's "Iron Battle":

> He took a board, pasted it with pieces of military cards, pieces of caramel and national flags, attached a children's house in the form of a fortress and black sticks, symbolizing guns, and traced bloody rivers and mountains, in the form of some red layers. The result was "a military toy," which a child would have done much better, because in the

17 Kazimir Malevich (1878–1935)—avant-garde painter, creator of Suprematism. Aleksey Morgunov (1884–1935)—avant-garde painter, a member of the Jack of Diamonds and Donkey's Tail.
18 From 1914 to 1924, St. Petersburg was called Petrograd.
19 Vasily Kamensky (1884–1961)—Russian Futurist poet, painter, playwright, and one of the first Russian aviators (he is credited with the Russian word for airplane: *samolyot*). Kamensky was a member of the Futurist group together with David Burlyuk, Velimir Khlebnikov, and Vladimir Mayakovsky.
20 Undated, 1915, RGALI: f. 769, op. 1, no. 283, 1–2. A copy of the letter is in Kandaurov's archive. An inscription in pencil in the right-hand corner reads, "on the 1915 exhibition."

name of the decorative side of the war, he would have forgotten about its blood.[21]

When Nadezhda Lermontova read such reviews describing the antics of the artists who had been invited to exhibit alongside the Zvantseva group, she sent an angry telegram from Petrograd to Kandaurov in Moscow:

> I consider the presence of the Futurists an absurdity. I ask that measures be taken to separate me and like-minded [exhibitors] or return my works. A letter will follow.
> Lermontova[22]

The letter that followed was no less angry. In it, she accused Kandaurov of an excessive "liberalism" that was harmful to her and her group of artists because both the public and the press were holding them responsible for the pranks of the Futurists. "I hate the Futurists," she wrote, "and consider them to have nothing to do with art, and therefore I consider their appearance at a serious exhibition the purest absurdity."[23]

Even Magda, sensitive, considerate, the last person to wish to offend anyone, could not condone the Futurists' presence at the exhibition and followed Lermontova's example. She wrote to Kandaurov that it was impossible for her to exhibit under the same roof with them. Magda's letter has not survived, but we know about it because Magda received a reply, not from Kandaurov, but from Vladimir Rogozinsky, their mutual friend from Koktebel. Rogozinsky began by addressing Magda with her less charitable Koktebel epithet "Executioner," perhaps underlining the baleful effect of her letter.[24] Although in the end, everyone agreed to participate in the exhibition, it took a great deal of back and forth between Petrograd and Moscow to persuade the enraged artists that Kandaurov did not hold Futurists in high regard either, and that to expose their art for what he thought it was, it behooved serious artists to exhibit side by side with them, thereby revealing their weaknesses. He thought them useful as provocateurs for others and as a stimulus for continued experiments and public debate; above all, he thought that they had a

---

21 Iakov Tugenkhol'd, "V zheleznom tupike," *Severnye zapiski* 7–8 (1915): 103.
22 End of March 1915, RGALI, f. 769, op. 1, no. 104.
23 Ibid.
24 Undated, 1915, RGALI, f. 769, op. 1, no. 440.

right to exhibit. Julia supported Kandaurov, although in a letter to Voloshin, she remarked that the exhibition "had been derailed by the Futurists and by the critics who took their bait—complaints, threats, and every sort of nonsense ensued."[25]

Nadezhda Lermontova's and Magda's letters echoed Bakst's views on art; the two women looked at the Futurists' "performances" with horror and disgust and considered them aesthetically and ethically unacceptable. That is not to say that the young artists of the Constellation Leo were conformists or prudes—they were Modernists, after all—and while they wanted their work to be provocative, they had a much more limited view of where the line was to be drawn.

In their private behavior, they, like their more vocal opponents, were questioning social norms. New approaches to gender roles had been discussed in Ivanov's Tower, and those conversations were well known to the Zvantseva Academy students. A number of the students were apparently homosexual, and all of them read and appreciated Kuzmin's homoerotic poetry. The traditions of the Voloshin dacha—with its nudist beach in the shadow of Kara Dag, Pra with her outlandish costume and pipe, as well as other women dressed in trousers and riding donkeys, and the host Voloshin clothed in a chiton after the fashion of ancient Greece—all provoked indignation among their neighbors, who expressed their opprobrium in the local newspapers. But these painters, poets, and musicians kept their ideas and experiments largely within their own circle. They did not proselytize or demand that others follow their example and seek the freedom from constraints that they sought for themselves. They did not exhibit themselves as objects of art.

Passions ran high, nevertheless. Insult, invective, attacks by one faction against another, are not, in the end, harmful to art. Perhaps it is even a good idea in general to organize exchanges of hostile views in an open exhibition like Kandaurov's and allow competing ideas to sort themselves out. In 1915, in spite of the world war, there still was vast scope for artistic expression in Russia. Aesthetic antagonisms did not yet threaten the physical annihilation of one side or the other. The Zvantseva school of artists could turn away from their nemeses and follow their own paths of experimentation.

But in just two years, the situation would change dramatically as the continuation of World War I was followed by the upheavals of the Russian

---

25   April 17, 1915, Pushkin House (IRLI), f. 562, op. 3, no. 900.

revolutions and the civil war and the privations of War Communism.[26] The scandalous behavior of the artists against which Nadezhda Lermontova and Magda objected, a direct assault on bourgeois taste, was a symptom of social unrest and simultaneously a weapon for the destruction of the status quo, as they thought, in aesthetics and ethics. But their desire for freedom had come close to a call for a social revolution. Then in 1917, the revolution came, and many of those artists eagerly welcomed the cataclysm that they had been anticipating and promoting. With their boisterous energy and political blindness, they soon occupied the aesthetic and political space available to art. Many former students of Bakst and Petrov-Vodkin would have to struggle for both their artistic and physical survival.

In the fall of 1915, Julia, Kandaurov, and his wife agreed to try to regularize their situation by living all three together in the Kandaurovs' apartment in Moscow, where a number of other friends took residence in a kind of a commune, which they called "Noah's Ark." And so a few months after *Exhibition 1915*, Julia began planning her move from Petrograd to Moscow. The experiment was a failure, and Julia soon returned to Petrograd. But she longed to be closer to Kandaurov, and in the spring of 1916, Julia, her mother, and her mother's common-law husband rented a large apartment in Moscow in which she arranged a studio for herself and Kandaurov, sometimes inviting a few other artists to share the space. Kandaurov became a frequent visitor. Indeed, he spent a good part of his life in that apartment. But it was the closest the lovers ever came to having a shared household.

Soon after Julia's move to Moscow, Magda followed suit. She rented a small house in a side street with one of her Koktebel acquaintances, Vera Efron, and the next few years saw a deepening connection between Magda and the Efron family—the sisters Vera and Elizaveta (Lilya) and their younger brother, Sergei, Marina Tsvetaeva's husband—and their circle of friends.[27] The year 1916 was a cloudless period of their friendship.

That fall, Sergei was drafted into the army and sent to officers' school. Before his departure, Magda finished a large portrait of him on which she had been working for several months (in a letter to Lilya, Tsvetaeva complained of

---

26 War Communism was the economic and political system of expropriation of private property including surplus food produced by peasants, established by the Bolshevik government in 1918–1921. It resulted in the appearance of a thriving black market and numerous uprisings of peasants and workers.

27 The Efrons: Elizaveta (Lilya) (1885–1976, Moscow), Vera (1888–1945, Urzhum region), and Sergei (1893–1941, executed during Stalin's purges).

Magda's slow pace: "Now Magda is painting his portrait, driving him crazy with her tortoise-like pace"[28]). In her memoirs, Anastasia Tsvetaeva, Marina's sister, described the moment when she first saw it:

> We are in Marina's room. Alya is snuggling up to her mother. Across from the small door, a bit to the right, over the magnificent spartan bed— nothing more than a box spring. There Seryozha's portrait, almost in natural size, is hanging on a wooden frame covered in rust-colored sackcloth.
>
> —Oh, Magda has finished (I, stepping aside to take it in better)— good ... her wondrous brush. And very like him.
>
> Seryozha, lying on a chaise longue, was looking at us, and there was in his glance a certain quietness.[29]

In 1937, during Stalin's purges, Anastasia, who owned the portrait after Marina's departure from Russia in 1922, was arrested. The portrait was confiscated and has never surfaced. The only image of it that has come down to our time, as far as I know, appears in a photograph of Anastasia taken in her room against a background of a wall covered with pictures. The canvas that stretches across almost the entire width of the wall is Magda's portrait of Sergei (figure 31).

One of the Efron sisters' acquaintances was a historian of literature, art critic, and translator named Boris Griftsov.[30] It is not clear exactly when Magda and Griftsov met, but after 1913, she was visiting Moscow regularly, where she would see the Efrons and their acquaintances. She mentioned Griftsov in her letters even before her 1916 move to Moscow. Was he the reason for her move? In any case, some sort of romantic relationship must have developed between the pair, for it is clear from Magda's letters that by the spring of 1917, the relationship had ended, and ended badly. The trauma of the breakup would reverberate in Magda's letters for years to come.

---

28 Marina Tsvetaeva, *Neizdannoe. Sem'ia: Istoriia v pis'makh.* (Moscow: Ellis Lak, 2012), 227–229.

29 Anastasiia Tsvetaeva, "Marinin dom," in *Neischerpaemoe,* ed. Stanislav Aidinian (Moscow: Otechestvo, 1992), 141.

30 Boris Alexandrovich Griftsov (1885–1950, Moscow) was one of the organizers of the bookshop Lavka pisatelya in Moscow in 1918–1920. In 1914–1916, Griftsov taught art history at Khalyutina's drama school and rented one of the rooms in the rascals' appartment in Malaya Molchanovka, where the sisters Efron were living at the time. Around 1915, he parted ways with his first wife.

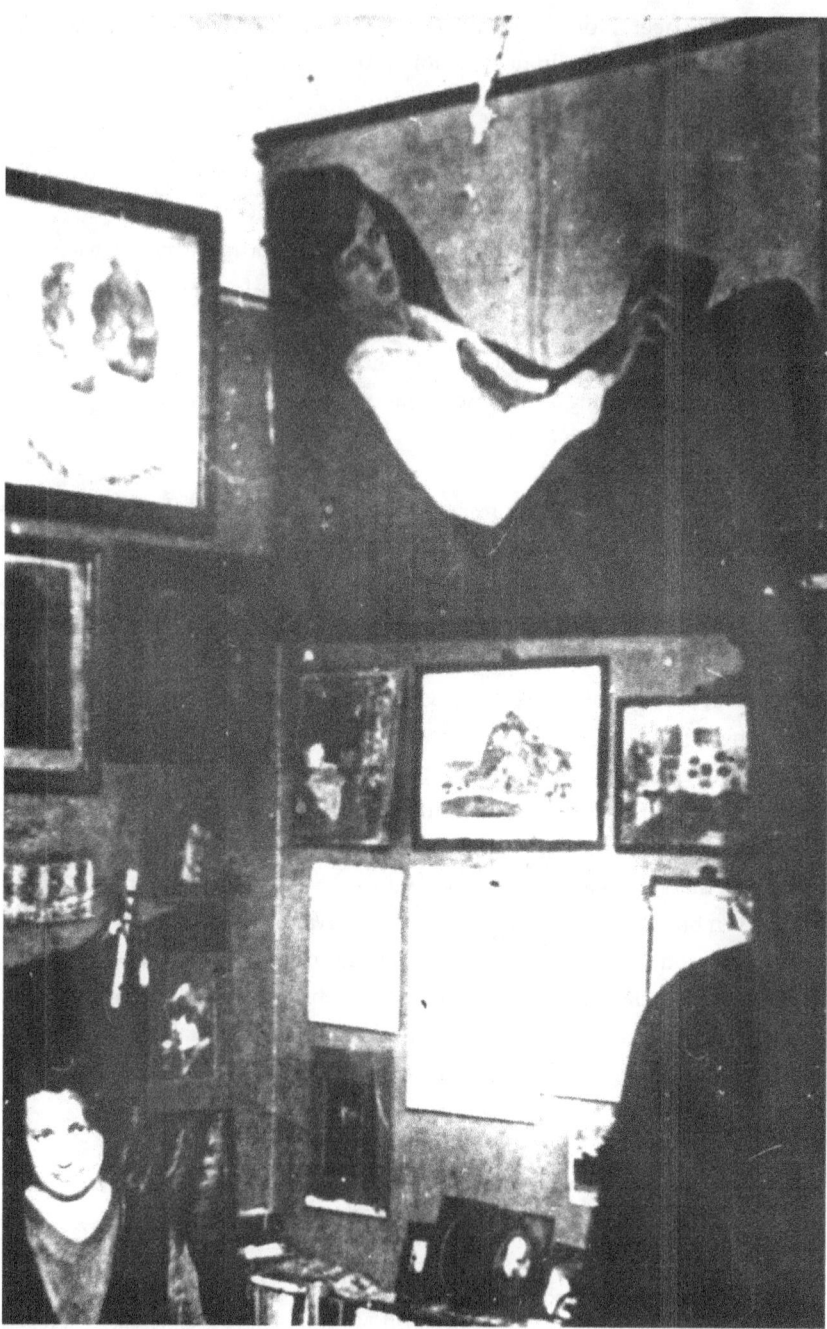

Figure 31. Photograph showing Anastasia Tsvetaeva (lower left corner) in her room; at the upper right is a portrait of Sergei Efron by Magda Nachman.

CHAPTER 7

The Revolutions of 1917 and Their Aftermath

Blessed is he who has visited this world in its fateful minutes!
—*Fedor Tiutchev*

Better to be a dog in peaceful times than a man in chaotic times.
—*Feng Menglong*, Stories to Enlighten the World

Along with other nineteenth-century European romantics, the great Russian poet Fedor Tiutchev believed that human history and civilization had arisen out of primordial chaos, that historic "fateful minutes," such as revolutions and similar upheavals, afforded the world a chance to replenish its energy and to reorder itself, and that for an individual, such events provided an opportunity to achieve a clearer and deeper understanding of oneself and human history. Out of the experience of "chaotic times," a wiser human being emerges, ready to behold the new shape of the world.

Which is all very well for those not hurled to their deaths by events, but even for those who survive, it may be that knowledge and insight will have been purchased at too great a price.

My young protagonists were coming of age as the world order was unraveling. Like countless others across Europe, they witnessed a descent into chaos. Some understood at the outset where events were headed, while others looked on in amazement and disbelief, waiting for the air to clear, while yet others threw themselves headlong into supporting and building the "new order."

Magda lived in Moscow through the February Revolution of 1917 and the abdication of Tsar Nicholas II, followed by the Bolshevik October Revolution later that year. The first two events did away with the Russian monarchy and the Russian Empire; they led to the establishment of the provisional government and the revival of councils—Soviets of Workmen's and Soldiers' Deputies—which had appeared initially during the 1905 Russian Revolution, to represent the interests of a variety of leftist, mainly socialist, parties and serve as watchdogs against counterrevolution.

The anticipation of the February Revolution is vividly described by Olga Freidenberg, a first cousin of the poet Boris Pasternak:

> Tsarist Russia was rotting and decaying. The revolution was being prepared throughout the land, from the first man to the last. Had I not been living in this era, I would not have been able to imagine the meaning of the unanimity of a nation of many millions, of all events, of everything that was happening. An enormous tsardom—steppes, forests, and mountains—everything rushed headlong toward revolution. I knew the soldiers from Nicholas's personal guard—his bodyguards; I had acquaintances among the Tsarskoye Selo imperial guardsmen. And they, and the great princes, Nicholas's relatives, and even the last common man—all wanted the revolution.[1]

The event that many had anxiously awaited had finally come to pass, and it all proceeded in a relatively orderly fashion, as Julia saw it. In a letter to Natalia Grekova, she wrote about the first days of the February Revolution as events unfolded in Moscow:

> Outside, the street was rejoicing and artillery trucks decorated with red flags were passing. There was a feeling of a whirlwind, a massive storm— and the desire to retreat into one's lair, as if it were an uninhabited island on which you had arrived by chance and were unable to communicate with anyone. This feeling of an "island" is of course a hyperbole of the first day, when nothing was clear, but in reality, even the phones did not stop working; stockpiles of candles and water, which had been accumulated by some, were superfluous because all was in perfect order. These circumstances added something more to the general harmony, the unreality of what was taking place.[2]

The disruptions to daily life that had been anticipated did not occur at once. The mood in Julia's letter is hopeful, for there was hope in the air. The

---

1   Ol'ga Freidenberg, "Fragmenty iz memuarov. God 17," *Voprosy literatury* 5 (2017). Annotations by Nataliia Kostenko.

2   March 20, 1917, RGALI, f. 2080, op. 1, no. 5, 1–2.

American journalist Ernest Poole reported from Russia that the whole country was hopeful, experiencing "immense and amazing happiness ... it was a dazzling revelation of the deep, deep powers for brotherhood and friendliness that lie buried in mankind."[3]

From letters and memoirs of that period, one gets the impression that all laws and customs had been suspended, that the events of February had given a push to the whole country and set everything in motion: soldiers deserting and returning home from the front; new governmental authorities and rival soviets sending their representatives and commissars to the front lines; private citizens experiencing an urge to meet, to discuss, to decide how to live from that day forward. The agitation and unrest seemed to have no definite goal.

This is how the literary theorist and writer Victor Shklovsky described the February Revolution in Petrograd in his memoir *The Sentimental Journey: Reminiscences 1917–1922*:

> And all around the city the Muses and Furies of the February Revolution were scurrying—cars and trucks, lined up and filled to overflowing with soldiers, going God knows where, obtaining fuel from God knows where, giving an impression of red chimes all around the city. ... The streets were seething with spontaneous assemblies.[4]

In her letter quoted above, Julia writes:

> Max [Voloshin] has been running from house to house, boiling and seething with news, plans, and projects. Magda, too, was running about for the first few days, and it seems that she has ended up with a cold.[5]

The turmoil following the February Revolution culminated half a year later in the October Revolution and Civil War, which upended all aspects of daily life. All these events took place during the final years of World War I, which Russia had been fighting on multiple fronts since August 1914. It was not long before events picked Magda up and ran her about—for three years in and out of Moscow into a number of provincial towns and villages—because Moscow had

---

3   Ernest Poole, *The Village: Russian Impressions* (New York: Macmillan and Co., Limited, 1919), 64.

4   Viktor Shklovskii, *Sentimental'noe puteshestvie. Vospominaniia 1917–1922* (Moscow: Gelikon, 1923), 22.

5   March 20, 1917, RGALI, f. 2080, op. 1, no. 5, 1–2.

little to offer besides hunger and cold—followed by two years during which she lived primarily in Moscow. Finally, in the fall of 1922, Magda left Russia altogether, never to return. Here is a summary of Magda's wanderings from summer 1917 to fall 1922:

Summer 1917:	Bakhchisarai, Crimea
Winter 1917–1918:	Moscow
Spring through Fall 1918:	Likino/Tyurmerovka, Vladimir gubernia
Winter 1918–1919:	Moscow
Spring 1919:	Ivanovo-Voznesensk, Vladimir gubernia
Summer 1919:	Likino/Tyurmerovka, Vladimir gubernia
Fall 1919–Fall 1920:	Ust-Dolyssy, Vitebsk gubernia
Spring 1921–Fall 1922:	Moscow and the Russian North
Fall 1922:	Berlin, Germany

Julia remained in Moscow in those years. The support of her family and Kandaurov provided some stability. Letters sent by post or carried by chance travelers were the only way to stay connected. Thus, Julia wrote to Magda about her life in Moscow, and Magda reported to Julia on her wanderings and her life among the peasants in the provinces. Both were accomplished writers, and the immediacy of their writing makes their correspondence an astonishing document of the epoch.

After the events of February 1917, travel in the country had become perilous. As Victor Shklovsky wrote:

> People, like fruit in picturesque baskets, hulk up like mountains on the roofs of train carriages. All space on the buffers was taken. Our small carriage, wretchedly dangling at the train's tail, was overfilled.[6]

The great difficulties of travel notwithstanding, Magda left that summer of 1917 for Bakhchisarai, Crimea, a thousand miles from Moscow, as she had done previously for a couple of summers.

Perhaps it was imprudent to leave Moscow when so much was in flux, but Magda was fleeing the aftermath of an ill-starred love affair with Boris Griftsov. She wrote to Julia from Bakhchisarai:

---

6   Shklovskii, *Sentimental'noe puteshestvie*, 36.

I will never forgive myself that this year I even began talking about leaving Moscow. I should have stayed. Yet I am convinced that I have to separate with all this because this man does not need me. Still, it is unbearable that fifteen hundred versts[7] lie between me and Moscow, and I have to go on living. If you hear about Griftsov, write to me. Although there is nowhere you can hear about him.[8]

Evidently, something decisive had taken place between Magda and Griftsov. She wrote to Julia that her feeling of loneliness was caused by "pain from a wound and injustice." That wound appears not to have healed even two years later, when she wrote to Julia:

How strange that you see Griftsov. What kind of man is he? What impression do you have from your meetings? I saw him recently in a dream. I dreamed of a friendly meeting, as if he had repented and begun treating me like an ordinary decent person. Of course, that will never happen. Oh, why did I ever meet him in this world? God forbid that anyone should have such a meeting.[9]

Magda told herself that she was being "unreasonable; one should not suffer over the past,"[10] yet every so often she acknowledged that past pain in her letters. As I followed the lives of Magda and her friends in this time of upheaval, I became more and more aware of the growing tension between public events and personal concerns. The personal was immediate and pressing, and frequently the background noise without could be ignored for a time, though they could little imagine at the outset how the revolution and its aftermath would affect their personal lives. And so Magda left for Crimea that summer as usual.

Vacationers flocked to Bakhchisarai that summer in larger numbers than in previous years, although food was beginning to become scarce. Magda salved her wounded feelings by immersing herself in work, producing studies and portraits, with no plan for the future. She had no job to return to in Moscow and no place to stay there. She wrote to Julia that the uncertainty of the next winter was tormenting her. "Where will I be?"[11]

---

7   One verst is almost exactly two-thirds of a mile.
8   1917, RGALI, f. 2080, op. 1, no. 45, 197.
9   May 23, 1919, ibid., 122.
10 June 7, 1919, ibid., 126.
11 Undated, summer 1917, ibid., 197.

Two years later, writing to Julia from yet another refuge, the village of Ust-Dolyssy, Magda returned to the same theme:

> Dear Julia, somehow I cannot get around to writing properly to you. I travel a lot on foot 8 and 9 versts, putting on plays 9 versts away from here, and now it seems time to part with Dolyssy for good. The situation here has become intolerable. ... I don't know yet how to arrange the future.[12]

But in chaotic times, it is often events, not oneself, that do the arranging. In another letter, from the same village, Magda wrote:

> The past is so vivid and irretrievable. Again I am visited by ancient memories: the gymnasia, the Liteinyi Prospect era; I want to say like an old person: how much hope there was! I see the main error of my recent years: I have been organizing my life provisionally, in expectation of coming changes and possibilities. And years are passing. ... If only I could get rid of the feeling of uncertainty. ... To live awaiting an uncertain future and old age?[13]

This feeling of uncertainty, which had imperceptibly infiltrated Magda's life around 1916 with her move to Moscow, had become a defining feature of all aspects of life—political, social, and private. To live in a highly volatile environment without any latitude to make reasonably viable plans even for the near future can become unbearable; to make long-term decisions when you are always on the move is impossible. Such uncertainty would persist for another twenty years, until Magda finally landed in Bombay and established herself there as an artist.

But we are still in Crimea in the summer of 1917, from where Magda reported on her work:

> As far as my work is concerned, it is not at all bad: I haven't lost a single day, although I get very tired. I believe I will have good painterly results this summer.[14]

And in another letter, she wrote about the general state of mind of those in her immediate surroundings:

---

12 April 9, 1920, ibid., 112–113op.
13 June 11, 1920, ibid., 114–115op.
14 Undated, summer 1917, ibid., 160, 160op.

Everything is so quiet and peaceful, as if the revolution had taken place in a far-off land, and Bakhchisarai dwellers regard it with suspicion. When some orators spoke to them about freedom and that now one can do as one likes, they questioned the usefulness of such an innovation, and the old men are shaking their heads. They hardly read newspapers. Only everything has become more expensive.[15]

In Petrograd, it was not quiet and peaceful that summer. From the newspapers, Magda learned what was going on in the capital, and her own political fears grew clearer. In a letter to Vera Efron, she wrote, "and in Petersburg the Bolshevik villainy is again brewing."[16]

The dual power of the provisional government and the soviets provided no stability. The Bolsheviks tried to use the Petrograd Soviet to bring about another revolution that would topple the government. However, the soviets united several heterogeneous party-affiliated factions, in which, for the time being, the Bolsheviks were in the minority. Nevertheless, their efforts to bring about a coup added to the volatility of the situation. Bloody uprisings took place in July in Petrograd followed by numerous arrests. Uncertainty about the near future settled in. And so even the more optimistic Julia wrote:

I am happy that you are working because ultimately, that is the main thing. From what I see and hear, life has turned melancholy. I don't want to give in to lamentation, and so I am keeping silent; one day, unexpected joy will come even to Russia.[17]

Magda was concerned about her return to Moscow: "I worry about how we will leave here—they write about a new wave of refugees from Galicia—which means on the southern roads."[18] And in her reply to Julia, she wrote:

But then again, to judge by the newspaper reports, by that time life will have come to a standstill, and we will have died or even before that will be hanging on the lampposts. However, in spite of everything, I do not believe in doom and Russian villainy. Secretly, I prefer a chimerical

---

15 Undated, summer 1917, ibid., 197.
16 July 7, 1917, RGALI, f. 2962, op. 1, no. 395.
17 Undated, summer 1917, RGALI, f. 2080, op. 1, no. 7, 92.
18 Undated, July 1917, RGALI, f. 2080, op. 1, no. 45, 154–155op.

Slavophile dream of Tsaregrad, about Great Russia, to these questionable embodiments of socialist symbols of faith.[19]

Magda wrote this still hoping for a turn of events and "unexpected joy" for Russia, still thinking that a change was possible, regardless of what the papers reported, since life in Bakhchisarai had not yet changed drastically.

Magda managed to return from Crimea to Moscow in August, at the time of yet more dramatic events unfolding in Petrograd. Lavr Kornilov, a general who had been appointed commander in chief of the Russian army only in July, ordered his troops to move on Petrograd to establish order and to support (or perhaps to topple; historians' interpretations of the affair differ widely) the provisional government. The government, fearful of losing power to Kornilov, moved against him and appealed to the Bolsheviks for help. Kornilov was defeated and arrested, mainly through the efforts of the Bolsheviks and the Petrograd Soviet. The Bolsheviks were now in a position to seize power.

Julia received her first impressions of the October Revolution in Petrograd from her and Magda's friend Nadezhda Lermontova, who replied to Julia's description of the bloody Bolshevik coup in Moscow that had taken place between October 25 and November 2, 1917, and about which Julia's friend the poet Vladislav Khodasevich wrote: "Seven days and seven nights, Moscow raged in fire and madness."[20] Here is Lermontova's description of how October 25, 1917, unfolded in Petrograd:

> I received your letter after the destruction of Moscow. I suggest that you do not put down your brushes and pencils, not even for a minute, for otherwise, you will be swallowed up by our current monstrous, shapeless, stateless, amoral, and senseless Russian life; and you will lose forever the last hope to swim to shore one way or another. I saw Alexander [Ziloti] at the ballet on October 25, on day one, or more accurately on night one, of Leon Trotsky's accession to the Russian throne of sufferings. He [Ziloti] was sure that everything would disappear by itself in short order. On October 25, everyone in the theater was sitting as if on a blazing pyre; many of the performers were unable to get there because of the raised drawbridges. But the principals—Karsavina and Obukhov—surpassed the possible in

---

19   Undated, summer 1917, ibid., 155.
20   Vladislav Khodasevich, "Vtorogo noiabria," in *Sobranie sochinenii*, vol. 1 (Moscow: AO "Soglasie," 1996), 165.

their virtuosity, refinement, and unattainable height of their art. We shall surely remember till the end of our days this dazzling light in the gloom of the night, in the darkness of frightened souls, accompanied by the sounds of gunfire at the Winter Palace. They were heroes in the service of art, and their hearts were bleeding, for they, too, were certainly suffering; they showed us art's timeless and spaceless existence, cold, free, and self-sufficient.[21]

Lermontova, Julia, Magda, Natalia Grekova, Alexander Ziloti, and their friends and correspondents witnessed the unfolding events as bystanders. Ziloti believed that the precipitous changes would have no lasting repercussions and would blow away in short order. They did not, of course, and he ended up emigrating to France. Julia looked for any positive sign in the new shape of the world. (After the revolution, her brother joined the Bolsheviks and became one of the first diplomats of the new regime. Kandaurov was sanguine about the situation and believed that politics would not affect their lives too greatly.) In the end, Julia made her peace with the new reality and lived out her life working inside it.

Grekova, uncertain how to react, with brothers in the White Army, which was fighting the Bolsheviks, moved with her siblings' families from place to place, from their ancestral home into a stranded railroad car, and finally to Constantinople. Magda rarely wrote about politics in her letters to Julia, perhaps out of sensitivity to Julia's loyalty to her brother. Yet ever observant of human conduct, she constantly reported on life as it was falling apart under the new social norms. What offended her was the cruelty and loutishness of those who were now in control in a world gone topsy-turvy. Although Magda and her group of friends had divergent responses to their shattered world, their art continued to unite them.

Lermontova opened and closed her letter to Julia on such a note. Art, creative engagement, and the work ethic developed in Bakst's school had become a safe haven and shield for these artists. Their letters may speak of cold, hunger, pain, and death, but always also about their work and art. Just as Magda reported from Bakhchisarai on her work, and Julia responded with approval, writing that "ultimately [the work] is the main thing," Natalia Grekova wrote in a letter to Julia, wondering whether her brothers were alive and how she would manage after having been dispossessed of her home:

---

21 November 20, 1917, RGALI, f. 2080, op. 1, no. 40, 42–43.

When for whatever reason I don't manage to get any work done, I fall apart completely. But usually, I lock myself up in my room and work. One has to seize the time while one can. Once, in a moment of doubt and low spirits, I came across a letter from K. S. [Petrov-Vodkin]. He writes, "As far as I know you, you have nothing else to do but paint, that is, all your life is pulsating within and around you, and to express it outside yourself is the salvation and 'realism' of your (of our) life. That you have the right and obligation to work at this and that you are able to paint a 'living' picture is guaranteed by …" and so on. These words comforted me greatly. Otherwise, I think often whether I have a right to work as an artist, especially at this time when life is so difficult for everyone. But now, it seems, I have to prove that these words of K. S. are true. Will I really be able to prove this? Will I be able to create a "living" picture?

The "homesickness" that suffocated me during the initial period of our living here has abated—all thanks to work. I attach a small sketch of the picture on which I am currently working—my entire family are horrified at the purple head, but I think that it will remain purple, perhaps changing its shade. The length of this piece is 2 arshins [56 inches], and the width is 10 vershoks [17½ inches]. The whole business now is to beat this head into shape.[22]

Around the same time, in August 1918, Grekova wrote to Julia about her visit to Lermontova at a sanatorium—the kidney disease from which she had been suffering for years had worsened, due at least in part to the lack of adequate food and medicine. However, Lermontova continued painting, and Grekova saw a great many interesting ink drawings, with some simple color illustrations for Ovid's *Metamorphoses*, and many other oil paintings. She concluded that Lermontova "need[ed] to organize an exhibition; there [were] many pictures, and taken all together, they define[d] her as an artist."[23] But there was to be no exhibition. Nadezhda Lermontova died in 1921, and her work would have to wait until the twenty-first century before it was rediscovered and appreciated.[24]

---

22 July 12 and July 25, 1918 (old and new styles), RGALI, f. 2080, op. 1, no. 24, 105. Like many letters written shortly after the calendrical reform of early 1918, Grekova's letter includes both the old- and new-style dates.

23 August 11, 1918, ibid., 96.

24 And as for Grekova's work, it was long believed that all her paintings had been lost. But I recently discovered two works: an oil self-portrait—a response to Petrov-Vodkin's portrait of Grekova ("Kazachka")—and a watercolor illustration for the popular story "Konek-Gorbunok." See "Dve raboty Natalii Grekovoi," *Nashe nasledie* 129–130 (2019): 144–145.

Magda and her circle continued working and exhibiting for a few more years. Exhibitions that had been planned before the October Revolution were not canceled, and many more were mounted in rapid succession, in some of which Magda participated.[25] However, it was becoming harder to find a place in a show or obtain a commission, which now depended on the state and on personal connections within the state apparatus.

Magda nonetheless tried to continue her life as an artist. As she wrote to Julia from the village of Likino in June 1919:

> Today I took out the paints and it seemed as if there arose the fragrance of some great motherland. Resinous oily scent! Am I an artist or not—these aromatic little tubes are my motherland. I have no other. This poverty does not make me unhappy.[26]

Magda managed to continue painting in every village and provincial town in which she found herself during the civil war, even when occupied in manual labor or as an office clerk. A student of Rudolf Steiner's anthroposophy, steeped in Symbolist poetry, she described to Julia her destiny as a fulfillment of herself as an artist:

> On the one hand is our destiny, on the other—chance events. Through them, we have to embody our destiny. It is high time to understand that we cannot change facts, but we have to use all we get to the fullest. To pine for the impossible means to lose what is possible and accessible, and be left a beggar. All this has become especially clear to me this summer.[27]

These words echo Magda's youthful meditations on the nature of time— about past, present, and future—her own admonition to herself to look at the present with eyes open and use every opportunity for self-fulfillment. From these early letters to the tributes that appeared in Bombay newspapers on her death, Magda's life can be seen as a confirmation of a belief that the winds of chance should not, must not, be allowed to blow one off one's chosen course. She fought to stay on that course in her quiet way—out of necessity. And fight she had to.

---

25 Magda's works were exhibited in Moscow at the "Mir Iskusstva" show that opened on December 26, 1917, and again in May–July 1918 at a show put on by the artists' union; her pictures were also included in the Fourth State Art Show in 1918–1919 and in the Second State Exhibition of Art and Science in Kazan, 1920.

26 June 6, 1919, RGALI, f. 2080, op. 1, no. 45, 96.

27 September 8/21 (old and new styles), 1918, ibid., 94op.

Those artists who sought to yoke themselves to the political revolution, seeing it as a medium for revolution in aesthetics and in human values and relationships, soon began working with the new regime. Even the World of Art association by this time was dominated by those who styled themselves revolutionaries. Those who were less political or whose work could be associated with bourgeois values were left out in the cold. Thus in January 1918, Obolenskaya wrote to Voloshin's mother about the World of Art's recently opened exhibition, whose jury had been presided over by former members of the avant-garde group Jack of Diamonds. She wrote that it was hopeless to submit any of Voloshin's paintings to such a hostile and belligerent jury.[28]

The antagonism between the radical avant-gardists and Magda's group that was revealed at the Exhibition 1915 became even more pronounced in the time immediately following the revolution (1918–1921), not so much because of aesthetic disagreements, though those should not be minimized, but because many key posts that controlled commissions and appointments had been quickly occupied by the more ideologically attuned. Many of those artists considered themselves in the vanguard of the builders of the "new man" who would people a society freed from bourgeois prejudices. In their thinking, they came close to the ideas of the Bolshevik leader and theoretician Leon Trotsky, who foresaw an actual biological rebirth of mankind. Trotsky assigned a pivotal role to the arts, which would assist in the merger of politics and aesthetics. He wrote:

> To master one's feelings, to understand instincts, to render them transparent, to run the wires of volition into what is hidden and underground, and thereby raise man to a new biological stage, to create a higher sociobiological type—a superman, if you will—that is the task mankind will set for itself.
> ...
> Art—verbal, theatrical, plastic—will give this process a corresponding form. More precisely, the form in which the process of cultural construction and self-education of the communist man will embody itself will absorb into itself and develop all vital elements of today's arts. The human body will become more harmonious, movements more rhythmic, the voice more musical, and the forms of everyday life will acquire dynamic theatricality.[29]

---

28 January 1918; Voloshin, *Sobranie sochinenii*, vol. 12: *Pis'ma 1918–1924* (Moscow: Ellis Lak, 2013), 64.

29 Trotsky wrote this in 1922. Lev Trotskii, *Problemy kul'tury. Kul'tura perekhodnogo perioda* (Moscow: T8RUGRAM, 2018), 265.

There was no shortage of artists eager to produce great new works for the "new man" with all their creative energy and enthusiasm.

During a time that saw soup kitchens multiplying to serve the growing population of orphans and shortages of coffins for the growing number of the dead, optimism about the future nevertheless ran high. The artists and writers who sided with the new regime felt that they were harbingers of a new era and that they held its reins in their hands. Revolutionary optimism attracted giant poetic voices, like those of Vladimir Mayakovsky and the constructivist Vladimir Tatlin, who designed a grandiose 400-meter spiral tower (never built)—the "Monument to the Third International." The nineteen-year-old Andrei Platonov, who would become perhaps the greatest twentieth-century writer of Russian prose, called for a revolution in the sphere of arts. The fires of that revolution were supposed to burn away the corpse of the bourgeoisie with its obsolete art, thereby doing away with all that was trite, filthy, and vulgar. Platonov believed that those fires would clear a space for creating the "beautiful and sublime" future:

> This will be the music of the spheres; an element that knows no limits or borders; a torch burning through a depth of mysteries; a flaming sword of the human struggle against darkness and the encroachment of blind forces. In order to begin building a common temple of universal creativity, a common dwelling of the human spirit, let us begin small for now, let us begin with the foundation for that future sunny temple in which heavenly universal joy will reside, let us begin with small bricks.[30]

However, the spirit of the time, bent on destruction, was in no mood to build. Following the revolutions of 1917 and the onset of the civil war and the Bolsheviks' systematic program of torture and murder known as the Red Terror the following year, the destruction began. The promised new and glorious world arising on the ruins of the old was nowhere in sight. Even in 1923, in his "Letters on Survival," the Russian anarchist Volin (V. M. Eikhenbaum) wrote:

> The Russian revolution, in an economic sense, hurtles back and forth between revolution-destroyed capitalism and revolution-destroyed state

---

30 Cited in A. N. Varlamov, *Andrei Platonov* (Moscow: Molodaia gvardiia, 2011), 21.

socialism—in the void and chaos of the wreckage of the one and of the other. ... Total destruction and no creation ... the revolution ... has brought total devastation: economics, politics, law, culture, labor, ethics, religion, gender, family, individuality—all has been reduced to a pile of smoking ruins.[31]

Later, in the 1930s, Platonov would portray characters who dreamed about building a beautiful future, but all they could create was a deep hole, exemplified in the title of his most famous novel, *The Foundation Pit.*

During that period, Magda received a letter from Julia with news about a mutual friend, the artist Raisa (Raya) Kotovich–Borisyak, who was unable to find artistic employment and was working as a clerk in a health education office and had just learned that Magda was in similar straits, working as a clerk in the village of Likino: "Raya took it surprisingly philosophically and said that it's time we all retire from the scene because our epoch no longer needs us."[32] In her next letter, Julia again wrote about Raya:

Raya called. Tired, broken. Work is eating her up. ... I agree with her that it is worse than the accounting office, but still I cannot imagine how you manage with accounts.[33]

To this Magda replied, directing her spleen particularly at the constructivists Vladimir Tatlin, Sofia Dymshits-Tolstaya, and Vera Pestel:

I am sorry for Raya, for myself. Everywhere you turn, there are the Efroses, and we are barred totally from everywhere. In part, this is the punishment for our former overly aesthetic and pampered life. We have not figured out ways to earn money, to assert ourselves, and we do not have teeth to bite and bite back; our teeth are not sharpened. And so she is without a position, and I am in an office, flicking the beads on an abacus, and we are useless. However, we have taste, and skills, and education. But it turns out that we are not needed. Efroses and Gogels are needed, and impostors in art and illiterates like Tatlin, and Sofia, and Pestel.[34]

---

31 V. Volin (V. M. Eikhenbaum), "Pis'ma o perezhitom," *Anarkhicheskii vestnik* 1 (1923): 30–31.
32 May 30, 1919, RGALI, f. 2080, op. 1, no. 7, 30.
33 June 16, 1919, ibid., 32–35op.
34 Undated, early fall 1919, RGALI, f. 2080, op. 1, no. 45, 137.

The names that Magda invokes in her letter are of individuals who, unlike Magda and Raya, were making it under the new political circumstances. The Constructivist Vladimir Tatlin (1885–1953) was in the ascendant, about which Julia comments in a letter to Voloshin:

> And artistic life is at a boil: Tatlin and Sofia Isaakovna are arranging things. Tatlin already calls K. V. "comrade" and has let me know today that he could have given us a dressing down in five newspapers that are at "his service," only he doesn't want to.[35]

Abram Efros (1888–1954) was an art historian, translator, and poet. After the revolution he was actively engaged in the protection of ancient monuments. Nikolai Efros (1867–1923) was a theater historian and playwright who in 1918 became an employee of the Theater Division of the People's Commissariat of Education. Sofia Dymshits (1884–1963) and Vera Efremovna Pestel (1887–1952) were painters who worked with Tatlin after the revolution. The Gogel to whom Magda was referring was perhaps the playwright and theater critic Konstantin Sergeevich Gogel (1888–1929).

The disdain for Tatlin and his ilk voiced by Magda and her circle, instilled by their teacher Bakst, was principled and conceptual. They objected to an abstraction divorced from the study of nature. The intervening century, however, has judged that the Russian avant-garde—the artists whom Magda disparaged—produced some of the great works of the twentieth century. The excitement of what appeared to Magda as nothing but hooligans breaking all the old rules and taboos is still as fresh in the canvases of the Futurists, Rayonists, Suprematists, and Constructivists as it must have been a century ago.

It was not only their artistic aesthetics that provoked the Bakstians' displeasure. Their politicization of art went against the grain as well. In 1920, writing in the new *Bulletin of the Executive Committee of Moscow Higher State Art Studios*, Malevich declared, "Long live the construction of the new and away with painterly culture—a useless aesthetic accoutrement."[36] And his colleague, the book designer Sergei Senkin, wrote in the same journal an article titled "Why We

---

35 This letter is cited in M. Voloshin, *Sobranie sochinenii*, vol. 12, 134. Julia's letter was written on May 20/June 2, 1918 (old and new styles). In the same letter Julia wrote that she had exhibited a portrait of Kandaurov, "which moved even Efros." In her letters, Magda names Efros as one of their nemeses.

36 Kazimir Malevich, "Ot redaktsii," *Vestnik ispolkoma moskovsk. vysshikh gosudarstvennykh khudozhestvennykh masterskikh* 1 (1920): 2–3.

Stand for the Organization of a Party," in which he called on the art association UNOVIS (Champions of New Art) to organize itself like a political party, taking for its model the Russian Communist Party of the Bolsheviks in its desire to eradicate all opposition, stating, "New forms of being must have one and only one new art."[37]

The quarrel between Bakst and his school and the radical avant-garde, which began as a disagreement over the objectives of art, had left the gallery walls and studio easels and splashed over into politics and the struggle for survival. Magda recognized how unprepared she and her friends were to compete for work. Most of them were women from well-to-do families who had never had to think about earning a living. As late as 1915, the twenty-six-year-old Magda, still living with her mother, wrote to Julia that she would like "at last to earn money at some point. …" But at the time there was no real necessity, and she finished her sentence with a shrug: "… but there is no way for me to do so."[38]

Bakst's students found themselves unwanted, cast out by history. In 1919, for example, Magda wrote:

> As the fates decree, I am cast out here in the woods, and what will become of me further? I have no money, I haven't found a paying job. And when will I be able to live again? Am I no longer an artist and will I never paint again?[39]

Life without the possibility of painting would be mere existence. But without a commission, all of which depended now on political connections, there was no paper, no paints, no buyers, and no money. Each time Magda left Moscow for the provinces, leaving behind those she loved and valued, it was after a harsh winter that had left her longing for greener pastures and emotional respite. But her letters to her friends in Moscow repeatedly express her feeling of abandonment and loneliness. After a time, her insatiable longing for companionship would cause her to return to the struggle that was life in the capital. Yet each time she returned to Moscow it was to a hopeless situation.

In August 1917, after her return to Moscow from Bakhchisarai, Magda rented a room in an apartment in Merzlyakovsky Lane that she shared with

---

37 Sergei Senkin, "Pochemu my stoim za organizatsiiu partii," *Vestnik ispolkoma moskovskikh vysshikh gosudarstvennykh khudozhestvennykh masterskikh* 1 (1920): 3–4.

38 August 18, 1915, ibid., 90–91.

39 Undated, spring 1919, RGALI, f. 2080, op. 1, no. 45, 156–157.

Vera Efron and several other women of long acquaintance. In years past, such shared apartments had been abodes of youthful gaiety and mutual support. But now, on the eve of political and social cataclysm, such carefree days were no longer to be had. Quarrels arose. Factions formed. A commune was metamorphosing into a soviet-type communal apartment.

As time passed, all the roommates in Magda's apartment attributed their misunderstandings and quarrels to outside events, which kept them in a state of nervous agitation. After all, they were all, if not close friends, then at least cordial acquaintances. Food had become scarce in the city already in August, and there was not much in the way of fuel; everyone was dreading the cold of winter. In the fall, street fighting in the bloody October Revolution went on in Moscow for seven days. Sergei Efron took part in the fighting on the side of the counterrevolution, which was defeated. He had to flee the city, and no one knew whether he was dead or alive (only later came the news that from Moscow he had headed south, where he soon joined the Volunteer Army, a faction of the White movement against the Bolsheviks). To earn money had become increasingly difficult.

Magda had to fend for herself, taking whatever jobs came her way. Sometimes she found work painting stage settings, and sometimes it was covering railroad carriages with agitprop posters. Finally, after the 1917–1918 winter of hunger, cold, and illness, she and Julia, who also needed money, took part in decorating Red Square for the May Day celebration. That turned out to be the last straw for the strained relationship between Magda and her roommates. The sisters Efron—along with a large part of the Russian intelligentsia—considered any support of the new regime indefensible, especially because their brother was fighting against it. They concluded from her participation in the decoration of Red Square that Magda was a tool of the Bolsheviks, and they, and even their visitors, refused even to speak to her. Magda, sensitive and gentle, suffered terribly from the ostracism. This silent treatment is mentioned in her correspondence with Julia, without any details. More can be learned from Julia's letter to Voloshin:

> I don't see the "rascals." They are boycotting us for having participated in decorating the city for May 1. Marg[arita] Vas[ilievna] [Sabashnikova] also wanted to help in this but didn't manage it, and so it seems they left her alone. The worst came down on Magda Max[imilianovna], who painted little stars and ornaments: Vera and Lilya haven't spoken to her for a month now, and their guests avoid her. … As for me, Mikh[ail] Solom[onovich]

[Feldstein] seems to have seriously taken offense because despite my requests ... to telephone me, he remains silent. Apropos this, Borisyak[40] suggests a talk on the theme "Bolshevism and Russian ornament." All joking aside, I would be very upset if they set Seryozha [Sergei Efron], who now is God knows where, against us.[41]

In May 1918, at the end of her tether, hurt and disheartened, Magda left for Likino, a village in Vladimir gubernia, 145 miles east of Moscow, where her brother-in-law worked in the management of a large forest. In summers past, Likino had been one of the vacation retreats where Magda and her mother would visit her older sister Erna and her family. But she could not stay in Likino indefinitely. Over the summer, her art supplies—paper, paints, even erasers—diminished, and it was difficult to find a source for replenishing them even in Moscow, let alone in the village. She had no money and was dependent on her brother-in-law, who himself had a large family to feed. The prospect of spending the winter buried deep in the woods was horrifying to her. Returning to Moscow would mean to live again in the unfriendly apartment in Merzlyakovsky Lane. But Magda decided to give it a try.

The Moscow winter of 1918–1919 was especially difficult. To survive, she attempted to sell her books (among them, an album of Canaletto's etchings and a collection of St. Petersburg cityscapes produced by the World of Art artists), and she obtained some freelance work for stage and costume design for some of the theaters in and around Moscow (for example, she painted sets for Molière's *Tartuffe* for the theater cooperative).[42] However, not knowing how to ingratiate herself with the administration of the evanescent theaters, she was rarely paid for her work. She tried unsuccessfully to find private art students. She painted murals promoting literacy on railroad cars, likely under the auspices of the Soviet artistic institution Proletkult, the Office for Proletarian Culture. In her memoirs, Margarita Sabashnikova, who worked for a time with Proletkult as coordinator of painters, wrote that the wonderful idea of painting the sides of railroad cars with propaganda, which would then be

---

40 Andrei Borisyak (1885–1962)—cellist, student of Pablo Casals. First husband of Raisa Kotovich-Borisyak.

41 This letter is cited in M. Voloshin, *Sobranie sochinenii*, vol. 12, 133. Julia's letter was written on May 20/June 2, 1918 (old and new styles).

42 In a letter to Voloshin, Julia wrote: "an extraordinary event: my *Snow Maiden* as well as Borisyachka's *Mermaid* and Magda's *Tartuffe* have been bought by the theater cooperative." (Borisyachka was a nickname of Raisa Borisyak.) See ibid., 13, not later than January 12, 1918.

seen throughout the country, had come from her office. In exchange for that work, a Red Army soldier's ration and some money were promised. Sabashnikova recalled:

> The frost was severe [that winter]. It was my job to write down the names of the painters and direct them to their place of work. People were waiting, trembling from cold and fear that they wouldn't be hired. It was excruciating to see these painters, among whom I met many acquaintances, so humiliated by privation.[43]

Magda became weak and ill. Julia wrote in her journal: "Went to see Magda. They were all sitting at the dinner table in their winter coats. … It was freezing in Magda's room."[44]

Magda and Julia's circle of friends tried to maintain some semblance of normal life. They made a paper Christmas tree and exchanged presents. Among their guests was the poet Vladislav Khodasevich, whom both had known from their Koktebel days and who would emigrate to Berlin in a couple of years; the artist Raisa Kotovich-Borisyak and her husband, the cellist Andrei Borisyak; the epidemiologist Leonid Isaev, who provided them with work painting medical posters, and his wife, Vera, Raisa's sister. They frequented the Poets' Cafe. Julia's improvised art studio in one of the rooms in her apartment had become a common space where Magda, Kandaurov, Sabashnikova, and Eva Feldstein painted together. They attended concerts and lectures.

Here is Julia's journal entry for the day of a lecture by the famous Symbolist writer Andrei Bely, who had become a serious student of Rudolf Steiner and a follower of anthroposophy. His talk, "The Paths of Culture," was an attempt to define culture in anthroposophical terms. Julia begins with a vivid description of a different path, a literal one, winding among the ruins of their former civilization, that she and her companions had to traverse to get to Bely's talk:

---

43 Margarita Sabashnikova, *Zelenaia zmeia* (Moscow: ENIGMA, 1993), 269. Later, in a letter to Magda, undated, March 1920, Julia wrote that she saw carriages painted by her at one of the Moscow railway stations. RGALI, f. 2080, op. 1, no. 7, 60–62op.

44 Obolenskaya's diary, February 20, 1919: GLM, f. 348, op. 1, no. 4. She wrote again in a few days, February 29, 1919: "visited Magda; she is sick in bed lying in a cold room; a doctor came to see her."

In the evening, a talk by Bely. We hobbled in single file along a terrible icy, bumpy path in the middle of the street (between former streetcar rails), flanked by lakes. [Our] feet kept breaking through the ice. The sidewalk was impassable. A[ndrei] B[ely] read his paper "The Paths of Culture— History of the Formation of the 'I'—tribal, personal, collective" (just as now, dove's steps inside us and a storm outside). At intermission I saw Margarita Vasilyevna [Sabashnikova]. She looked terribly worn out, frazzled. Her parents are literally starving. Could not recognize her. She, like Magda, wakes up at night in horror. How strange now to read books, old novels. I read sometimes at night to feel all their unreality, childishness. All this is a plaything in comparison with present-day life.[45]

Apart from the scarcity of food and firewood, the city's infrastructure was collapsing. Broken pipes turned the Moscow streets into a frozen sewer, and no one cleared them.

By now, communal apartments had become commonplace, especially in urban centers. Since all real estate had been nationalized, former owners or tenants of larger apartments, whose rooms were in danger of being assigned by the authorities to strangers, would invite friends and acquaintances to move in. None of these people were accustomed to communal living, but some were better able than others to adapt to the new conditions. Neighbors who were related or knew each other well sometimes were able to form a friendly cooperative fellowship. Besides her immediate family and Kandaurov, Julia's apartment housed her brother and his family, her stepfather's brother and his family, and some friends who needed a room for a time. There were misunderstandings and tensions, but Julia had her mother, who was also her close friend, and Kandaurov, both of whom loved and supported her, and thus while describing the difficulties of communal life to Magda, Julia wrote:

I imagine to myself with horror ideal circumstances, but without K. V. [Kandaurov] or mama by my side—no, then better nothing. And now I want a better [situation] mainly for their sake.[46]

---

45 Ibid., no. 3. The phrase "dove steps inside us and a storm outside" is a reference to Nietzsche's *Also Sprach Zarathustra*: "It is the quietest words that bring the storm. Thoughts that come on dove's feet govern the world."

46 Undated, 1920, RGALI, f. 2080, op. 1, no. 7, 113–115.

Magda's brothers and her eldest sister had remained in Petrograd; another sister lived in Likino, to which Magda could periodically escape. Yet another sister had married and moved to Switzerland. Their mother moved between Petrograd and Likino to be with her older daughters. Magda, however, was alone. She had to put up with the apartment in Merzlyakovsky Lane, where tensions ran high and where she felt under constant attack. In March of that cold and hungry year, to escape waking up in horror at night and to avoid unwanted yet unavoidable encounters with Boris Griftsov (with whom she had many acquaintances in common), but mainly to flee squabbles in the communal apartment and to find a way to support herself, Magda left for Ivanovo-Voznesensk, a city about 150 miles northeast of Moscow, where a friend had promised her a job as a painter. Later, Magda would write to Julia about her flight:

> When I was on my way to Ivanovo, I was in a frenzy. There was much that tormented me last winter, and even now, it horrifies me to think about my life on Merzlyakovsky. That room cost me dearly. After all, my soul has become calmer now that I no longer hear the endless criticism and hostility, and endless old wives' judgments and an atmosphere of obnoxious female nature. They don't write; perhaps they have found new reasons to be dissatisfied with me. But let them be.[47]

She left on the advice of Mikhail Feldstein, who had connections with the Ivanovo Polytechnic Institute, which had moved there from Riga in 1918, and who introduced Magda to a friend and colleague, Eduard Pontovich, whom Magda mentions in her letters with affection.[48] Feldstein himself managed to work in Ivanovo as a guest lecturer in 1920–1922, between repeated arrests on trumped-up charges of counterrevolutionary activity.

On her arrival in Ivanovo-Voznesensk, Magda learned that Pontovich had been unable to arrange a job for her, but official restrictions on travel, lack of money, and the unlikelihood of being able to survive in Moscow made a speedy return impracticable. And so once again, as in the summer of 1918, Magda joined her sister's family in Likino. But this time, like almost everyone else, her family were having trouble making ends meet. Her brother-in-law found her a job as a tally clerk in the office of the forestry division where he worked. To

---

47 June 7, 1919, RGALI, f. 2080, op. 1, no. 45, 123–126.
48 Eduard Pontovich (1886–1941, Magadan, Gulag)—jurist and philosopher of jurisprudence, professor of law.

work as an office menial was certainly not the life that Magda had envisioned for herself when she left Zvantseva's academy five years previously, but it was that or starvation. As she wrote to Julia:

> With horror I think that I won't be able to return to Moscow in the fall. It seems to me that I won't be able to survive the winter here. There is not even any electricity here. I should not have gone to Ivanovo. But I was so desperate then. It did me in; I could not return without money. And now I have to save from a meager pittance in order to repay my debts. I won't be able to save enough by the fall. So you can see that what is left to me is to plant a cross over myself and remain an office clerk, because no beautiful prince will come to save me from my imprisonment.[49]

A month later, Magda wrote again of her feeling of being trapped in Likino:

> Our local train stopped running. No engine is available. So one can walk the thirty versts from Volosataya [the last train station] if one likes. They are delivering the mail by Soviet horses, but only until July 1, after which, who knows? A final separation from the world. … Day and night, I pray for deliverance from captivity.[50]

And a few days later: "The mail is again being delivered, but there is no train, and so our imprisonment continues."[51]

By the fall of 1919, Magda again thought of returning to Moscow. In order to travel during the civil war, one had to have an official document stating the identity of the traveler and the purpose of the journey. Magda attempted to obtain such a document, which had been difficult even the year before: "Everything is very complicated here because of a terrible attitude toward the intelligentsia—watch out or you will be in prison before you know it."[52] According to a new decree, one could not resign from one's job unless one had already found another position. Travel was allowed only on business. Furthermore, to Magda's surprise, it turned out that she had become subject to military service: "In taking this job," she wrote to Julia, "I never thought that all of a sudden I would become liable for military service and would be treated like a serf."[53]

---

49 May 23, 1919, RGALI, f. 2080, op. 1, no. 45, 119–122.
50 June 19, 1919, ibid., 97–97op.
51 July 2, 1919, ibid., 55–57.
52 September 8/21, 1918 (old and new styles), ibid., 93–94op.
53 September 25, 1919, ibid., 105–106op.

On top of these complications, life in Moscow had become even more difficult. Julia advised Magda against returning:

> In general, to tell the truth, it would be insanity for you to come to Moscow for the winter. What cultural life?! Don't deceive yourself by looking at the starving poets warmed by the summer sun reading their poems to the public. In summer, even near the poles some cranberries grow; so we now follow nature in everything. If we make it till spring, then come, if it is possible.[54]

And so Magda remained and continued her work in the local forestry office, suffering bitterly from the drudgery and the impossibility of painting:

> As to the realities of my work, I check accounts, receipts, and account books. Calculate how much so-and-so many horses cost, so-and-so much flour ground at the mill, what and how much of everything is [stored] in various barns—so constant exercise in arithmetic; I calculate livestock and dead stock.[55]

Magda was witnessing the destruction of the countryside at first hand. In spring, summer, and fall of 1919, she observed with dismay the rapid disappearance of the forest, which, under the supervision of her brother-in-law and his cousins, and before that of their grandfather, had been renowned as a model of forest management. Having spent summers in Likino visiting her forester relatives, she knew how much knowledge, labor, and love had gone into maintaining the forest and how much easier it was to destroy than to preserve:

> And they have ruined everything with their own hands. Obtuseness, brutish nature, short memory—all this comes not only from ignorance; there are some better-educated people who behave in the same way. This entire vast and once exemplary forest economy has been totally ruined; no work has been conducted; and everything depends on fraud. And all around it is the same—no work is done anywhere. Even for themselves, they do

---

54 Undated, fall 1919, RGALI, f. 2080, op. 1, no. 7, 97–99.
55 Undated, fall 1919, RGALI, f. 2080, op. 1, no. 45, 137.

not have firewood. Yet there is forest all around! In the past, they exported firewood to Moscow from here.[56]

It is astonishing how swiftly what was to become the Soviet way of life—"no work has been conducted, fraud, and loutish behavior"—settled in after the revolution, as if it had long been lying dormant.

What Magda saw with her own eyes was described in one of the first accounts of the Russian Revolution by I. F. Nazhivin, published in Vienna in 1921. The author witnessed the events of 1917–1918 in Vladimir gubernia and in particular the destruction of the Likino forestry:

> A pointless felling of trees had begun; cattle were grazing in protected plantations within V. S. Khrapovitsky's large and cultivated forest preserve, destroying them; in the forests and fields, birds and beasts once protected by law were aggressively exterminated—"now everything is ours," and that's why everything was being wiped out, ruthlessly and pointlessly.[57]

Magda's last letter from Likino was most likely written in September 1919. Around the beginning of October, she received a surprising invitation from Lilya Efron to work as a set and costume designer in a people's theater that Lilya had been invited to direct in the village of Ust-Dolyssy, near Nevel, in the Vitebsk gubernia, about 500 miles to the west of Likino and 325 miles west of Moscow.

---

56 Undated, fall 1919, ibid., 136–137. The Muromtsevo forestry management had been considerably improved by Karl Türmer, grandfather of Magda's brother-in-law A. P. Knorre, and was one of the best and richest in the country. In his honor, Likino acquired a second name—Tyurmerovka.

57 I. F. Nazhivin. *Zapiski o revoliutsii* (Moscow: Kuchkovo pole, 2016), 50.

CHAPTER 8

The People's Theater at Ust-Dolyssy

Someone took us in his palm, like seeds, and scattered us over the earth. Ah, how one wishes to grow into a ripening stalk, I think that such is the dream of even the smallest seed.

—Magda Nachman

Lilya Efron's invitation to work in the Ust-Dolyssy people's theater gave Magda authorization to leave her job in the forest office. In early October 1919 she was in Moscow, staying in "her room" at Julia's apartment for a few days before traveling together with Lilya to their destination. Her letters to Julia began to arrive from Ust-Dolyssy in late October.

Ust-Dolyssy is a little village of about a thousand inhabitants situated in a picturesque lake region, about fourteen miles from Nevel, the nearest town. The town was created about 500 years ago in the reign of Ivan the Terrible at a crossroads of languages, religions, and empires. For the next 200 years, the town and its environs were fought over by Russia, Lithuania, and Poland, reverting finally to Russia in 1772 after the First Partition of Poland, becoming part of the eastern border of the Jewish Pale. Nevel and the surrounding villages were populated by Catholics, Uniates, Russian Orthodox, Old Believers, and Jews. Old paintings of the cityscape depict churches with tall steeples, a monastery, and low wooden and brick provincial townhouses. Nevel was also home to sixteen synagogues and prayer houses.

Very little physical evidence of Nevel's history survived the twentieth century. The Soviets began by destroying the churches. During World War II, the town was heavily bombed, and the Jewish population was murdered not far from the town and buried in a mass grave. In the center of town more mass graves can be found, of soldiers killed in the war. A statue of Lenin stands nearby. Most of the remaining churches, those that survived the first years of the revolution, were destroyed decades later under Khrushchev and Brezhnev.

Today, Nevel is something of a ghost town. Its center has lost its principal buildings, and the streets have become wide and somehow gap-toothed, built up mostly with three-story Soviet-style gray brick apartment buildings. The streets still carry the names of Communist luminaries—Lenin, Marx, Engels—although the street named "International" has a plaque underneath its name saying "formerly Kagalnaya" (the Russian equivalent of the Hebrew *qahal*, or congregation), a reminder of the Jewish Pale. Away from the center, the town resembles a village, its rustic wooden houses surrounded by orchards and vegetable gardens.

In 2011, I gave a talk on Magda's year in Ust-Dolyssy at a conference in Nevel on local history organized by the historian Lyudmila Mironovna Maksimovskaya, author of *Ust-Dolysskie istorii* (Ust-Dolyssy stories) and founder and director of the Nevel historical museum. After the conference, Maksimovskaya accompanied me to Ust-Dolyssy, where she introduced me to a ninety-five-year-old woman who as a five-year-old girl had known Magda and despite her young age at the time and the intervening years, remembered Magda well, because she had taken part in children's theatrical productions that Magda had supervised and because her mother had worked as a seamstress for the people's theater, sewing costumes from Magda's designs. Magda had also painted portraits of her whole family.

The annual conference in Nevel was established in honor of the important Russian literary critic and philosopher Mikhail Bakhtin, who lived in Nevel during the civil war. In the spring of 1918, Bakhtin fled Petrograd, away from hunger and toward safety. He went to Nevel to join some friends who had arrived there earlier, and he remained there for over two years before moving on, in the fall of 1920, to Vitebsk, whose walls Malevich, Chagall, El Lissitzky, and their students were then covering with paintings. Bakhtin's sojourn in Nevel coincided with Magda's stay in Ust-Dolyssy. In fact, on November 8, 1919, Magda attended a lecture by Bakhtin on music followed by a concert, as she reported in a letter to Julia: "On the 8th, there was a concert, relatively good. The pianist was a privatdocent from Petersburg named Noskov."[1] Ninety years later, Lyudmila Mironovna would describe the same event in *Ust-Dolysskie istorii*:

> Of course the Nevel Symphony Orchestra also gave performances in the Ust-Dolyssy People's House, since the natives of Ust-Dolyssy had fixed up their People's House in the best possible way. The November concert in Ust-Dolyssy was a big event that inspired both the performers and the

---

1 November 20, 1919, RGALI, f. 2080, op. 1, no. 45, 131–131op.

audience. M. M. Bakhtin gave a lecture. The newspaper *Molot* wrote that "on November 8, to mark the second anniversary of the October Revolution, the first free public concert and lecture were organized by the Board of Directors of the Ust-Dolyssy Central Cooperative in a building that is being remodeled as a theater."[2]

In Nevel, an unlikely place, a group of young intellectuals forced by circumstances to lead a peripatetic life came together to form a circle that studied philosophy and religion, organized symphony concerts and theatrical spectacles, gave public lectures on music and literature, and sponsored public debates on religion. Here Bakhtin conceived ideas that defined his early philosophical work. And so the conference was named in honor of the great philosopher, which gives it a certain prestige. Although the papers presented each year at the conference may include talks on Bakhtin and his circle, they are for the most part on different aspects of the local history and local sons and daughters (such as the pianist Maria Yudina, who was born in Nevel).

As mentioned in the previous chapter, Magda had gone to the village of Ust-Dolyssy in the autumn of 1919 at the invitation of Lilya Efron, who had been invited by the local theater enthusiast Alexander Vasilyevich Kotov to direct a newly organized "people's" theater.[3] Lilya, in turn, had proposed Magda as a stage and costume designer. With this offer, Magda was permitted to leave for Ust-Dolyssy. Life in the village was full of hardship for Lilya and Magda, but they made a sincere effort to bring high art to the villagers.

The village of Dolyssy appeared on the map in 1852, when a posting station was built as part of a highway tract engineered by order of Nicholas I along a route, straighter even than the crow flies, connecting St. Petersburg with Kiev. The original station was built in a deep forest, several versts away from the old village of Dolyssy. Within half a century, however, Ust-Dolyssy had attracted settlers and businesses, and the old Dolyssy diminished in importance.

On October 6, 1919, the Nevel newspaper *Molot* (the Hammer) reported that "actors of Moscow State theaters and other professionals have been invited

---

2   L. M. Maksimovskaia, *Ust'-Dolysskie istorii* (St. Petersburg: Nestor-Istoriia, 2009), 74.

3   The Efrons and Tsvetaeva were friendly with two families whose estates were in the vicinity of Ust-Dolyssy—the Trupchinskys and Zhukovskys—and it is likely through them that Kotov got the idea to invite Lilya. Anna Yakovlevna Efron married Alexander Vladimirovich Trupchinsky, nephew of Karp Trupchinsky, owner of the Dolyssy estate. Adelaida Gertsyk, poet and friend of Tsvetaeva and Efron, was married to D. E. Zhukovsky, whose estate, Kanashovo, neighbors Dolyssy.

to the newly organized Ust-Dolyssy people's theater under the direction of the famous actress Efron." However, all those advertised actors were embodied in one person, Lilya Efron herself, who had almost no theatrical experience. The "other professionals" comprised Magda and no one else. In 1923, Lilya wrote to her brother Sergei:

> I became an actress because of hunger. I would never have gone on stage, but that's how it happened: either die, or act and lie that you are an experienced actress. I became an actress and ... a Khlestakov.[4] In the newspapers, they wrote about me as an actress of the Art Theater. This is my unbelievable epic. I was at once director, heroine, and comic old woman. Magda was the stage designer.[5]

Hunger, especially in larger cities, and a craze for the theater all over the country are two common characteristics of this period frequently mentioned by memoirists and scholars. Even before the revolution, inspired by Wagner and Nietzsche, many Russian intellectuals were preoccupied with the reform of the theater and its role in society. Many wanted to introduce high art into low culture by bringing theater closer to the masses. After the revolution, people's theaters and puppet shows sprung up in towns, villages, schools, even military organizations. There was a high demand for performers. Thus, before arriving in Ust-Dolyssy, Magda wrote to Julia from Likino:

> Recently, two 15-year-old high school students appeared before me and declared that they had elected me an honorable member of their cultural–educational circle. ... They are very talkative and self-assured. Of course, they are starting with theater, and of course with Chekhov.[6]

The railroad connection to Likino had been discontinued; nevertheless, Magda wrote that

> the commissar begs to find him a theater instructor. Salary is 2100 rubles minimum. He promises to send horses to the Vladimir station. So one would go to Vladimir by train and then 40 versts by horse-cart.[7]

---

4   Khlestakov, a character from Nikolai Gogol's play *The Inspector-General*, is an incorrigible liar.
5   Tsvetaeva, *Neizdannoe*, 300.
6   June 19, 1919, RGALI, f. 2080, op. 1, no. 45, 97–97op.
7   July 6, 1919, ibid., 98–99.

Some village theater enthusiasts believed that people needed spectacles "to keep them from rioting. Fun was a good safety valve. Give the people a good time and keep them out of trouble."[8] Since notions of the individual's relationship to society were changing, there appeared yet another reason for bringing theater to the masses: to explain the new roles that each individual was now supposed to play and to promulgate Communist ideology, although the repertoire for such theater took some time to appear. In another letter, Magda expressed the idea that "chastushki," four-line folk rhymes, reflected the histrionic nature of life during the period of War Communism. She wrote:

Here are some *chastushki* for you:
He used to be a greaser
Who oiled railroad cars,
But now he's at the front,
On his shoulders stripes and bars.

He used to be a pickpocket,
A no-good petty thief;
But now he's in the Soviet
As commissar in chief.

He used to be a cook,
Wielding knives and spoons and pots;
But now he's in the Soviet,
Handing down diktats.

She used to be a laundress,
Or even something worse;
But now she's at the front,
Serving as a nurse.

She used to be a laundress,
Washing linens till she's numb;
But now she's in the Soviet,
A commissar become.

8   Poole, *The Village*, 131–132.

This is a creation of the locals; the children sing these songs and evidently express quite precisely the attitude of the populace to the current situation.[9]

It was as if, as Trotsky wrote, everyday life had acquired dynamic theatricality. The Russian–American anarchist Emma Goldman, who traveled around Russia in 1920 and 1921, noted that

> in the case of the theatres no reservations have been made. All were permitted to continue their performances when factories were shut down for want of fuel. The opera, ballet, and Lunacharsky's[10] plays were elaborately staged, and the *Proletcult*—organized to advance proletarian culture— was generously subsidized even when the famine was at its height. It is also true that the Government printing presses were kept busy day and night manufacturing propaganda literature and issuing the old classics.[11]

Theaters in Nevel and the villages around it—Chuprov, Chernetsovo, and Ust-Dolyssy—appeared as if by spontaneous generation, often as the result of grassroots activity. *Molot* published a notice from the local office of "enlightenment" (education) announcing special courses for "the laborers of the stage in villages."[12] Theater was thus intended not so much to entertain as to educate, and as an institution, it fell under the guidance of the state educational departments and specifically their offices of extramural affairs, which were responsible for education outside regular schools. Performances were followed by discussions of the plays and critiques of the directors and actors—all published in the newspaper.

The issues of *Molot* for the years 1918 to 1920 provide an interesting flavor of the time and place where Magda lived and worked. Like many similar publications that sprang up in the Russian provinces immediately following the October Revolution, *Molot* was reworking the Russian language to express the fiery optimism of the time. It was yet another stage on which writers, many of them barely literate and new to their task, performed public roles and endeavored to fashion public opinion. The "Department of the Press" of the

---

9   August 19, 1919, RGALI, f. 2080, op. 1, no. 45, 104–104op. I have known such *chastushki* since my youth and was pleasantly surprised to find them in Magda's letter.

10 A. V. Lunacharsky (1975–1933)—Bolshevik, first commissar of education, from 1917 to 1929, also a playwright.

11 Emma Goldman, *My Disillusionment in Russia* (New York: Doubleday, Page & Company, 1923), 113.

12 *Molot*, July 16, 1918.

Commissariat for Foreign Affairs disseminated information for the local papers about cases of political and social unrest abroad in imperialist countries and the territories under their control. The dissemination of national news was in the hands of the Russian Telegraph Agency (ROSTA). Marguerite Harrison, an American journalist based in Moscow, wrote in her memoir:

> The Rosta has agencies in every town and city and receives full reports of local happenings all over the country. There were often accounts of strikes, peasant uprisings, meetings and events unimportant in themselves, but straws pointing which way the wind in the provinces was blowing, which were either suppressed for various reasons, or not printed for lack of room in the next day's papers.[13]

Controlled from the center, publications like *Molot* produced an impression of worldwide proletarian unity and boosted the fighting spirit of the populace.

Life seemed to have taken on a carnivalesque aspect, as reflected in the pages of *Molot*. An announcement requesting the whereabouts of the writer's brother, who was removed from the Petrograd–Nevel train by Red Army soldiers and has not been seen since, is followed by a request for information about a runaway horse. Throughout 1918, the local Cheka, that formidable "Extraordinary Committee for Combating Counterrevolution and Sabotage," publishes in *Molot* lists of executed counterrevolutionaries in the Nevel area; publication of such lists would end in 1919. There are also calls for the reorganization of secondary education and for universal literacy from the "Department of Enlightenment," which laments that many children do not attend school because of hunger and because they are being sent to work in the fields. There is a report that Bakhtin and his friends have staged Sophocles's *Oedipus at Colonus*, a spectacle presented under the open sky, employing 500 volunteer performers. "Nicholas Romanov" (the deposed tsar) is reported to have been shot, but his wife and son have been taken to a safe place (this was, in fact, disinformation: the tsar's entire family had been murdered). A music school and a sculpture studio have opened, as well as a studio for the aesthetic education of children. A directive appears that one egg is to be collected from each household to be sent to the starving children of Petrograd. Every day sees the publication of new decrees, bylaws, and ordinances: every household is required to clean its stretch

---

13 Marguerite Harrison, *Marooned in Moscow: The Story of an American Woman Imprisoned in Russia* (London: Thornton Butterworth Limited, 1921), 66–67.

of street; all doctors, engineers, and those not engaged in labor for the benefit of the people must register with the authorities; all bicycles, spare parts, linen, and horses must also be registered. Each decree concludes with the threat that anyone guilty of disobedience or negligence will be called before a revolutionary tribunal.

One may also read in *Molot* that the Nevel Symphony Orchestra has given twenty concerts of classical music in just one year, 1919, not counting chamber music performances (Beethoven, Haydn, Mozart), and the local theaters have staged fifty plays. Peasants who did not comply with the requisition plan have been shot as a warning to others. A public disputation on "God and Socialism" has taken place in the new "Karl Marx" people's club; the house was full, and the dispute lasted into the wee hours. Priests of the Orthodox Church have been ordered to vacate their houses, which are needed for public use. The next disputation on religion, "Christianity and Its Critics," lasted two days with a full house. During that event, Bakhtin and the philologist Lev Pumpyansky delivered lectures on the history of Christianity, German religious philosophers, and Nietzsche's attitude toward Christianity. At the same meeting, the Marxist Yakov Gutman delivered a counter-lecture from the point of view of historical materialism. War bulletins, government decrees, and news about revolutionary developments and labor crises abroad accompany local ordinances and directives. Reports of revolutions and crises in the capitalist world are written in a highly metaphorical language with a clear ideological slant ("imperialist sharks," "counterrevolutionary bandits").

The decrees demanding the equitable redistribution of people and goods, as published in *Molot* and elsewhere, began with registration and requisition, but they seldom resulted in the desired redistribution, for which there was no workable mechanism apart from the hated and therefore unusable capitalist one. The writer and critic K. I. Chukovsky commented on the situation in a diary entry of November 30, 1919:

> I am arranging a library for the House of Arts. With this in mind, Kolya [his son] and I went to the book depository yesterday—oh, how cold it is there, cluttered, hopeless. Expropriated books have been thrown into a nonsensical pile over which a woman, cold through and through, prowls like a bird— and pecks—a book here, a book there, and tosses them onto another pile.[14]

---

14 K. I. Chukovskii, *Sobranie sochinenii v 15 tomakh*, vol. 11 (Moscow: TERRA—Book Club, 2006), 276.

In fact, there was no bread and there was no fuel, and so there were hunger, cold, and a witch hunt to find those on whom to pin the blame. Nonetheless, those in power held onto the naive belief that a reeducation of the populace would render market forces obsolete and that each would take only according to his need.

Under the rubric "The Red Army Soldier's Corner," an announcement in *Molot* informs readers about a new workers' library called "Knowledge Is Power" and reports on a meeting of soldiers:

> There sounded calls to all thinking comrades to give of their knowledge and energy to awaken those languishing and slumbering in ignorance and darkness.[15]

Theater, too, is called upon to form the New Man:

> The Soviet authorities have taken theatrical affairs into their hands, aspiring to that ideal of the proletarian theater, which, like a lodestar, lights the path of the dramatic arts. The variety show and cabaret are dying out and are closing. The theater has revived; the repertoire has been rejuvenated and cleansed of all rubbish. The theater has become a means of the moral and artistic education of the masses.[16]

The "renewed repertoire" meant that a censorship bureaucracy had been established. A comprehensive decree on Soviet theater policy for Russia appeared in 1921, according to which the theater was declared to be

> agitator and propagandist of the Communist ideology, educator of the new man, creator of a new way of life. There is no theater for entertainment; there is a school, a podium, a bright, artistic, strong mouthpiece of the ideology and will of the working class.[17]

Molot called on the theater to bring its enlightenment to those mired in greatest ignorance—the peasants:

---

15 *Molot*, June 27, 1919.
16 *Molot*, December 17, 1918.
17 "Organy upravleniia teatral'nymi organizatsiiami Vitebskoi gubernii v 1917–1924," *Uchenye zapiski* [Vitebsk University] 10 (2010): 109–114.

The People's House is the center of village education. Traveling theater, bringing joy to the village, must drive out boredom and show life in all its manifestations.[18]

Similar ideas were active in cinema, where in the early Soviet years, teams traveled the country, showing films and filming local communities in newsreel style.[19]

The theater in Ust-Dolyssy, organized in autumn 1919 with the arrival of Lilya and Magda, occupied a former posting station built in 1852. At the beginning of the twentieth century, a post and telegraph office had opened in the building, and a local resident, Alexander Vasilyevich Kotov, had been named postmaster. In spite of some difficulties with the Cheka immediately after the revolution, Kotov became an important community organizer. He founded the Ust-Dolyssy Central Consumer Cooperative, which was to combine modernization with cultural enrichment: the former posting station was to house a generator to bring light to the local peasantry, while a people's theater producing concerts, lectures, and plays would bring light of a different kind. The handsome station building, although now somewhat run down, still boasts gothic windows, some with stained glass, several spacious rooms, and a large hall that housed the theater (figure 32).

Lilya jumped at the opportunity offered by Kotov. In Moscow, she had no means of supporting herself. In turn, Lilya saved Magda from languishing in the Likino forestry office. When Lilya wrote to her offering a job at the Ust-Dolyssy people's theater, Magda accepted with alacrity.

The peasants of Ust-Dolyssy and other nearby villages had never seen or heard—and would never see or hear again—local theater performances, symphony concerts, and lectures on music and literature the like of which they experienced during 1918–1920. Lilya Efron and Magda Nachman were among a number of other refugees from Moscow and Petrograd who were living in Nevel and its environs. As mentioned above, Bakhtin and members of his circle traveled with the city's symphony orchestra to nearby villages, including Ust-Dolyssy, with lectures on art, literature, and music. The concert on November 8, 1919, to commemorate the second anniversary of the October Revolution was followed by another concert a week later accompanied by a lecture

---

18 Iosif Gurvich, "Narodnyi dom—tsentr prosveshcheniia derevni," *Molot*, December 3, 1918, 2.

19 Alexander Medvedkin (the subject of Chris Marker's documentary *The Last Bolshevik* [French—*Le tombeau d'Alexandre*] is the prime example. (I am grateful to Eric Laursen for pointing this out.)

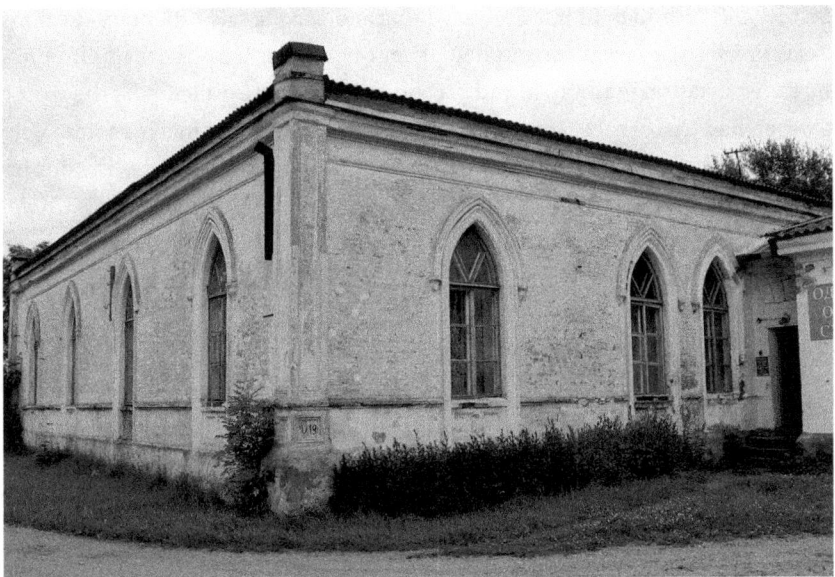

Figure 32. The Ust-Dolyssy theater was located in this building, constructed in 1852 as a posting station (*photograph by Lena Nekludova, 2014*).

on the Russian scientist and poet Mikhail Lomonosov by a local historian and teacher of literature, N. I. Zorin.[20] In a letter to Julia, Magda wrote, "I hear more music here than in Moscow."[21] Local schools hired university professors, for example the St. Petersburg University law privatdocent M. M. Noskov, who became Magda's close friend. He was also an accomplished pianist who accompanied vocal recitals in Ust-Dolyssy, and he taught in the Chernetsovo village school. Valentin Ivanovich Presnyakov, a ballet dancer and choreographer in St. Petersburg and formerly a frequent guest at the nearby Trupchinsky estate, organized a successful school–sanatorium in the village of Semyonovo (1919–1921) for mentally handicapped children, hiring excellent teachers, who were in great supply among the refugees. (The school was closed in 1921 for being out of step with Soviet ideology.)

However, the majority of newcomers to the area remained in Nevel, where music and disputation on philosophy, religion, and socialism fell on

---

20 Zorin's lecture was denounced in *Molot* as superfluous at the present moment and detrimental to the peasant masses on account of its religious content. Zorin persevered in his educational endeavors until 1930, when he was arrested and sent to the Belomor–Kanal penal building site. See Maksimovskaia, *Ust'-Dolysskie istorii*, 79–80.

21 January 29, 1920, RGALI, f. 2080, op. 1, no. 45, 175–178.

fertile soil. Although in Ust-Dolyssy Lilya and Magda saw other city-dwellers occasionally, they were surrounded primarily by peasants. There was no public transportation in the area, and private travel became difficult. So the young women had to work with the material at hand: Lilya with amateur actors who had never been in a theater; Magda without stagehands and with diminishing supplies of paints, paper, kerosene for her paints, and canvas. *Molot* announced that paper would be distributed only to holders of a special ration card. Magda often complained about the lack of materials and difficulties of production:

> There is almost no electric light, so we sit in darkness rather often. The most essential items for work are absent. I have finished two studies for the stage design and many costumes (also for the children's play). I have to supervise their construction. So I am very busy. Now I have to paint the stage sets, without evening light and not even a house painter to help. How to manage? I do not know.[22]

And again:

> The participants are amateurs, almost none of them has ever been to the theater, totally uncultured. To make them comfortable, to explain gestures, diction, playing, ensemble—this is already a great deal—it is a great achievement that there is no falsity and bad taste in the performances.
>
> Watercolors and paper are coming to an end. And I dreamed of painting in the summer. Now I won't be able to make sketches even for the theater. As if someone had chopped off my hand and fingers with an axe—terrible hopelessness! How do Moscow artists survive? Not everyone has a store of supplies! I don't know how to be and what to think next. … I frantically want to paint. … I dread the moment when the theater has no supplies left: there is very little canvas left, little paint.[23]

Magda had sent requests to Julia for paints and paper from all the provincial towns in which she found herself. But such things had disappeared from open distribution together with everything else. Julia tried to help and at the

---

22 Undated, November 1919, ibid., 173.
23 March 30, 1920, ibid., 150–154op.

same time admonished Magda for her frequent requests for items that had disappeared even before Magda had left Moscow.[24] In a letter that she titled "Memoirs of an unfortunate executor of commissions, volume one," Julia wrote:

Dear Magdochka,

They just brought your letter [there was no reliable mail service and so letters and parcels were often brought by local peasants traveling on business] and a hundred rubles for paints, paper, and other non-existent-in-nature items. Tomorrow I'll trot about in search, although I doubt very much that erasers, for example, could be found for sale without some special cards or permissions. As to "some simple paper"—one can immediately see that the supplicant is a country bumpkin. ... As to paper, I don't know what to think, one needs all kinds of documents.[25]

One of the first decrees of the Bolshevik government, issued two days after the seizure of power, was a Decree on the Press, aimed at suppression of all opposing views. The decree was accompanied by the disappearance of paper from free circulation. That was the first measure of successful censorship introduced by the Bolsheviks. As Vladislav Khodasevich wrote:

Having nationalized printing houses and registering paper reserves, the Soviet government appropriated to itself the right to control all means of printing. From now on, in order to publish books, journals, newspapers, one had to obtain a special "allocation" for a print shop and for paper. ... The Bolsheviks did not yet dare to introduce direct censorship—they introduced it only at the end of 1921. But using paper and fuel shortages as a pretext, they at once obtained the ability to deny allocation orders to unwanted publications to motivate their closure not by censorship but for economic reasons. All anti-Bolshevik newspapers, and then journals, and then simply private publishing houses were gradually wiped out.[26]

---

24 "As for paper, it was impossible to find it even when you were still here—the shops are closed and one needs some special permits, certificates, and the same for erasers" (June 16, 1919, RGALI, f. 2080, op. 1, no. 7, 32–35op.).

25 June 11, 1919, ibid., no. 7, 36–45op.

26 Vladislav Khodasevich, "Knizhnaia palata," in *Literaturnye stat'i i vospominaniia* (New York: Chekhov Publishing House, 1954): 335–336.

Meanwhile, Magda wrote that she was aching to paint and was doing so on the reverse sides of some certificates of recognition of the former ministry of agriculture in exchange for food.[27]

Although such hardships continued, she and Lilya were filled with ambition. In one of her first letters to Julia from Ust-Dolyssy, Magda listed the plays they had chosen to perform:

> We are rehearsing for Christmas; the costumes for the children's evening (Krylov's fables …) are being sewn according to my design; they are coming out nicely. Then we'll have *The First Distiller*, by L. Tolstoy, *Miser Scrooge*, by Dickens, and *At Night*, by Stakhovich. I have to finish all the stage designs by the first. But there is no electricity and it's not clear when it will appear because there are no workers.[28]

From Magda's letters to Julia and Lilya's letters to her sister Vera, we know more of their theater's repertoire—it was remarkably rich. Apart from the above-mentioned works, they staged Chekhov's *The Bear*, *The Proposal*, and several short stories; Ostrovsky's *At an Advantageous Place*, *There Was Not a Penny and Suddenly There Was a Pound*, and *Guilty Without Fault*; Gogol's *May Night*; Pushkin's *Queen of Spades* in tableaux vivants, *Angelo*, and *The Bridegroom*; Tolstoy's *From It Come All Qualities* ("a terribly boring piece," as Magda noted); and a play about peasant life by A. Potekhin, *Ill-Gotten, Ill-Spent*. For children, they reworked a number of fables by the famous Russian fabulist Ivan Krylov (1769–1844). They adapted several folk songs for the stage and performed them to great acclaim, and their musical and poetry-reading events were very popular. Magda persuaded her colleagues to organize a puppet theater as well:

> Please write to me whether it would be possible to get a set of puppets and how much it would cost. Or is it hopeless? Tell them that this is for the People's House at the Ust-Dolyssy Cooperative. … The Cooperative will pay for it no matter how much it costs.[29]

It was an ambitious program, carried out with a minimum of human and material resources. Almost all the actors and stagehands were local peasants.

---

27 July–August, 1920, RGALI, f. 2080, op. 1, no. 45, 184–185.
28 Undated, ibid., 163–163op.
29 January 29, 1919, ibid., 175–178.

Even Lilya—the main producer and actress—was not a professional theater director, although no one suspected this. Magda wrote thus about her principal collaborator: "Lilya is talented and very beautiful on stage and somewhat monotonous; sometimes she laughs with delight and says, 'If they only knew that I am not an actress.'"[30] In a letter of June 9, 1920, Magda sums up the results of the 1919–1920 season: "There were quite a few productions: large and small—altogether 24 … some were repeated."[31] And as if that were not enough, Magda would walk long distances to another village to help with a theater there: "I frequently walked for 8 and 9 versts; I produced shows 9 versts from here."[32] Lilya and Magda were making an earnest attempt to put on productions of serious works that could nevertheless appeal to their unsophisticated audience.

In *Molot*'s reports on cultural events in the villages surrounding Nevel and reviews of concerts and plays, the Ust-Dolyssy theater won special praise for the quality of its productions and in particular its professionally executed costumes and stage sets. Just as they would have done in normal times, such reports inspired envy and rivalry in similar establishments and excited ambition in aspiring actors. Thus Magda reported to Julia, "Life here is not without little storms, namely, the theater has enemies."[33] She went on to report on a forester who was hoping to become an actor and when denied a dramatic role for lack of ability, began to criticize everything and everyone, writing threatening letters, lodging formal complaints, and giving speeches about his desire to serve the people. Lilya, too, wrote to her sister Vera, quoting this "enemy": "You invite professionals, but we are against professionals, down with them! We do not know what lies are concealed behind their profession!"[34] In one of her letters to Julia, Magda wrote about an attack against the theater by a rival people's house.[35] And again in a few weeks:

> Recently, there was a new attack, namely from the regional department
> of people's education. The head of the department organized a people's
> house, but his enterprise is not going well, and he is burning with envy.
> One fine day, he appeared and began to demand to be allowed to put on

---

30 March 30, 1920, ibid., 150–154op.
31 June 9, 1920, ibid., 112–113op.
32 Ibid.
33 January 29, 1920 RGALI, f. 2080, op. 1, no. 45, 175.
34 December 23, 1919, RGALI, f. 2962, op. 1, no. 23, 9–11op.
35 January 29, 1920, RGALI, f. 2080, no. 45, 175.

a production in our theater (he is a tailor by profession). When he was told that the stage was occupied and since we consider ourselves responsible for the artistic standards of the productions, an unvetted production could not be allowed, he became filled with anger and began to threaten and intrigue, but we repelled all his attacks victoriously. This is the second attack. People are curious creatures; they cannot bear someone else's success.[36]

The success of the theater was due partly to the enthusiasm of the participants but most of all to the serious, professional approach Magda and Lilya took in choosing the repertoire, reading and interpreting the plays for the "actors," and working with each of them individually on their roles. Even so, the critics voiced their opinions, and Magda wrote to Julia defending herself and Lilya:

We had to select every play, to read and to think it through, then to teach each actor individually—this they [the critics] don't understand. And the human material here is unrewarding. I am reproached that I make stage sets not as they appear in popular books, but in my own way![37]

However, the local authorities in Nevel were pleased. Magda continued:

The local chair of the trade union admired our work and invited us to his newly opened theater; and then I have been invited to become a theater instructor for the regional theaters. I still do not know whether to take a job here or return to Moscow.[38]

The hope of returning to Moscow was a leitmotif of Magda's letters. Yet she hesitated. She knew only too well what hardships would await her there. As matters stood, she was in a position to send food to Julia, for which her friend was grateful:

Dear Magdochka, I don't know how to thank you for the parcel that I received today together with the letter. You can guess the degree of gratitude, imagining how we trudge along. ... Your room [in which Magda had

---

36 Undated, ibid., 167–170, 170op.
37 June 9, 1920, ibid., 112–113op.
38 Ibid.

stayed on her way to Ust-Dolyssy] is covered in frost, the snow is falling in your room, water and plumbing froze long ago. We live as if in a posting station on our way through a faraway village, with one difference, that the courtyard is five stories down, and each basin of slops has to be taken down from a considerable height. The absence of water is not as bad as the fact that there is no place to dispose of it ... and here is a new adventure: The Borisyaks' house has been ordered to be taken apart for firewood. You won't recognize Moscow: ruins are everywhere. In one place, a wall opened, showing a stove and two water closets hanging in the second floor. I say we will have to climb up there for lack of these facilities in frozen apartments. ... We feed ourselves mostly on frozen potatoes and acorns.[39]

In another letter, she wrote:

My diet is frozen potatoes cooked with fish oil of yesteryear vintage, frozen bitter cabbage and claylike bitter bread (190 rubles for a pound!). Do whatever you wish: get better or die and get in line for a coffin. ... Also, in honor of the holiday, I drank coffee with a rusk and sugar (they issued a small amount). The rusk smells of soap, the sugar of kerosene, and the coffee does not smell, because there is no coffee in it. One is always hungry—but don't think that I'm complaining.[40]

Julia's letters are peppered with such descriptions. Here is one of Magda's replies:

I received your letter, and after it, even sugar here has become bitter for me, I feel so much pain for you. How well I know all this! Carrying and sawing the firewood, feeding the furnaces, ice on the window, and slowly freezing hands and feet. Besides, this year the food supply is worse. The cold and feeding the furnace I have mastered.[41]

Magda's hesitation about returning to cold and hungry Moscow is understandable. Julia's reports on the situation in the city, on how their mutual friends were faring, and on what might await Magda were discouraging:

---

39 February 9, 1920, RGALI, f. 2080, op. 1, no. 7, 50–53op.
40 January 1920, ibid., 113–115.
41 End of 1919 or beginning 1920, RGALI, f. 2080, op. 1, no. 45, 167–170.

These days, for example, it seems we live in London, because if you look out the window, the horizon stops behind St. Basil's of Caesarea at best, and now one cannot see even St. Basil's; just a golden cross glimmers in the milky whiteness. All this "soaring of vapors" is perhaps due to uncleared snow that has turned into an ocean of water. What is going on in the streets—you won't believe. I think days are coming when we will have to stay at home, that's an agreement between me and Kot [Kandaurov].

But tomorrow, I have to go to my stint at hard labor, that is, to clear the railroad tracks from snow. I don't know what to put on my feet: today, I hadn't even made it to Sadovaya Street when my feet were soaked through. I regret quite inhumanely that you are not here: together, we would have worked the day away cheerfully. The only thing that my soul revolts against is roof cleaning: with my giddiness, I will fall for sure. Besides that, we clean manure in the yard; that is, we're obliged to clean … but there are no tools and no means of transportation, so we have to harness ourselves, but the cart is so heavy that all our men cannot budge it even without a load. Such is the state of public affairs.[42]

Julia had a happy talent for finding humor even in desperate situations. In a later letter, she made light of that day of "hard labor" on which a crowd of ill-clothed and poorly equipped Muscovites had been ordered to clean one of the Moscow railway lines, which in winter had become a dumping ground. She delighted in folk turns of phrase that she heard or read while working there, for example the declaration in a poster that "handshakes have become obsolete." Julia reported on Khodasevich, who had cut a hole in the wall between his room and the kitchen so that the warmth of the stove would reach his emaciated body. She found humor in that situation as well:

We have been dreaming of going to visit Vladislav. I thought of a drawing with the following content: Night. Intérieur: in the background, one sees a wall with a cutout into the kitchen. The window is frozen; icicles are growing on the water ducts; there are puddles under the window. There is the cook: she is sleeping under fur coats. In front of the wall with the cutout stands a desk. An electric lamp is hanging but is not giving any light; instead, a candle stub is burning in a small bottle. Vladislav is sitting at one side of the table. He is wearing his fur coat, hat, felt boots; he looks

---

42   March 9, 1920, RGALI, f. 2080, op. 1, no. 7, 54–55op.

dejected and woebegone. Pushkin is sitting across from him, bundled in the shawl that is on his shoulder in the portrait by Kiprensky. He is bright, somewhat surprised, and very delicate.

Khodasevich (from *The Inspector General*):—Well now, brother Pushkin?

Pushkin:—Well, brother. ... That's how it is.[43]

Julia's lightheartedness and readiness to laugh at the absurd were supported by real human warmth. Her mother—her dearest friend—was with her, and taking care of her mother during her illness was for Julia an act of self-fulfillment. The greatest support, however, she found in her lover, Kandaurov. In reading Julia's letters recommending that she stay put in Ust-Dolyssy, Magda felt the allure of Moscow, the hope of significant human relationships, which she so thoroughly lacked in her village. Her youth was slipping away as she wandered about the Russian provinces, alone, just trying to survive. She suffered from loneliness and homelessness, feeling that life, with friends and poetry, was elsewhere. There was envy, to be sure, but more than that, she felt a profound need to love and be loved. She wrote from Ust-Dolyssy:

> How well I know all these horrors of Moscow life. I feel pain for you and for the waste of your life forces. For this suffering—but even so, when I think that there is such an exalted light as love, I am envious, because that great joy is not given to me.[44]

Magda returned often to the theme of loneliness and lack of love, no matter how much Julia tried to persuade her that she was not alone in the world, that her friends remembered and loved her. At some point, she began to think that her friend Noskov might become a source of the love and friendship that she so sorely desired.

---

43 February 9, 1920, ibid., 50–53op.
44 February 17, 1920, RGALI, f. 2080, op. 1, no. 45, 110–111op.

CHAPTER 9

The Noskov Affair

Magda met Mikhail Mikhailovich Noskov shortly after her arrival in Ust-Dolyssy, at a concert where he performed as an accompanist. He stood out among her new acquaintances and soon became a focus of her attention. As she wrote to Julia:

> There is one person here, rather pleasant and very musical—a legal scholar at the university, a former jurist and an educated man; however, he comes here only for concerts, and there is something about his appearance that reminds me strongly of a rat.
>
> But of course, I have not yet found "one of us"; I have yet to meet anyone approximating a real person. Everyone here seems to be in some other category.[1]

In a few weeks, however, Magda appears to have accepted Noskov as sufficiently "one of us." She wrote that here she had found "a new Mikhail instead of the old one, and much better than the last." The "old" Mikhail was Mikhail Mikhailovich Isaev (1880–1950), jurist and specialist in criminal law, a casual Moscow acquaintance. In their letters to Magda, her friends often teased her that she was in love with him. Isaev had a wife and children, and I have no idea whether such a flirtation between him and Magda was real or imaginary. In her letters she referred to this Mikhail Mikhailovich as M. M.–1, and to Noskov as M. M.–2. She began writing warmly about M. M.–2, informing Julia that before escaping to the countryside, Noskov, like M. M.–1, had been attached to St. Petersburg University, where he taught law. But in addition, Noskov was an accomplished pianist, performing with singers in the surrounding villages. Noskov had settled in a village five miles from Ust-Dolyssy and was working

---

1   Ca. December 1919, ibid., 175–178. According to the documents from a Pskov regional archive in Velikie Luki, Noskov was a graduate of Tartu (Yuryev) University (F. R.–608, op. 1, no. 19). In the Imperial School of Jurisprudence graduates' roll, Noskov is listed as a graduate of 1915. See http://genrogge.ru/isj/isj-091-7.htm.

there as a schoolteacher. Magda praised him as "a restrained, modest, and gentle person":

> He likes music very much, which is the reason for our acquaintance, because he comes here as an accompanist. He lives eight versts from here and works as a schoolteacher. He shares one room with an invalid mother who is bent over with rheumatism. She adores her "Mishenka," and he is extremely gentle and patient with her, like a woman. He is not handsome at all and somehow looks very young, almost always disheveled, looks a bit like Gogol. His smile and glance are beautiful. See how much I have written about the new Mikhail, who has quite consoled me in the loss of the former one. Only I beg you not to derive any conclusions from this. It is good that a person to my taste has appeared.[2]

She described in detail their first encounter:

> We have met some people here, though somehow exclusively men. I have written to you already about one, the "new Mikhail." But I was taken aback when he rechristened me "Maria." I thought he had not heard my name correctly, but it turns out he likes it better this way. It is significant that he addressed me thus at once. Now on the one hand, it is rather strange to rename a stranger so precipitously; on the other hand, he did it so endearingly that I allowed him to call me by that name. So I am now "Maria," to my great surprise. And to yours as well, I should think. I am unalterably no longer in love with the "old Mikhail"; let Kopelman stop dreaming of arranging a love affair; it seems he had something like that in mind.[3]

Whenever Magda referred to Noskov, it was always with warmth. Indeed, she wrote about him so sympathetically that Julia and other friends in Moscow could not help but "derive conclusions from this," and they began to tease her, Julia even offering to send Magda the *fleurs d'orange*—a souvenir of Magda's mother's wedding—that she unearthed every time she rummaged in Magda's trunk for something Magda had requested. As if with the intention of putting a stop to the teasing, Magda described Noskov to Julia as more of a fragile, childlike figure than a potential lover:

---

2   December 23, 1919, ibid., 107–109op.
3   December 1919, ibid., 172–174op. Solomon (Monya) Yulyevich Kopelman (1881–1944), journalist and publisher, was a mutual acquaintance.

Dear friend, your suppositions about *fleurs d'orange* are premature, nothing of the kind is foreseen, so please refute the Borisyaks' fabrication regarding a certain attorney-at-law and of facts in general. M. M. is a very lovable grownup boy and I like him very much, but it is a long way from that to such an event.[4]

And she wrote again, at the end of March, with more detail on Noskov's immaturity:

M-2 was here recently. He will be here again one of these days. He was sick for 3 days and lost a frightening amount of weight, and he is sad, I don't know why. Lilya immediately took hold of him and dragged him to the piano to accompany, while he, poor thing, wanted simply to sit and rest, but with a meekness typical of him, he could not bring himself to refuse. He has not become more handsome from his thinness. His nose has become even longer, completely Gogolian. I have now a feeling of great compassion and tenderness toward him: he is so unlike a grownup and a scholar. He is very sensitive to good treatment and positively glows from any gentle word, so that it would somehow be a sin to offend him.[5]

Despite his deficiencies, Noskov had found a friend and musical colleague in Alexander Pakhomovich Kazakevich (1889–1959), a singer from Petrograd who was a native of the Nevel area and had returned there with his wife and son at the time of hardships. As Magda had written to Julia a month earlier:

There is another teacher where M. M.–2 is—a former singer at the Russian Opera in Petersburg. He recently returned from Kiev; and now we have met. This is one genuine "dashing fellow." He is friends with M. M., on whom he has a strong influence in practical affairs. If he had not appeared, poor Mikhail would have been completely enmeshed in his own absurdity.[6]

With time, Magda became ever more puzzled about Noskov's character ("M. M.–2 turns out to be awfully strange"). His childishness and meekness

---

4   February 17, 1920, RGALI, f. 2080, op. 1, no. 45, 110–111op.
5   March 30, 1920, ibid., 150–154op.
6   Late February–early March, 1920, ibid., 145–149. After 1921, Kazakevich had a successful singing career, appearing in many opera houses of the Soviet Union.

bordering on otherworldliness and his inability to stand up for himself made her compare him to Dostoevsky's Idiot:

> I often find him exasperating and often just throw up my hands. There is in him an excessive innocence, an excessive benevolence, a certain absurdity. I scold him behind his back, but when I see him, it is very difficult to be angry with him, because he allows himself to be scolded uncomprehendingly and submissively. Furthermore, he is such a bungler, the like of which the world has never seen. It's hard to figure him out, and falling in love with him would be a heavy cross to bear. I don't want this, and so let Raya stop rejoicing. But sometimes in his gentleness and sense of fun there is a sort of a childishly touching charm. In some respects, he is exceedingly uncultured; he totally does not understand art (for a long time, he thought that some Japanese prints were my drawings); he asks whether Holbein is a contemporary painter. I don't think it has ever occurred to him that paintings are done with "brushstrokes." He knows little about literature and philosophy, especially modern. And yet he is knowledgeable: he is studying Roman law, comparative linguistics, theology, and he is preparing for a professorship. His character is so undemanding and weak that it's enough to make you weep.[7]

Noskov was indeed a bungler. To teach in a village school was certainly not the ideal employment for someone of such weak character as his. Magda wrote to Julia that his school had made some difficulties for him, and he wanted to quit. In compensation, he was offered a reassignment to a school of his choice, and he asked to be transferred to Ust-Dolyssy. However, as Magda reported:

> It seems poor Mikhail will be transferred fifteen versts from here. He wanted to come here so much that he overdid it and as usual blundered, and it seems the whole thing fell through, although I am still hoping. Such holy fools are sometimes lucky. Still, he is so touching with all his absurdity, which sometimes exceeds all bounds. I cannot imagine his future life under conditions like today's.[8]

Noskov was in fact transferred fifteen versts away from Ust-Dolyssy, as one can infer from Magda's letter of March 30 ("He walked halfway, that is,

---

7 Spring 1920, ibid., 145–149op.
8 March 12, 1920, ibid., 142–143op.

8 versts") and from the following letter; but despite the distance, he managed to come to the village on occasion:

> Yesterday #2 came with Kazakevich. In the evening, K. sang, don't know whose piece, to words by Pushkin, *For the Shores of a Distant Homeland*. It was something very beautiful. And some other things. It was a nice evening, and they left late. Lucky Mikhail! His father sent him white flour. He'll come for it one of these days. He and Kazakevich invited me to visit them in Chernitsovo for Easter and promise to treat me to tea with sugar and kulich. I want to go on foot, because to hire a horse is beyond my means. Fortunately, K is only 8 versts from here, I cannot walk 15. M-2 is in a melancholy state, I don't know what's with him.[9]

From Magda's descriptions of Noskov and from how their relationship played out, it seems that his charm and musicality, his kindness, his touching treatment of his invalid mother, his sincerity and openness, may have been as far as he was able or willing to go in relating to others, and that he may have been too timid to initiate a romantic attachment. And so although Magda sympathized with Noskov and appreciated his kindness, decency, and friendliness, her relationship with him was unsatisfactory. Her despair—to run, somewhere, anywhere—finds its way into a letter to Julia:

> Dear friend, of course I would never say that I am completely alone in this world as long as I have you and K. V. [Kandaurov]. I have written to you in that vein before. But I have such a feeling of being cut off, of remoteness; so little hope of seeing you again, that it seemed: loneliness then, okay, loneliness; does it matter where: in Irkutsk or here. If I cannot live with those I love, and here I am suffocated by such scum, wouldn't it be better to travel to the end of the world, at least I would see something new. ... Anyway, no one needs me as K. V. needs you and you need him.[10]

Indeed, all that had been precious to Magda in her prerevolutionary life had vanished. Moscow, friends, and art were beyond her reach. Her own family—mother, siblings, and their families—were far away, some in Petrograd,

9 April 8, 1920, ibid., 138–139op. The setting of Pushkin's poem is by Alexander Borodin. Chernitsovo is a village near Ust-Dolyssy.
10 Summer 1920, ibid., 186–188.

some in Likino, some in Vilna. They, too, were struggling for survival. Their rare letters were filled with descriptions of everyday hardships. Her brother-in-law and supporter in Likino had been harassed and even briefly arrested. Her nephew from Petrograd had contracted relapsing fever while traversing the countryside in search of food and died: "My sister has lost a second son; the first drowned in 1917. I am so terribly sorry for her."[11] Her mother was in despair. And no help was coming from anywhere.

Even in the best of times, although there was a strong family attachment, her brothers and sisters had not taken Magda's engagement with art seriously. And although her second sister, Erna, invited her to return to Likino, Magda wrote—recalling the previous year there and especially the drudgery of her work as a clerk—"to return there would mean to put a tombstone on my life and say farewell to everything."[12] Moreover, Magda experienced a feeling of guilt at having left her mother behind in Likino. She wrote to Julia that her dream was to earn enough money to be able to bring her mother to live with her. Magda, ever sensitive, was hurt by the conduct of her siblings, who, in her opinion, did not pay enough attention to their mother. In early July of 1920 she wrote to Julia:

> First I want to thank you for corresponding with Mama: you have greatly comforted and cheered her up. My brothers and sisters have turned out to be swine; a hard life is no excuse for not writing to one's mother. It's difficult for everyone, not just them, but others manage to write. Now in particular love and memory are dearer than ever. What a joy your letters are.[13]

But even Julia had become remote. Their shared youth was a distant memory, and their lives had diverged in those calamitous years. Having lived in Moscow, Magda was able to imagine Julia's life, but Julia seemed incapable of fathoming Magda's struggles in the village and often made light of her complaints and occupations. Kandaurov had become her prime concern, and nothing else could command serious attention, although she faithfully tried to carry out Magda's requests for art supplies and sent her books and clothes. At times, her letters were even dismissive. Yet Magda expressed no anger or

---

11 Early March, 1920, ibid., 145–149op. James Schmidt, Magda's nephew, a son of her elder sister Eleanor died in spring 1920.

12 June 11, 1920, ibid., 114–115op.

13 Ibid., 184–185op.

disappointment in her replies to Julia's sometimes uncharitable letters. Her writing about Noskov—about his idiosyncrasies and about her own feelings toward him—was confessional, perhaps because there was no other outlet and no other source of advice or comfort. She thereby laid herself open to jokes and teasing, and yet she continued to open her heart. Noskov held an important place in her life and in her letters.

As the months wore on, the Ust-Dolyssy theater was becoming ever more uncertain to Magda and Lilya as a source of livelihood and sense of purpose. That uncertainty and her ambiguous relationship with Noskov contributed to Magda's feelings of abandonment and isolation, which became so strong that by late summer, she could write that without close human relationships, without friendship and love, without giving and receiving real human warmth, life had little meaning:

> Why is my feminine nature becoming ever more dominant within me, as if I am inexorably turning into a different sort of creature, and it's not in my power to stop this transformation. Why do I know now that I can give up my soul, and art, and all other possibilities for love. If I do not obtain it, then my art and my soul will die, because they need nourishment from real life. The whole thing is hopeless.[14]

Yet she still had some hope. Despite her ridicule of Noskov, of whose shortcomings she was painfully aware, if he had exhibited any tender feeling for her, had intimated that he desired her friendship, Magda would perhaps have found a deeper feeling for him. Even in summer, when it had become clear that their theater career was coming to an end, she wrote to Julia:

> M-2 very much does not want me to leave, although his ultimate attitude toward me is unclear. If it were clearer, I wouldn't leave, because this is now the only thing of value to me. You and Moscow are far away; art—where is it? And see, there has appeared a person toward whom there is within me such tenderness—should I lose him in pursuit of a materially better life? To sweep away this possibility of my soul like smoke and ashes and live awaiting an uncertain future and old age? How can I leave and lose the last remaining precious thing?[15]

---

14 Ibid., 185op.
15 June 11, 1920, ibid., 114–115op.

Magda sought to persuade herself that tender friendship was better than nothing. Following the cry of despair quoted above, she argued with herself for and
against attaching herself to Noskov, writing to Julia:

> As for M.—I don't know. We will definitely be leaving here, and at every
> meeting he is trying to persuade me to settle where he is.[16] He wants to
> send his mother to his father in Vilna[17] (she is from there). His father will
> have an important position in Vilna, and besides, they have old connec-
> tions there; he graduated from gymnasium in Vilna. He proposes a com-
> mon household. However, in this way, we would be living off him, since
> he has everything and we have nothing. His mother really desires this, but
> Lilya does not. She hungers for a theatrical career in Nevel, although in
> my opinion, such a career would be physically impossible for her. I don't
> know how to persuade her. To me, she says, "And as for you, it would be
> madness to bury yourself in a village, and so on." As if in Nevel it would
> not be a burial of oneself to an even greater extent because there would
> be less free time. I know that I will be necessary to M., and for me that
> is serious. If my feeling toward him is not passion, still it is a great joy to
> him and a great tenderness. Why, indeed, should I deprive myself of that?
> When as things are, I am poor in joy. Granted, he is extremely spoiled and
> it's difficult for him to break certain habits. I am not repelled by that. After
> all, he works like a simple peasant in the fields, dresses God knows how.
> To establish oneself in town is impossible; otherwise, of course, it would
> make no sense to remain in a village. But I would like by all means to drag
> Lilya along. She cannot live alone. Say that I soon become disappointed in
> him; I think even that wouldn't be so terrible.[18]

That letter, written in late summer 1920, in which Magda's confusion and
conflicting feelings are so evident, marks the end of her correspondence about
Noskov. Although Noskov remained in the Nevel area and worked there as a
teacher until at least the end of the 1921 school year (after which his traces are

---

16 On June 9, 1920, Magda wrote: "M-2 is trying to persuade me to take a job where he is work-
    ing; I don't know whether it will work out" (ibid., 112–113).

17 Noskov's father visited Ust-Dolyssy on his way to Vilna. Magda wrote to Julia: "Tomorrow M-2
    promised to appear with his father, an old general who is returning from the front on leave. It
    will be interesting to see him. I like meeting parents of those who are dear to me. Somehow, one
    feels a person more deeply when one sees his roots" (July 7, 1920, ibid., 117–118/op).

18 July–August 1920, ibid., 186–188op.

lost), Magda never mentions him again in her surviving correspondence, as if he had disappeared from her life completely.

In November 1919, at the time when Magda was first becoming acquainted with Noskov, the stage was being set for a tragedy in Lilya's family in which Magda became embroiled. Lilya's brother Sergei had fled Moscow in November 1917 after participating in the failed counterrevolutionary action against the Bolsheviks, and the family had had no word from him for several months. They then learned that he had joined the White Army, which was fighting against the Bolsheviks, and had moved with it to the south. Two years later, in November 1919, with Sergei still absent, his wife, Marina Tsvetaeva, placed their two young daughters, Irina and Ariadna, in an orphanage near Moscow, saying that she could not care for them in the starving city. In January 1920, Tsvetaeva brought home her older daughter, Ariadna, who was ill, leaving Irina behind, prompting Sergei's two sisters, Lilya and Vera, to think even more energetically than before about how they might arrange to extract their niece from the orphanage—despite Tsvetaeva's likely lack of cooperation—and bring her to Ust-Dolyssy, especially since they had learned that the orphanage was suffering from a shortage of food.

Both sisters had cared for Irina in the past. Vera's nieces had lived with her on several occasions when Marina was absent from Moscow, and Lilya had spent several months with Irina at a dacha near Moscow in the summer of 1918. Under Lilya's care, Irina's health and development had improved considerably, and Lilya became deeply attached to the child. Later, she wrote to Sergei about Irina:

> She had become like a daughter to me. She was a bright, timid, and gentle girl. When I brought her she was quite sick and weak; she slept all the time, she couldn't stand on her feet. After three months, she had become unrecognizable, had begun talking and running. She was uncommonly quiet. All summer long I could not do anything, even read, I delighted in her presence, in her life, and in her development. My dream was to take her for good and bring her up.[19]

Lilya was bitterly hurt when Tsvetaeva unexpectedly appeared at the dacha and took away her daughter, saying that she did not need her sister-in-law's help any longer.

---

19 Marina Tsvetaeva, *Neizdannoe*, 511.

Now, eighteen months later, with Irina abandoned to an orphanage, Lilya decided that Irina's place was with her. In addition to her own love for the child, she felt responsible to her brother to provide security for his daughter while he was away fighting the Bolsheviks.

But if Irina were brought to Ust-Dolyssy, where would they live? Lilya and Magda were living with Kotov's family in their tiny apartment, which served also as a cooperative office, a shop for the production of theater props and costumes, a post office, and a space for any other need that might arise. They depended on Kotov's support and goodwill, which was diminishing, since he had fallen in love with Lilya, who did not reciprocate.

Happily, in January 1920, a room for her and Magda was found, and Lilya began writing to Vera with plans and instructions how to arrange Irina's move and what would be needed to accommodate her. Lilya's letter brims with love for the child and the expectation of having her again.

However, the first obstacle was her mother's consent, without which Irina could not be extracted from the orphanage. In their correspondence, Lilya and Vera decided that Vera, who was in Moscow, would approach Marina. Meanwhile, Vera and Mikhail Feldstein, who were living together, both fell ill with the influenza, and Vera suffered severe complications. To add to their problems, in January 1920, Feldstein found himself under threat of arrest—the Bolshevik Red Terror[20] was sweeping Moscow, and he, a jurist and legal scholar, was a prime target. Many who were arrested at this time were never seen again. He was arrested on February 28 and was in and out of prison until August.[21]

But Lilya and Vera's efforts to extract Irina from the orphanage had ended on February 15, with Irina's death. An excerpt from a March 1920 letter in which Magda informed Julia about the child's death appears frequently in the scholarly debate about Tsvetaeva:

> Seryozha's daughter, Irina, died in an orphanage—have you heard of it? Mikh. Sol. [Feldstein] is under arrest—Vera wrote about it. Lilya wanted to bring Irina here and now blames herself for her death. I am terribly sorry for the child—in two years of earthly life nothing but hunger, cold, and beatings.[22]

---

20 Although the term "Red Terror" was coined to describe the Bolshevik repressions and killings in September–October 1918, it is frequently applied to the whole period of the civil war (1917–1922), since persecution of those deemed counterrevolutionaries did not cease in 1918.

21 Feldstein was arrested again in 1922, 1927, and 1938, when he was executed.

22 March 12, 1920, RGALI, f. 2080, op. 1, no. 45, 142.

In the lines quoted above, Magda does not mention the child's mother except obliquely and unflatteringly: "nothing but hunger, cold, and beatings." The correspondence between Magda and Julia suggests that it was general knowledge, or at least rumor, that Marina had treated her younger daughter badly, in fact abused her. Even though she is writing from the point of view of Sergei Efron's sister Lilya, and so understandably refers to Irina as "Seryozha's daughter," it is as if with these words Magda were additionally repudiating Tsvetaeva's claim to motherhood.

Having shared an apartment with Vera when she and Lilya had been taking care of Irina, and now sharing her life with Lilya, learning all the details of Irina's death from her, and understanding Lilya's feeling of hurt and guilt, Magda did not hesitate to take the aunts' side in their view of what had happened, although no one stated baldly that Tsvetaeva was to blame in her daughter's death. However, Magda's omission of Tsvetaeva's name and the mention of physical abuse and Julia's response, in which she implies that the child would eventually be returned to her mother only to be abused, show that both Magda and Julia faulted Tsvetaeva:

> I understand Lilya's frustration about Irina, but to save someone from death does not yet mean to do someone a great favor: what did this unhappy child have to live for? After all, at the end of the day she would not have been given to Lilya forever. Lilya would have expended the last drop of her own strength only to delay the child's sufferings. No, this way is better. But thinking about Seryozha, I understand Lilya very well. But she is not to blame. What is happening with Mikh. S. [Feldstein], for heaven's sake? I do not understand anything.[23]

Neither Magda nor Julia had warm feelings toward Tsvetaeva. Whenever she is mentioned in their correspondence, which is not often, it is always with a distance and some coolness. Irina was dead, and now it was time to save Feldstein, who was still alive but in prison with a death sentence handed down by the red tribunal. On April 30, Julia wrote to Magda, "Just came back from my brother. I caught him between meetings to plead for M. S. God willing, we'll succeed in helping him."[24] Thanks in part to Julia's brother Leonid, who now occupied an official position in the Soviet government, Feldstein was released.[25]

---

23 March 19, 1920, RGALI, f. 2080, op. 1, no. 7, 57.

24 Ibid., 73.

25 See L. Bernstein, "'Umerla v priiute Seriozhina doch'—Irina': tekst i kontekst," *Toronto Slavic Quarterly* 56 (2016), http://sites.utoronto.ca/tsq/56/Bernstein56.pdf.

Magda and Lilya continued their work in Ust-Dolyssy, although the situation was becoming insupportable. A strained relationship with their host, Kotov (whose unrequited love for Lilya had been transformed into hatred and vengefulness), dwindling financial support (salaries were irregular, and in any case, money could not buy much in what was then a barter economy), lack of paints and other materials for painting and building stage sets (Magda's raison d'être for going to Ust-Dolyssy), a shortage of food, alienation from their "public," and mounting criticism, all conspired against their remaining in the village. Yet they tried to make a go of it. Magda described to her correspondents in Moscow her latest attempt at survival:

> We bought a cow! On which we spent four-months' salary (half of which we took as an advance). She is quite wretched, but the local requisition commissar promises to exchange her for a good one. Here they requisition cows for slaughter, and he will take ours and give us a good one. A cow is a great salvation from hunger, and I think that with it, one can survive. …
>
> If only you could get here to drink our cow's milk. I myself take her out to pasture, milk her, and take her back. Even so, it is difficult to imagine me in the role of a Homeric princess.[26]

Even two years earlier, such a situation would have been incomprehensible to Magda, a young educated woman and aspiring artist from a "good" family, and to her friends—from the upper crust of the Russian intelligentsia. Now she takes to new notions—"requisition commissar" and "they requisition cows for slaughter"—as if they had always been ordinary features of daily life.

It is difficult indeed to see Magda as a "Homeric princess," but roles had been reassigned, and there was no predicting what the next one would be. As the owner of a cow, Magda failed miserably: its yield was a mere four glasses of milk a day. However, she defended herself thus:

> Don't think that I do not milk the cow properly; my milking has been examined not once by experienced people, and they say that I milk her correctly—it's just the nature of the beast. In compensation, she is quick with regard to others' vegetable gardens. At the first opportunity, she helps herself in forbidden places. Usually she is with the herd, but we

---

26 June 19, 1920, RGALI: f. 2080, op. 1, no. 45, 112–113op.

have nothing else to give her. I began dreaming of exchanging her for a she-goat—good she-goats give more milk—and it will be like the man in the fairy tale who exchanged and exchanged until he was left with nothing.[27]

Magda saw the absurdity of her situation and the futility of her endeavors, and yet she persevered. Meanwhile, Julia, always finding a bit of humor even in a grim situation, could not help but tease Magda on her new acquisition:

We were in stitches over your Homeric occupations, and at the Patriarch's Ponds, they exclaimed unanimously, "poor cow." So, you acquired a cow and still think about returning to Moscow? Alas, I am not fated to taste her milk, but I wouldn't mind if you could send me her other products to fertilize my house plants.[28]

I imagine how you drive her into the barn: "Please, would you be so kind as to enter? I am in a bit of a hurry."[29]

Perhaps it was difficult for their friends in the city to imagine Magda and Lilya's situation in Dolyssy, where, if they remained, the cow would be their hope for survival:

I get up before sunrise and am seriously not getting enough sleep, but I do not regret or repent the purchase; if we stay here, she can save us in winter.[30]

But even in the height of summer, the cow did not meet their hopes:

We are living like birds of the air. It's three weeks since they gave us our last rations, and we eat what the grateful public offers us, which comes in the guise of vegetables and apples, curdled milk, and pastries, but we cannot live like this forever, they won't feed us forever. It is two months since we received our last firewood allotment, and I collect twigs and use them to make a fire. In a word, true penury, because they do not give money

---

27 July–August 1920, ibid., 184–185op.
28 Julia to Magda, June–July 1920, RGALI, f. 2080, op. 1, no. 7, 84–85op. Patriarch's Ponds is a Moscow neighborhood where their mutual friends the Borisyaks and the Isaevs lived.
29 Late June, 1920, ibid., 120–121.
30 June 11, 1920, RGALI, f. 2080, op. 1, no. 45, 114–115op.

either. … For two days we were guests of the priest and ate our fill there. Otherwise, we are starving. The devil knows what is going on.[31]

The cow seemed to Magda a reasonable investment, and she tried profit from it without Lilya's help. But that did not stop her from criticizing one of Lilya's schemes: "Lilya is dreaming of raising rabbits!! She got a brochure about rabbits and assures me that it is profitable. Imagine us having a rabbit farm!"[32]

There was no inconsistency in Magda's acquiring a cow, hoping to exchange it for a she-goat, and thinking about returning to Moscow or to her sister's to work again at the abacus in the forestry department or moving to the nearby village of Chernetsovo to teach art to the peasant children and be closer to Noskov or becoming a theater consultant in the Nevel district, all of which she discussed in her letters: each possibility was as reasonable and fantastic as any other. The instability and controversies of her current situation—a serious desire to bring classical repertoire to the villagers even though she had come there only to escape hunger and unemployment in Moscow, serious work with peasant actors along with complaints about the "defective human material" among them, the enthusiasm of the audience coupled with attacks on the theater by rivals, an attachment to Noskov but with no sign he had much to offer in return—naturally led to Magda's vacillation between trying to arrange her life somehow in the Nevel area and fleeing it as soon as possible.

By June 1920, after the end of the theater season, Magda and Lilya felt that their stay in Ust-Dolyssy had become untenable. A lack of money, food, and materials for the theater and for painting convinced them that it was time to leave. On June 9, Magda wrote:

> Now it looks as if we have to part with Dolyssy for good. The situation has become impossible. The attitude toward Lilya here is terrible. They complain about her ill health (they do not believe her) and her character, that she pushes people away, that there are too few performances. All this is unfair, although things would have been much better with more restraint on her part.[33]

---

31 July–August 1920, ibid., 186–188op. The priest whom Magda mentions in the letter, Mitrofan Ivanovich Shirkevich, lived in the village of Kubok, not far from Ust-Dolyssy. Here Lilya and Magda met his daughter Zinaida, who became Lilya's closest friend and shared the rest of her life with her.

32 June 11, 1920, ibid., 114–115op.

33 June 9, 1920, ibid., 112–113op.

A few days later, Magda confirmed their decision:

> We are thinking that we will be leaving here for sure. Lilya wants to obtain
> leave to travel to Moscow to take a look around, hunt for possible jobs,
> and finally decide whether to remain in the area or move somewhere else.
> I think there is no point in returning to Moscow to live. To begin a new
> life in a new place—there wouldn't be sufficient will to live. If we could
> arrange things here so as not to die of hunger in winter, I would stay.[34]

By the fall of 1920, the Ust-Dolyssy interlude was finally coming to an end:

> And so our future is not yet known; I don't want to lose heart, but I do
> want to clear out of here: it is too painful to remain under such circum-
> stances. I think that after us, the People's House will cease to exist.[35]

Having obtained all the necessary papers, Lilya left Ust-Dolyssy in early
September to scout for work for both of them, while Magda remained to look
for employment in the Nevel district and to keep an eye on their common
household: if they were to stay another winter in a village, it would have been
impractical to get rid of their semblance of "home," including the cow. In her
last letter from Ust-Dolyssy, Magda wrote about a possible situation for both
of them:

> My dear friend Julia, I have been sitting here without Lilya for the fourth
> week and haven't heard a peep from her. I am very angry. My situation here
> is ridiculous. A place has been offered in the Forest school-sanatorium for
> 8–12-year-olds, in our district. The head of the school is the Petersburg
> conservatory teacher Presnyakov. He is very pleasant. In general, the
> teachers are from the intelligentsia. Completely in the woods, on the shore
> of an enormous lake. Dinner and supper are provided, 1.5 lb. of bread per
> day. Classes two and a half hours a day and duty obligations for 24 hours
> once every six days. To teach children drawing and modeling. I want Lilya
> there too; but I am afraid that her vacancy will soon be occupied; they
> won't wait long.[36]

---

34 June 11, 1920, ibid., 114.
35 June 9, 1920, ibid., 112–113op.
36 September 28, 1920, ibid., 179–179op.

However, it appears that nothing worked out. The fact that Magda's last letter to Julia from the Nevel district is dated September 28 suggests that Magda followed Lilya to Moscow that autumn.

It was not ideology, but the possibility of professional work and the desire to paint that had led Magda to Ust-Dolyssy, and her letters spoke of enthusiasm and pride in their theater for several months after her arrival. But by summer 1920, worsening economic conditions had made it clear to Magda and Lilya that their People's Theater could not survive another winter and that the time had come for them to leave.

The heyday of the people's theater as an experimental institution was brief, and not only in Ust-Dolyssy, but all over the country. In 1918, shortly after the revolution, Iosif Gurvich, a painter and member of the extramural educational office in Nevel, had expressed in *Molot* the general enthusiasm for the arts:

> We, who live on the land and in the forest green, who for centuries carried silence in our hearts and fetters on our bodies, we, exhausted, demand art. Come to us, singers, come to our liberated fields and tell us about the beauty created by you.[37]

That same year, Julia joined forces with Kandaurov and her mother, Ekaterina Ivanovna Obolenskaya, to organize a puppet theater. At first, it was successful. Ekaterina made puppets; Julia and Kandaurov wrote texts and painted scenery. They even produced a book based on a puppet play about playing-card characters, *The War of Kings*. Vladimir Sokolov, an actor whom Magda and Julia had befriended in Koktebel in 1913 and who later moved to Berlin and then to Hollywood, was one of the puppeteers. They persisted until July 1920, when their space was expropriated by another Soviet organization not related to theater.

By 1921, the People's Commissariat of Education's budget for theater had swollen to twenty-nine trillion rubles, while only seventeen trillion was allocated for higher education. Lenin decided that the theater had gotten out of hand and sent a message to Commissar of Education A. V. Lunacharsky:

---

37 L. M. Maksimovskaia, "Nevel' v kontse 10-kh–nachale 20-kh gg. XX veka," *Nevel'skii sbornik* 12 (2007): 221. Gurvich (1895–1978/80) left Nevel in 1922 to become chair of the Petrograd Regional Committee of the Union of Art Workers (1922–1925) and then director of the Russian Museum (1932–1934).

I suggest that all the theaters be put into a coffin. The people's commissar of education should occupy himself not with theaters but with teaching reading and writing.[38]

And thus the theater mania ended, in Ust-Dolyssy as elsewhere.

≋ ≋ ≋

In Ust-Dolyssy, ninety-five-year-old Nina Dmitrievna Galaktionova, whose mother, Sofia Fedorovna Morozova, had volunteered as a seamstress for the Ust-Dolyssy theater and who remembered both Magda and Lilya, recalled playing a fox in one of Krylov's fables as a five-year-old; she recalled her mother under the kerosene lamp—Kotov's dynamo had not been powerful enough to bring light to the villagers—sewing costumes from Magda's designs. Magda complained all the time of the difficulty in working with insufficient light. Yet she also wrote to Julia, "they are sewing costumes for the children's performance according to my designs (Krylov's fables, the little goat and others); it's coming out nicely."[39] In exchange for food, Magda painted portraits of the Morozov family. Alas, they were destroyed by fire along with the Morozovs' house during World War II.

Nina Dmitrievna's recollections attest to the theater's influence on those who participated in its productions and on their audiences. There were 120 seats in the hall, and it was always full: people would walk several versts to attend a play or concert. Even the Old Believers living in several communities around Ust-Dolyssy[40] would come to the "People's House," or the "Station," as they called it. Inspired by the theater, the local population continued to produce amateur performances and organize dance classes long after the theater had officially closed.

---

38 Vladislav Ivanov, *Russkie sezony teatra Gabima* (Moscow: Artist, rezhisser, teatr, 1999), 76.
39 1919, RGALI, f. 2080, op. 1, no. 45, 163–163op.
40 In her letters, Magda mentioned Old Believers several times. For example:

> The bearer of this letter is an interesting person—he is a rich peasant, old-believer deacon. He has a wonderful house, with huge rooms beautified with a gazebo of curious grapevines. Surikov's *Boyarynya Morozova* and old believer lubok prints adorn his walls. Nothing tasteless: diptychs, copper crosses, icons. On the table, there is a huge folio of *Acts of the Apostles*. The whole family made a vow of celibacy, and so all the brothers and sisters live together in a kind of a family monastery. There is the grandeur of a church in their house, as if you had found yourself in ancient Rus'. They are all somehow dignified. I dream of getting myself into their chapel; I don't know whether I will be able to manage it (1920, ibid., 163–163op.).

Until 1932, long after Magda had left for Berlin, Lilya would return occasionally to Ust-Dolyssy or to the nearby village Kubok and direct a play for the local amateurs. After Magda's time, the "Station" was taken over by a long succession of organizations. At one time, it was used as a sanatorium; the stables and hay barns that surrounded the station became dormitories. During World War II, the Germans used it as a military hospital. By 2011, Ust-Dolyssy had lost much of its population; the building was occupied by local offices, a library, and a general store, and the former stables were used as apartments. When I entered the store, whose shelves were half-empty, the saleswoman, to whom I was of course a stranger, approached me and began complaining bitterly about life in the village: the bus connection had been cut; all who could leave had left; the village was populated by only the old and drunkards; there was no agriculture, although a few kilometers across the border in Belarus they tilled the land and reaped rich harvests. Then she stopped and said, "And who are you?" On learning that I had come from America on a visit, she quietly said, "I'm getting the hell out of here."

CHAPTER 10

M. P. T. Acharya

Within two years of Magda's departure from Ust-Dolyssy, she had married an Indian Brahmin, M. P. T. Acharya, with whom she left Russia, never to return. Acharya, an Indian nationalist, had arrived in Bolshevik Russia with a group of Indian comrades in search of ideological partners in their struggle to drive the British out of their country and give birth to an independent India.

Mandayam Parthasarathi Bhayankaram Tirumal Acharya (figure 33) was born in Madras in 1887 into a Brahmin family with nationalist leanings. His father was a civil servant, a supervisor in the Public Works Department. The Brahmins were at the top of the Indian caste system, and many Brahmins were priests and teachers. (Indeed, the name Acharya means teacher or spiritual leader.) Under British rule, educated Brahmins held many positions requiring a command of English. As V. S. Naipaul wrote:

> South Indians, Brahmins especially, had a better grasp of English because they were more exposed to it, and they would get jobs as secretaries, stenographers, or even typists. These were probably the most widely followed professions for the South Indian or Tamil Brahmins in British times. Otherwise, as a class South Indian Brahmins worked as teachers or as priests or as petty clerks. Or, if they were lucky enough, they would take up a job in one of the government departments. ... They were dominant in Indian social life, the professions, and in the beginnings of the national movement.[1]

With such a background, it is unsurprising that Acharya became politically engaged at a young age, running the political weekly *India* and the journal *Bala Bharat* (New Party), the organ of the nationalists. A fiery revolutionary from the start, he had been exposed to a variety of opinions about how to achieve national liberation. He learned about ideological controversies among Indian

---

1   V. S. Naipaul, *India: A Million Mutinies Now* (New York: Viking, 1991), 121, 223.

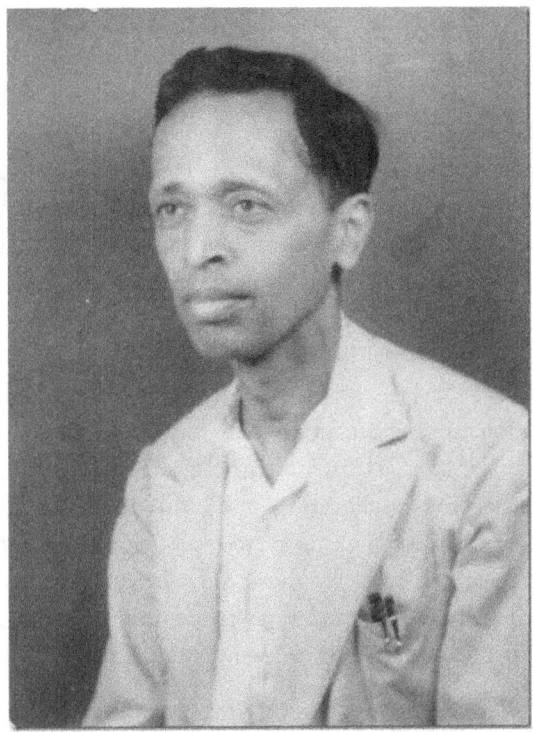

Figure 33. Photograph of M. P. T. Acharya (*courtesy of Sophie Seifalian*).

nationalists in his youth at the side of his teacher, the nationalist and social reformer Lokmanya Tilak, with whom he studied in Poona in 1906–1907.[2] Acharya received no formal education beyond secondary school; however, he was a quick study: residing in Germany, France, and Turkey, he became fluent in the languages of those countries. While living in Stockholm in 1917–1919, he hired a private tutor to help him learn Swedish. And he read voraciously. According to Victor Garcia, a prominent anarchist, Acharya "was above all a very informed connoisseur of Western socialist theories."[3]

---

2   Lokmanya Tilak (Bal Gangadhar Tilak, 1856–1920) was a leader of the left wing of the National Congress. In 1908, he opened negotiations with the Russian envoy to Bombay, V. O. von Klemm, about possible education for Indian officers in Russian military schools. Tilak also studied trading markets and sought the widening of trade between India and Russia. See T. N. Zagorodnikova and P. M. Shastiko, eds., *Russko-indiiskie otnosheniia v 1900–1917 gg.* (Moscow: Russian Academy of Science, 1999), documents 124–138, pp. 168–187.

3   Quoted in Nirode K. Barooah, *CHATTO: The Life and Times of an Indian Anti-Imperialist in Europe* (Oxford: Oxford University Press, 2004), 116.

Finding himself under threat of arrest by the Indian colonial authorities for his nationalist agitation, Acharya left Madras for Pondicherry, a French enclave in British India. But Pondicherry proved no safe haven, and in 1908, he sailed to Marseille. The following year, Acharya briefly joined the informal Indian nationalist organization India House, in London, quickly becoming a key member. With the closing of India House after the assassination of Sir William Hutt Curzon Wyllie, political aide-de-camp to the secretary of state for India in July 1909 by an India House inmate, Acharya moved to Paris, where he became a close associate of the prominent Indian nationalist Bhikaji Cama (1861–1936). He assisted her in the publication and dissemination, especially in India, of her nationalist newspaper *Bande Mataram*. During a trip to Berlin to meet Indian nationalists, he persuaded them to print another of Bhikaji Cama's newspapers, the *Talvar* (Sword), which he also helped to publish. Acharya managed to smuggle these publications into India, disseminating them, as well as other seditious texts, among Indian troops. Such activity led to the Indian Press Act of 1910, which restricted the importation of seditious literature into India. Nevertheless, Acharya found a way to continue his work, sending publications from different addresses in different countries to make tracking by the authorities difficult.[4]

Acharya moved between Paris, Morocco, Portugal, Germany, the Ottoman Empire, Egypt, Jerusalem, and the United States, always in pursuit of the liberation of British India.[5] The conflict in Europe during the Great War had provided Indian nationalists with the possibility of obtaining assistance from enemies of the British. The Berlin Indian Committee, formed in 1914 by Indian political activists residing in Germany, had sought assistance from Germany, the archenemy of Great Britain.[6] Making use of the enemy of one's enemy is, of course, nothing new in political struggles. Indeed, in 1915, the Irish nationalist Roger Casement traveled to Berlin to try to persuade the Germans to supply arms to

---

4   M. P. T. Acharya, *Reminiscences of an Indian Revolutionary*, ed. Bishamber Dayal Yadav (New Delhi: Anmol Publications, 1991), 36–38.

5   For more details see C. S. Subramanyam, *M. P. T. ACHARYA: His Life And Times: Revolutionary Trends in the Early Anti-Imperialist Movements in South India and Abroad* (Chennai, India: Institute of South Indian Studies, 1995); Maia Ramnath, *Decolonizing Anarchism* (San Francisco: AK Press and the Institute for Anarchist Studies, 2011), 125–133, and Acharya, *Reminiscences*. According to Yadav, Acharya came to Turkey in 1911 to seek Turkish help for the Indian cause.

6   After 1915, the committee changed its name to the Indian Independence Committee. It was formally attached to a branch of the German Foreign Office, the Nachrichtenstelle für den Orient.

the Irish nationalists and to assist Irish prisoners of war in Germany in forming an anti-British brigade. As Acharya would later mention in one of his political surveys written for the *Vestnik NKID* (Herald of the People's Commissariat for Foreign Affairs), Ireland and India—both under British rule—had common goals and common methods of attaining them. Like their Irish counterparts, some Indian nationalists, Acharya among them, hoped to influence British Indian troops to turn against their masters. Both the Indians and the Irish failed in those attempts.

For their part, the Germans had begun courting Indian nationalists even before the start of hostilities with Great Britain. The Germans, intent on weakening the British Empire in any way possible, had been working since as early as 1910 to unite Turkish and Persian forces, with Afghanistan as their base, to threaten British India. In the process, Germany began attracting Indian nationalists as well. Indians continued working with the Germans throughout the war, in what became known as the Hindu–German Conspiracy. However, after the establishment of the anti-British Bolshevik government in Russia in 1917 and Germany's defeat the following year, the Indians abandoned the Germans to try their luck with the Soviets.

In May 1917, after the February Revolution in Russia, Acharya traveled to Sweden to work with the European socialists who were preparing for a peace conference to be held in Stockholm. There, he met the Ukrainian Bolshevik Konstantin Troyanovsky, whom historian Nirode K. Barooah calls "one of the earliest Russian propounders of spreading the revolution to the East." Troyanovsky associated closely with Acharya and his colleagues and developed a project to bring India and revolutionary Russia closer together. Soon Troyanovsky was back in Russia, arriving there together with Lenin on the notorious sealed train sponsored by the Germans. In Russia he published a book, *Vostok i revoliutsiia* (The East and Revolution),[7] in which India occupied a central position. His ideas influenced Trotsky, "the person responsible for giving permission to the Indians to travel to Russia."[8] For their part, the Indians were enthusiastic about Bolshevism, which encouraged subjugated nations to rise up against their colonial masters at once, without waiting for the Marxist stage of industrialization to occur. And so, in early 1919, with Troyanovsky's encouragement and Trotsky's support,

---

7   Although the book is known as *Vostok i revoliutsiia*, which is what appears on the title page, the title on the front cover reads *Vostok pri svete revoliutsii* (Moscow: Izdatel'stvo vserossiiskogo tsentral'nogo ispolnitel'nogo komiteta sovetov R., S., K. i K. deputatov, 1918).
8   On Troyanovsky and Acharya in Stockholm, see Barooah, *Chatto*, 107–116.

Acharya along with several other nationalists traveled by air from Sweden to somewhere in Russia and proceeded to Moscow.[9]

Decades earlier, Acharya's teacher Tilak had advocated a military alliance between India and Russia. Acharya and his comrades now set great store by the Bolsheviks, in particular by what they saw as the new regime's dedication to the liberation of oppressed peoples and its success in beating back the forces of imperialism.

The interest was mutual. The British had many rivals for their Indian possessions, but the main one had been the Russian Empire, which had conquered vast territories in Central Asia in the second half of the nineteenth century and maintained a presence in the border regions between India and Afghanistan. Since the second half of the nineteenth century, the so-called Great Game—the Russian–British rivalry in the region, with both empires conducting intelligence and counterintelligence activities and vying for the support of the emir of Afghanistan and the leaders of Central Asian tribes—had been a fixture of the two empires' national policies. But Russia's devastating 1905 defeat in the Russo-Japanese War led within two years to the Anglo-Russian Convention, a treaty that brought the Great Game to an end. Russia and Great Britain became allies against the Central Powers in the years leading up to the Great War, and Russian ambitions for dominance in Asia and the acquisition of Indian territories were put aside.[10]

After the war and the October Revolution, however, the Bolsheviks abrogated all tsarist treaties. Fired with revolutionary zeal and geopolitical ambition, they took up the moribund Great Game with renewed energy, hoping to export revolution to the Indian subcontinent and thus weaken the British. According to Lenin, the loss of colonies and resultant economic downturn would create a favorable revolutionary climate in the colonizing metropolises.[11] And so in summer 1920, at the Second Congress of the Comintern, one of the main items on the agenda was the anticolonial national liberation struggle,

---

9   War Office, Whitehall, February 17, 1926, IOR: L/E/7/1439/0021.

10 The term "Great Game," which today is used to describe the struggle between Britian and Russia for imperial dominance in Central Asia, was coined by Arthur Conolly (1807–1842), a British intelligence officer, although the meaning of the term evolved over time. On the history of the term, see Seymour Becker, "The 'Great Game': The History of an Evocative Phrase," *Asian Affairs* 43, no. 1 (March 2012): 61–80.

11 Vladimir Lenin, "Draft Theses on National and Colonial Questions for the Second Congress of the Communist International," in *Collected Works*, vol. 31, trans. Julius Katzer (Moscow: Progress Publishers, 1965), 144–151.

on whose success (according to the Bolsheviks) hinged the fate of world revolution. As early as 1919, Trotsky suggested the opening of a "second front" of world revolution in Asia. He believed that "the road to Paris and London lay through the cities of Afghanistan, Punjab, and Bengal."[12] The Bolsheviks revived the espionage infrastructure from tsarist times and more-recent channels installed by the Germans. The Comintern and the Red Army were seen as the political and military arms at the eastern gates to world revolution. The road to India lay through Afghanistan, and the Soviets' base of operations was nearby Russian Turkestan.

The first Soviet legation to Afghanistan, headed by the former tsarist diplomat N. Z. Bravin,[13] arrived in Kabul on August 21, 1919. On their way to the Afghan capital, they met the last of the Germans leaving the country, having failed to achieve anything of significance in their goal of fighting Great Britain on Asian territory. The Germans had established the Provisional Government of India (a provisional government-in-exile), with whom the Soviets continued to work.

Despite the difficulties and dangers facing all travelers in the region, Acharya managed to crisscross half of Asia several times. On his arrival in Moscow in July 1919, he and his fellow nationalists met with Lenin. At that meeting, it was decided that some of them, including Acharya, would accompany the new Soviet minister plenipotentiary and envoy of the Comintern in Central Asia, Yakov Surits (1882–1952), who was to replace the earlier legation to Kabul. Surits's letter of credence, composed by Lenin himself, authorized him to conduct negotiations not only with the Afghan government but also with many other indigenous peoples of Central Asia who were living under the yoke of British imperialism. In fact, Surits had been appointed to act on behalf

12 Quoted in Iurii Tikhonov, *Afganskaia voina Stalina: Bitva za Tsentral'nuiu Aziiu* (Moscow: Iauza, 2008), 48. The idea of engaging Great Britain in Asia was not new for Russia. In 1855, in response to growing commercial privileges for British traders in Persia and Afghanistan, Colonel N. P. Ignatiev, a Russian military attaché in London, proposed extending Russian political control to the Amur River. He believed that "only in Asia could Russia fight England with any hope of success, and only in Asia could Russian commerce and industry compete successfully with those of the other European states" (Seymour Becker, *Russia's Protectorates in Central Asia: Bukara and Khiva, 1865–1924* [London and New York: Routledge Curzon, 2004], 16). That idea eventually led to Russia's political and military conquest of Central Asia (1863) and opened the "Great Game" between the two empires.
13 N. Z. Bravin, after being dismissed from the post of Soviet envoy, defected from Soviet Russia and was assassinated in Afghanistan in 1921 on the eve of his departure for India.

of the Comintern more than on behalf of the Soviet state.[14] He was instructed to make contact with representatives of the oppressed nationalities, either personally or through agents approved by him. The Indians who accompanied the new minister were one such group of agents.

The mission left Moscow in December 1919, with the plan that the Indians would carry out agitation and propaganda along the Indian border, mainly with Pashtun-speaking tribes; deliver arms to tribal fighters; and continue to assemble an Indian revolutionary army. Thus, after his meeting with Lenin, Acharya traveled to Kabul to continue the same kind of work in which he had been engaged since 1915 under German auspices.

Following the safe arrival there of the Soviet Afghan mission, Acharya and another Indian nationalist, Abdur Rabb Barq, formed the Indian Revolutionary Association (IRA), combining several factions of nationalists already present in Kabul. This was accomplished with the assistance of Yakov Surits and Soviet funding.

Despite the IRA's acceptance by the Soviets, Surits insisted that it not be ideologically rigid. Cooperation among all factions, none of which would lose their autonomy as members of the IRA, would be guaranteed by their shared hatred of British rule. The IRA's membership grew rapidly, enabling it to commence propagandizing activities among the Indian border tribes in early spring 1920.

The Bolsheviks wanted the Afghans to allow the IRA to use the country as a staging point for shipment of arms and other materiel into India. But Amānullāh Khan, the new emir of Afghanistan, had to navigate between two shoals. He wanted what the Soviets were offering: gold and arms. But he did not want to spoil relations with the British. Following the three-month Third Afghan War (May–August 1919), initiated by Amānullāh, which ended in a standoff, the British had signed a generous peace treaty in which they at last recognized Afghanistan as an independent kingdom. British generosity and concessions were occasioned by their fear that Afghanistan would throw in its lot with the Bolsheviks. Emir Amānullāh had to walk a thin line if he wanted to benefit from both sides.

Amānullāh continued playing his game with Surits for quite some time, with some success for both countries: a treaty of friendship was signed in 1921. But ultimately, under pressure from the British, he forbade the Indians to continue propagandizing among the border tribes, and in May 1920, he expelled

---

14 Such double appointments of Soviet envoys to Afghanistan continued into the 1940s.

them from his country altogether. The IRA, with its rank and file of over a hundred members, moved its headquarters to Tashkent.[15]

With its tree-lined streets and network of canals, the city had been prosperous, with a large district populated primarily by Uzbeks, Turkmens, and Tajiks, and a smaller Russian quarter. But during the time Acharya lived and worked there, Tashkent and its surrounding region had become a seething cauldron. The repercussions of the Great War and the Bolshevik takeover were experienced in Tashkent particularly keenly. The Bolsheviks established their hegemony over the city within a few weeks of the October Revolution. The Turkestan government, headed by Fedor Kolesov (who later would play an important role in Julia's life), was dominated by the Russian Bolsheviks and Left Social Revolutionaries, almost to the exclusion of the indigenous politicians, and these Bolsheviks were laying down the new law. To disseminate information about themselves and what they had to offer to the Central Asian border nations that were not yet free from their bourgeois oppressors, the government established the Soviet International Propaganda Bureau (Sovinterprop). The Cheka was particularly harsh, acting independently of the Turkestan government, so that even local officials had something to fear. For three months after mid-October 1917 and again for five months after mid-April 1919, Central Asia was cut off from European Russia by the White Army, which occupied the southern Urals (Orenburg). All communication lines with the center were severed, and the Cheka acted with unchecked cruelty, its overcrowded cells regularly vacated by summary executions. The city also hosted the Turkestan Bureau of the Comintern, which was actively seeking to export revolution to India and China. In the mountains around the city, the Basmachi, the local anti-imperial force that had been formed to oppose military conscription in 1916 and who following the revolution had become anti-Bolshevik guerrillas, understanding that the Soviets had recognized national self-determination only in theory but were not going to set the area free from Russian hegemony, responded to the new colonizers with firm determination, their ranks swelling with each new atrocity. The Cheka and the Red Army, whose detachments were quartered in the city, conducted punitive raids into the mountains and waged a guerilla war against the Basmachi. The 1920 "revolutions" in Bukhara and Khiva were staged mainly

15 Emir Amānullāh continued working secretly with the Soviets against the British through Djemal Pasha, one of the three Turkish generals who led Turkey into World War I and had been sentenced to death in absentia in Turkey. Djemal Pasha first escaped to Germany and from there was helped by the Germans to move to Soviet Russia. For a time, Soviet and Pan-Turkic interests coincided. Cf. Tikhonov, *Afganskaia voina Stalina*, 63ff.

by the Red Army, with headquarters in Tashkent. All the trees that had made Tashkent so beautiful were gone by now, having been cut down for fuel. Expropriation of private property was going at full throttle. The Cheka considered all private commerce illegal speculation, and food had become scarce.

To add to the complexity of the situation, around 28,000 German and Austro-Hungarian prisoners of war had been settled in prison camps in the city and many more in the area around it. The abominable camp conditions and hunger among the inmates, who after Russia's withdrawal from the war and its peace agreement with the Central Powers were free to go but had no means to return home, pushed many prisoners to join the Red Army. The German officers among the prisoners of war were conducting their own espionage activities, attempting to organize military groups to fight the British, with whom Germany remained at war until November 1918.

Concerned about their Indian possessions and fearful of thousands of former prisoners of war in Central Asia returning to active duty and reinforcing the Central Powers' front lines, the British sought to negotiate an agreement with the new government in Tashkent that would preclude that possibility. They sent a mission to request that the authorities exercise firm control over the movements of former prisoners; the envoys were also instructed to report on the character of the new Bolshevik power and on its anti-British activities. The British had ample indication that the Bolsheviks were pouring anti-British propaganda into India. The viceroy in New Delhi, responding to anxious telegrams from the India Office in London as to what measures had been taken to prevent such literature entering India, wrote:

> with our vast frontier we must rely in the main on the evil being tapped at its source by means of [an] intelligence system at all chief centers of Bolshevik activities. We ourselves are attempting to set up one such intelligence agency at Tashkent, now apparently [the] most active center where India is concerned.[16]

Years later, in Berlin, when Acharya was trying to obtain a British passport, the Foreign Office and emigration authorities asked him to explain his conduct during and immediately after the war. Acharya was evasive. However, information on Acharya had been collected during the years in question and

---

16 Quoted in Peter Hopkirk, *Setting the East Ablaze: Lenin's Dream of an Empire in Asia* (London: John Murray, 1984), 119.

especially during his stay in Tashkent, where, on his arrival from Kabul, he had at once begun participating in the work of the Comintern, becoming one of its most active propagandists. The British closely watched everyone who participated in the Comintern's activities. They knew that Acharya had facilitated the transmission of propaganda and arms across the border through Afghanistan to Pashtun-speaking border tribes. When in March 1921, the president of the Board of Trade, Robert Horne, signed the Anglo-Soviet Trade Agreement, he presented a letter to the people's commissar for foreign trade, Leonid Krasin, with a description of anti-British activities perpetrated by the Soviet representatives, many of whom, like Surits, doubled as members of the Comintern, and Indian nationalists in Turkestan and Afghanistan. Acharya's name, along with Rabb's, was among them. The British knew that the Indians had sought to establish a military center at Pamir and Chitral, south of the Hindu Kush, and that they had expected and received Soviet help in that endeavor.

What Acharya did not write in his report to the British Foreign Service is that after the war, in Tashkent and in the town of Andijan, southeast of Tashkent, he continued organizing and providing military training for a revolutionary group, assembling it out of heterogeneous elements—mainly Indian, Afghan, Iranian, and tribal traders, smugglers, and seasonal workers, as well as Indian Sunni Muslims who crossed the border on their way to join forces with Turkish Muslims fighting for an Islamic caliphate, all stranded in Afghanistan during the Russian Civil War. The Turks were outraged by what they perceived as the unpardonable treatment of Turkey by the British after the defeat of the Central Powers. They were fearful for the future of the caliphate, whose spiritual head was in danger of losing both his titles: Sultan of the Ottoman Empire and Caliph of Islam. Many of them had been stranded in Afghanistan without any means of support, plagued by hunger and disease. The Turkestan Bureau of the Comintern, and Acharya among them, helped these fighters cross into Russian Turkestan, at which point an attempt was made to reeducate them and recruit them to the Bolshevik cause.

Shaukat Usmani, who had hoped to fight for the restoration of the caliphate and instead had been recruited by the IRA as a "soldier of revolution," wrote from Andijan, where he was recruiting together with Acharya:

> As for my Hindu brethren here, I have found them no better than the Caliphate agitators there [in Tashkent]; these are nothing but idlers, drunkards, and debauchers. By writing all this I do not mean to disgrace the fellows but want to bring the truth to light; otherwise I love them very much

because they are Indians. After C[omrade] Acharya's departure I have been relating them the English atrocities played by them during these 6 years ... and I, on my part, try to add some Indian heroism in these stories.[17]

The heterogeneity typical of the "revolutionary" forces of the East is well described in the report on The Congress of the Peoples of the East that took place in Baku in the fall of 1920:

> There were two thousand delegates present at the First Congress of the Peoples of the East organized in Baku by the Communist International. These delegates belonged to many various and highly heterogeneous ethnic entities. They were classified into Communists and non-Party members, according to somewhat doubtful criteria. We can point out five groups: the "profiteers"; Muslims of Russia and Central Asia, fiery champions of the positions of national Communism; delegations of Transcaucasia consisting mainly of representatives of small ethnic groups protected by Bolsheviks; foreign Eastern delegates—in this group, the only ones to raise their voices were the Turkish nationalists; and the representatives of the Comintern and of the Western Communist parties who got all the credit.[18]

The Turkestan Bureau of the Comintern was attempting to work with a motley crew. Nevertheless, the Soviet government spent large sums of money to recruit fighters against the British, sending arms and ammunition, even airplanes, organizing military and ideological training, and providing shelter and financial support for the future revolutionaries.

Around October 1, 1920, a new member of the Turkestan Bureau of the Comintern arrived in Tashkent from Moscow and became head of the Indian section; his name was Manabendra Nath Roy (1887–1954). He had been appointed by the Comintern to aid Acharya and Rabb in their work among Indians—in fact, to take control over their work. Roy had been selected by a Bolshevik agent, Mikhail Borodin, in 1919 in Mexico City, whither Roy had arrived from Bengal via Japan and the United States, and where he had been a

---

17 Shaukat Usmani, letters 1920–1921, RGASPI: f. 495, op. 68, no. 17, 33.
18 Edith Chabrier, "Les délégués au Premier Congrès des peuples d'Orient," *Cahiers du monde russe et soviétique* 26, no. 1 (January–March 1985): 21–42.

founding member of the Mexican Communist Party.[19] According to Ruth Price, Roy assumed a leading position among Indian revolutionaries at the time of the American government's crackdown in 1917 on Indian nationalists in America. While his comrades-in-arms were under surveillance, arrested and indicted, or awaiting trial, he escaped to Mexico and persuaded the German legation there that he was the main contact with his American comrades and thus should manage the German funds that had been steadily supporting Indian nationalists since the beginning of World War I. The tall, handsome self-promoter with fiery eyes was installed by the Germans to oversee the Indian revolutionary work in Mexico and given 50,000 dollars to distribute as he saw fit. Roy established himself in a luxurious house in an affluent part of Mexico City and "was passing himself off as an Indian prince and mingling in the upper echelons of the local society."[20] As Roy wrote later in his autobiography, when the two men met in 1919, the Bolshevik Borodin was leading a similar life, supporting himself with party funds and giving himself out as an American merchant. The mutual appeal was cemented by each man's personal cynicism. In 1920, Borodin brought Roy to Russia and introduced him to the highest echelons of power.

Before traveling to Tashkent, Roy attended the Second Congress of the Comintern in Petrograd and Moscow, where he was elected to the executive committee. He twice met with Lenin, who approved and supported him as a leading Indian representative in the Comintern and a member of its Turkestan bureau responsible for ideological education and revolutionary agitation among the Indians. (A point of explanation: although all the activities of the Comintern were planned and controlled by Moscow, formally it presented itself as an independent international body. So the Bolsheviks could keep an innocent face in their relationship with Great Britain—whose recognition they sought and with whom they signed a trade agreement in March 1921—and at the same time conduct their aggressive policies through the Comintern.)

Roy and Acharya met at the congress. Together, they wrote a letter addressed to the congress delegates in which they exposed a system of indentured labor that

---

19 The party, founded as the Socialist Workers' Party, changed its name in 1919 to the Mexican Communist Party. Roy proclaimed himself a communist after Borodin had taught him the rudiments of Marxism. The party, as Ruth Price remarks, "had six members and a calico cat," but with Borodin's support it had won affiliation with the Communist International. Subsequently, Roy was chosen as adviser to the Comintern on India and began receiving its coveted funds. Ruth Price, *The Lives of Agnes Smedley* (Oxford: Oxford University Press, 2005), 86.

20 Price, *Lives*, 64.

had been widespread in colonial countries and was little known in the West, which they called a "modern form of slave-labor." They charged the Comintern "to investigate and expose the appalling conditions prevailing under these systems of contract coolie and indentured labor" and to support those laborers in their action against their state of servitude.[21] Roy and Acharya's meeting promised a fruitful collaboration. However, events took a different turn once Roy left Moscow and arrived in Tashkent, by which time Acharya had returned east and was working in Andijan. He left Andijan for Tashkent to welcome Roy, his new boss.

By that time, Acharya had considerable experience organizing revolutionary groups, both armed troops and civilians. In particular, he was experienced in working with Muslims. In 1909 and 1911, and then again in 1915, Acharya went to Jerusalem, Istanbul, and the Suez Canal, where his efforts were directed at forming the Indian National Volunteer Corps, for which he recruited among Indian prisoners of war and among Muslim Indians, who would travel in large numbers to the Ottoman Empire every year for the hajj. For this work, Acharya assumed an alias—the Muslim-sounding name Mahomed or Muhammed Akbar.[22] However, with the arrival of Roy, recruitment among the Muslims in Tashkent deteriorated dramatically, undermined by the rigid class ideology and antireligious rhetoric of Roy and his Comintern backers.

A few statements from Roy illustrate his understanding of Marxism and what Acharya characterized as the warped logic of a rigid ideology. In his autobiography, Roy wrote:

> The hardships experienced in Moscow [during the civil war] were mainly due to the resistance to war communism in the countryside. The peasants simply would not produce more than they needed for subsistence.
>
> In those early days, communist conviction, though very largely emotional, did not exclude attempts at understanding. Lenin's was an appeal to reason as well as to faith. That was dialectic.
>
> Only on the eve of his own death did Danton feel the cruelty of the terror. Dzerzhinsky was a more sensitive man; he wept his heart out every time he sent a man to the gallows.[23]

---

21 "Resolution on the Contract Coolie and Indentured Labor Systems in the Colonies and Subject Countries," RGASPI, f. 495, op. 68.

22 Acharya, *Reminiscences*, 36–38.

23 See M. Roy, *M. N. Roy's Memoirs*, Delhi: Ajanta Publications, 1984, 316, 318, 324. Felix Dzerzhinsky (1877–1926) established the Soviet secret police (Cheka) and served as its director from 1917 to 1926. He was responsible for summary murders, especially during the Red Terror and the civil war.

Roy knew very little about Russia. He learned about Marxism and Bolshevism from Borodin a few weeks before his arrival. Yet through his self-assurance, he found favor with the leading revolutionaries there and rose to a high position in the Comintern. Usmani reported in his autobiography, "I can say this with confidence that the Comintern had granted tremendous aid for the Indian cause and the keys of such a treasury were in the hands of M. N. Roy."[24]

In Tashkent, Acharya worked hard, trekking with leaflets to Andijan, looking for routes into India through the Pamir Mountains and for knowledgeable guides, organizing other centers for work among the Indians in Skobelev (today Fergana, in Uzbekistan) and Osh (in Kyrgyzstan, on the border with Uzbekistan), trying to send people to Kashgar, in westernmost China, to establish a secret center there as well, and agitating and recruiting for his cause. Before his final departure from Tashkent in 1921, he traversed the road from Tashkent to Moscow and back several times. He managed to get to Moscow and Petrograd to attend the Second Congress of the Third International in July and August 1920 as a nonvoting member and a member of the propaganda section.[25] While there, he sent a letter to Lenin answering the leader's call for opinions, suggestions, and criticisms regarding his (Lenin's) thesis on Colonial and National problems, taking up the issue of the fight against pan-Islamism.[26] Acharya cited his vast experience working among pan-Islamists and anti-Islamists in such countries as "Morocco, Turkey, Syria, Palestine, Mesopotamia, Turkestan, Bokhara, and Afghanistan." In addition, he wrote, "I have also taken great interest in the national political and religious movements of Tunisians, Egyptians, Persians, and Tartars." He suggested that at the moment, the idea of pan-Islamism was impotent and utopian. Just as the European countries before the Great War had every reason to unite "for further conquest and plunder of all non-European peoples of the world, they could only organize a war against each other." In the same way, "all Islamic governments have all opposite interests" and would never be able to come to an agreement and unite for the victory of pan-Islamism.[27] (As history

---

24 Shaukat Usmani, *Historic Trip of a Revolutionary (Sojourn in the Soviet Union)* (New Delhi: Sterling Publishing Private Limited, 1977), 46.

25 The Second Congress took place from July 19 to August 7, 1920; the opening ceremonies were held in Petrograd, after which the proceedings shifted to Moscow.

26 See Lenin. *Theses on National and Colonial Questions.*

27 Acharya's letter to V. I. Lenin, July 24, 1920, RGASPI: 2-1-24686-012:014. The Soviets' interest in pan-Islamism disguised a deeper agenda. They wished to use pan-Islamic forces in their own fight against the British in Central Asia. At the same time, they did not want to have Islamic fighters, like the Basmachi, on their own territory.

showed, he was right. Resistance to the Bolsheviks by Turkestan's indigenous Muslim populations was broken largely due to disagreements among the different groups and internal power struggles.)

In October 1920, in Tashkent, Acharya had joined forces with Roy in forming the Indian Communist Party (ICP), which consisted of seven members, two of whom were European.[28] The first organizational meeting was a solemn occasion; its minutes state that it "adjourned with singing the 'International.'" However, by the second meeting, in December, disagreements arose as to who should be eligible to join the ICP. It was decided by a majority of votes that one could not be a member of the party if one belonged to another political organization that was not under party control. At the time, Acharya was still a member of the Indian Revolutionary Association, headed by Abdur Rabb. Both men had been careful not to disenfranchise their Muslim constituencies and were exceedingly tolerant in religious matters. After all, the majority of the people they worked with were Muslims. Acharya's actions and writing show him to have been essentially an antiauthoritarian nationalist willing to work with any party or ideology that supported his goal of the liberation of British India. "We are not against Communism," he had stated—presumably on behalf of the Indian Revolutionary Association—on December 5, 1920, "and we do not make a distinction between a Communist revolutionary or just a revolutionary. All we object to is forcible conversion to Communism; at least in the form dictated by Roy and the Comintern."[29]

Roy and his Comintern backers insisted on a one-party system and manipulated recruits by financially rewarding the faithful while leaving others without support. Roy's actions led to the complete destruction of the IRA, which had functioned successfully before his arrival. A petty tyrant and unscrupulous manipulator with a predilection for luxury, Roy believed that all dissent should be crushed. His tyrannical treatment of his "inferiors" (he came from a Brahmin family of hereditary priests) fit in well with the methods employed by the Soviets, who chose to support him as the leading Indian revolutionary.[30]

---

28 Comrades Ellen Trent Roy and Roza Mukharjee were the wives of two Indian members.

29 Quoted in Maia Ramath, *Decolonizing Anarchism* (San Francisco: AK Press/Institute for Anarchist Studies, 2011), 131. Ramath maintains that "Acharya's differences with Roy had developed into differences with the Communist International and with the Communist regime in Russia itself." Acharya's letters to the Comintern committees and his subsequent writings in the German and Indian press support this assertion.

30 One Indian revolutionary, Abdul Qadir Khan, who knew Roy well, wrote this about him: "arrogant, self-important, and ill-tempered in discussion ... often vehement in seeking to

After his Indian affair in Central Asia failed, Roy was installed in Moscow as a functionary of the Comintern. On his next assignment, after the Fourth Congress of the Comintern (November 5–December 5, 1922), in which he participated, Roy was sent to Berlin as a Comintern agent and stayed there on and off till August 1924.[31] Later, he was sent to China in the same capacity, returning to Moscow after the failure of the Chinese operation and remaining there until 1928, when the political situation in Russia became too hot even for him. With the help of Nikolai Bukharin, he managed to leave the country, first for Berlin and from there, in 1930, to India, knowing that he would face an arrest warrant there, issued in 1924. But he considered arrest in his homeland preferable to trying his luck among the murderous Russians and Germans.

Acharya attempted to salvage the deteriorating situation in Turkestan. In January 1921, he was back in Moscow, where he took part in negotiations between the Indian nationalists and representatives of the Soviet government on transporting arms and ammunition through Afghanistan to India. The negotiations were proceeding well until they were brought to an end by the theft of Acharya's notebook containing the code names of his Indian contacts. The perpetrator was an agent of the British Secret Intelligence Service, which was conducting espionage in Moscow.[32]

Still trusting the Bolsheviks, Acharya wrote letters to the state, party, and Comintern officials in Moscow, pointing out that the actions of the Turkestan Bureau of the Comintern were contrary to professed Bolshevik ideals. He believed that Roy and his acolytes had been planted by the British, so detrimental to the goals of Indian national liberation had their actions been. It was difficult to explain their behavior otherwise.[33] In one of his letters, Acharya

---

impose his opinion on others." Quoted in Gene D. Overstreet and Marshall Windmitter, *Communism in India* (Bombay: Perennial Press, 1960), 32. Ruth Price writes about Roy: "Aside from his desire for Indian independence, the well-bred Brahmin was in no way a radical, and he retained a firm belief in child marriage, the caste system, and other institutions that held India back" (Price, *Lives*, 60–61).

31 On December 18, 1922, in a letter from Berlin to his friend Igor Reisner in Moscow, commenting on the high cost of living, Acharya described Roy's grand lifestyle: "Roy is living in a first-rate boarding house on the corner of Kurfürstendamm and Ulandstraße (like a *kurfürst* in the middle ages) ... he rides around in an automobile, supposedly on business of international aid for workers" (RGASPI, f. 495, op. 68, no. 64, 44).

32 Tikhonov, *Afganskaia voina Stalina*, 127.

33 Acharya kept up his accusations against Roy for quite some time. In 1932, he wrote a letter to Trotsky denouncing Roy and his staunch supporter Michail Borodin, a member of the Comintern: "In my experience with Roy, I came to conclude he was a provocateur and saboteur of Imperial England." See Acharya's letter in Houghton Library, "Trotskii coll.," bMS Russ 13.1 (95).

identified himself as "one of the original members of the so-called Indian Communist Party [who] was thrown out for criticizing Roy's and his lieutenants' methods."[34]

Acharya soon understood that "Roy's and his lieutenants' methods" were also the Bolsheviks' methods. He had witnessed the staging of "revolutions" by the Comintern and the Red Army in the emirate of Bukhara and the khanate of Khiva, former Russian protectorates, resulting in their eventual incorporation into the Soviet Union. In September 1920, Acharya had been a delegate to the Congress of the Peoples of the East in Baku, where he was elected to the presidium as a representative of Indostan. There he had ample opportunity to witness the "methods" by which Soviet and Comintern officials ran such assemblies: full dictate by Moscow, total suppression of all opposition or dissent. He saw that the new colonizers were more dangerous than the old ones. Their ideological rigidity allowed no compromise. Moreover, the new Soviet authority treated the Central Asian peoples as backward children possessing no culture of their own, as barbarous and violent, fanatically religious, and therefore in need of the civilizing guidance of the Russian revolutionaries. Few local politicians were allowed to take part in the governance of their own territory. Despite their anti-imperialist rhetoric, the Bolsheviks' imperialist aims were clear. In 1920, for example, Grigory Zinoviev, the head of the Comintern, stated, "We cannot do without the petroleum of Azerbaijan or without the cotton of Turkistan. We take these products not as former exploiters, but as older brothers bearing the torch of civilization."[35]

Acharya's work with Roy and the Comintern and his experience of the Soviet methods of conquest and subjugation of the colonized peoples led to his thoroughgoing disenchantment with Soviet Russia and the Comintern. He began engaging more seriously with the ideas of anarchism, describing himself thereafter as an anarcho-syndicalist. From a militant fighter, he had become a pacifist. In his correspondence from Berlin with the British passport authorities, he sincerely denounced the Bolsheviks' methods and insisted that he was no friend of theirs. In his writing, he turned to economics and away from politics.

Within a few years, the Bolsheviks conquered and pacified—in fact beat into submission—the mostly nomadic peoples of Central Asia and defined the

---

34 Acharya to the Secretariat of the Comintern, August 3, 1921, RGASPI: 495-68-45-006.
35 Quoted in Stephen Blank, "Soviet Reconquest of Central Asia," in *Central Asia: Its Strategic Importance and Future Prospects*, ed. Hafeez Malik (New York: St. Martin's Press, 1994), 41.

borders of the five Central Asian Soviet republics that today, after the fall of the Soviet Union, are independent states. Thus Acharya's fears of "forcible conversion to Communism" were well founded.

In January 1921, Acharya was back in Moscow. And so was Magda. Julia's diary entry of June 28 of that year reads:

> In the morning Magda and I went to Vera Isaeva's, where they gave Magda a haircut and Leonid teased her (how she had bowed, how she had torn down a curtain from the window and made a dress for herself out of it and departed with the Comintern).[36]

By "Comintern," Julia is jokingly referring to a person or a group of persons, most likely foreigners, associated with that organization. Whether Acharya was one of them is unclear. Julia's comment suggests that Magda may have met Acharya that spring, or if not, then possibly in August, after she returned to Moscow from a medical research expedition in which she was employed as a poster painter.

---

36   Obolenskaia's diary, GLM, f. 348, op. 1, no. 5.

CHAPTER 11

Exeunt Stage Left

W hether or not Julia's June 28 diary entry referred in any way to an acquaintance between Magda and Acharya, it seems that the two most likely met sometime in 1921. In the fall of that year, Magda confessed to Lilya Efron that her life "had been becoming exceedingly unreal."[1] Whatever that meant, it would seem that Magda was ready for a change in direction. And that change might be in the direction of love, for as she had written to Julia in the summer of 1920, during the Noskov affair, "I can give up my soul, and art, and all other possibilities for love. If I do not obtain it, then my art and my soul will die."[2]

On her return to Moscow from Ust-Dolyssy, Magda settled in a room in Julia's communal apartment. In her letters, Julia had frequently reminded Magda about "your room," even though Magda had been away from Moscow for well over a year and had stayed in "her" room for only a brief period a year previously on her way from Likino to Ust-Dolyssy. Thereafter, the room was periodically occupied by other tenants, as indeed it was when Magda finally returned. A young German engineer had just left "Magda's room," and an acquaintance of Magda's, Lydia Brodskaya, had moved in. And so Magda found herself sharing her room with Lydia.[3] Soon that room had a third occupant: Acharya.

In the 1970s, Viktoria Schweitzer and Lydia Brodskaya were sitting together in that very room, in which Lydia had been living for the past half-century. Viktoria had come to see and take a photograph of Magda's portrait of Tsvetaeva, which was hanging in Lydia's room. She was working on the poet's biography. The portrait's author was a side interest for her at that time, and so Magda was not the focus of their conversation. On learning from Lydia that she

---

1   Undated, RGALI, f. 2962, op. 1, no. 91, 10–11.
2   July–August, 1920, RGALI, f. 2080 op.1, no. 45, 185op.
3   L. M. Brodskaya (1892–1977) was at times an aspiring artist, a medical military nurse (in 1916 in Ukraine), a secretary to high-positioned Soviet functionaries, and a translator, as well as a correspondent of the great Symbolist poet Alexander Blok and later a friend and correspondent of the writer Varlam Shalamov.

had shared this room with Magda and her Indian lover, Viktoria asked whether she had found the situation awkward. Lydia replied that in those times, one didn't have the luxury of privacy. It was their youth, and they were not going to let it slip away.

It was not difficult to meet a foreigner in Moscow in 1920 and 1921: communists, socialists, trade-unionists, and nationalists from colonizing and colonized countries flocked to the congresses of the Third Communist International. As Marguerite Harrison wrote:

> Moscow is probably today the most cosmopolitan city of Europe. I certainly found it so during the summer of 1920. The meeting of the Third International brought delegates from every part of the world, as well as hosts of sympathizers and foreign journalists. There were peace delegations, labor delegations, business men, representatives of oppressed nationalities and political minorities, propagandists, crooks and idealists from the four quarters of the globe.[4]

In a letter from Moscow to Magda in Ust-Dolyssy, Julia painted a vivid picture of the Second Congress delegates marching through the streets of Moscow that summer:

> Outside, there are festivities (the Third International). Processions, fabulous scarlet silks are waving; music. Just now I was astonished by a tiny occurrence not noticed by anyone: A detachment was marching with music and banners. All of a sudden, two barefoot girls around 8 or 10 years old ran out from the archway with a doll and a puppy wrapped in a small blanket. They rolled right up to the soldiers' feet, and one of them began to dance to the music in a heavenly manner with a childish lack of bashfulness (Dalcroze), eagerly drinking up the rhythm and coming closer and closer, impossibly close, up to their very feet. Long, thin arm-branches flew up, waving like willows in the wind; some sort of bleached-white, too-short skimpy pinafore without sleeves; long, thin little legs flew over the stones. Is this a street of the future? Then this is indeed fabulous. And can a human being in tune with rhythm be rude and clumsy inside and outside? That is what proletarian culture means (many ask such a question with annoyance or irony); that is what it means after all.

---

4   Harrison, *Marooned in Moscow*, 193.

The processions continue without end. Now they are in 2 rows: women workers and the like, and on the left side are artillery decorated with garlands, horses with red plumes and roses on their heads. Unfortunately, they stuck pitiful little pictures cut out from cardboard into the gun barrels. Guns and cardboard! The artist is an idiot!—On our balcony, a photographer is taking pictures of all this; F[edor] K[onstantinovich][5] is helping him. Tanks are passing by, some sort of motley green monsters all out of cylinders—it's a camouflage color for the forest. Music, the sun. White columns of "preconscript youth [born in] 1902" are passing— young girls in shorts in the front, followed by [an English banner] "cadets recruited 1903"—[and a German one] *allgemeine Waffenausbildung*, with the "a" curling around the pole. All of Tverskaya Street is swarming with columns—the silhouettes revolve against the light and the banners are illuminated. There are inscriptions in Arabic, French, German, all sorts. This flow of people stirs me, as always. Oh, there is no end of them, but my paper has been used up.

No, I cannot stop. Now the entire street is swarming with shapely columns of half-naked people: they are all wearing absolutely identical dazzlingly white shorts, and their brown bodies and legs sparkle in the sun. Hordes of naked children, young men, grownups—they are free, stepping easily—a sort of Rome. They don't even have sandals on. Imagine such a Moscow, such a street. And here are oarsmen, apparently—their banners have oars and they are wearing jerseys. It's already 12:15. On workdays, too, I often see children dancing in the streets. No, such a state is not criminal. *Ich würde nur an einen Gott glauben, der zu tanzen verstünde, Zar.*[6] Airplanes flew low, right above the roofs. Drag chutes were hanging, and toward evening there were fireworks.[7]

While the culture in which she had been raised was crumbling around her, Julia believed that a new, vigorous proletarian culture was being born to take its place, revealing the inner beauty of those who had won freedom. For such a future, no sacrifice could be too great. She was taken by the beauty of

---

5   F. K. Radetsky—common-law husband of E. I. Obolenskaya, Julia's mother. He was a good amateur photographer.

6   The quotation is from Nietzsche's *Also Sprach Zarathustra*: "I would believe only in a God who knew how to dance."

7   July or August 1920, RGALI, f. 2080, op. 1, no. 45, 107–111op. The Second Congress of the Comintern took place in the summer of 1920, from July 19 to August 7.

the uninhibited human body and by the festiveness and power of the display of artillery, airplanes, camouflage, and soldiers. She did not seem to perceive any menace in those scenes. Among her acquaintance were many who opposed the new regime and had already felt its persecution. For example, at that time, Mikhail Feldstein was awaiting sentencing on trumped-up charges; indeed, she mentioned him in that very same letter. So when she writes, "No, such a state is not criminal," perhaps she is defending the revolution to many of her circle—despite her direct experience of physical hardship, violence, and the persecution of her friends.

Indeed, the same letter begins with Julia's habitual litany of the hardships she and her loved ones had to endure: hauling water from downstairs to the fifth-floor apartment to wash and cook and hauling the slops downstairs, running around the city trying to buy milk, indulging her family with an egg ("at home there was one egg, Mama brought it"),[8] and working all the while on some silly diagrams for which wages had been promised. Yet no matter the hardships, Julia seems to regard them as a down payment on universal freedom. Julia's brother had been inclined toward the Bolsheviks from the time of the October Revolution. Her strong sense of humor and the mutual moral support within her immediate circle sustained her faith and hope.

Magda by now had quite a different perspective. Alone and far from everyone and everything she loved, she had witnessed the total destruction of the countryside (for example, the plundering and destruction of the Likino forest, and the destruction of the Ust-Dolyssy peasantry through requisition, expropriation, and outright murder), numerous arrests and near escapes (village priests in the Nevel area and Feldstein in Moscow). She saw no future for herself under the current state of affairs.

By the time Acharya and Magda met, his faith in the Bolsheviks had weakened. His experience working with Roy and the Comintern and his revulsion at the Soviet thirst for power had left him ever more disenchanted with developments in Russia, especially with the Bolsheviks' brutal methods of eliminating all potential rivals for power or influence. By the time Acharya left Tashkent for Moscow, a large number of American anarchists, some of whom Acharya had known from his European and American days and with whose views he had sympathized, had arrived in Russia following their deportation from the United States. At first they and their Russian anarchist comrades were tolerated by the regime, and according to Marguerite Harrison, they even were

---

8   Ibid., 107.

operating a restaurant "open to the public, where a very good meal could be had for thirty-five rubles, astonishingly cheap for Moscow."[9] She writes further that they

> held open meetings every Sunday, and were allowed to preach their doctrines undisturbed, though to tell the truth, at their meetings there was at least one Checkist to every Anarchist or impartial listener, and they held debates with corresponding prudence and due realization of this fact. ... Numbers of them had already been arrested, and during my own term of imprisonment [which began in spring 1921] a general roundup of all Anarchists was made by the government.[10]

And again Harrison, from within her prison cell:

> Meanwhile, the political situation continued to be very interesting. Nearly all the prisoners were Socialists, Mensheviks, Right Social Revolutionaries and Jewish Bundists, belonging to the seceding faction of the Bund which did not unite with the Third International. ... The Socialist room [at the Lubyanka prison], which held twenty-four, was occupied by Right and Left Social Revolutionaries, Mensheviks and Anarchists.[11]

Emma Goldman and Alexander Berkman, two prominent anarchists deported from America,[12] arrived in Moscow in January 1920 and left, after a prolonged house arrest, in December 1921 in horror of what they had seen: both in Russia and Ukraine they met with abuse of power, repression, inequality in food rations and educational possibilities, the impossibility of speaking out freely, and corruption. Goldman quotes Lenin:

> "But as to free speech," he remarked, "that is, of course, a bourgeois notion. There can be no free speech in a revolutionary period." Free speech, free Press, the spiritual achievements of centuries, what were they to this man?

---

9 Harrison, *Marooned in Moscow*, 141.
10 Ibid., 140.
11 Ibid., 278, 292.
12 In 1918, the American Congress passed the Sedition Act, which forbade the use of "disloyal, profane, scurrilous, or abusive language" about the United States government, flag, armed forces, and war effort. One of the results of this act was the deportation of 249 anarchist and communist activists to Soviet Russia. Goldman and Berkman were among them.

A Puritan, he was sure his scheme alone could redeem Russia. Those who served his plans were right, the others could not be tolerated.

Anarchists filled Bolshevik prisons; many had been shot and all legal Anarchist activities were suppressed. The Tcheka especially was doing ghastly work, having resurrected the old Tsarist methods, including even torture.[13]

Undoubtedly, Acharya knew about the fate of anarchists and members of other revolutionary parties, the Mensheviks, Right and Left Social Revolutionaries, and the Bundists, who experienced the same kind of repression. First in Tashkent and now in Moscow, he witnessed the ubiquitous and all-powerful Cheka suppressing and persecuting every private initiative, be it political, commercial, or educational. Not only Russians but also foreigners who had disagreements with the Bolsheviks and tried to escape from Moscow's influence were in harm's way. In his journalistic work later in Berlin, Acharya openly accused Moscow of suppressing any attempt at dissent from the Bolshevik line. He accused the state and party leadership of foul play, naming individuals who after their arrival in Russia had never been seen again.

Acharya's political views might also have undergone changes due to his friendship with Magda, who introduced him to her circle. Within this milieu, he could witness the destruction under the Bolsheviks of the Moscow intelligentsia, for whom August 1921 was a fateful month: August 7, the death of the great Russian poet Alexander Blok, whom the authorities did not allow to go abroad for medical treatment for fear that he would disseminate unwanted truth about their regime;[14] August 25, the execution by the Cheka of another prominent poet, Nikolai Gumilyov, along with sixty-one other alleged members of a monarchist plot.

Magda's own family—her mother and siblings—were struggling to survive. Her mother wrote from Likino to her daughter Adele in Switzerland, "Every day it becomes more and more difficult to live. Everything is very expensive and difficult to obtain, and there is no money at all, we have lost

---

13 Goldman, *My Disillusionment in Russia*, 67.

14 See Yevgeny Zamyatin's letter to Kornei Chukovsky, written on August 8, a day after Blok's death:

> Yesterday, at 10:30, Blok died. Or more correctly: was murdered by our primitive, brutish life. Because it was still possible—possible to save if he could have been taken abroad in time. August 7, 1921 is as monstrous a day as the day in 1837 when they learned that Pushkin had been killed (https://arzamas.academy/materials/941).

everything."[15] Many close acquaintances were in and out of jail, suffering from dispossession, internal displacement, and starvation. Some were trying to leave the country. Marina Tsvetaeva left in May 1922, Vladislav Khodasevich the following month. Magda's beloved friend Natalia Grekova left even earlier, in the fall of 1920. Either in 1921 or in 1922 Magda received a letter from Grekova from Constantinople in which she described horrific times before her departure from Crimea, on a boat across the Black sea.[16]

In January 1920, Julia wrote to Magda, who was still in Ust-Dolyssy, about Elizaveta Zvantseva, the founder of the Petersburg art school they had attended:

> Elizaveta Nikolaevna was here. They [Zvantseva and her lifelong friend Elena Ivanovna Karmin] have been finally kicked out and had to move in with some miserly doctor who treats them as if they were boarding-school girls. What they endured is difficult to imagine: those people spent the night in their rooms, spat at them, smoked, called them idiots, threatened to throw a bomb at them, etc., etc., and finally kicked them out altogether.[17]

Zvantseva, who was at the time working with children at an orphanage, died the following year.

It must have been about a year after Acharya and Magda first met that they left the country together. Both had tried to eke out an income. After she left Ust-Dolyssy in the late fall of 1920, Magda had been in and out of Moscow, taking whatever jobs she could find. In summer 1921, she joined an expedition to the Russian north as a poster painter. In her diary, Julia noted that Magda left Moscow on June 29, and an entry of July 11 reads, "Magda writes that they feed themselves by stealing potatoes at railway stations."[18] The expedition, like many of her endeavors to support herself, ended in failure. On August 26, 1921, Julia, who together with Kandaurov had left on an expedition to Central Asia, received a letter from her mother:

> Yesterday Magda came back, this time for good. Waiting in Vologda for the provisions and money for the expedition, she spent all of her own, but

---

15 April 24, 1917 or 1918, family archive.
16 Undated fragment, Kandaurov collection, RGALI, f. 769, op. 1, no. 424, 1–4. Published in *Nashe nasledie* 122 (2017), letter no. 25.
17 January 29, 1920, RGALI, f. 2080, op. 1, no. 45, 46–49op.
18 Obolenskaya's diary, August 26, 1921, GLM, manuscript division, f. 348, op. 1, no. 5.

she waited in vain and went on to catch up with her companions. As soon as she left, a messenger came with money and left with it again. Thus the whole expedition had to return to Moscow because they did not have a kopek. To top off all her disasters, at her departure, all twelve of her drawings for which she was supposed to receive piecework wages in Moscow disappeared from the railroad car. She is left without a kopek and only with some bitter oat flour that she received for rations. Now she has set out to look for money; I don't know how it will work out. That's her luck, what can you say![19]

In Moscow, Acharya first was allowed to work as a journalist, and he published surveys of the political and economic situation in India, about its liberation movement, its party politics, and its national leaders. His articles appeared in *Pravda* and in *Vestnik NKID*.[20] It was during those years that Gandhi was restructuring and democratizing the Indian National Congress, which resulted in an expansion of membership and participation in the Congress's offices and activities irrespective of caste and economic level. Bal Gangadhar Tilak, Acharya's teacher in nationalism and one of the main opponents of Gandhi, died in 1920. Although Tilak had been revered by the nationalists, including Gandhi himself, new leaders who were more attuned to the latter's teachings had been emerging and changing the shape of the national liberation movement. Gandhi turned the nationalists' attention to social issues—the caste system, illiteracy, lack of medical care, the seclusion of women, and poverty—that had to be addressed in the struggle for freedom. Although Acharya had lived outside India since 1908, he was aware of the latest political and social developments in his country. His erudite, comprehensive reports drew on a great variety of sources including Indian

19 RGALI, f. 2080, op. 1. no. 46.
20 *Vestnik NKID* (Bulletin of the People's Commissariat for Foreign Affairs) was a bimonthly published from June 1919 to June 1922. The editor in chief who invited Acharya to write for this publication was B. F. Lebedev, one-time anarchist, whose first wife was the daughter of the famous activist, scientist, and philosopher of anarchist persuasion Petr Alekseevich Kropotkin. Lebedev knew five European languages and also Persian and Arabic. Until 1928, when he was expelled from his posts for party nonaffiliation, he worked as an information officer at the Commissariat for Foreign Affairs.

periodicals and British, German, French, and American newspapers. Moving freely among European languages, he read widely and offered a lucid analysis of the complex political situation in India.

Foreign journalists and foreign specialists had been shadowed by agents working for the Cheka and for the People's Commissariat for Foreign Affairs, whose "Department of the Press," established at the end of 1917, controlled Soviet information and propaganda issued for export and supervised the work of foreign correspondents. In his memoirs, M. N. Roy reminisced about the Second Congress of the Comintern in 1920:

> A bevy of young women was attached to the foreign delegates to act as interpreters. Apart from the service they were to render and which they did satisfactorily, most of them were physically attractive. They were to spy on the leading foreign delegates and with that purpose worm into their confidence through their cupidity, if not hearts. The abominable practice led to some happy unions, although generally it resulted in debauchery and some cases of heart-breaking tragedy.[21]

Journalists were accompanied by "guide-interpreters" who were supposed to report every movement of their charges. For that purpose, a special form had been devised that had entries for time, place, names, and the content of conversations or utterances.[22] Marguerite Harrison reported from Moscow how journalists worked there in the early 1920s:

> Our dispatches to our papers, after being read by Rosenberg [head of the Western Section of the Foreign Office], who often made changes or erasures, were sent to Chicherin [Commissar for Foreign Affairs] for approval, with the result that there were sometimes further cuts. Then they had to pass the "Military Censorship," which meant in plain English that they were subjected to the scrutiny of an agent of the Extraordinary Commission [Cheka], after which such portions as were considered fit to print were sent out by the government radio, to take their chances, if favorable to the Soviet Government, of being picked up and intercepted by various governments en route … it was impossible for us to write anything except

---

21 M. N. Roy, 355–356.
22 A. S. Romanov, "Inostrannye korrespondenty v Moskve: Otchety gidov-perevodchikov NKID. 1920 g.," *Istoricheskii arkhiv* 2 (2009): 119–147.

straight news or interviews unless we went in for tangential stuff favorable to Communism.[23]

Acharya would not have been treated differently from any other foreign journalist, all of whom were under suspicion and surveillance, although he was not yet sending his dispatches to non-Soviet publications. If that had been the case, Magda would likely have become a target of surveillance as well.

At times, Soviet paranoia made it difficult for foreign journalists, and other foreigners as well, to leave the country, as Marguerite Harrison discovered. It was not easy for Acharya either. Following some disagreements with the Soviets, he could no longer publish in their periodicals and had to find other employment. In 1922, he worked with the American Relief Administration, which was trying to ease famine in Russia, all the while looking for ways to escape the country.

On December 4, 1922, Lev Karakhan, deputy secretary of the Peoples' Commissariat for Foreign Affairs, sent a letter to G. E. Zinoviev, secretary of the Executive Committee of the Comintern.[24] In this letter (with "urgent; top secret" at the heading), Karakhan informs Zinoviev that a group of Indian nationalists who had been expelled from Afghanistan to Russian territory in 1920 but who had not joined the Comintern were stranded in Moscow without any financial support or opportunity to work for their cause. For fifteen months, they had been trying to obtain exit visas while receiving meager support and shelter from the Commissariat. This intolerable situation, compromising for the Commissariat for Foreign Affairs, must come to an end. The Commissariat had come to an agreement with the GPU [a successor organization of the Cheka] about the Indians' departure. However, the Comintern had objected to that decision, and the Indians now faced eviction from the Commissariat's premises, where they had been housed. Karakhan suggested that the Comintern take all the responsibility for them from now on. He was making a case for the Indians, noting that as a result of negotiations between his department and the GPU, several Indians from the same group, "Acharya and two other nationalists who sided with him, were allowed to leave for Germany."

I don't know exactly when Acharya and Magda met, nor when they were wed. But on May 9, 1922, Magda was in Likino, where she completed and signed a portrait of her mother, which she took with her into exile (Figure 34). Two months later, in a letter to Voloshin of July 5, 1922, Julia mentioned that

23 Harrison, *Marooned in Moscow*, 61.
24 RGASPI, f. 495, op. 213, no. 232, 12–12op.

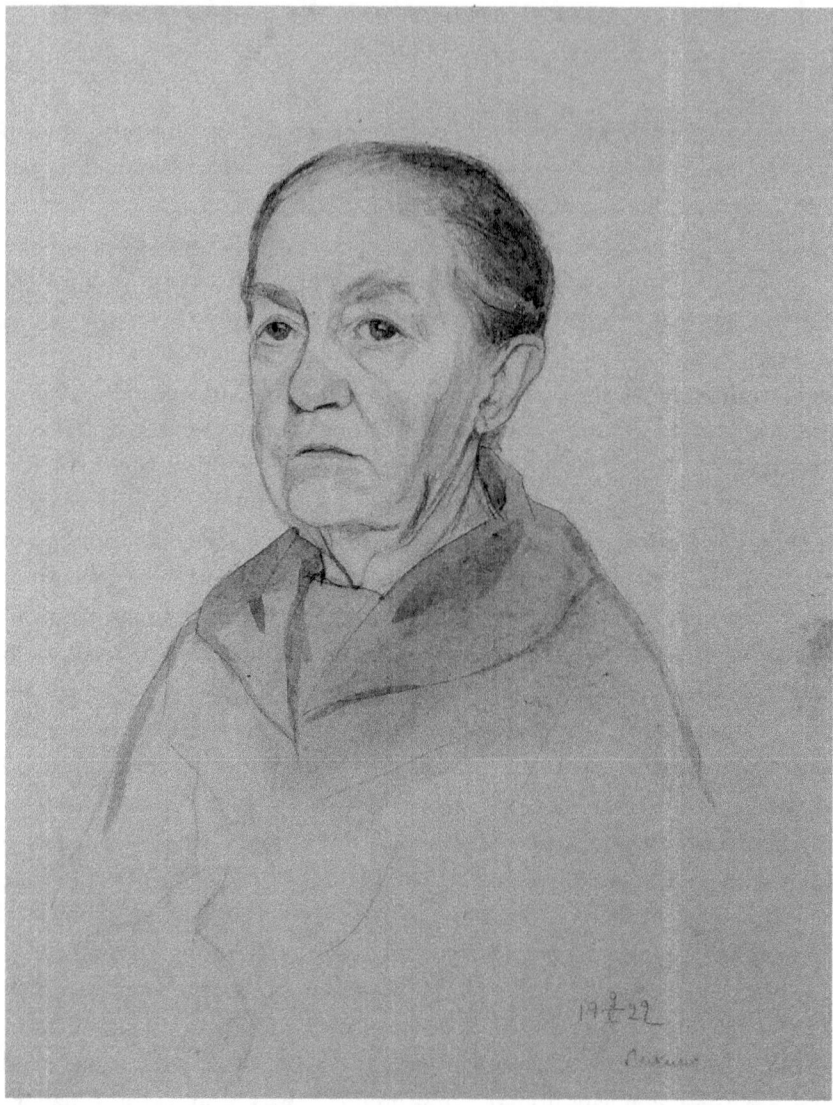

Figure 34. Magda Nachman. Portrait of the artist's mother, Klara Emilia Maria Nachman, née von Roeder, 1922 (*courtesy of Sophie Seifalian*).

Magda had married a Brahmin.[25] And the couple almost certainly left Russia together in November 1922, as attested by the German diplomat Kurt Max

---

25 On July 5, 1922, Julia Obolenskaya wrote to Maximilian Voloshin: "Do you know that Magda Maximilianovna married a Brahmin?" (IRLI, f. 562, op. 3, no. 902).

Prüfer, to be introduced in the next chapter, who wrote that the Acharyas had arrived in Germany in November 1922.

To leave Russia was not a simple matter. In his letter to Igor Reisner, his colleague and friend in Kabul, written on December 18, 1922, from Berlin to Moscow, Acharya described their precarious border crossing and first weeks in Berlin.[26] In that letter, Acharya reported that Karl Moor, a Swiss banker who had helped the Bolsheviks before and after the October Revolution and who might have been a double agent,[27] had called the GPU to ask them not to allow him to leave Russia and that a telegram to that effect had been sent to the border police. In any case, Acharya and Magda managed to leave the country. In that same letter, Acharya informed Reisner how perilous the situation had become since then:

> I have just heard that an Egyptian delegate to the 4th Congress of the CI disappeared suddenly in Russia. ... I wouldn't be surprised if something happens with the revolutionaries coming to Russia. I myself have gone through this all, but with open eyes and concentrated attention, and if I managed to escape, I am obliged to these open eyes and not only to luck. What happened with Mahmud Husni el-Arabi, the Egyptian delegate to the Fourth Congress of the International, whom I do not know, happened or will happen to two Sikh delegates from America, who, just like Husni, have not returned to Berlin. ... These Sikhs wanted to write a report for me on their difficulties with Roy in Russia. [bottom of the page damaged] a possibility to run away from Russia if they are not in Butyrki.[28] But if they are still "at large," the way we were "at large" for a long time, they are under surveillance. ... They will roam the streets of Moscow the way we did in our time.[29]

26 RGASPI, 495-68-64. This letter exists only in a Russian translation in the Comintern archive. For several years after 1917, I. M. Reisner (1898–1958) served in the People's Commissariat of Foreign Affairs, working in Afghanistan from 1919 to 1921 as a translator and intelligence officer, where he and Acharya became close colleagues. He became a Soviet Orientalist.

27 H. Schurer, "Karl Moor—German Agent and Friend of Lenin," *Journal of Contemporary History* 5, no. 2 (1970): 131–152. In his letter to Reisner, Acharya in fact calls Moor an Entente agent (but then he suspected many Comintern functionaries because he believed that their course of action was counterrevolutionary).

28 The formidable Butyrskaya prison housed many political prisoners.

29 RGASPI, 495-68-64, 39.

Acharya wrote that he had no desire ever to return to the land of the revolution, which he considered a failure, a "bankruptcy of communist politics," and added, "Let them call me an anarchist." As to Magda, he wrote that she had begun painting to earn money and so as not to become rusty. Acharya's first Indian and German publications began to appear early in 1923.

The two close friends Magda and Julia parted ways not only geographically, but geopolitically as well. Julia remained in Russia. Like Magda, she lived through cold and hunger, through dispossession, through arrests, imprisonment, and even execution of her friends, through all the disturbing and frightening realities of the new Soviet life, and yet she emerged from that experience with a surprisingly benign judgment. For example, she perceived the subjugation of Central Asia as a progressive step in bringing enlightenment and civilization to places where there had been none. She knew the area well, having participated in several expeditions in Turkestan, but like so many Russians before and after the October Revolution, she remained estranged from the native populations, regarding them as half-savage.

Magda rarely wrote to Julia about politics. But she had experienced the workings of the new regime firsthand in her years in the Russian provinces, and she had linked her fate with that of the Tashkent witness Acharya, who had stated openly that unscrupulous Bolshevik colonizers had brought disaster to Central Asia. She had turned her back on a country that offered her no future.

CHAPTER 12

The Emigrants

Aﬁer their successful crossing of the Soviet border in the fall of 1922, the Acharyas settled in Berlin.[1] In the early 1920s, the Charlottenburg and Tiergarten districts of Berlin were flooded with Russians fleeing first the Bolshevik Revolution, then the Red Terror and the Civil War. Charlottenburg even acquired the telling epithet "Charlottengrad." This is how the composer Nicholas Nabokov (Vladimir Nabokov's first cousin), who arrived in Berlin in the spring of 1921, writes about émigré life at that time:

> They lived in cheap boarding houses, pensions, hotels, furnished rooms, and flats, or, in some rare cases, sumptuous villas in the Tiergarten and Grunewald. But the Russian refugees were by no means a humble, frightened lot that fretted and trembled in a hostile environment. They seemed to have taken over Berlin and transformed it into a Russian camp. ... The center of Western Berlin, from the Wittenberg Platz past the Gedächtnis Kirche and down the Kurfürstendamm, seemed to have surrendered to the Russian takeover.[2]

Russian newspapers, Russian publishing houses, Russian theaters and art galleries, Russian restaurants and stores, were proliferating and competing for business. As Vladimir Nabokov writes in his novel *Glory*:

> But perhaps the most unexpected thing about this new, much expanded, postwar Berlin ... was the free-mannered, loud-voiced Russia that chattered everywhere, in the trams, in the shops, on street corners, on the balconies of apartment houses.[3]

---

1 From this time on, Magda often signed her works Magda Nachman Acharya. Some letters written to her by friends in Germany are addressed to Magda Acharya as well. The name in German would sometimes be spelled Atscharja, Atschariya, or Atscharia. Nachman sometimes acquired another, Germanizing, "n" at the end: Nachmann.

2 Nicholas Nabokov, *Bagázh: Memoirs of a Russian Cosmopolitan* (New York: Atheneum, 1975), 119.

3 Vladimir Nabokov, *Glory* (New York: McGraw-Hill International, Inc., 1971), 135.

At the time of the Acharyas' arrival, Russian émigrés constituted about twenty percent of the city's two million residents. Berlin was attractive for its relative proximity to Russia, low cost of living, and the relative ease with which a German entry visa and residency permit could be obtained. And Acharya had resided earlier in Berlin, where he had been financially supported by the German government as a member of the Hindu–German conspiracy, and he had connections to other Indian expatriates there.

A decade earlier, in 1911, when her younger brother Walter was sick and thinking of traveling to Germany for medical care, Magda had written to Julia:

> You know, my brother wants to go to Karlsruhe, and Mama wants to jour-
> ney there with me and him and remain there for several years. But how
> could I, bred in Russo–Petersburgian soil, live for such a long time in
> European realms?[4]

Much had changed since 1911: revolution, civil war, hunger, had destroyed in her any hope of living even a semblance of the life that she had expected to lead in Russia. No longer was she wondering how she could possibly live abroad—and not even in upper-middle-class luxury. As for Acharya, he considered himself for-tunate to have escaped the Bolsheviks, and as he wrote to Igor Reisner in the letter cited above, nothing would induce him ever again to set foot on Russian soil.

Magda's decision to leave Russia for an unknown future was not out of charac-ter. When tried to the breaking point, her otherwise quiet, patient, and understand-ing nature became determined and unyielding, and rather than accommodate her-self to unacceptable circumstances, she broke decisively from them. So it was when she left for Bakhchisarai, in Crimea, in the summer of 1917 after her break with Griftsov. So it was in the spring of 1919 when she left Moscow for the country-side, pushed by the strained relationships in her communal apartment. And so it was now after her difficult experience in Russian villages during the civil war and the impossibility of working as an artist even after her return to Moscow. Julia had noted Magda's propensity to run away from difficult situations and was not sympa-thetic. In one of her less charitable letters, in 1919, she wrote this to Magda:

> You sometimes make things worse for yourself as if on purpose; that's how
> it was, for example, with this trip to Ivanovo-Voznesensk, so obviously
> pointless. ... Of course, if you manage to remain a clerk for all eternity, it
> will be only on account of the particularly strong force of this stubborn-
> ness that is so injurious to you.[5]

---

4   July 8, 1911, RGALI, f. 2080, op. 1, no. 45, 51–53.
5   May 30, 1919, RGALI, f. 2080, op. 1, no. 7, 30–31.

Julia's criticism seems to me unjustly harsh. By her own admission, Magda's decision to leave Moscow in 1919 was rash. Yet it was eminently reasonable, given the difficult conditions in Moscow. And perhaps a similar charitable construction can be placed on many life-altering decisions from that tumultuous time.

And now Magda had made a final break with Russia. Within a rather brief span of time, she had met Acharya, married, and left with him for Berlin. Was Magda in love with her husband? Or was her marriage simply another act of despair, a means of leaving Russia? From her subsequent history and a few comments in letters from friends and relatives, it seems that whatever else it was, the relationship was one of loyalty and friendship. In his autobiography, their friend Shivaram Karanth wrote that Magda "doted on her husband."[6] There is no evidence that this was merely a marriage of convenience, and indeed, in both Europe and later in India, Magda and her husband were considered a "normal" married couple. For example, in all the family photographs in which Acharya appears, Magda's niece Clara has identified him as "my uncle Acharya." And Acharya wrote kind letters to his and Magda's nieces after Magda's death. In a handful of surviving notes written to Magda, her friends in emigration Vladimir Nabokov and the artist Vadim Falileev send their regards to Acharya or invite the couple to visit.

Very little is known about Magda's years in Berlin. None of Magda's letters from Europe survive, although Julia Obolenskaya mentioned having received such a letter. Writig to Voloshin, she says:

> Do you know that the temple in Dornach burned down on New Year's Eve? Everyone was at Dr. Steiner's lecture at the time. Magda Max[ilianovna] wrote from Berlin.[7]

Moreover, in her diary covering Magda's first months in Berlin, Julia recorded the first two of the Acharyas' Berlin addresses. There is also a 1930 letter from Julia to Magda, which survived among Magda's sister Adele's papers, that informs Magda of Kandaurov's death. In it, Julia laments, "Magdushka, why do you write so rarely?" Indeed, Magda could have been writing rarely, or some letters might have been "lost," that is, confiscated by the authorities. In any

---

6   K. S. Karanth, *Ten Faces of a Crazy Mind. Autobiography*, translated by Sri H. Y. Sharada Prasad, Bombay: Bhatatia Vidya Bhavan, 1993, 157.

7   January 1923, Pushkinskii Dom (IRLI), f. 562, op. 3, no. 1026. The Goetheanum in Dornach, Switzerland, the main building of the Anthroposophical Society, was destroyed by fire on December 31, 1922–January 1, 1923.

case, there are no letters from Magda's years abroad in Julia's archive, in which so many documents were preserved. It is possible that Julia destroyed them at some point in the 1930s out of fear that they could be used against her as incriminating evidence of contact with foreigners.

Furthermore, though it is difficult to imagine that she would not have corresponded with her mother and siblings, no letters have surfaced from these years. In fact, there is a letter of 1928 from Magda's mother, in Leningrad (as St. Petersburg was now called), to her granddaughter in Switzerland in which she thanked her granddaughter for writing, which indicates that there was a correspondence at that time. If Magda described her life in Europe to family and friends in Russia, that account has been lost.

Nevertheless, some traces of the Acharyas' life in Berlin survive. Their first address appears on the envelope of the December 1922 letter to Igor Reisner and in Julia's diary: Leibnizstrasse 42 (bei Frau Witte), Charlottenburg. As of July 30, 1923, their address is given on an official document as Bochumerstrasse 5, 4; Treppen bei Schwabe (Tiergarten).[8] In September 1923, Julia entered yet another address for Magda into her notebook: Kantstrasse 90 IV bei Schneider, Charlottenburg.[9] In July 1926 they resided at 3a Landgrafenstrasse, Berlin W. 62, and the next month, in August 1926, they moved to 4 Ringbahnstrasse, Halensee. In December 1928, on a postcard from Vadim Falileev, the Acharyas' address is given as 17 Kaiser Platz 12, Berlin-Wilmersdorf.[10] And yet in another card of 1930, a friend asks Magda whether their search for an apartment had been a success, which means that the Acharyas had been planning to move yet again. In 1932, the return address given in a letter that Acharya wrote to Leon Trotsky is Grossbeerenstrasse 56c, Berlin SW 61.[11] The same address is given by Acharya in his letter to the British Consul General in May 1931.[12] The Acharyas' last address in Berlin was Kronzprinzendamn 19, Berlin-Halensee. Like many other émigrés, the Acharyas moved frequently.[13]

---

8   Politisches Archiv, Auswärtiges Amt, vol. R 287476: Abteilung III, Indien Privata.

9   Obolenskaya's diary, GLM, manuscript division, f. 348, op. 1, no. 5.

10 Family archive. In 1924, Vadim Falileev left Russia for Stockholm with his wife, the artist Ekaterina Kachura-Falileeva, and their daughter, Ekaterina. In 1926 they moved to Berlin, and in 1938 to Rome.

11 Harvard University, Houghton Library, Trotskii collection, bMS Russ 13.1 (95) and IOR, L/P&J/6/1968/0069.

12 IOR, L/P&J/6/1968/0069.

13 For example, between 1919 and 1937, the Nabokovs moved more than half a dozen times in Berlin. The historian Simon Dubnov moved five times between 1922 and 1930. See Karl Shlegel', *Berlin, Vostochnyi vokzal* (Moscow: NLO, 2004), 387.

The acute shortage of residences even for native Berliners led to restrictions on housing and high taxes on foreigners. A foreigner not holding a foreign national passport had to have two documents: a permit from the central Berlin office to reside in the city and a permit from the district office to occupy a specific lodging. Such permits were not given for an entire apartment, but only for one or two rooms. Procuring the needed documents usually took months, during which the petitioner could live only in hotels or pensions. In March 1923, a new residence tax was introduced that was five times higher for foreigners than for Berliners. As time passed, the situation was somewhat ameliorated as the result of appeals by different Russian organizations in Germany, but in general, Berlin landlords were not eager to rent rooms to stateless persons who might have difficulty in obtaining proper documentation and in paying rent and taxes.

Magda was not stateless, in contrast to many other Russians in Germany who either had left their country under the old regime and were in possession of obsolete documents, or had more recently crossed the border illegally. Magda had left Russia as the wife of a departing foreigner and likely arrived in Germany with a Soviet passport. Such passports began to be issued with the commencement of the New Economic Policy introduced in 1921. They were valid for a certain period of time and could be reissued in countries that had diplomatic relations with Soviet Russia or had Soviet trade representation offices. Such passports gave certain privileges to their holders according to international laws of reciprocity. At the time, most countries had not yet recognized the Soviet government. Germany, however, under the burden of war reparations and restricted trade agreements imposed by the Western powers, had turned to Russia, with the two countries, badly in need of international markets, signing a treaty on May 6, 1921, in which each waived claims against the other due to the war and called for an immediate resumption of diplomatic and consular relations.

Many Russians who left the country legally with Soviet passports after the end of the civil war did not think that they were leaving forever, and for a time, it was possible to validate one's passport in a foreign consulate, giving the holder the possibility of returning, as did the writers Maxim Gorky, Alexei Tolstoy, and Andrei Bely, among many others.[14]

---

14 For example, Khodasevich, the famous poet and Magda's acquaintance from Moscow, and his wife, the writer Nina Berberova, left Russia in 1921 for Berlin with Soviet passports, which they renewed a couple of times. But when in 1923 or 1925 they moved to Paris, deciding that there was no way back, they simply allowed their passports to expire. According to another account, in 1925, the Soviet embassy in Rome refused to renew their passports.

It would seem that Magda's Soviet passport, if she in fact had one, did not help the couple greatly, if at all, in finding a place to live. Acharya's legal position in Germany was complicated. He had forfeited his status as a subject of British India when he fled his homeland under the threat of arrest for subversive political activity. At times, he traveled with forged documents in Europe and the United States. During the period of his cooperation with the Germans in wartime, he may have been issued a legal document that allowed him to reside in Germany. However, after his sojourn in Russia, he possessed no valid passport. And so it was not easy for the Acharyas to find a place to live, and they were not exempt from paying the high tax on foreigners.

In January 1926, Acharya applied for a British passport. It is possible that by that time, Magda no longer possessed a valid Soviet passport, and Acharya initiated his pursuit of legalization from a simple desire for normalcy, for the rights that legal status would have given them to live, travel, and work within Europe. In reply to a request by the passport office for information on his wartime activities, he wrote, "I am also a convinced anti-Bolshevik. ... I am only concerned with assurance of my steady living for the rest of my years and that peaceably."[15]

In March 1926, an emergency certificate for one-time travel to India (without a guarantee of not being arrested and imprisoned on arrival) was offered to him. But he declined it, knowing that legal procedures would be taken against him in India. All he wanted was free passage and the right to live somewhere in Europe, other than Soviet Russia. This the British denied him. A telegram from the War Office informed the Under-Secretary of State for Foreign Affairs that issuing such a passport to Acharya was "very undesirable."[16] The same sentiment was expressed in a memorandum of the Economy and Overseas Department, a part of the India Office, which stated that "in view of this man's record the Secretary of State for India is not prepared to recommend that he [Acharya] be granted an ordinary British passport."[17] Eight years passed before Magda and Acharya received British passports and permission to travel to India.

Meanwhile, Acharya attempted to obtain an exemption from the foreigners' tax by claiming that he had been a long-time German resident. He had indeed resided in Germany sporadically before and during the war. The most

---

15 February 15, 1926, IOR, L/E/7/1439/0007.
16 February 17, 1926, ibid., 0020.
17 February 19, 1926, ibid., 0032.

dependable account of Acharya's whereabouts throughout his career inside and outside India can be traced in a detailed dossier on his movements created for Great Britain's India Office by the Military Intelligence Office in London, based on reports from their own agents in Berlin and on reports from India, for the British kept close tabs on Indian nationalists abroad. Their records show that Acharya first arrived in Berlin in November 1910. A year later, he was in Munich, and shortly thereafter, he left for Constantinople, Egypt, and the United States. He left the United States for Germany in 1914, at the beginning of the war; and in April 1915, after receiving military training from experts in the kaiser's army under the assumed name Muhammad Akbar (or Ali Haidar), he accompanied a German mission on behalf of the Berlin Indian Independence Committee to the Suez Canal to found the Indian National Volunteer Corps with Indian soldiers and prisoners of war. In March 1916, Acharya was back in Constantinople, traveling from there in 1917 to Stockholm, with a brief stop in Germany. His claim to have been a permanent resident of Germany was rather thin.[18]

Nevertheless, Acharya turned for support to the German diplomat Curt Max Prüfer (1881–1959), with whom he may have been working in Egypt and Constantinople during the war. Prüfer had been sent to Cairo in 1907 as a specialist in Semitic languages. While in Cairo, he developed strong anti-British sentiments and developed strategies to sabotage British rule in Egypt. He organized attacks on the British post at the Suez Canal, where Acharya was present as a member of the Hindu–German mission to the Suez Canal, Palestine, and Persia. If they indeed met in Egypt, Acharya and Curt Prüfer would have found common ground in their hatred of the British.

The upshot of Acharya's appeal was that in June 1923, Prüfer wrote a letter to the tax authorities asserting (falsely, whether knowingly or otherwise) that Acharya had been long in residence in Germany, first in 1910–1911 and then from 1914 to 1919. He wrote that Acharya had left Germany in 1919 with the intention of quickly returning, but due to unforeseen difficulties had managed to do so only in November 1922. Prüfer's correspondence with the tax authorities on behalf of Acharya and his wife may or may not have been successful.[19] But whatever their documentation and tax status, the Acharyas somehow managed to survive in Berlin, which was teeming with writers, artists, and other

---

18 Undated, ibid., 0021. In the United States, Acharya was indicted in absentia in the San Francisco conspiracy case of 1917–1918.

19 Politisches Archiv, Auswärtiges Amt, vol. R 287476: Abteilung III, Indien Privata.

intellectuals competing for attention and resources. As one of Nabokov's biographers writes:

> Russian Berlin, 1921–1924, was a cultural supernova without equal in the annals of refugee humanity. A few hundred thousand very temporary settlers in a Berlin already well supplied with its own books and periodicals published more in three years than most countries publish in a decade. ... It was the intellectuals—the artists, writers, and scholars—who made the Russian emigration a mass exodus unique in history.[20]

To make it in this boisterous Russian crowd—at the mercy of impoverished, defeated Germany, itself in need of resources for reconstruction and war reparations—one had to have sharp elbows. The Berlin economy could not support the superfluity of writers, painters, and actors who flooded the city. One researcher of the period quotes a Russian littérateur thus:

> To get into literature is like squeezing into an overcrowded trolley car. And once inside, you do your best to push off any new arrival who tries to hang on. Communities in exile are not renowned for their generosity of spirit.[21]

How did Magda fare in the hustle-bustle of émigré Berlin? As the scholar of twentieth-century Russian history and Russian émigré literature, journalism, and culture Lazar Fleishman wrote to me about Magda, "She definitely was not part of the Russian artistic milieu; if she appeared, then only episodically."[22] That rings true. It is hard to imagine quiet and sensitive Magda pushing to make room for herself in an overcrowded trolley car.

Berlin was also home to a large Indian political émigré community, to which Acharya had belonged since 1910. On his return to Berlin in 1922, he at once reconnected with former comrades to renew his activities in pursuit of

---

20 Brian Boyd, *Vladimir Nabokov. The Russian Years* (Princeton: Princeton University Press, 1990), 196, 198.

21 Stacy Schiff, *Véra (Mrs. Vladimir Nabokov)* (New York: Random House, 1999), 34. According to other sources, the phrase belongs to the poet Nikolai Gumilyov and refers to Russian literature in general. See Vasilii Ianovskii, *Polia Eliseiskie* (Moscow: Astrel', 2012), 44.

22 Lazar Fleishman, email to the author, January 13, 2018.

Indian independence. As he wrote to Reisner, and as Prüfer confirmed in his letter to the authorities, Acharya joined the Indian News Service and Information Bureau (INSIB),[23] which had been the brainchild of his friend and colleague the Indian nationalist Virendranath Chattopadhyaya, known as Chatto. Acharya and Chatto had known each other since Acharya's residence in India House, in London, in 1909. They had roomed together in Paris, Berlin, and Stockholm. Both men had shaped the Indian revolutionary movement abroad before and during World War I and had continued working together for some time in postwar Berlin.

The INSIB emphasized education over military action, a shift in emphasis that reflected Acharya's own views at the time as well. It published and disseminated in India pro-German newspapers, such as the *Indo-German Commercial Review* and the *Industrial*, and later its successor, the *Trade Review for India*. The bureau supported Indian students in Germany and businessmen from India, sent news and information free of British influence to India, and promoted Indian–German cultural ties.

Acharya began writing for the INSIB newspapers and other papers published in India, for example the *Hindu*, in Madras, sometimes under the pen name Muhammed Akbar, which he had used earlier in Egypt, and sometimes as "Mr. Bhayankar."[24] He later became a Berlin correspondent of the *Bombay Chronicle* and contributed to the Indian papers *Forward* and *People*. The main thrust of his articles, written shortly after his departure from Russia, was to report on his experiences with the Comintern with the goal of discrediting its methods and leaders, as he had promised to do in his letter to Reisner of December 18, 1922, in which he wrote:

> but who are the leaders of the Comintern if not several fools and plenipotentiary agents of the British Empire. If nothing is undertaken to clarify this, the Comintern will continue to be esteemed by its paid "revolutionaries."[25]

---

23 Indisches Nachrichten- und Informationsbüro, G.m.b.H. Berlin-Halensee, Georg-Wilhelm-Str. 9. Politisches Archiv, Auswärtiges Amt, vol. R 287476: Abteilung III, Indien Privata. INSIB was organized in spring 1921.

24 Acharya corresponded with and later in India befriended K. S. Karanth (1902–1997), an Indian writer, social activist, and filmmaker. Acharya sent articles to Karanth for placement in Indian periodicals.

25 RGASPI, f. 495, op. 68, no. 64, 39.

Acharya reserved particular vitriol for M. N. Roy, a ranking member of the Comintern, exposing him as an "Entente agent" in league with the British whose actions were detrimental to the goals of Indian liberation. As Acharya was sending his critical articles to India, Roy, in his capacity of Comintern agent, was sending Communist propaganda there. Acharya never eased up on Roy, continuing to denounce him even in the 1930s.

His articles were also critical of the Russian Revolution, whose vaunted idealism he exposed as nothing more than a grab for power by a band of scoundrels, above all Lenin himself:

> They fought for political power and not necessarily for communism, and they gained the first without the second. And now they have declared that this is communism, that it has been accomplished and the heaven has been restored (for them). But with such authority (money and bayonets) other bandits and scoundrels ruled in their time and fooled masses till they were kicked out of their saddles.[26]

Scholars have given some glimpses of Acharya's political engagement on behalf of Indian liberation and a shift in his views to a wider international perspective in books on Acharya's like-minded comrades.[27] Two of these colleagues were Chatto and Agnes Smedley, Chatto's common-law wife, who was an American radical working with the Indian anticolonial movement abroad.

Although with time, both Chatto and Smedley would begin working with the Comintern, in 1921 Smedley published an article in which she indicted the Third International as an organ of Russia's national self-interest rather than "an instrument of world revolution":

> The Communist (Third) International represents nothing more than a collection of political communist groups in each country, many of which have no connection with the working class but sprang into being only after receiving Russian money.[28]

---

26 Ibid., 41.
27 See, for example, Barooah, *Chatto* and Price, *Lives.*
28 Alice Bird (pen name of Agnes Smedley), "The Baltic Sea a British Lake," *Modern Review,* December 1921, 710.

Thus Acharya was not alone at that time in his analysis of the goals of the new Soviet government and its use of the Comintern as its tool.

In December 1922, shortly after Acharya's arrival in Berlin, a meeting of anarcho-syndicalist groups from across the world was held there, at which the International Working Men's Association (IWMA, sometimes known as the Anarchist-Syndicalist International) was established. This event marked a decisive break between the international syndicalist movement and the Bolsheviks. Acharya attended the weeklong founding meeting of IWMA with a group of other Indians.[29] Soon they set up a committee and began sending anarcho-syndicalist literature to India. Among the Indian nationalists Acharya had become the strongest adherent of anarchism. As he wrote to an editor of the radical Bengali paper *Forward,* his political belief was now "anarchism, pure and simple."[30] He began contributing to anarchist magazines with an international perspective in America, France, Argentina, and Spain, and to Russian-language anarchist publications abroad. His vast knowledge of colonized peoples of Africa led to his concern for freedom transcending the specific issues of Indian liberation. Acharya established ties with the Dutch-American labor activist Nicolaas Steelink, with whom for many years he exchanged information and literature on the activities of American and Indian syndicalists. (Steelink was sending Acharya literature for dissemination in India at least through 1948.) Acharya's growing faith in anarchism, his rejection of military approaches in the fight for freedom, and his condemnation of Bolshevism in Communist clothing distanced him from many of his fellow nationalist revolutionaries.

In 1926, Acharya had a major falling out with his colleague Chatto, who was working toward an international conference to establish a "League Against Imperialism and for National Independence" (LAI), which took place in February 1927 in Brussels. Although many in LAI, including Chatto, did not want the Soviets to play a central role in its work, the league was in large part financed by the Comintern and the Soviet Union. By 1929, the Soviets and their allies had obtained full control over the LAI, and when this was exposed at the 1929 LAI congress in Frankfurt am Main, several members of the executive committee resigned, including Jawaharlal Nehru, who had given an address

---

29 "Mandayam P. Tirumal Acharya, anarchist; activities and passport application," India Office Records (IOR) L/P&J/12/174, file 7997/23. After the congress, Berlin became the headquarters of the Revolutionary Syndicalists' International. Two prominent anarchists, Emma Goldman and Alexander Berkman, lived in Charlottenburg and attracted many comrades there. Acharya claimed to have known them.

30 IOR, L/P&J/12/174, file 7997/23.

and an extensive report on the situation in India at the Brussels Congress, and Albert Einstein, who was one of the league's honorary presidents.

Acharya's position on Soviet-style Communism never changed. He was opposed from the beginning to the League's acceptance of Soviet sponsorship, and he cut his ties with Chatto. This is how the situation is described in the files of the India Office:

> His [Acharya's] hostility to the Comintern has resulted in his attacking the League Against Imperialism, and through this he has fallen out with his former friend Chattopadhyaya, and is in fact completely isolated in Berlin.[31]

But even earlier, in a September 4, 1923, letter to a friend in India (P. Parthasarathy), intercepted by the British, Acharya wrote:

> I go to very few Indians and very few come to me—as all are busy enjoying themselves with those who can afford to pay for enjoyment and have a mind to do so.[32]

For those Indians, such as Roy, who were more interested in a comfortable life than political ideals, fealty to Soviet ideology kept money flowing from the Comintern. Acharya, in contrast, honest and ascetic in habits acquired during a long life of revolutionary devotion and meager means, disdained unearned luxury and deviation from the path of righteousness.

In 1923, the British sources commented thus on Acharya's journalistic diligence and its dearth of financial reward:

> Indeed, he seems to have done little else [except writing articles], for we never hear of him having an employment, regular or otherwise; and the great length of his articles and letters indicates that he was a man of leisure, who expressed himself on paper for lack of listeners to the spoken word.

In 1924, another report stated that he was "earning a little by acting as secretary to Indian and Egyptian revolutionaries, and by teaching English and Oriental language." And the report of a few years later was just as stark: "Ever since [his arrival in Berlin] he has eked out a decidedly precarious existence by

---

31 IOR, L/P&J/12/174/0007.
32 Orientals in Berlin and Munich: SIS and DIB reports, IOR, L/P/12/102: Jan.–Oct. 1923.

teaching English."[33] Acharya's dire straits were also noted in a 1933 memorandum: "He has eked out a precarious existence in Berlin for the past seven years, teaching English, doing translations and latterly, a little film work."[34] There was nothing unusual or special in the Acharyas' poverty. Few others among Indian and Russian émigrés fared better, and not for lack of entrepreneurship. Acharya's friend Chatto, a talented organizer and inspiring journalist, was often on the brink of starvation. And Vladimir and Véra Nabokov experienced dire poverty, despite Vladimir's literary publications and Véra's working a number of jobs.[35]

And Magda was apparently not earning much from her painting either, if one is to judge from a letter of May 1928 in which Agnes Smedley pleaded with the Indian National Congress (INC) for financial support on behalf of Acharya. As reported in the files of the India Office, she wrote to the INC that "he was lying seriously ill as a result of years of starvation."[36] Another person who wrote to the Indian National Congress with similar information and a request for support for Acharya was Chatto's sister Sarojini Naidu, a famous Indian poet and politician. I do not know whether the INC took any action. By that time, Acharya had repeatedly chastised Jawaharlal Nehru for having connections with the Soviet Union and misleading the Indian National Congress. He sent two articles to the Indian periodical *People* criticizing the Congress's foreign policy, described thus in an India Office note for January 1928: "both [articles] harped on the connection between Britain and Russia—he is more than a little mad on the point."[37]

Acharya would lash out in print at anyone who was financed by the Comintern or even had friendly dealings with it. As noted in the British files, "The general impression which is borne out by his writings, is that owing to ill-health, undernourishment and isolation, he is definitely a mental case." But while it may be madness to believe in the anarchist dream that all forms of governmental restraint can be replaced by voluntary cooperation and free association of individuals, that does not qualify Acharya to be considered a "mental case." Acharya's articles reveal an uncompromising logic, a determined single-mindedness, and a utopianism that may seem like madness to hard-nosed realists. In response to the query from the British Consul General's office in 1931 as to why he needed a British passport, Acharya entered on a long explanation

---

33 Ibid., 6, 11, 12.
34 IOR, L/P&J/2/174/0019.
35 Schiff, *Véra*, 75.
36 IOR, L/P&J/12/174/0014–0015.
37 Report of September 1929, IOR, L/P&J/12/174/0015.

of his ideas on restructuring the economy, abolishing money, and doing away with any type of government—the only measures that could, in his opinion, prevent the coming bloodshed.[38] He required, he wrote, a British passport to ensure his freedom to disseminate his ideas through the British press. While the British agents may have viewed Acharya's ideas as symptoms of madness, they may have had second thoughts when Acharya was soon proved right about the coming bloodshed.

Perhaps Magda, ever sensitive and compassionate, found in Acharya, lonely, ill, and misunderstood, a person who really needed her. Before her acquaintance with Acharya, in her letters of 1919 and 1920 to Julia, Magda wrote that she longed to be needed by another human being:

> In general, I do not have a feeling of my overarching necessity in this world. After all, I am not needed by anyone in the way that you are by K. V. [Kandaurov] and he by you. Of course, Mama needs me but this is still not an overarching tie. It is a bond of kinship and not one of choice.[39]

And of course Magda's relationship with Noskov revolved primarily around his neediness.

The British intelligence documents tell us that Magda was a working painter ("his wife made a little money by painting"),[40] supporting both herself and her husband by her art. Who purchased her art? Where is it now? And what was Magda's relationship with the Russian, Indian, and German communities?

The Russian emigration was largely a self-contained world, mixing little with the German population. At first, many émigrés believed that the Bolsheviks would not last long in power. They worked to support their language and culture, to provide their children with a Russian education, and to be ready to return home at a moment's notice. Many knew little German and had no interest in learning it, since such knowledge was superfluous to their aspirations.

It is unlikely that Magda was among those preparing to return to the lives they had left behind. Everything we know suggests that she shared her husband's antagonism toward the Bolsheviks, and she was surely influenced by his belief that Lenin and his regime would not be easily dislodged from power. In

---

38 February 17, 1931, IOR, L/P&J/6/1968/0071, and especially ibid., 0067, May 20, 1931.
39 End of July 1920, RGALI, f. 2080 op. 1 no. 45, 186–188/op.
40 IOR, L/P&J/12/174/0013.

his letter to Reisner, Acharya wrote that both he and Magda were relieved to be outside Russia, where he could begin to speak the truth about the Bolsheviks.

There is no evidence that Magda assisted her husband in his political activities, nor that she actively participated in the political ferment in the émigré community. As noted in the British intelligence reports, "his wife is a non-political entirely concerned with art."[41] But a lack of political engagement was no barrier to friendly relations with her husband's acquaintances, as evidenced from a 1947 letter to Acharya from Ruth Fischer, a former German and Austrian Communist who had been active in Berlin in the 1920s and, like Acharya, had ultimately denounced Soviet Communism. The letter had been typed on Fischer's behalf by "K. R.," who added the following note:

> I hope that Magda is in good health and spirit and painting as always. Why don't you send us photos of her pictures … ?[42]

The emigration from Russia was anything but homogeneous. It comprised many groups, principally ethnic Russians, Russians of German background, and Jews. Those in the two last categories had an easier time associating with the local population than those in the first; the Russian Germans shared a language and cultural sympathy, and many Russian Jews made connections with the large Jewish community. Magda, with her Jewish father and Baltic German mother, belonged to both groups.

Magda Nachman had readily available links to German life. She had been educated in a German gymnasium in Petersburg, and her German was as fluent as her Russian. Her knowledge of German culture was deep. In many letters to Julia, she referred to Goethe and Nietzsche as her teachers and dear friends. She knew Heine's work, and seriously studied the writings of Rudolf Steiner. Thus it comes as no surprise that her 1928 solo exhibition was held in a gallery that did not specialize in Russian art and that she was engaged by a German-Jewish publishing house to illustrate their books.

Many painters, musicians, and even some actors and theater directors who at the beginning of the 1920s poured from Russia into the German capital transcended the language barrier and attracted the attention of their German counterparts and the general public. In describing his years in Berlin, Nicholas Nabokov,

---

41 January 2, 1927, IOR, L/P&J/12/174/0058.
42 Harvard University, Houghton Library, Beq. Ruth Fischer; *81M–37, 1961 (bMS Ger 204 [1024]).

whose mother was a Russian German, mentions many Germans to whom he was introduced and became friends with. The Russian émigré cabaret theater Der Blaue Vogel (The Blue Bird), which flourished from 1921 to 1937, attracted German actors and directors and a German audience. Many émigré Russian painters in Berlin—Vassily Kandinsky, Alexej von Jawlensky, Marianne von Werefkin, among many others—had studied at German art schools before the Russian Revolution and then remained in the country for long periods of time. Thus they had well-established connections with the German art world. And of course, for these Russian artists, there was no language barrier to the appreciation of their creations such as there was for writers like Vladimir Nabokov, and their works were readily displayed in galleries alongside the work of other European artists.

There was an endless stream of important painters of the Russian avant-garde, including such temporary visitors as Kazimir Malevich, El Lissitzky, and Alexander Rodchenko, who returned eventually to the Soviet Union, and émigrés such as Ivan Puni (Pougny), Xenia Boguslavskaya, Naum Gabo, Antoine Pevsner, and the artists mentioned above. These are names largely associated with the aesthetics and polemics that Magda opposed. But there were other Russian artists, including a number who had connections with and were ideologically closer to the World of Art association. They participated in the Berlin art journal *Zhar-Ptitsa* (Firebird),[43] which presented articles by leading art critics and featured high-quality illustrations. In its spirit, the journal echoed the original *World of Art* journal published by the World of Art association at the turn of the century. It also reminded Russians about their past and present-day artists and showed the Western reader that in spite of war and revolution, Russian art was something to be reckoned with. The journal had sections in German, English, and French, thus broadening its readership. Fourteen issues of *Zhar-Ptitsa* appeared between 1921 and 1926. Magda knew many of its contributors, among whom were her teachers Bakst and Dobuzhinsky. Had she made any attempt to see them? That would not have been easy, of course. Bakst had settled in Paris, and Dobuzhinsky in Riga (but he made several visits to Berlin and Paris). Was she connected in any way with the journal and artists and publishers associated with it?

Exhibitions of the work of Russian artists in Berlin were reviewed in various Russian-language newspapers, such as *Rul'*, *Russkaya kniga* and its successor, *Novaya russkaya kniga*, *Spolokhi*, *Teatr i zhizn*, *Beseda*. Magda participated in at

---

43 Perhaps this title suggested to Kandaurov and Obolenskaya in Moscow the name for their artistic organization—Zhar-tsvet (Fireflower)—established in December 1923, which exhibited the work of former members of the World of Art who had remained in Russia.

least two exhibitions. One was a group show in the gallery Amsler & Ruthardt organized by the Deutsche Gesellschaft für Osteuropakunde (German Society for the Study of Eastern Europe), an association established in Germany in 1913. A brief favorable review appeared in the May 10, 1929, issue of *Rul'* (The Rudder), the foremost Berlin Russian-language newspaper. In it, the anonymous reviewer praised each artist, including Magda: "Some pastels by Mrs. Nachman are pleasing (particularly her 'Courtyard')." Among the exhibitors were Magda's friends and fellow émigrés Vadim Falileev, Ekaterina Kachura-Falileeva, and Magda's Zvantseva classmate Sergei Kolesnikov,[44] who back in Moscow had become Falileev's apprentice in the art of engraving.

Another review of a solo exhibition of Magda's work in 1928, in Galerie J. Casper, was written by none other than Vladimir Nabokov, and it appeared in *Rul'* on November 1, 1928. In the 1920s, the gallery was run by Johanna Casper (née Heimann), the sister-in-law of the renowned Austrian philosopher and novelist Robert Musil, who moved between Berlin and Vienna in those years. Galerie J. Casper specialized in solo exhibitions of lesser-known artists, and according to the Berlin newspapers of the time, there was always something of interest to be found there. In the 1920s, the gallery began showing more Jewish artists (for example, the surrealist Felix Nussbaum had two shows there). There are few surviving traces of the existence and exhibitions of Galerie J. Casper. In addition to Magda, three other Russian artists had exhibitions there: Nikolai Glushchenko in 1924, Ivan Babij also in 1924, and Elena Makovskaya in 1931. At the time of Magda's show, the gallery was situated at Lützowufer 5, in the heart of the Berlin art-trade district Lützowviertel. The gallery closed in 1932. In 1941, Johanna Heimann-Casper was deported to the Theresienstadt concentration camp, where she perished.[45]

In his review of Magda's exhibition Nabokov wrote:

> A person who has a feeling for colors is fortunate in a fortunate world, in which a pouring rain is not a harbinger of a runny nose but a wonderful iridescence on the asphalt, and in which an enticing speck of light burns on the most insignificant object of everyday life. Mrs. Nachman-Acharya possesses such a feeling, and she knows how to use it to the full. I especially liked two still lifes: a bottle made of transparent glass, all pierced by light,

---

44 Sergei Kolesnikov (1889, China–1952, Germany); Magda writes about him in her letters to Julia.

45 I am grateful to Lisa Weiß for information on Galerie J. Casper.

and a bunch of blue grapes coated with a precious glaze. Superb also are some portraits—a woman in a black kerchief against the background of a northern landscape; a smoky-green pudgy-faced Buddha; a thin Indian in profile. A very pleasant show, which demonstrates once more the high standing of Russian art.[46]

Magda had been introduced to the Nabokovs by a friend, Anna Feigin, a pianist, a graduate of the St. Petersburg Conservatory and a cousin of Vladimir's wife, Véra. Magda makes an occasional cameo appearance in biographies of Nabokov. The first biographer of Nabokov, Andrew Field, describes Magda Nachman as "a friend of the family. ... The Nabokovs described her to me as 'a tremendously sensitive person.'"[47] Field also mentions that in 1933, Magda fetched books from the library for Nabokov when he was ill. Nabokov writes about this as well in a letter to his wife: "I met, for example, P. de Reul, whose book about Swinburne I remember well (Magda brought it over when I was sick)."[48] From this casual mention of Magda's name it is clear that she was a familiar figure in their lives. At the time of his illness, Nabokov was beginning research for one of the major novels of his Russian period: *Dar* (The Gift). In an interview with Nabokov's later biographer Bryan Boyd, Véra Nabokov recalled that

> Magda Nachman-Achariya lugged from the state library volume after volume of Chernyshevsky and the enormous tomes in which Russian explorers—Miklukho-Maklay, Grand-Duke Nikolay Mikhailovich, and especially Nikolay Przhevalsky and Grigory Grum-Grzhimaylo—recount their Central Asian expeditions.[49]

Around the same time, Magda painted pastel portraits of Vladimir, Véra, and Vladimir's mother, Elena Ivanovna. Magda's is one of only two known portraits of Vladimir from his Berlin years (figure 35).[50] This is how Andrew Field describes it:

---

46 Vladimir Nabokov, "Vystavka M. Nakhman-Achariia. Galereia Kaspar," *Rul'*, November 1, 1928, 4.

47 Andrew Field, *Nabokov: His Life in Part* (London: Hamish Hamilton, 1977), 187.

48 See the letter of January 18, 1936, in Vladimir Nabokov, *Letters to Véra*, ed. Brian Boyd and Olga Voronina (New York: Alfred A. Knopf, 2015), 233. In a letter of October 24, 1932, Nabokov makes a casual reference to Acharya as well: "Khodasevich looks like a monkey or even like Acharya, and all those Hindu movements too" (ibid., 193).

49 Boyd, *Vladimir Nabokov. The Russian Years*, 400.

50 The other is a portrait by M. Dobuzhinsky (1937), Magda's teacher.

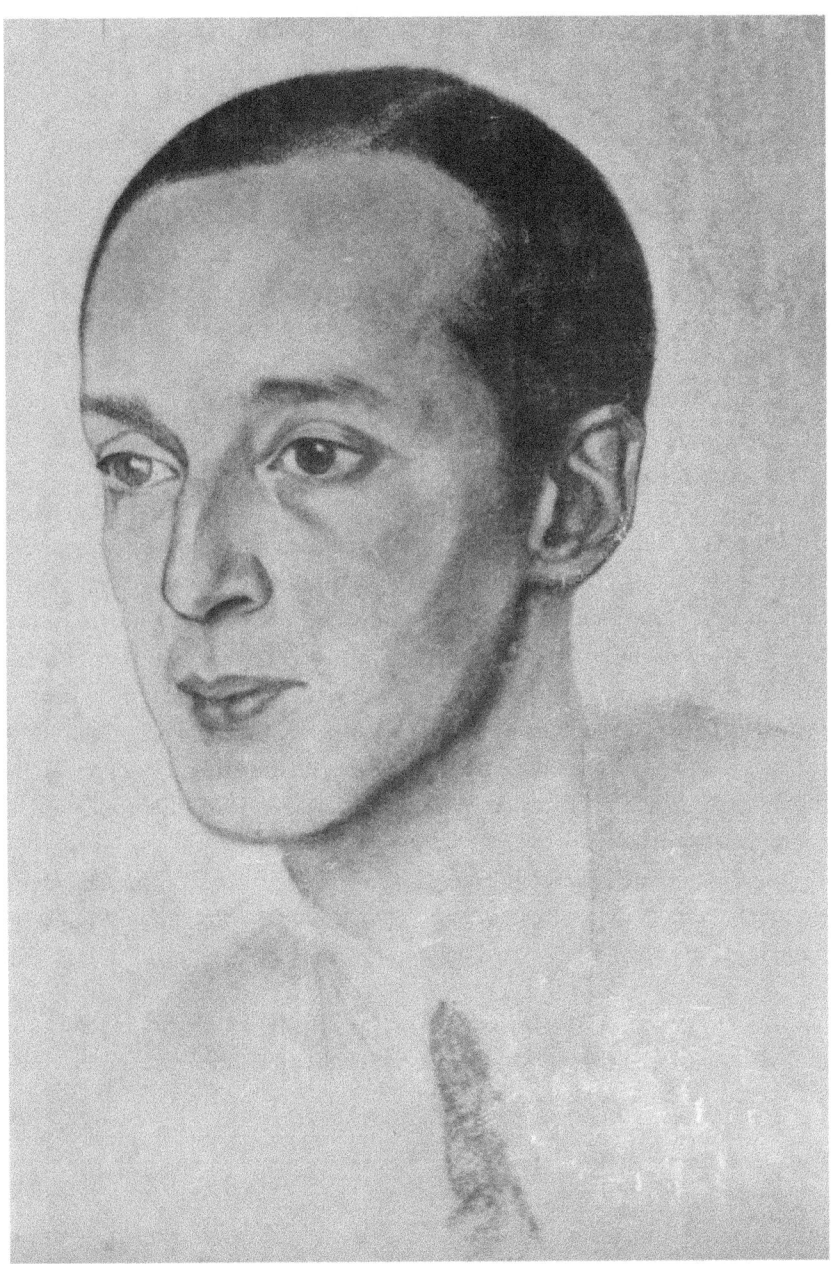

Figure 35. Magda Nachman. Portrait of Vladimir Nabokov, Berlin, Germany, 1933 (*Copyright © 1971 by Vera Nabokov, used by permission of The Wylie Agency LLC*).

The picture has two striking characteristics. Nabokov, not only because his hair is slicked back and very close to his head, somehow appears wet in the picture, as though he has just emerged from the water. This is a matter of style, of course, and in the other Indian pictures [by Nachman] which I have seen one sees this same air or posture of being a little out of place and very conscious of oneself in many of her subjects. It is a style that suits Nabokov's personality quite well. The other characteristic emanates from the subject: Nabokov looks at us in the picture not only as a man who knows precisely who he is and what he can do, but also what he has done. He is still a young man, but he has a different assurance about him. The snapshots of this period, mostly with tilted shoulders and patient smile, do not capture this aspect of his personality nearly as well as Magda Nachman-Achariya's study.[51]

The sitter indeed seems to possess a certain self-assurance. However, here, as in the portrait of Tsvetaeva, Nabokov is not really looking at us. With a slight smile on his lips, he seems rather to be looking inside himself and into the future.

The fate of the Nabokov family portraits was the same as that of many works by Magda: they disappeared. The Nabokovs took them from Berlin to Paris when they moved there in 1937. On leaving for the United States in 1940, they left a trunk with their papers and pictures with their friend Ilya Fondaminsky. When Fondaminsky was taken by the Gestapo in 1941, the trunk with its contents went missing.

Years later, the Nabokovs tried to recover Magda's works through advertisements in the Parisian Russian-language newspaper *Russkaya mysl* (Russian thought): the following appeared on January 29, 1971:

> I collect works by Magda Nachman-Acharya (pastel, oil, pencil). In your offer include a description and a photograph, if possible. Reply to the office of *Russkaya Mysl*.

On September 16, 1976, yet another announcement appeared:

> VLADIMIR VLADIMIROVICH NABOKOV is seeking three portraits—of himself, his wife, and his mother—by the artist Magda NACHMAN-ACHARYA. All three portraits are done in pastel, the approximate size is 50 by 60 cm. The portraits were stored in the

---

51 Field, *Nabokov*, 187–188.

basement of I. M. Fondaminsky's apartment and disappeared during the occupation of 1940 and 1942. Reply to *Russkaya mysl.*

Fortunately, a photograph of Nabokov's portrait survived (Field's description of the portrait quoted above was based on that photograph). In a letter of May 11, 1971, to an editor at McGraw-Hill, Véra Nabokov wrote:

> Enclosed please find a glossy print of a portrait (pastel) of my husband by Magda Nachman-Acharya. It was made in 1933, in Berlin. He thinks it would be nice to use it on the jacket of Glory, which was written a couple of years earlier. It is an excellent likeness, and has never been published before. This is what VN asks me to tell you, but he also wants me to add that the ear is too large. The portrait was lost during the German occupation of Paris, and our efforts to retrieve it have been fruitless so far.[52]

By placing a portrait of himself by Magda on the dust jacket of his novel and placing Magda's name inside, Nabokov was in part paying tribute to Magda as a courageous artist, who, like the author and his novel's protagonist, allowed herself to be driven by fate only so far.

Magda's niece Irene (Irina in Russian) may have been to some extent the prototype for one of the characters in *Glory*. Born in 1918, the year of her father's death from influenza, she contracted the disease herself in infancy and was left mentally impaired. In the novel there is a girl, also called Irina and also left mentally impaired around 1918—in this case as a result of witnessing her father being pushed out of the window of a moving train by Red Army soldiers.

By the end of 1923, that is, within a year of Magda's arrival in Berlin, Russian émigrés began to leave Germany in large numbers. Inflation, which had been rampant since the end of World War I, was drowning the country in despondency. What could buy a loaf of bread in the morning wouldn't buy a crust by midday. Only those with foreign currency could buy food comparatively easily. All the rest were selling anything there was to sell: jewelry, clothing, themselves. Magda and Acharya again were surrounded by hunger and misery. Then in the fall, the inflation was finally put in check. The German mark was revaluated and stabilized, and the country became as expensive as other European countries. Rents increased. German state welfare, for which some Russian

---

52 Letter to Anne Dyer Murphy, editor of the Trade Books Division of McGraw-Hill Book Company, Berg Collection, New York Public Library. Copyright © 1971 by Vera Nabokov, used by permission of The Wylie Agency LLC.

émigrés were eligible, had become less generous and threatened to be cut off altogether. Support from various Russian charities diminished. It became even more difficult to find remunerative employment. The cultural opportunities that had been available at the beginning of the 1920s dwindled along with the book and art markets. There was no longer a compelling reason to remain in Berlin, and many moved to Paris, Prague, Great Britain, or the United States. As Nicholas Nabokov wrote, Berlin "was reverting to the natives."[53]

Magda and Acharya remained. Several friends were still in Berlin, including the Nabokovs, who, like Magda, were among the last Russian holdouts. Other friends included Anna Feigin, Vadim and Ekaterina Falileev, and Sergei Kolesnikov. Magda may also have maintained friendly relationships with Vasily Masyutin (1884–1955) and Konstantin Gorbatov (1876–1945), two artists who had taken part in the group exhibition of 1929 and had also remained in Berlin.[54] And there were others with whom she associated through her husband.

During her years in Berlin, Magda became acquainted with many more Jews than she had known in Russia. In 1923, Jews constituted about one-fourth of the approximately 360,000 Russian émigrés in Germany, most of them in Berlin, and many of them occupied prominent positions in various aspects of Berlin émigré life. Among them were doctors, bankers, jurists, scholars, publishers, writers, poets, and artists, many of whom also had contact with German Jews.

Beginning in 1928, Magda produced illustrations for several issues of the *Jüdischer Jugendkalender* (Jewish Calendar for Young People), which included poems, plays, and short stories as well as a Jewish calendar illustrated by Jewish painters. It was published by the Berlin publishing house *Jüdischer Verlag*, among whose founders were Martin Buber and Chaim Weizmann. In the issues for 1928–1929 and 1930–1931 there are four stories illustrated by Magda (figures 36 and 37).

Although Maximilian Nachman was Jewish, Magda, along with all her siblings, was baptized and raised as a Lutheran. But if the editors of the *Jugendkalender* had been looking for a Jewish artist, they would have assumed that Magda, with her outspokenly Jewish surname, was in fact Jewish, which to some extent, of course, she was.

Which leads to the question of how Magda identified herself in ethnic and religious terms and how others identified her. In her letters she often

---

53 Nabokov, *Bagázh*, 124.
54 There was one more participant in that show, named Berenson, whom I have been unable to trace.

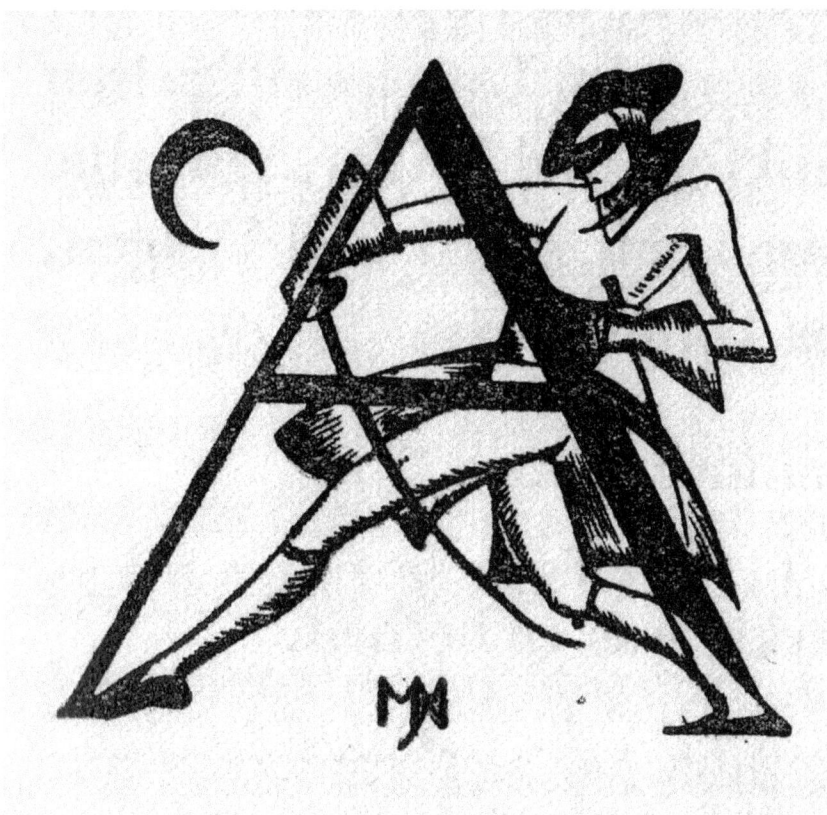

Figure 36. Magda Nachman. Initial capital letter in the story "Aus den Tagen des Schinderhannes."

speaks about the beauty of church services, and she marks time by the church holidays that the family celebrated (Christmas, Easter, Pentecost). Her closest friends back in Russia were aware that Magda had something of a Jewish background. For example, Julia wrote to her in Likino about an exhibition of Jewish artists in 1918 in which Magda had been invited to participate: "Lyonya Feinberg wanted to have your paintings for the Jewish exhibition, overlooking your Lutheranism for the sake of the culturedness of your art."[55] That awareness is also evidenced by the fact that the reflexive anti-Semitism that her friends exhibited in their letters to each other was never voiced in their letters to Magda.

---

55 July 23, 1918, RGALI, f. 2080, op. 1, no. 7, 23–25op. Leonid Feinberg (1896–1979), artist, one of the organizers of the *Exhibition of Painting and Sculpture by Jewish Artists* (Moscow, 1918).

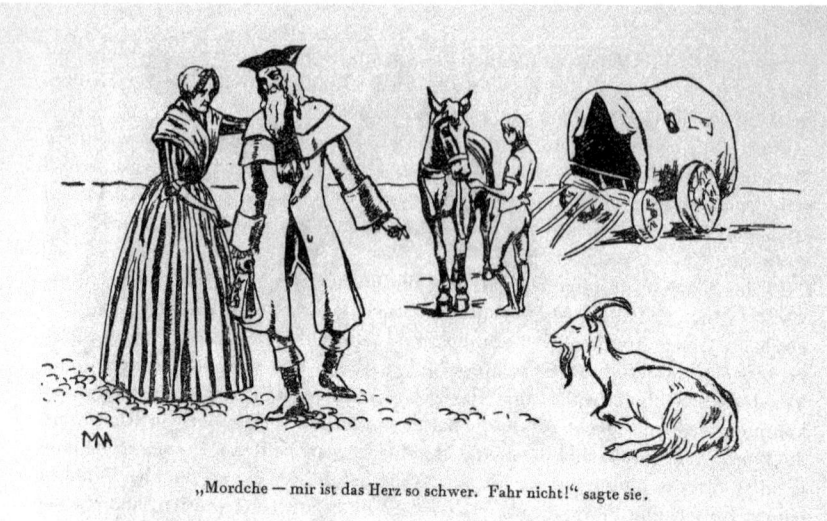

„Mordche — mir ist das Herz so schwer. Fahr nicht!" sagte sie.

Figure 37. Magda Nachman. Scene from the story "Aus den Tagen des Schinder-hannes."

Whatever the extent to which Magda may have considered herself Jewish, that part of her must have felt increasingly vulnerable as anti-Semitism in Germany became more and more overt toward the end of the 1920s. In anti-Semitic monarchist circles, the leading Russian-language newspaper *Rul'* was considered "Jewish." For even though such a prominent figure from the Russian nobility as Vladimir Dmitrievich Nabokov, the writer's father, was among its founders, its editorial board was predominantly Jewish. The son, Vladimir Vladimirovich, was referred to as a "half-Jew" because his wife was Jewish.[56]

With the rise of Nazism in Germany, such anti-Semitic utterances among the Russian emigration became more pronounced:

> By the spring of 1933 there were perhaps fifty thousand émigrés left in all of Germany, and only about ten thousand in Berlin. The dominant political element was extreme right, the dominant national element the Russian Germans. Few other émigrés could find in the Third Reich either a place of refuge or a center of culture in any way resembling that offered by Berlin ten years before.[57]

---

56 Oleg Budnitskii and Aleksandra Polian, *Russko–evreiskii Berlin, 1920–1941* (Moscow: NLO, 2013), 244.

57 Robert C. Williams, *Culture in Exile* (Ithaca: Cornell University Press, 1972), 285.

Acharya's situation had also become precarious. Before and during World War I, Germany had made use of Indian nationalists in its fight against the British. After the war, the relationship between Britain and Weimar Germany tended toward cooperation rather than hostility. One reason was that before the war, Indian trade had accounted for a substantial share of the German economy, and the Germans were eager to restore and expand their commercial relations with the subcontinent. For their part, the British expected the Germans to clamp down on anti-British propaganda by Indian nationalists, and they demanded that information regarding Indians in Berlin be shared. For a while, the Germans walked a thin line between mollifying the British and protecting their former Indian allies. (Thus, for example, Curt Prüfer was willing to help and protect Acharya in the early 1920s.) But increasingly, Indians were finding themselves unwanted and harassed. With the advent of the Nazis, the situation became dire:

> [Nazis were] in a special sense against the Indian national struggle for freedom. ... Hitler, in his capacity as the supreme Nazi leader, went out of his way to declare [in 1931] that the Indians' move for self-determination was an undesirable development, and he held the view that any weakening of British hold on India would be a calamity.[58]

Hitler's declaration on India appeared in both German and British newspapers. In December 1931, his private secretary, in his response to a protest letter from the Federation of Indian Chambers of Commerce and Industry, confirmed that "Herr Hitler remained convinced that it was in the interest of the civilized world to keep British rule over India intact."

Many of the Indian nationalists in Germany lacked legal documents and were wanted in India as political fugitives, thus making their departure from Germany nearly impossible. Moscow, on the other hand, offered a safe haven to those willing to promote the Communist ideology. Thus, for example, Acharya's old friend and colleague Chatto felt that he had no choice but to escape from Berlin to Moscow, where he eventually perished in Stalin's purges.[59]

For the Acharyas, returning to Russia was out of the question. And not only because Acharya's political views would not allow it. By that time, Magda might have learned the fate of her family back in Russia. Her niece, little Magda, whom she had tutored in the summer of 1908, had been arrested in 1924 as a

---

58 Barooah, *Chatto*, 283–284.
59 Ibid., 284.

German spy and sent to Solovki, one of the earliest and most formidable Soviet labor camps. Magda's sister Erna's family fled Likino, and their older son was arrested and sent to a labor camp, where he perished (in the 1940s, their second son suffered the same fate). The repressive policies of the Soviet government, its suspicion of anyone with foreign ties, and its establishment of labor camps for political prisoners had become general knowledge. Magda must have understood that there was no going back. But with the rise of Nazism, the Acharyas could not remain in Germany much longer either.

Fenner Brockway,[60] a former member of the British Parliament and chair of the Independent Labour Party, who was born in India and sympathized with the Indian nationalists, pleaded on behalf of Acharya and his wife with the British authorities. In letters of July and September 1931 to under-secretaries of state for foreign affairs, he wrote, "From [Acharya's] letters he appears to be a pacifist anarchist, quite harmless sort of person." And again: "I understand that he is a pacifist anarchist and wishes to go to India to preach integral co-operation."[61] Indeed, an India Office agent noted in Acharya's file that "he had given up all idea of violence, thinking that everything could be accomplished by the pen."[62] In his own statement to the British authorities in Berlin, Acharya wrote, "Since 1922, having seen the uselessness of politics and danger of agitators who want to [promote?] violence, I have become a convinced and logical pacifist."[63] Thanks to Brockway's support, Acharya was promised a passport in November 1931, but one that would be valid only for travel within Europe (except Soviet Russia). But for some reason, Acharya did not remit the fee, and the passport was never issued.

By 1934, the rate of growth of Acharya's fat dossier at the India Office had slowed. In their reports, British agents characterized Acharya as no longer a danger to the established order: "as an extremist [he] can be regarded as a spent force."[64] In a 1929 report, this phrase elicited doubt on the part of a reviewing officer of the India Office, who scribbled in the margin, "Will this remain true if he got back to India?" In 1933, the same phrase reappeared with absolute assurance: "he may certainly be regarded as a spent force."[65] The India Office's

---

60 Archibald Fenner Brockway (1888–1988) was a British politician, peace activist, chairman of the Independent Labour Party, member of Parliament (1929–1931), member of LAI, an outspoken supporter of Indian independence.

61 IOR, L/P&J/6/174/0064, 0058.

62 IOR, L/P&J/12/174/00116. Entry for July 1928.

63 IOR, L/E/7/1439/0084. Fall 1929.

64 IOR, L/P&J/12/174/0006.

65 Ibid., 0019.

interest in him dwindled, and the reporting became skimpy. The fear that if Acharya were granted permission to return to India he would shed his pacifistic sheep's clothing seems to have spent itself. Permission to return to India was not granted, but on January 10, 1934, on the basis of the 1931 approval of passports, Acharya and his wife received documents for travel within Europe.

That same month, the Acharyas left Germany for Switzerland, where they joined Magda's sister Adele in Zurich. There was little hope, however, that they would be able to reside permanently there. Switzerland's laws on immigration and the status of refugees were quite stringent, having been passed with the goal of minimizing the number of foreigners in the country. Even Adele—who had resided in Switzerland for decades—and her family were not secure in their residency. Adele's first husband, a Prussian national, had died in 1918. Adele then married a Swiss citizen, at least in part, according to family lore, to obtain permanent legal residency. Her three daughters from her first marriage retained their father's Prussian nationality, and despite their mother's Swiss residency were subject to deportation to Germany. One of them, Klara, married a Swiss citizen and, like her mother, secured Swiss residency. A second, Stella, obtained a counterfeit residency permit for Switzerland, but she then married an Englishman and moved to the United Kingdom. The third, the feeble-minded Irene, lived with her mother and was left alone by the authorities.

On February 18, 1934, Acharya wrote to his fellow anarchist Émile Armand, to whose newspaper *L'En-Dehors* he had frequently contributed, about the precariousness of their situation:

> I have to prepare for wandering life this year. I am living at my sister-in-law here who is also married to a Swiss. These are poor people and they offered roof for some weeks. They have at present no money at all. I had to take advantage of their offer as I had no income and was in danger of arrest perhaps. They had to borrow money to pay railway fare. It was luck I got British passport (for Europe only)—as otherwise I could not come here. It is not allowed to work here either and I can only remain as visitor for 2 months—till end of March.
>
> ... I am sure in a few months all mankind will be at the grave ... If nothing comes, I will have to go back to India to get into prison or gallows, for the Government does not give safe conduct.[66]

---

66 Archives Nationales, Paris, Institut Français d'Histoire Sociale, E. Armand papers. 14AS/211/1.

Back in 1926, when Acharya had begun his campaign for a British passport, he hoped that with proper documentation he would be able to legalize himself in Germany and be able to travel freely in Europe. He knew that in India he was subject to prosecution: a warrant for his arrest had been issued in 1909 and reissued in 1925, and it was up to the government of India to lift it, which for years they had adamantly refused to do. Now, with Hitler in power and an extended residency in Switzerland out of the question, the couple sought permission to travel to India.

In November 1933, still in Berlin, Acharya wrote to the British Consul General:

> As I intend to go to India, I wish to know the following, since this condition is made for going to India:
> 1) If there are any charges against me, whether they will be rescinded as they refer only to the past which I have broken with.
> 2) If an unconditional going to India is not permitted, what are the conditions under which I will be permitted.
> As I am seriously intending to go home as soon as possible, I shall be much obliged to your favouring me with an answer at your earliest convenience.[67]

His letter was forwarded to India on November 2, and on February 27, 1934, a letter from the British Consul in Berlin was sent to Acharya, which began:

> With reference to your recent application for a passport, I have to inform you that I am now authorized to endorse your passport as valid for India on your furnishing satisfactory evidence that you intend returning to that country. I am further instructed to say that the Government of India, while they are not prepared to grant you amnesty in respect of your past conduct, have decided that you would be left in peace in India unless you embarked on treasonable or seditious courses.[68]

Acharya might have received this letter with some delay, since it had been sent to his Berlin address when he was already in Zurich. But by May, the Acharyas

---

67 IOR, L/P&J/6/1968/0047.
68 Archives Nationales, Paris, Institut Français d'Histoire Sociale, E. Armand papers, 14AS/211/1.

had obtained tickets for the SS Victoria, which was to sail for Madras from Genoa on May 28. All that remained was to have their passports endorsed at the British consulate in Paris. They were expected in India on June 8.

On June 16, the following telegram from the government of India was received in England at the office of the secretary of state for India:

> Madras Government report person and wife not passengers on "Victoria." We would be glad to know by telegram present whereabouts of the individual as no information is available here.[69]

One senses some nervousness in the bureaucratese of this telegram. They would be held responsible if a well-known subversive had sneaked into the country undetected to resume his subversive activities.

The Acharyas were still in Europe. It is difficult to reconstruct precisely what happened. First of all, it seems that Magda's passport had not been endorsed in Paris, for on July 6, the British secretary of state for foreign affairs in London directed his office to inform "the secretary of state for India that in the absence of any decision by him regarding the grant of facilities to Mrs. Acharya no authority has been given for the endorsement of her passport for the journey to India."[70] A week later, on July 13, a letter from the Foreign Office in London to the General Consul in Paris requested that Mrs. Acharya's passport for India be endorsed, the Paris office replying that Mrs. Acharya's passport had in fact been endorsed on May 15 in accordance with the instructions received from Zurich on April 14 and was valid for travel to India. But if the passport had been endorsed, why did the Acharyas not continue on to Genoa? It seems likely that Magda's documents were not in order by the time they had to embark on their journey. The Acharyas returned to Zurich, as attested by an October 1934 memorandum from the British Foreign Office confirming their residence there. Sometime thereafter, Acharya arrived in India, alone, and an envelope survives dated April 2, 1935, addressed by Acharya in Bombay to Magda in Zurich.

Also from the period between Acharya's arrival in India and Magda's arrival there about a year later, there remain a couple of picture postcards and some photographs of Acharya in India. Two of the photographs are inscribed to Irene: "An meine liebe Irenle. Onkel Acharya. Bombay 13–9–35."[71]

69 IOR: L/P&J/6/1968/0014.
70 IOR, L/P&J/6/2419/0047.
71 Family archive.

Why did Acharya settle in Bombay and not in his hometown Madras, where his family still resided? Bombay would have been attractive as a cosmopolitan city, and returning to Madras would have been problematic, because at age 15, Acharya had been wed to a young girl in an arranged marriage.

Magda remained in Zurich at least until April 1936, a date that appears on a portrait of a lady that she left with her sister (figure 38). Also in that month,

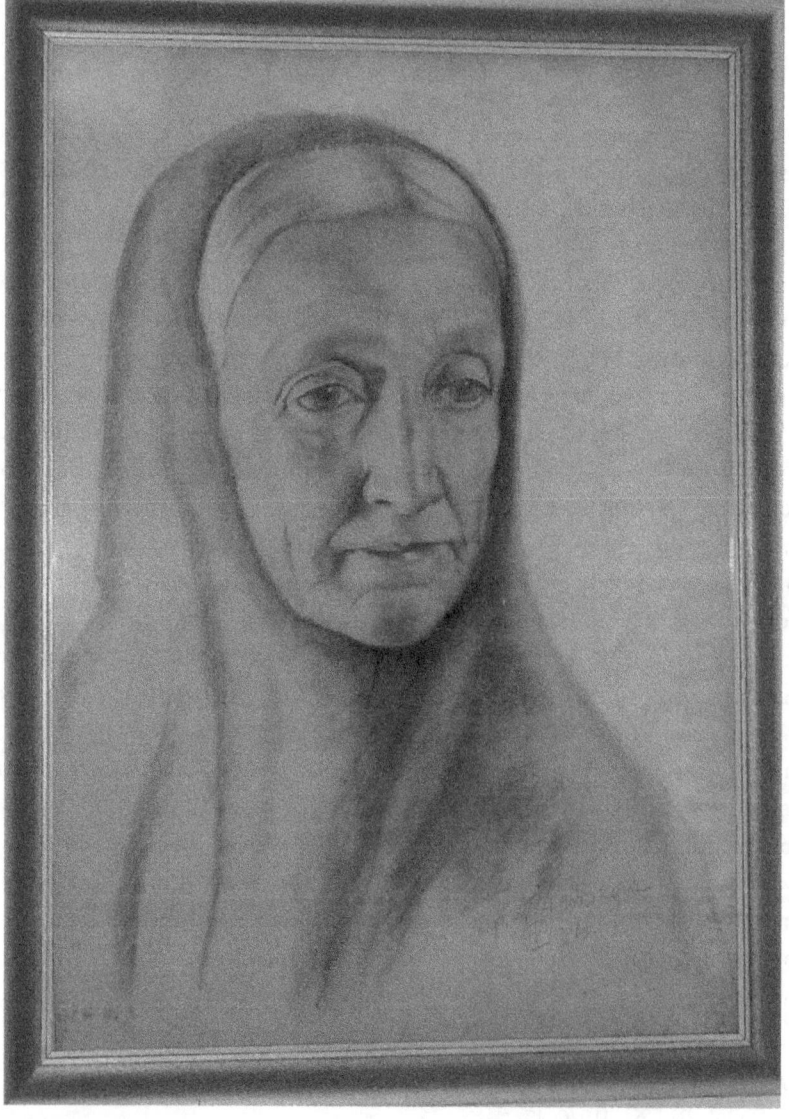

Figure 38. Magda Nachman. *Portrait of a Lady*, Switzerland, 1936.

Acharya posted a letter addressed to Magda in Zurich. She sailed to India sometime after that. Magda left her paintings with her sister Adele in Zurich, who
sold some of them and sent money to Magda in Bombay.

Other Russian émigrés were also fleeing Germany. A letter to Magda dated
December 16, 1937, confirms that by that date, the Nabokovs, too, had left Berlin and were living in the south of France.[72] The year 1937 was a trying period
for their marriage. Vladimir had been carrying on an affair with Irina Guadanini,
a Russian émigré whom he had met in January on a trip to Paris. The affair had
ended in September, and typically of the Nabokovs, there was not a hint in their
letter to Magda that their relationship had gone through a crisis.

Véra explained their long silence by stating that they had both wanted to
write, but "V. V. had been so terribly busy, and so we postponed a letter until a
free minute, which does not want to arrive." She told Magda about their difficult departure from Berlin, recounting step by step their progress toward Paris:
Vladimir's business trip to Paris in January, her and Anna Feigin's preparations
to leave Berlin, fighting for visas, traveling first to Prague and reuniting there
with Vladimir, and their journey to Menton, in the south of France. She wrote
about their son, Dmitri, and sent a photograph. She wrote that Vladimir had
been working harder than ever, cataloging in detail what he had written in the
last five months, including the number of pages. All of that was true, yet there
was not a hint of the turmoil precipitated by Vladimir's affair.

Years later, when her husband's biographer Brian Boyd showed Véra a copy
of her letter to Magda, she tore it to pieces, saying that she did not want to talk
about that time.[73]

The first part of the letter was written by Véra. Then Vladimir wrote that
he agreed with everything that Véra had written, and went on to write of being
glad to be out of Germany ("thrice damned Germany is far away") and about
his dental problems ("they extracted two teeth, and so I am staying home with
a crooked mouth"). He told Magda that in Paris he had met Dobuzhinsky, and
they had spoken about her. He also said that they would be "terribly happy" for
any news from her, and ended by saying that they had heard about her successes
(presumably from Anna Feigin or other mutual friends with whom Magda was
corresponding). In closing, he "kisses her little hand" and gives regards to her
husband.

---

72 The Nabokovs' letter to Magda is in the Berg collection, NYPL, Manuscript box,
    Nachman-Achariya, Magda, ALS to 1939(?), Dec. 16, 1 p, correspondence out.
73 Brian Boyd, private communication.

There are a few surviving letters from Adele to Magda, written in 1940 and 1941, that eventually found their way from India back to Magda's nieces in Europe (Adele died in Zurich in 1942), perhaps sent by Acharya after Magda's death. There is a sense of doom in them, for although safe in Switzerland, she was distraught at the destruction raging in places that had been dear to her. She lamented in particular about Finland, which was now under attack by the Soviet Union. Adele wrote to Magda on February 20, 1940, during the Winter War, which ended in Finland ceding territory to the Soviet Union:

> The fate of Finland also upsets me. We spent so many happy summer months there. You could say that our entire childhood passed there. No one comes to their aid, and alone, they will lose the war. I have a feeling that the whole world is about to disintegrate. What will remain?

And on July 22, 1941: "Magda, Magda, write what's going on with you. What is happening in Russia? In what times we have landed!"[74]

---

74 Family archive.

CHAPTER 13

Bombay

It seems Magda had left a difficult life in Russia for a difficult life in Europe. And now she was settling in for a difficult life in Bombay. The Bombay of Magda's time echoed her previous experiences in Russia, including the wartime shortages of painting materials, the all too familiar political rhetoric, and the enormous difficulty in making one's living by one's vocation. According to Hilde Holger, "Magda was poor her whole life and never earned enough to live on." As the historian Gyan Prakash writes about Bombay of that time:

> Intellectuals and artists were drawn to Bombay's pulsating modernity, but they also viewed it as deeply contradictory. If the city's promise of progress and freedom attracted them, they were also repelled by its depredations and injustices. ... By the 1930s, Bombay was a place to be if you were a writer, an artist, or a radical political activist. Already a preeminent center of commerce and industry, the Backbay Reclamation and the Improvement Trust's housing and transportation projects had imparted it the urban form of a metropolis by the early thirties.
>
> The elites heard swing and jazz sounds in clubs and restaurants and watched Hollywood films in the new Art Deco theaters. The world of workers in chawls and slums lay far away from the cosmopolitan glitter of the elites, but there too the winds of change were blowing. While the Congress activists mobilized the working-class neighborhoods for national agitations, the Communists organized the mill hands for militant industrial actions. Politically energized by anti-colonialism and Marxism, many middle-class intellectuals found stimulation in the modern metropolitan milieu of Bombay. Writers and artists from North India flocked to the city, seeking opportunities to practice their craft in newspapers, literary journals, and the growing film industry.[1]

---

1   G. Prakash, *Mumbai Fables* (Princeton: Princeton University Press, 2010), 128, 119.

In 1942, the critic Rudolf von Leyden expressed a similar opinion, writing, "Bombay appears to be an art minded city. One exhibition follows the other."[2]

Magda might well have felt that she had gone back in time to her student years in the St. Petersburg of the 1910s or to the Berlin of the 1920s. The political engagement and debates and the experimentation with "avant-garde" approaches to art in Bombay in the late 1930s and 1940s mirrored those that had taken place in St. Petersburg and Moscow earlier in the century. Also familiar to Magda would have been accusations hurled at contemporary Indian artists of having become epigones of the West, or the opposite— revivalists of ancient traditions that had lost their vitality in the modern world. The urgent question, "how to stay Indian and become modern," echoed the earlier question, "how to stay Russian and become modern." Both countries were "Oriental," as it were, experiencing an anxiety of influence, looking longingly at Western modernity and at the same time reinventing, and also inventing, their folk traditions as part of an expression of national identity. As Partha Mitter writes, "If sympathy for the poor was nothing new, the elite discovery of the peasant in the 1920s as the 'authentic' voice of the nation was altogether novel."[3]

Cities and their elites had become bastions of urban colonial civilization in India, just as cities had become Westernized in Russia. And it seemed that one should therefore look to the countryside to find a "pure" India untouched by colonial influence and a "pure" Russia untouched by Western influence. Mitter continues:

> It is the vision of primitivism as an alternative to Western "rationality" promised by non-Western thought that formed the crucial bridge between Western and Indian primitivists.[4]

Russians, too, looked to the countryside for the authenticity of the low-brow that could stand in opposition to bourgeois, middlebrow, values. They found it, or imagined it, in the folk life of the village. Thus Jamini Roy, in his primitivist paintings, and Sergei Diaghilev, in producing such ballets as *Les Noces* and *Le Sacre du Printemps*, had the same agenda: to stage a revolt against the bourgeois worldview through exaltation of the primitive. Magda may

---

2   *Times of India*, February 7, 1942.
3   Mitter, *The Triumph of Modernism*, 29.
4   Ibid., 34.

have arrived as a stranger in a strange land, but these questions about art and authenticity would have been familiar.

In the 1930s, when Magda was in Berlin, modernism in Europe fell victim to Nazism, which had relegated all of modernism to the category of degenerate art, and to Soviet Communism, which insisted on socialist realism as the only legitimate "method" of artistic expression. Yet at this time, the arts in India were experiencing the fervor of new discovery. New ideas were encouraging experimentation in India of the sort that Magda had witnessed first in Russia and then in Berlin.

In Russia, Magda had become an unwilling participant in the revolution and its aftermath, in which she witnessed the politicization of all the arts, with the theater in the vanguard. Russian society was trying out—or being forced into—new roles, while life, imitating art, had become histrionic. And now, twenty-five years later, the political left in India was promoting similar ideas about "people's theater." The following words, declaimed at the convention of the Indian People's Theater Association (IPTA), an organization formed under the aegis of the Indian Communist Party in Bombay in 1942, could have been—might well have been—cribbed from any number of Soviet revolutionary leaflets:

> IPTA recognizes the urgency of organizing a people's theater movement throughout the whole of India as a means of revitalizing the stage and the traditional arts and making them at once the expression and organizer of our people's struggle for freedom, cultural progress and economic justice. ... For the achievement of these aims it is necessary that not only the themes of our songs, ballads, plays etc. be suited to the purpose in view, but it is also essential that our production be simple and direct so that the masses can easily appreciate and understand and also participate in the creation and production of these.[5]

Just as happened in Russia after 1917, the theater in India was called upon to reeducate the masses and to mobilize them for struggle in the face of a political danger ("Fascist hordes and alien [i.e., British] bureaucracy") that threatened to take away all freedoms. In the words of the historian and art critic Geeta Kapur:

---

5   *IPTA Bulletin*, July 1943, in *Marxist Cultural Movements: Chronicles and Documents 1936-1947*, ed. Sudhi Pradhan (Calcutta: Santi Pradhan, 1977), 148 (quoted in Dalmia, *The Making of Modern Indian Art*, 40).

In the 1940s and 50s IPTA mediates folk traditions, especially in performances, to progressive, clear socialist ends. A narodnik style of politics is
played out in India as it is in other colonized cultures.[6]

These folk traditions are "mediated" by the middle and upper middle
classes in the name of the people. The same was true for literature. The Progressive Writers' Association had its first all-India meeting of writers in different
Indian languages in 1936. According to the art historian Yashodhara Dalmia,
"It resolved to look at literature as part of social reality and to struggle against
obscurantist tendencies." In the words of the writer Mulk Raj Anand, those
included "the almost indestructible superstructure of religion in anthropomor-
phic form, antiquated [i.e., feudal] customs and beliefs."

Both Magda and Acharya had heard and seen such manifestos before,
whose rhetoric was borrowed from European revolutionary artistic and political movements earlier in the century. And now the same tune was being
replayed in India, with the educated classes becoming the voice of the nation.

The leftist leanings of well-meaning literati and artists were accompanied
by a much cruder expression of support and admiration for Stalinism on the
pages of the *Times of India*, a widely circulated national newspaper, in which one
could find articles with titles such as "I Found Myself Seated Third from Stalin"
(a self-satisfied essay by Shaukat Usmani, Acharya's nemesis from the old days
in Moscow and Tashkent) and biographical sketches of Stalin and his cohort in
which their motives and actions were praised. How Magda and Acharya must
have blanched at the bald propaganda expressed in pictures of women manag-
ing impossibly heavy building materials with the caption "In Moscow Women
Build Houses," alongside a discussion of gender equality, when in fact, those
women were doing the work of the millions of men who had fallen in the war
and Stalin's purges. How might Magda and Acharya have reacted on reading
"Stalingrad—Scenario for an Epic," which appeared in the *Bombay Chronicle* on
June 22, 1947, the sixth anniversary of the Nazi invasion of the Soviet Union,
and portrayed Stalin towering over his general Vasilevsky as the genius master
strategist of the victory at Stalingrad? Yet another headline proclaimed that the
"Liberation of Asia Lies in Democracy and Socialism."

In the world of Indian modern art, the word "progressive" became a code
word for movement away from the artistic values that had been established under

---

6   Geeta Kapur, *When Was Modernism: Essays on Contemporary Cultural Practice in India* (New
     Delhi: Tulika Books, 2000), 272.

British rule through art education. In fact, the Progressive Artists' Group forged an alliance with the Communist Party and had its first meetings at the Friends of the Soviet Union office in Bombay. The Progressive Artists' Group's Communist connections were short-lived, however, and Magda lived to see the disillusion that appeared as early as 1948, when in the group's exhibition catalogue, the artist Francis Newton Souza stated that art should not serve any ideology. Nevertheless, the general aspiration of the newly independent India was toward Soviet-style socialism, which for Magda and for her husband was "déjà vu all over again."

One day, I was in the studio of Gieve Patel (in Magda's old neighborhood, off Walkeshwar road). Gieve had practiced medicine for thirty-five years, while also painting, exhibiting, and writing poetry and plays. He appeared modest, quiet, and sharp, and he exuded gentleness and compassion. He looked like an Eastern European, a bit like Václav Havel, in baggy pants and an open-collar shirt. And he also demonstrated a knowledge of Russian literature.

While talking about Magda and showing copies of her paintings to Gieve, I lamented her lonely, difficult, perhaps even tragic life, to which Gieve replied, "Well, she had met Acharya and they were together to the end. Whatever else happened, isn't that good luck?" I suppose it was. The way I had looked at it, there was Magda, wholly devoted to her art, and then there was Acharya, preoccupied with his utopian ideals and political writing—like the components of a binary star, each in the other's orbit but light years apart. But now I called to mind Magda's portrait of her husband in a pose of oriental serenity and meditation. There was so much warmth in it. I thought about what Acharya had written after Magda's death and his letters to her sister in Switzerland; how ardently he had wished to mount an exhibition of Magda's paintings in London so that she would not be forgotten. Acharya wrote to a friend:

> I want to keep this house as Magda's memorial gallery. ... I want to keep alive [unclear] exhibitions and publicity which were difficult to make when she was alive. Thanks to her, people are now more friendly to me than before. I am trying to finish my autobiography [unclear] perfect or not as Magda wished me to do so. [unclear] it will be a record.[7]

Typically, as Acharya's biographers remark with regret and puzzlement, after his arrival in Berlin from Moscow, he distanced himself from the active fight

---

7   C. S. Subramanyam, *M. P. T. Acharya: His Life and Times* (Madras: Institute of South Indian Studies, 1995), 146.

for Indian liberation. At that point, they either lose interest in his political involvement or lose sight of him altogether, becoming confused even about the year of his return to India and the year of his death. Thus, C. S. Subramanyam, Acharya's biographer, notes with puzzlement and disappointment:

> His participation in and contribution to the struggle for freedom in this period has been surprisingly very little. He was in Germany till the beginning of 1935 and for another 19 years in India.[8] … His life ended in 1954 but his political activities, which had any relevance to the freedom movement, would seem to have ceased years before.[9]

The fact is that Acharya remained politically engaged until the very end of his life. A tireless agitator in the international anarchist movement for almost thirty years, in India he became a lonely fighter for ideals that went beyond Indian liberation and addressed forms of self-governance, rather than the formalities of government, that might bring lasting change to all human communities.[10] In a fitting testimony to Acharya, a fellow anarchist wrote in his obituary that

> it was impossible to comprehend the difficulty in standing out against the tide so completely as was necessary in a country like India. It was easy for former "nationalist revolutionaries" to assert their claims to the positions left vacant by the old "imperialist oppressors." This Acharya would not do. He remained an uncompromising rebel, and when age prevented him from speaking, he continued writing right up to the time of his death.[11]

In India, Acharya continued the work he had begun in the mid-1920s as a dedicated anarchist. Although at times he called himself an anarcho-communist, his experience in Soviet Russia had made him a dedicated follower of Bakunin—and Proudhon, for that matter—who considered that "socialism without liberty would be the worst form of slavery."[12] On that, he and Magda

---

8   Ibid., 16.

9   Ibid., 13.

10   For a collection of Acharya's writings, see M. P. T. Acharya, *We Are Anarchists: Essays on Anarchism, Pacifism, and the Indian Independence Movement, 1923–1953*, edited by Ole Birk Laursen (San Francisco: AK Press, 1996).

11   Internationalist (pseudonym of Albert Meltzer), "M. P T. Acharya," *Freedom*, August 14, 1954, 3.

12   A warning from both Proudhon and Bakunin as quoted in Paul Avrich, *Anarchist Portraits* (New Jersey: Princeton University Press, 1988), 238.

were in agreement: when they decided to leave Russia, both had witnessed a terrorized country turning to tyranny. As the historian Paul Avrich writes, characterizing anarchists as a group:

> Examining the careers of anarchists, both well known and obscure, one is struck above all by their passionate hatred of injustice, of tyranny in all its forms, and by the perceptiveness of their warnings against the dangers of concentrated power, economic and political alike. They were among the earliest and most consistent opponents of totalitarianism, both on the left and on the right, marked by the growth of a police state, the subjugation of the individual, the dehumanization of labor, and the debasement of language and culture—in short, by what Herbert Spencer described a century ago as "The Coming Slavery."[13]

Avrich also remarks that all the anarchists whom he studied "led interesting lives and were endowed with remarkable human qualities." Avrich mentions Acharya in connection with other "comrades-in-arms" during his work in America, and Avrich's assessment of the anarchists as a group applies to Acharya in full measure. Acharya's life was indeed interesting, filled with risk, privation, and political fervor. He brought his convictions with him to Bombay and was active there in their propagation.

In Mumbai, Acharya is frequently labeled with the epithet "Communist." The Indian historian Indira Chowdhury even went so far as to brand Magda a Communist as well: "Nachman, a communist, was an Indian citizen by marriage and had spent more than two decades in India."[14] Wrong on two counts. In 1947, the year about which Chowdhury is writing, Magda had been in India for only eleven years. And a Communist? Poor Magda! She would have been horrified! With her highly developed religious feeling and leanings toward anthroposophy, she had seen what the Soviets had done to her country, her friends, and her family and did not mince words in writing about them in her Russian letters. True, Acharya had been an ambivalent founding member of the Indian Communist Party, in Tashkent, in 1920. However, he had ideological and moral differences with his comrades and

---

13 Ibid.
14 Indira Chowdhury, "The Laboratory and Its Double: The Making of the Scientist-Citizen at TIFR," Center for the Advanced Study of India, University of Pennsylvania, Casi Working Paper Series, Number 12–01 06/2012.

very quickly dissociated himself from them. The label "Communist" simply doesn't apply.

Of course, during World War II, the majority of the free-thinking world was on the side of the allies, and thus on the side of Stalin and against Hitler (although India was so far away from the Nazi atrocities that fascism gained ground with some Indian reformers; even Gandhi made a nod in that direction, and Subhash Chandra Bose, an important Indian nationalist, became an open fascist sympathizer). The choice between Stalin and Hitler was a choice between two evils (both of which Magda and Acharya had experienced at first hand). Why India turned to the Soviet Union and not to the West in the postwar years is a complicated question.

India remained, nonetheless, a part of the free world, and the same newspapers and journals that carried articles about the Soviet Union published Acharya as well. He also published a short autobiography that covered the years of his initiation into the fight for national liberation. Furthermore, in 1945, Acharya obtained a position at the Institute of Indian Sociology, becoming its secretary. Libertarian tendencies within the institute were strengthened by his influence, which was seen in its statutes of 1947 and in the decision to change its name to the Libertarian Socialist Institute. That position gave Acharya a free hand in promoting his views, albeit in a narrow arena. He maintained connections with the Industrial Workers of the World (IWW), receiving their publications for dissemination, namely from the IWW activist Nicolaas Steelink,[15] and published his writings abroad in various anarchist publications (such as *Tierra y Libertad*, in Mexico, and *Contre Courant* and E. D. Armand's papers *L'Anarchie* and *L'EnDehors*, in Paris). In the mid-1940s, Acharya and fellow anarchist Albert Meltzer (in London) ran an international committee for political prisoners in Asian countries. That project was discontinued after Acharya's death, for as Meltzer noted, Acharya had been the engine behind it.

Acharya's writing clearly delineates the political conviction with which he returned to India and that he held till his death. In his autobiography, *Reminiscences of an Indian Revolutionary*, written at Magda's suggestion,

---

15 Nicolaas Steelink (1890–1989), a Dutch-American labor activist and a member of the Industrial Workers of the World (IWW). In his letter to Steelink of March 1948, Acharya acknowledges receiving bundles of IWW publications and outlines his plan for their dissemination. Although the letter contains a business discussion, it is also personal. Acharya writes about his deteriorating health and his need to go to a sanatorium to cure his tuberculosis (Nicolaas Steelink Collection, chief correspondence from 1922 to 1953, Newberry Library, Chicago).

Acharya made light of his revolutionary activities from 1907 to 1912 (at which point, unfortunately, the autobiography ends). With humor, irony, and self-detachment, he describes the escapades of a young Indian boy who had come to Europe with an ardent heart and a muddle of ideas in his head. Later, his Russian experience—including the unethical behavior of his Indian comrades, his work with the Communist International in Central Asia, the fate of the Moscow intelligentsia under the Soviets, all of which he witnessed, and his work for the journal of the Russian People's Commissariat of Foreign Affairs—cured him of any desire to foment revolution or any other militant action.

In Bombay, he worked to propagate the ideas of libertarian socialism, the only system, in his view, that could lead to the abolition of the state and the emergence of true socialism. In his brochure *How Long Can Capitalism Survive?* (published by the Free Society Group of Chicago in 1951), Acharya insisted that the Soviet version of socialism was indeed state capitalism with a sugar-coating of insincere promises of freedom. Writing in the *Times of India,* he calls Bolshevism a dictatorship while criticizing all current democracies:

> Democracy as understood by politically minded people is a mixture of
> Fascism and Bolshevism—a veil for both. Being a mixture, it cannot be
> stable but must disintegrate into its component elements. Even if Bolshe-
> vism is destroyed in Russia, the Bolshevist menace will continue.[16]

His ideas of social organization led him to envision free workers' associations that would abolish wages and come together freely as a federation of equal members that would not create any controlling body or hierarchy. It was to that end that he was working in the Libertarian Socialist Institute in Bombay.

Magda's devotion to Acharya and her support for him had been noted even in the official correspondence of the British Intelligence Service, but it is not clear to what extent Magda shared her husband's political views, or even the extent to which they interested her. While there is no written record of Magda's political views (other than her revulsion at the new Soviet reality, as expressed in her correspondence with Julia Obolenskaya), there is an artistic record, the work itself, in which Magda's viewpoint shines forth as essentially apolitical. This is what Lama Anagarika Govinda, who will be introduced more fully in a later chapter, had to say about Magda's work:

---

16 M. P. T. Acharya, "McCarthyism," *Times of India,* July 4, 1953, 6.

Her love and understanding for the poor has thus two sources: the one is based on her ideal of simplicity and sympathy; the other on the fact that she herself has shared their sorrows and tribulations more than once in her life. If, therefore, she feels for the poor, it is without the condescension of the sophisticated or the shocked outcry of social reformers, who see poverty only in terms of dirt, crime and ugliness. She is not concerned with social problems but with individuals, and what she discovers is much more important than the squalid sights of slums: it is the dignity of man, even in the poorest, the heroism of endurance, the cheerfulness as well as the silent tragedy of a bravely accepted fate. The understanding of these human values in the poor is certainly more important than the well-meant creation of mass movements in which the individual is nothing—or the sentimental outbursts of compassion which move people to easy tears but not to action.[17]

---

17 *Aesthetics* 5, no. 1 (January–March 1951): 9.

CHAPTER 14

A Case of Identity

When I met the artist Akbar Padamsee in Bombay, as I mentioned in an earlier chapter, he described Magda at the moment of her bitter outrage on her work being rejected for inclusion in an international exhibition in England. Mr. Padamsee recalled the rejection as being from the Bombay Art Society. He also remarked that Magda had exhibited with that society. And so she did, beginning shortly after her arrival in India and continuing for the rest of her life. Her pictures appear in each of the society's catalogues of that time. In 1940, she won an important prize from the society for her painting *Red Shawl*. She also had regular solo exhibitions at the society's salon and at the Institute of Foreign Languages, and also one at the Chetana gallery in 1947. Reviews of these shows can be found in the *Times of India*, in the art quarterly *MARG*, and in the *Bombay Chronicle*. Magda had become an accepted and respected painter in Bombay. But it was not the Bombay Art Society that had rejected Magda, as Mr. Padamsee had recalled so insistently when he first shared with me his recollection of the indignant Magda as she shouted, "Who are they to reject me? What do they know about art? They rejected my work!" It was the selection committee for an international exhibition in London. The archive of Bombay's Tata Institute of Fundamental Research houses documents related to the decision not to include Magda's paintings in that exhibition. The institute stands at the edge of the Indian Ocean, in the Colaba area of Mumbai, on a street named after its founder, the famous Indian physicist Homi Bhabha (1909–1966). Homi Bhabha was also an accomplished amateur artist and a discerning collector. In eulogizing him, his younger brother Jamshed wrote:

> For Homi Bhabha, the arts were not just a form of recreation or pleasant relaxation; they were among the most serious pursuits of life, and he attached just as much importance to them as to his work in mathematics and physics. For him, the arts were, in his own words, "what made life worth living."

Jamshed noted that for his brother, those

> who had the insight and judgment to recognize the seeds of greatness in
> others, long before the world found evidence of it, and to help and stimu-
> late the latent genius to flower, were creative geniuses in their own right.[1]

And Dr. Bhabha acted accordingly. His collection of works by members of
the Bombay Progressive Artists' Group, and those of other twentieth-century
artists, adorns the walls of the spacious vestibule of the institute. There is a large
mural by M. F. Husain in the mezzanine.

The Tata Institute archives contain the correspondence between Homi
Bhabha, Magda, and Acharya that detailed the story of Magda's rejection. In
1947, Magda had applied to be included in the *Exhibition of Art Chiefly from
the Dominions of India and Pakistan, 2400 B.C. to 1947 A.D.*, which was to be
mounted at the Royal Academy of Arts at Burlington House, in London, in
the winter of 1947–1948. The selection committee rejected her application on
the grounds of her European roots, education, and ethnicity. In other words,
although an Indian national living and working in India, she was not sufficiently
Indian.

That Magda was enraged by her rejection, as witnessed by Mr. Padamsee—
"She was standing there … terrible"—is not surprising. How many times had
she been uprooted? How often had she been on the run? How many times had
she experienced a sense of homelessness? And now, after all that sorrow, having
finally established herself in far-off India, with an Indian husband, as an Indian
artist, to be told that here, too, she was a stranger, an outcast.

Acharya wrote to the art collector Kekoo Gandhy, asking him to inter-
vene on Magda's behalf. Mr. Gandhy suggested to Acharya that he write to
Homi Bhabha, who was a member of the selection committee for the London
exhibition.

Acharya's letter, which is now in the Tata Institute's archive, provoked a
series of letters by Homi Bhabha. He wrote in defense of Magda to the prominent cultural figure, poet, and politician Sarojini Naidu, who stood at the head
of the all-Indian committee for the London exhibition, and to Maulana Azad,
the minister of education. Homi Bhabha saw the case of Magda Nachman
Acharya as an important touchstone for working out the principles that should

---

1 Jamshed Bhabha, ed., *Homi Bhabha as Artist: A Selection of His Paintings, Drawings and
Sketches* (Bombay: Marg Publication, 1968).

underlie Indian law for future approaches to such "cases." At stake was the very definition of the notion of an "Indian artist" and hence the very notion of who is Indian. How far removed from Europe had one to be in order to represent India? After all, Bhabha wrote, "half a dozen of the pictures chosen by the committee are painted in purely European style, and practically all the others show the unmistakable influence of European art."

As a member of the tiny ethnic minority of Parsis, Homi Bhabha well understood Magda's predicament and the predicament of his country. Furthermore, Bhabha was living in his native Bombay quite by chance. In the summer vacation of 1939, he had returned home from the Cavendish Laboratory at the University of Cambridge, where he had been conducting research in atomic physics. The outbreak of war in Europe that September kept him in India, where he eventually decided to remain. And so instead of becoming a British scientist of Indian extraction, Bhabha became the father of the Indian nuclear program.

India would have to decide where its artists, many of whom spanned two civilizations, belonged. This public and private dilemma is vividly exemplified in the life and art of the eminent Indian artist Amrita Sher-Gil, herself of mixed parentage and cultures. In her painting *Two Girls*, Sher-Gil portrayed her divided heritage and "double" identity: a dark-skinned girl with brown eyes is sitting next to a standing light-skinned girl with blue eyes whose arm embraces the dark girl's shoulder, yet their bodies are separated by a white cloth. Does this dual portrait address the artist's feelings about herself (Who am I? Where do I belong?) or the public perception of her?

The predicament of Magda Nachman Acharya is similar to that of Sher-Gil. Magda does not seem to fit comfortably anywhere. In her notes, Hilde Holger wrote that

> the European community did not give much support [to Magda] because she was married to an Indian and for the Indians her art was too westernized; but in my opinion she was the artist with the deepest understanding for the suffering of the Indian people.

In his 1947–1948 laudatory essay "Magda Nachman: A Russian Interpreter of India," Hermann Goetz, curator of the Baroda Museum and Picture Gallery and member of the executive committee for the 1947 London exhibition, made the case for Nachman, comparing her to foreigners in other nations who eventually became the pride of those nations. He wrote:

Magda Nachman is one of the best Bombay artists, highly esteemed by a small circle of art connoisseurs, critics and cultured people, but badly neglected by the average art public. She has been awarded many distinctions. Amongst her portrait-sitters are some of the most prominent people. Her pictures can be seen in several Indian embassies. But her name is only occasionally heard in the bustle of official art life and publicity. She has often enough been treated as an outsider by those trying to ride on the crest of a rising nationalism. She, who has to support an invalid veteran of the national movement, was pushed aside in the name of Indian nationalism. ... She has not bowed before any of those fashions which official art tends to favor and which in later generations arouse such a nausea of stale meretriciousness. She simply tries to be honest to herself, to her themes, to her art. And for this reason her art shows such a thorough understanding for the Indian soul. [Nachman] is an artist between two civilizations, an outsider in search of the Indian soul. She is quiet, humble, understanding.

Magda Nachman's is a mature art, far from the noise and bustle of the market, an art of silence, of the soul, Russian in its tradition, international in its qualities, Indian in its deep and warm understanding.[2]

In her letter to Homi Bhabha, Magda wrote:

I think that being married to an Indian for 25 years and going with him through all the sufferings, privations and dangers of exile and besides being an Indian national does entitle me to take part in an exhibition of Indian artists. Moreover, India is not a racial unit. So in the end, the prejudice against me is chiefly a color prejudice, and it is difficult to understand how people who have suffered from the color bar can apply it to others. It is inferiority feeling with utter want of imagination that leads to this result.—It is the power of mental inertia against which it is impossible to fight for an isolated human being. Only the awakening of the right kind of pride can improve matters.

The more grateful I am to you and Mrs. Thiroja Wadia for having the courage to stand up against the prejudice of the great majority and to fight out of idealism even a losing battle.[3]

---

2   Hermann Goetz, "Magda Nachman: A Russian Interpreter of India," *Bulletin of the Baroda Museum and Picture Gallery* 5 (1947–1948): 78–83.

3   Archive of the Tata Institute for Fundamental Research, ref. no. 271.

Not many Indians know that the following oft-quoted words of Homi Bhabha, which adorn art galleries and shine out as epigraphs in writing on modern Indian art, come from his letter to the minister of education, Maulana Azad, in defense of Magda Nachman Acharya:

> We all hope that with its newly achieved freedom, India will become the leading country of Asia and one of the leaders in cultural matters, and it can achieve this in the artistic sphere not by a mere repetition of its ancient forms but by the creation of new art forms, possibly through synthesis of the ancient Indian and European traditions in art.[4]

It wasn't just Magda. The modern art section of the exhibition could have cast a much broader net. A commemorative catalogue of the exhibition *The Art of India and Pakistan*, edited by Sir Leigh Ashton, consists of three sections—on sculpture, on bronzes and textiles, and on painting—each introduced by an opening essay. The introduction to the painting section is written by Basil Gray, who begins his wonderfully detailed and scholarly essay thus:

> In the following pages I tried to sum up the present state of knowledge of Indian painting during the centuries covered at the exhibition, that is from the eleventh onward.[5]

The last phrase of his essay sums up his view of Indian painting: "After 1820, there is a slow but steady decline."[6] Not a word on later developments (aside from a short piece on British artists in India by Graham Reynolds). The catalogue's long bibliography carries but a single reference to a modern Indian painter, an article by John Irwin on Jamini Roy (1944).

Modern Indian artists faced serious obstacles in obtaining recognition among their contemporaries at home and abroad. Indeed, as the following anecdote about the supporter and collector of modern Indian art Emmanuel Schlesinger, reported by Yashodhara Dalmia, shows, the view of what should be considered art that was genuinely Indian could be quite narrow:

---

4   Ibid., ref. no. 40.
5   Basil Gray, "Introduction to Paintings," in *The Art of India and Pakistan*, ed. Leigh Ashton (New York: Coward-McCann Inc., 1947), 86.
6   Ibid., 103.

Schlesinger married his Goanese housekeeper and lived in India till he died in 1963. Before his death he had offered to donate his large collection of paintings, some of them priceless today, to the Prince of Wales Museum. The offer, however, was rejected by the Museum authorities who felt that modern art was imitative and hence could not be considered part of the national heritage.[7]

Like all true artists, Magda continued to paint despite her disappointment, exhibiting widely in Bombay, as is well documented in the newspapers, catalogues, and posters of the time. Magda was not on the cutting edge of Indian art. She painted from models, recording their attire and poses; she arranged objects for still lifes and painted particular landscapes. Yet she was no academic painter. She was conservative, yet modern. Her models are set against flattened surfaces with stylized patterns and splashes of color. Magda was a superb draftsman. I want to think that here was the main connection between her and the young experimenting Bombay artists: she was attentive to their art and provided them with models of expert drawing.

She also had become popular as a portrait painter and had commissions from many elite Bombay families. The majority of the paintings I was able to find in Mumbai were such commissions. A versatile artist, she worked in oil, watercolor, pastels, gouache, pencil, and charcoal. Reviews remarked on her exceptional draftsmanship, on her subject matter—which for the most part was concerned with the Indian poor, the Indian natural world, and Indian classical dance—and on her extraordinary attention to her models' eyes, which expressed her sitters' innermost depths.

One of Magda's most important exhibitions was mounted in 1947, right around the time of her rejection by the London Exhibition Committee, in one of the most sophisticated cultural spaces in Bombay of the late 1940s—Chetana, which combined a restaurant, a bookstore stocked with books on philosophy in English and Hindi, a chess club, a display of Indian handicrafts, a space for a school for Indian classical dance (Bharatanatyam), and exhibition space for Bombay artists. It also published a small leaflet in which the various cultural topics featured at Chetana were discussed. This was the eve of independence, and the country was busy forging a new national identity (Magda's rejection by the committee was one of the signs of this painful process). The concept of Indian cultural revival and its implications for Chetana (which means "awakening") was due

---

7   Dalmia, *The Making of Modern Indian Art*, 64.

to Sudhakar Dikshit. In 1946, he purchased a shuttered restaurant in Rampart Row, in the city's cultural center, and it immediately became a meeting place for many prominent figures of the day, among them the writer Mulk Raj Anand, the poet Nissim Ezekiel, the anthropologist Evelyn Wood, and the writer Raja Rao. Chetana opened its doors for public discussions by Indian and European experts on such topics as "Philosophy and Science," "Psychoanalysis as an Introduction to Religious Experience," and "The Concept of Karma." At the same time, a chess club was actively recruiting members: "The game of chess is an ancient Indian game and it is because of this that Chetana is happy to encourage the club in its activities," wrote Homee Cooper in the Chetana leaflet. The Chetana restaurant professed a scientific approach to diet, at the same time boasting as its main attraction an atmosphere of art and intelligence that surrounds the diner:

> There are pictures on the walls, and the pictures are changed constantly with the various exhibitions—the books on one side, which make for intelligent and colorful associations—and the tapestries, which bring in a sense of intimacy and seriousness. When we have music or dancing or discussions, the Restaurant only goes into the background to emerge again into very friendly activity.[8]

There was no paucity of fine artists in Bombay. However, exhibition spaces were exceedingly limited in those years, and Chetana began showing contemporary Indian art. The first to exhibit there, in 1946, was K. H. Ara. Magda had a show at the end of that season, which opened on February 20, 1947. She exhibited fifty paintings, among them single and group portraits, still lifes, and landscapes in oil, gouache, and watercolor. The poster for Magda's show depicted one of several portraits by her of the famous dancer Shrimati Shanta Rao performing Bharatanatyam classical dance, a fitting subject for Chetana.

In opening the exhibition "before a distinguished gathering," Mr. Justice Chagla praised the art of Magda Nachman, saying, "The impressions of modern India conveyed through her paintings would be of very great significance for artists in this country."[9] The artist—he added—had a great part to play in the present period of transformation through which India was passing.

---

8   Homee Cooper, *The Chetana Leaflet*, undated, no pagination.
9   "City Art Exhibition," *Times of India*, February 21, 1947, 7. Mohammadali Carim Chagla was an Indian jurist, diplomat, and cabinet minister who served as chief justice of the Bombay High Court from 1947 to 1958.

How ironic! Mr. Chagla, unlike the members of the London Exhibition Committee who had rejected her, based his appreciation of Magda's art solely on what he saw in front of him on the walls of Chetana, and not on the provenance of the artist.

In the words of the Bombay arbiter of artistic taste, the preeminent art critic Rudi von Leyden, who wrote for the *Times of India* and who reviewed the show:

> To see the works of Mrs. Magda Nachman is always enjoyable because her drawing is pure, precise, and expressive. Her line gives contour and understates the plastic form it describes. Mrs. Nachman's portraits are fascinating in their idealized detachment. Her paintings of Indian men and women, single and in groups, share this dreamlike remoteness emphasized by their over-naturally large dark eyes. "Peasants" [figure 39] is a large composition in oil that appeals by its dignity and depth of sympathy.[10]

In the same review, von Leyden singles out the colored drawings "of a well known Indian woman dancer."

Rudolf von Leyden was not the only Bombay art critic who praised Magda's drawings. Another was R. Chatterji, who wrote in the *Bharat Jyoti* about Magda—"a well-known personality in the art-circles of Bombay":

> After all her wanderings, she chose India as her home. She has been living in this country for a number of years and therefore has been able to get a true insight into Indian character. Her portrayals of the poor and the destitute in so many of her compositions reflect her genuine social sympathies apart from her intrinsic interest in them as suitable subjects of artistic treatment.[11]

Hermann Goetz valued Magda's art highly:

> Like Amrit Sher-Gil she is not a painter of dreams, but a portraitist, an interpreter of things and of people observed. Like Sher-Gil she tries to penetrate to the heart and soul of her subjects. And yet her art is very different. It has not the high tension, the tragedy under a mask of arrogance of Sher-Gil's life and art. She is quiet, humble, understanding. She has not

---

10   "Mrs. Nachman's Paintings," *Times of India*, February 21, 1947, 7.
11   R. Chatterji, "The Art of Magda Nachman," *Bharat Jyoti*, February 23, 1947.

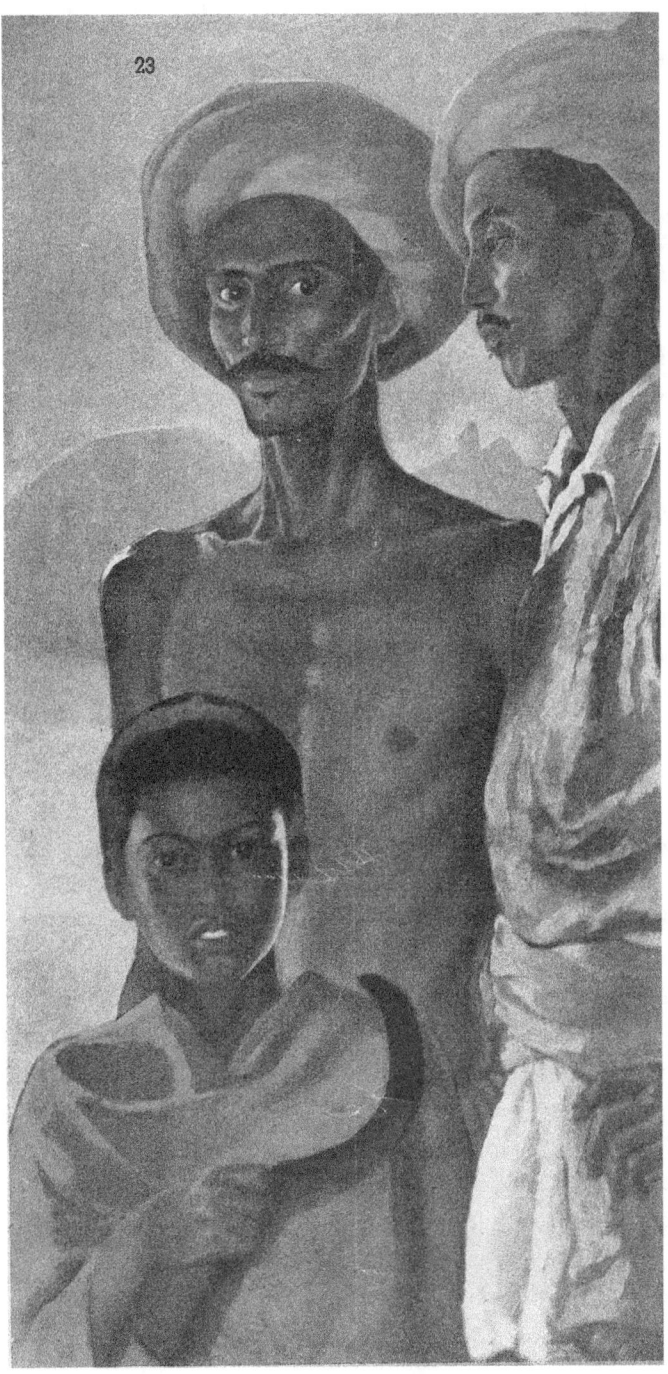

Figure 39. Magda Nachman. *Peasants*, 1946.

the sophisticated glorious colors nor the decorative self-display of Sher-Gil. Like Léon Bakst—who, however, was also a revolutionary colorist—she is first a draughtsman, an excellent draughtsman.

Her figures of villagers, artisans, beggars, dancers, etc. evoke, like those of Sher-Gil, quite a world of social atmosphere, of life experience, of the life of the soul, just through some slight, but intimately observed gesture, some almost imperceptible line of the face, a bending of the neck or of a hand, some other gesture or expression, some look, such as life shapes without our ever being conscious of it, so intimately caught that it is never toned down to the average standard of our social conventions nor exaggerated to the "picturesque," but just such that it speaks for all the throbbing life behind it.[12]

Squatting Boy is a superb example of Magda's art of drawing (figure 40). The artist's hand seems never to have left the paper before completing the unbroken curved line from the top of the boy's forehead to his foot. We see the same technique in the outline of Hilde Holger's dancing figure (figure 41), only here instead of transmitting repose, the line is moving in space. As Magda's teacher Bakst told his students:

Look how the Japanese do it. Handle your charcoal in such a way that it moves along the whole length of your line in one movement, so it does not consist of pieces pasted together. To make the line pour forth, draw it out in one strong motion.[13]

That is exactly what Magda does in these drawings.

Many of Magda's shows were reviewed in the Bombay newspapers. An art critic for the *Jewish Advocate,* a Miss H. Kohn, wrote in 1947 after attending Magda's show:

When we visit an exhibition of Magda Nachman's works, we are free to wander around and enjoy the beauty of what we see without having to worry our heads about whether the pictures are "modernist," "impressionist" or anything else ending in "ism." Magda Nachman, when asked about her tendency or her aim in art, replies simply that she has neither the one

12 Goetz, "Magda Nachman," 78–83.
13 P. V. Andreev, "My Recollections of Bakst," in Pruzhan, *Lev Samoilovich Bakst,* 92.

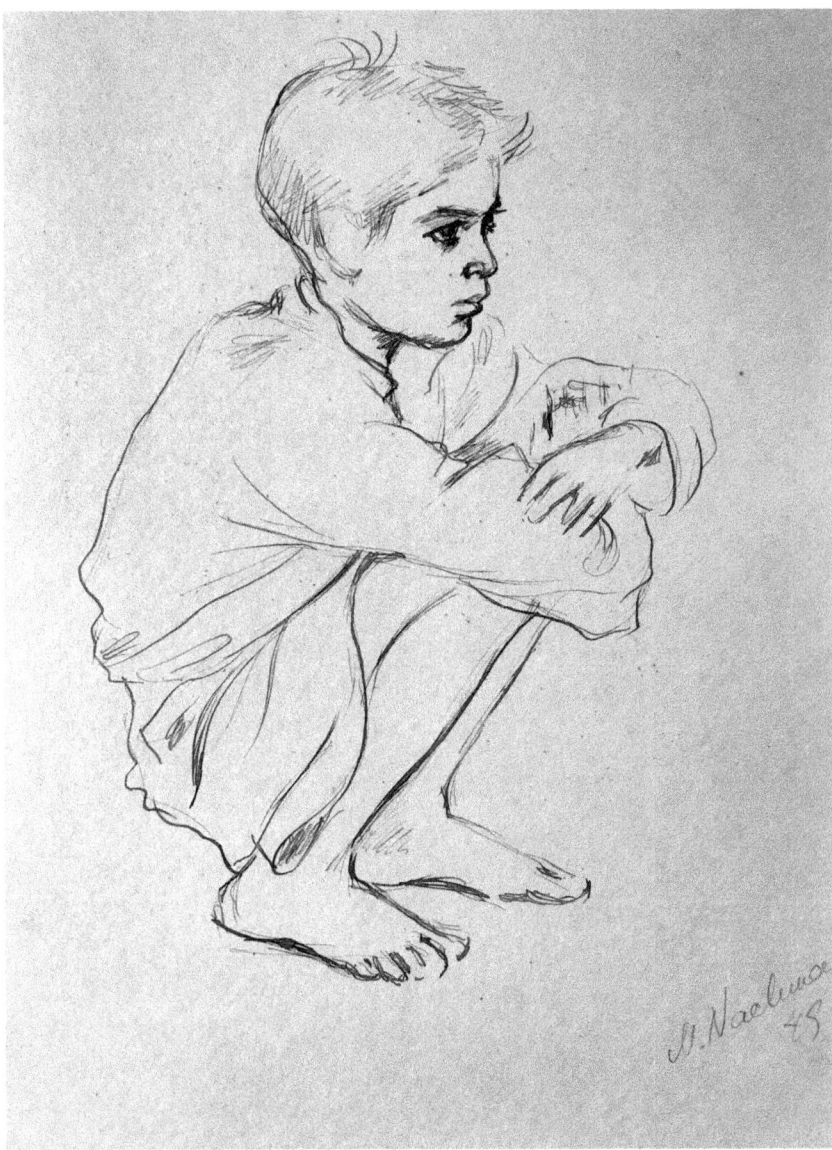

Figure 40. Magda Nachman. *Squatting Boy*, 1949 (*courtesy of John Burns*).

nor the other. She just paints what she sees and she goes on painting. When we see a portrait painted by Magda, we feel that she sees through the person painted and reveals his or her soul.[14]

---

14   H. Kohn, quoted in Magda Nachman's obituary in *Aesthetics* 5, no. 1 (January–March 1951): 14.

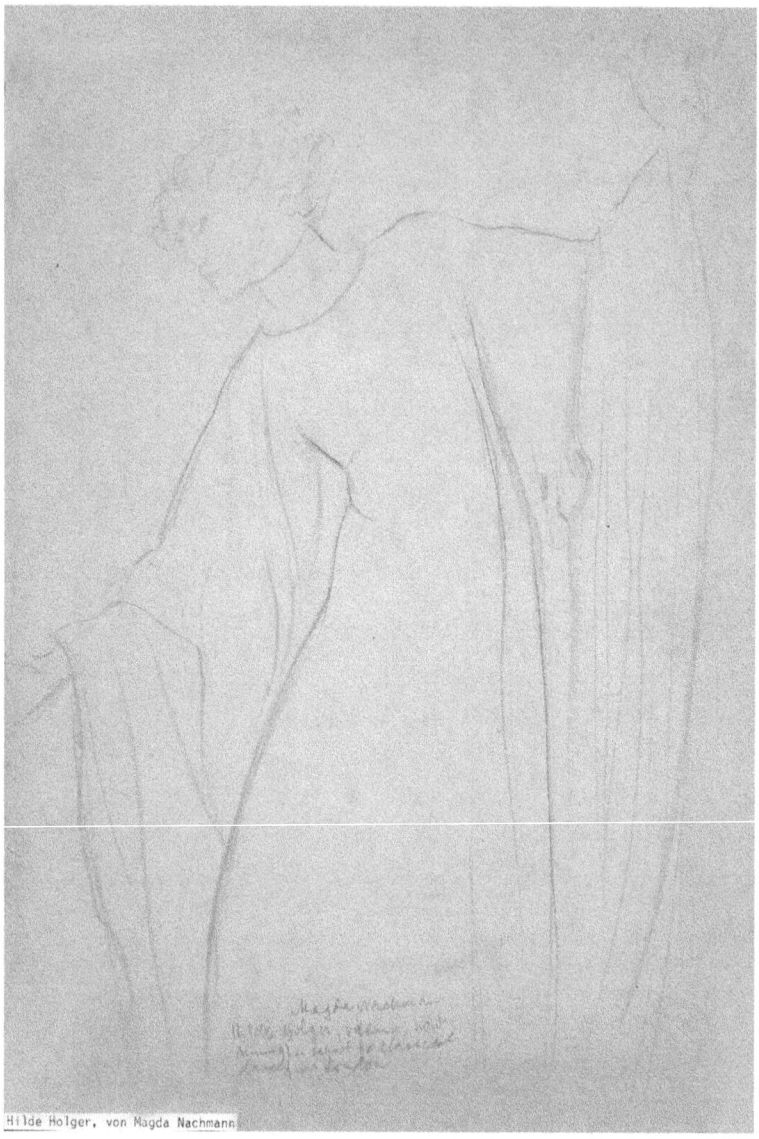

Hilde Holger, von Magda Nachmann

Figure 41. Magda Nachman. Drawing of Hilde Holger in blue angel costume designed by the artist (*Hilde Holger Archive © 2001 Primavera Boman-Behram*).

Elsewhere, the same critic wrote that being at Magda's exhibition is "like being in a beautiful place of worship listening to divine music and feeling involuntarily lifted to higher spheres." Magda had indeed become a strong presence in the Bombay art world. Lama Anagarika Govinda wrote this about Magda's art:

Magda Nachman's paintings are never sensational: they never try to force themselves on the beholder by extravagance in subject or composition, but they are always convincing. A quiet objectivity, an honesty of expression, which makes a clear statement of what the artist saw and felt, are reflected in her work. She does not try to force her own opinion or feeling upon the world around her, but rather tries to let her objects—be they men, animals, or inanimate objects—speak to her and reveal themselves through their own inherent forms.[15]

"A quiet objectivity," attention and respect for what is in front of her, and honesty in her attitude to herself and the world—these characteristics come up again and again in descriptions of Magda and her art.

---

15   Ibid., 8.

CHAPTER 15

In Quest of Magda's Paintings

Despite its wealth of artists, Mumbai lacks a modern art museum where some of Magda's works might have been expected to turn up eventually. The art scene in Mumbai seems to justify the accusation of social critics that the consumer society is turning—has turned—art into a commodity. Several prominent auction houses for art have established themselves in Mumbai (even Christie's has an office). In my six weeks there, I saw paintings by Indian artists in private galleries and auction previews that would be at home on the walls of any of the world's great museums of modern art. Yet they are displayed for only a few days before being sold into private hands as investments that will disappear into a vault until their next sale.

One of the oldest and most prominent art auctioneers in Mumbai is the Pundole Art Gallery. Toward the end of my stay in Mumbai, I received an email from a friend, a movie director whom I had met at Akbar Padamsee's:

> Tonight, there's an art auction preview at Tanna House (between Regal Cinema and Wodehouse Cathedral), 6.30 to 9.30. Also an Art Opening at Sakshi Gallery on Arthur Bunder Road.

Exhibition openings and auction previews have been social occasions for Mumbai's elite since the birth of the Bombay Art Society in 1888. And so it was that night at Tanna House, where the Pundoles had mounted a pre-sale exhibition of works by Husain, Badri Narayan, Ara, K. G. Subramanyan— one name more illustrious than the next—as well as ancient and more recent (nineteenth-century) Indian sculpture.

Such gatherings were typical in Magda's time as well. I entered to a deafening din of voices and blaring music. The visitors, smartly dressed, with wine glasses in their hands, were helping themselves from the trays of snacks offered by servants. Not many guests were paying attention to the art, or so it seemed. But someone must have been paying attention, for in four days, most of it was sold.

I had a knowledgeable guide in the dancer Jeroo Chavda, daughter of the artist Shiavax Chavda, who had collaborated with Magda in producing Hilde

Holger's performances. She took me from picture to picture and from sculpture to sculpture. In front of every picture, she gave me a brief lecture about the artist, and in front of every sculpture, she explained the myth depicted in the bronze. Some guests joined us who appeared to know very little about what they were looking at. We returned to the show the following day, when the rooms were empty of people and we could concentrate on the work.

That show was one of the highlights of my Mumbai visit, though it may have stood in the way of my discovering more pictures by Magda. Shortly before I arrived in Mumbai, the Pundole Art Gallery had auctioned the estate of Homi Bhabha's brother, Jamshed, who had been Homi Bhabha's sole heir. I wanted to know what had been put on the block, because it occurred to me that Homi Bhabha might have acquired some of Magda's pictures. I located the catalogue of the auction, which contained in its pages enough items to stock a museum: exquisite household items and furniture executed by notable Indian craftsmen, fabrics, carpets, and sculpture and paintings by modern Indian artists. Alas, Magda was not among them. Still, I put a call through to Mrs. Pundole, described Magda's connection with Homi Bhabha, and asked whether there might have been any pictures by her in the Bhabha estate. She said that there were some pictures that had not been included in the sale because they were unsigned and had remained unidentified. Would I please send her some examples of Magda's art? I did so at once—that is, as soon as my internet connection was working again, for connectivity was a constant trouble.

As I understood in retrospect, the Pundoles were too busy preparing the lucrative sale at Tanna House to pay attention to the unprofitable Magda. So our correspondence came to naught. Perhaps at some future date, some pictures by Magda will surface from the Pundole storerooms. Shireen Sabavala maintained that Magda had made several portraits of Bhabha's close friend and confidante Pipsy Wadia. Meanwhile, I had to turn my attention elsewhere.

I knew from a colleague who does research on Austrian refugees in Bombay that the Baroda Museum and Art Gallery, in the city of Vadodara, as Baroda is called nowadays, where Hermann Goetz had been keeper of the museum, had in its collection four pictures by Magda. I had written to a museum administrator and to a professor of art at the University of Baroda asking for confirmation of the museum's possession of the pictures and requesting an opportunity to see them if they were not on public display. After repeated emails went unanswered, I finally received a reply from the art historian that no such artist or her works were known in Vadodara. I never heard from anyone associated with the museum.

I had yet another connection to Vadodara. A combination of luck and the efficiency of the Google search algorithm had led me to Ashish, son of Mohan Khokar, an Indian dance historian and first head of the dance department at the University of Baroda. Ashish maintains his father's dance history archive, parts of which he periodically exhibits. In searching for Magda on the internet, I discovered that a portrait she had painted of an Indian dancer had been part of an exhibition organized by Ashish. I wrote to him, and through our correspondence, we became friends. And apart from the personal connection that Ashish and I now had, we quickly discovered a common professional interest—portraits of dancers.

Ashish was born in Baroda. He knew the museum curators there and was well connected in the life of the city. It also happened that Ashish had organized a dance conference at the University of Baroda during the time of my planned stay in Mumbai, and he invited me to give a talk at the conference on Magda as a portraitist of dancers.

In one of his letters, Ashish mentioned that he had been busy sorting and cataloguing his father's enormous archive on Indian dance and that while he was handling some papers at his desk, a newspaper clipping fell out on his lap. He had attached a scanned copy. It was an announcement from the *Free Press Bulletin* of February 3, 1951, of Magda Nachman's hospitalization and that an exhibition of her art had been mounted in the Institute of Foreign Languages of Bombay in support of the ailing painter. So Ashish's father knew of Magda.

It is not surprising that Mohan Khokar would have known of Magda and preserved the clipping. First of all, some of her pictures had been bought by Hermann Goetz for the Baroda Museum, among them two portraits of Balinese and Javanese dancers, and Mr. Khokar might well have seen them. Second, he would likely have heard of Magda through her portraits of Indian dancers, one of which had appeared on the cover of the first modern history of Indian dance, Govindraj Venkatachalam's *Dance in India* (1947). It features Magda's portrait of the famous Bharatanatyam dancer Shrimati Shanta Rao. When I arrived in Vadodara at last, Ashish presented me with the dust jacket of that book with the portrait by Magda. He had removed it from his father's archive. It was a very generous gift (figure 42).

Ashish sent me yet another copy of a portrait by Magda, from *Dance Magazine* (New York, October 1952), this one of an émigré Russian–Jewish dancer born in Brussels who called herself Xenia Zarina and who had toured Asia to study and make photographic recordings of Asian dance. Magda had posed Xenia Zarina in traditional Persian costume, her many-braided hair dancing around her body as

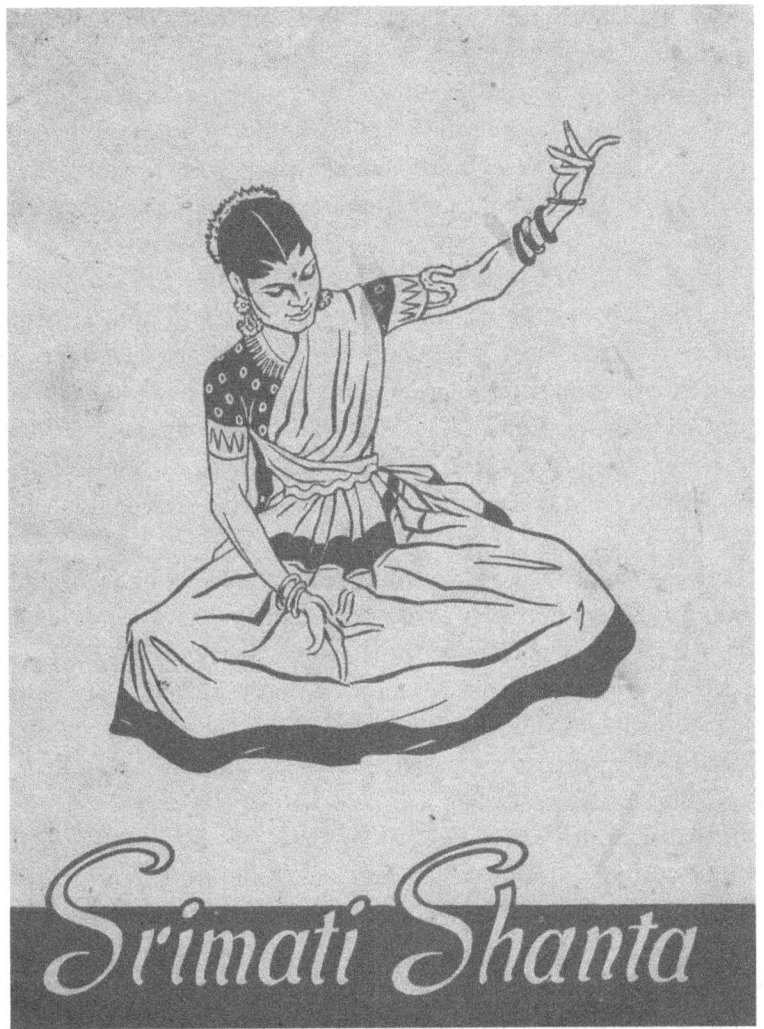

Figure 42. Cover by Magda Nachman. Portrait of the Bharatanatyam dancer Shrimati Shanta Rao.

she re-created a Persian classical dance. To my delight and astonishment, I found the original of that portrait in Mumbai, in the collection of Shared Patel.[1]

---

1 Roy Ernest Hawkins, editor and later general manager of the Oxford University Press office in Bombay (from 1937 to 1970), was also an art collector. He left his exquisite collection to his intimate friend Ms. Shared Patel, who kindly allowed me to take pictures of the two paintings by Magda in her possession: one of Xenia Zarina in Persian costume, the other of a girl kneeling on a striped blanket against a background of leafy plants.

Ashish kindly arranged my visit to Vadodara/Baroda, where I was to take part in the dance conference. Of course, my primary purpose in visiting Vadodara was to see Magda's paintings. By now, I knew for certain that her pictures were there, because Ashish had managed to procure photographs of two of them. I had also heard from another researcher, whom I had met in the United States, that he had visited the Baroda museum and located four pictures by Magda.

The museum was built and opened to the public in 1895 by Sayaji Rao Gaekwad III (1863–1939), maharaja of the princely state of Baroda. His model was the Victoria and Albert Museum in London, with the addition of some aspects of a science museum. There are numerous galleries, including art from Egypt, Greater India–Burma, Mali, and China; old Indian bronzes; carved wood; ivory; stone archeological objects; Indian miniatures (on which Goetz was a specialist); and Indian musical instruments. The museum is a national treasure.

Maharaja Sayaji Rao was a remarkable man. Besides being a powerful and successful social reformer and advocate of harmony between Muslims and Hindus, he was also an open-minded champion of art. At the height of the cultural debates over what should be considered authentic Indian art, he introduced to his museum, which was rich in precolonial Indian art, a collection of European paintings, as if to say that all art is authentic and has a place under the sun, or at least in his museum.

The door to the Indian modern art gallery, where Magda's paintings were supposed to be, was locked. A note on it said that there was no attendant available that day. It was obvious that the note had been there for quite a while. In a panic, I tried to find a curator, but to no avail, and the day was coming to a close.

The next day, I knocked on the door of the museum director's office. Two curators who were present led me upstairs and unlocked the room, which turned out to be a narrow corridor lined with treasures by some of the most important modern Indian artists. And there were two pictures by Magda, an oil painting, *Brother and Sister* (figure 17) (1944), and *Leaves* (pastel, undated). For the first time, I saw Magda's paintings on a museum wall, and in good company, too, along with paintings by Jamini Roy, N. S. Bendre, and Francis Newton Souza. It was no small matter to be represented in one of the best museums in the country.

Two more pictures, depicting Balinese and Javanese dancers, were in another room with the designation *Greater India*, which held objects from neighboring countries. I had already visited that room on my own, but I had missed Magda's pictures: they were hanging in an upper corner, over a display case containing objects from Bali, completely in darkness. Both pictures had been painted in 1948, which meant that they had been acquired after Magda's debacle with the selection committee for the London exhibition. What better confirmation of her qualification as an Indian artist could there be?

The curators helped me to find a professional photographer, and they all remained with me after hours, waiting for him to appear. The pictures he took were spectacular, especially the dancers, which had been invisible in their obscure corner (figure 43).

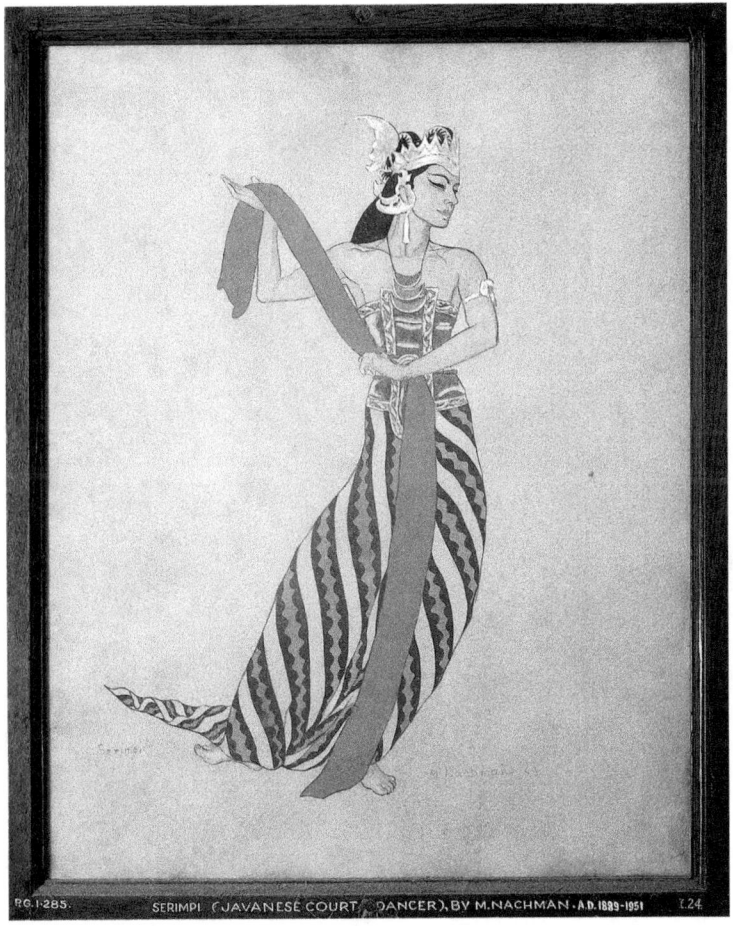

Figure 43. Magda Nachman. *Serimpi* (Javanese Court Dancer) (Watercolor, courtesy of the Baroda Museum and Picture Gallery, Vadodara, India).

The curators explained the lock on the door by saying that the modern art gallery had been "under renovations," which did not explain the note referring to the lack of an attendant. Inside, a window was open, and sticks had been placed in the opening to protect the room from pigeons. The walls were dripping with moisture. What a sad state of affairs for that gallery.

CHAPTER 16

A Kindred Spirit

A surprise awaited me in Mumbai's principal museum, formerly the Prince of Wales Museum and known nowadays as Chhatrapati Shivaji Maharaj Vastu Sangrahalaya. (For the most part, they call it simply "the Museum," since even the locals have difficulty in remembering or pronouncing such a long name.) It takes a while to see that the museum's rich and vast permanent collections fall into several categories: art, archeology, and natural history. In addition, there are spaces for temporary Indian and foreign art exhibitions and an art library.

Not knowing what I was looking for, I went from room to room, attracted sometimes by Mughal miniatures, sometimes by an ivory carving. I stumbled upon a room with a sign announcing that it contained Tibetan art. And all of a sudden, I found myself looking at photographs and sketches done by Li Gotami on her expedition to Tibet. She had been one of Magda's closest friends in Bombay, and Magda had painted her portrait. She and her husband, Lama Anagarika Govinda, spent the years 1947–1949 in Tsaparang and Tholing, in western Tibet, documenting, in photographs, rubbings, and sketches, a culture that was to vanish twenty years later in the Chinese Cultural Revolution. For a year, I had been trying to locate any surviving papers related to Li Gotami in the hope of uncovering some of Magda's letters. Here was a thread that might lead my steps aright.

There was an announcement on the gallery wall asking visitors to support the museum by purchasing a book, available in the museum bookstore, about Gotami's collection. I rushed downstairs to the bookstore, bought the booklet, read it then and there, and ran off looking for a director or curator who could tell me from whom Gotami's collection had been acquired. No luck. After several telephone conversations, emails, and more telephoning, I had arrived nowhere. No one in the museum could tell me the collection's provenance.

During all this back and forth, I was invited to a dinner party by a couple to whom I had been referred by Shireen Sabavala because they had a portrait by Magda, which I had photographed a few days earlier at their home. I began complaining about how frustrating it was to have gotten so close to Gotami and yet been unable to discover anything further, only to hear that my hostess was related to Li Gotami, that one of the guests had gone to school with Li Gotami's niece, with whom either of them could put me in touch. Roshan Cooper, Gotami's niece, lived in Pune, where I was going in a few days in any case in search of yet another painting by Magda.

My knowledge of that painting came from a colleague who had told me about Magda's work in the museum in Baroda. He had also mentioned that he had heard a rumor of a portrait by Magda of a Mrs. Wood, whose son, it seemed, was living in Pune. An internet search for a "Wood" in Pune, not a very common Indian name, produced Ananda Wood, a philosopher with an email address. I wrote to him and received a kind letter in response—this was all before my trip to India. Ananda was the son of Kamal and Evelyn Wood. Kamal had been a professor of English and the principal of Elphinstone College in Bombay, and her husband, Evelyn, had been an English anthropologist. Ananda told me that Magda Nachman was a name he had known since his childhood, having grown up with two portraits of his parents painted by her. Another portrait by Magda Nachman of which he was aware was of the late Indian painter Jehangir Sabavala, husband of his aunt Shireen in Mumbai. Ananda had suggested in his letter that I call Mrs. Sabavala on my arrival in Bombay (which is how I met Shireen).

I finally got myself to Pune, and I telephoned Ananda to arrange a meeting with him and Li Gotami's niece Roshan.

He told me that his sister Leela, who at the time was teaching art and art history at the Sahyadri school (founded by Jiddu Krishnamurti) in the Western Ghats, near Rajgurunagar, not far from Pune, had their mother's portrait in storage in Ann Arbor, Michigan. I had known about Leela from my previous correspondence with Ananda and had been trying, and trying, and trying to reach her by phone and email, to no avail. Finally, after talking with Ananda, I had decided just to show up on her doorstep, when suddenly she telephoned, and we had a lovely conversation. She had been familiar with her parents' portraits since her early childhood, and she recalled that everyone admired them. Indeed, her mother's portrait by Magda was in her possession. (Shireen Sabavala maintained that this portrait of her sister, Kamal Wood, was one of the finest works by Magda.) The portrait of her father, Evelyn Wood, had disintegrated, and she had thrown it away without even taking a picture of it, which she now regretted. (I had experienced Magda's paintings crumbling under my fingers in Hilde Holger's archive in London. Magda painted on the cheapest paper, perhaps for lack of money or because only such paper was available during the war years.) Leela said that she would be back in Ann Arbor soon and would call me and send me a photo of the portrait. That was the first and the last I heard from her.

It was in Bombay that the Acharyas met and befriended Li Gotami and her husband, Lama Anagarika Govinda. Like the Acharyas, Li Gotami and Lama Anagarika Govinda were a "mixed-race" couple. Li Gotami (1906–1988), originally Rutty Petit, was born into a prosperous Parsi family. She was an artist, a writer, a photographer, and an explorer (as a young woman, she began calling herself "Rati" and frequently signed her work with that name). I had seen her pictures in the Bombay Art Society catalogues together with Magda's paintings. Now I saw her original pictures in Roshan's house. Li had meticulously documented the expedition to Tibet that she had made with her husband in the years 1947–1949. Her notes, newspaper clippings (their reports had been published in the *Times of India, Illustrated Weekly*, which had underwritten the trip), and all the correspondence connected with the trip were carefully preserved. Unfortunately, no other documents had made it into those neatly bound albums that Roshan showed me. The collection of photographs and rubbings that I had seen in the museum's Tibetan room had been donated by Roshan and her sister.

Rati Petit had received a conventional upper-class upbringing, for a year attending the girls' finishing school Heathfield in London and then St. Xavier's College in Bombay. After dropping out of college, a stormy social life in Bombay, marriage, and divorce, the willful young woman enrolled, against her parents' wishes, at Santiniketan, the ashram and international university established by Rabindranath Tagore near Calcutta, where she spent twelve years, from 1934 to 1946. In 1942, she became the last student of the artist Abanindranath Tagore, Rabindranath's nephew, who had spearheaded the Indian revivalist art school in the 1920s.

I am inclined to think that Rati and Magda felt like kindred spirits with a shared past, and in spite of differences in their temperaments, did not have to explain themselves to each other. They had in common a similar upbringing and artistic sensibility. Magda's education at one of the top secondary schools in St. Petersburg and the art instruction she had received from Léon Bakst resembled Rati's educational experience. I believe that each of these two women's teachers was an important influence in her development as a representational artist who kept far from abstraction and the "isms" of the day. Each of them was grateful to her teacher for opening her eyes to new ways of seeing.

It was during a visit to Bombay from Santiniketan to collect a prize from the Bombay Art Society show that Rati met Magda. When Rati's sister told her that the artist Magda Nachman wanted to meet her, Rati replied, as she recalled in an obituary on Magda's death,

> How very strange, and I have been longing to meet Magda Nachman ever since I saw her pictures, goodness alone knows how many years ago. …
> As years passed, our friendship grew warmer and warmer, and I do not think there was any other friend so near and dear to my heart as Magda. Though the difference of age between us was considerable, there was complete affinity of thought and spirit, and I felt I could tell her anything at any time, just as if I was telling it to myself. … It soon became clear to me that Magda Nachman was a great soul, whose sense of understanding of all things, big and small, was something more than uncanny. Magda was no ordinary character.[1]

Rati fell in love with Lama Anagarika Govinda (1898–1985). She converted to Buddhism and changed her name to Li Gotami. The couple were married in 1947. Born Ernst Lothar Hoffman in Waldheim, Germany, he was the son of a German father and Bolivian mother. It was at Magda and Acharya's house on Walkeshwar Road that the wedding reception for Li and Govinda took place. (The marriage was a terrible blow to Li's family, and they did not attend.)

Around 1945 or 1946, Li took Magda to her family's country place in Matheran, in the Western Ghats, a place of breathtaking beauty. Roshan recalled that her aunt had told her that she and Magda would go to the market or into the village to paint peasants and artisans, or into wild spots to paint landscapes. The watercolor landscape that Roshan showed me had been painted there. It is characteristic of Magda that in her painting, the master's villa is barely discernible in the foliage behind the servants' quarters, which are in the foreground (figure 44).

Magda painted many pictures during that visit, including a large "well-known canvas" (according to Li) called *Underground*, and later in Bombay,

---

1   *Aesthetics* 5, no. 1 (January–March 1951): 10.

she painted a remarkable portrait of Li, who reproduced both paintings in her obituary for Magda. Where are those pictures as well as others painted in Matheran and in Bombay? The paintings in the show of Magda's work that opened at the Institute of Foreign Languages a few hours after her death sold for thousands of rupees. In 1952, Charles Petras, director of the Institute of Foreign Languages, mounted yet another show of Magda's works in the newly established branch of the institute in New Delhi. And finally, after her death, Acharya made a desperate attempt to organize a show in London, which was

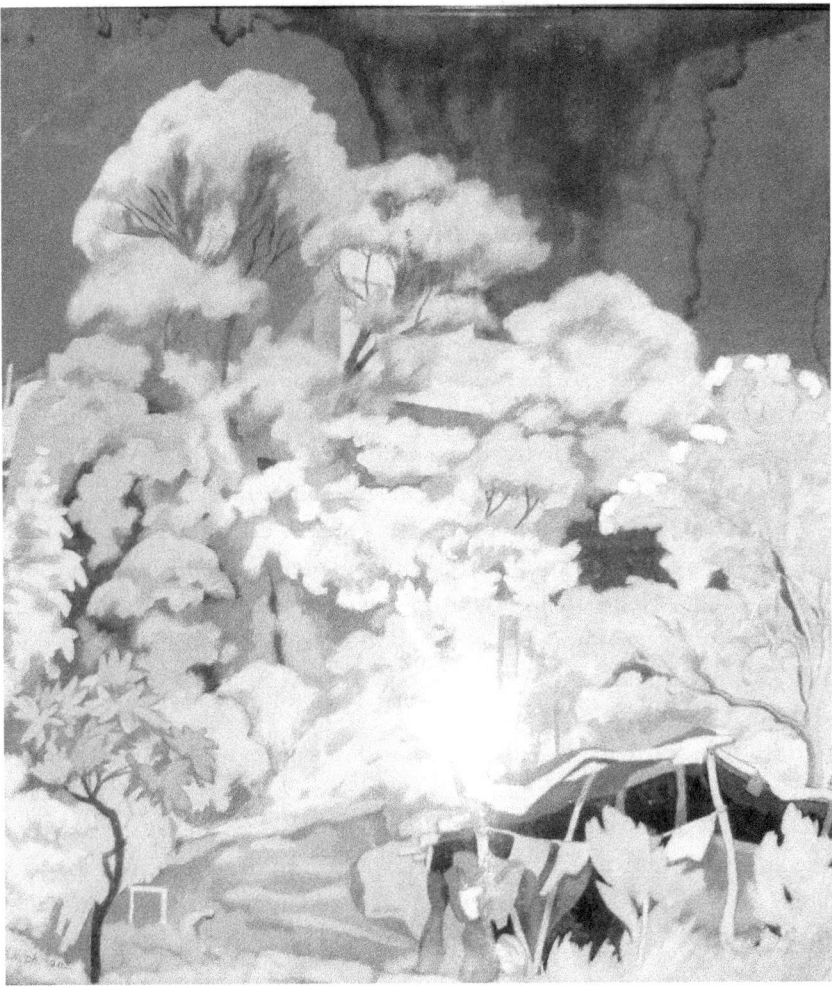

Figure 44. Magda Nachman. *Landscape in Matheran,* 1945 (watercolor, *courtesy of Roshan Cooper*).

described by Albert Meltzer in *I Couldn't Paint Golden Angels: Sixty Years of Life and Anarchist Agitation*:

> Suddenly I got a request from Acharya to stage an art exhibition for the works of his companion Magda Nachman, who had just died. She had joined him in Moscow in the early twenties, when he had been in the Comintern as a fervent young Indian nationalist until he lost his illusions in State Communism. They had moved to Berlin and had shared the problems of exile. She was making a name as an artist and was featured in Hitler's famous Exhibition of Decadent Art when they moved to Bombay. Starting again from scratch, she had specialized in Indian subjects. ... Acharya wrote me despairingly he could not bear to think she would be forgotten and asked me to arrange an exhibition in London. Unfortunately, Acharya died suddenly. The Indian authorities blocked the export of Magda's paintings and stated that they had been claimed by Acharya's legal widow, whom he had married at fifteen by parental arrangement and not seen for fifty odd years, and who thought she had come into unexpected treasure. So they vanished from sight.[2]

Meltzer's words gave me two directions to follow in my search for Magda's works: to look among the works exhibited in 1937 in the Nazi exhibition *Degenerate Art* and to try to locate Acharya's family in Chennai/Madras, where Magda's remaining works might have gone after his death.

Lists of works exhibited at the *Degenerate Art* exhibit are available from different sources. The lists differ from one another, and some indeed include Magda's name. Her participation in that exhibit is inconclusive. The exhibition's master ledger, now in the Victoria and Albert Museum, in London, does not contain Magda's name, although there are several paintings cataloged by unknown artists. Could Magda be one of those?

The second path led me to Acharya's relatives in Madras/Chennai. Through the wonders of the internet and my luck in finding dedicated archivists, I had a name and a phone number of an Acharya relative in Chennai even before I left for India. However, the person at the other end of the telephone line could not understand me, and I could not understand a word that he spoke, although we both were speaking English! What to do? Again I was

---

2   Meltzer, *I Couldn't Paint Golden Angels*, 128, 130.

in luck. The main language in Chennai is Tamil. The Tata Institute, which I had visited, has a mathematics department, and it just so happens that many Indian mathematicians are Tamil. Thus it was just a matter of asking a Tamil mathematician at the institute to make a call to Chennai on my behalf and speak with Acharya's relatives in Tamil. This call produced an email correspondent for me, and writing turned out to be a great improvement over telephone conversations. I finally received the following letter from a Mr. Srinivas in Chennai:

> Dear Prof. Lina,
> I have spoken to Mr. Parthasarathy. He states that when Mr M. P. T. Acharya died in Mumbai, none of his relatives were around. To this best of his knowledge, there are no paintings or any other belongings of Acharya with any of his relatives in Madras or Bangalore. It was said at that time that all his belongings were vandalized by locals.
> Therefore you need not make any trip to Madras for this purpose alone.
> With best regards
> M D Srinivas

So where is Magda's art? Once in a while, one of her works will surface, only to disappear again. A few years ago, there appeared a picture of an Indian boy on eBay that sold for $300 to an anonymous purchaser. In the 1990s, a portrait of Hilde Holger's student Nergesh in a buffoon costume had been bought by someone who then disappeared together with the picture. A collector in Israel found me on the internet because he has two pictures by Magda and hopes to find more: he is crazy about her. A colleague working in the Tata Iron and Steel Company Archives in Jamshedpur found and sent me a copy of Magda's picture *Poona Girl*, as reproduced in the company's 1962 calendar, which billed itself as "the fourth calendar devoted to the reproduction of fine examples of modern Indian Paintings." A few years ago, yet another picture was bought by an Indian journalist from a Mumbai street vendor (figure 45). Two collectors discovered my website dedicated to Magda and her husband[3] and sent me scans of several pictures by Magda in their possession. I, too, have acquired a picture by Magda: a portrait of an Indian boy painted in 1945 that I bought on eBay in 2015 (figure 46).

---

3   See: https://magdanachmanacharya.org.

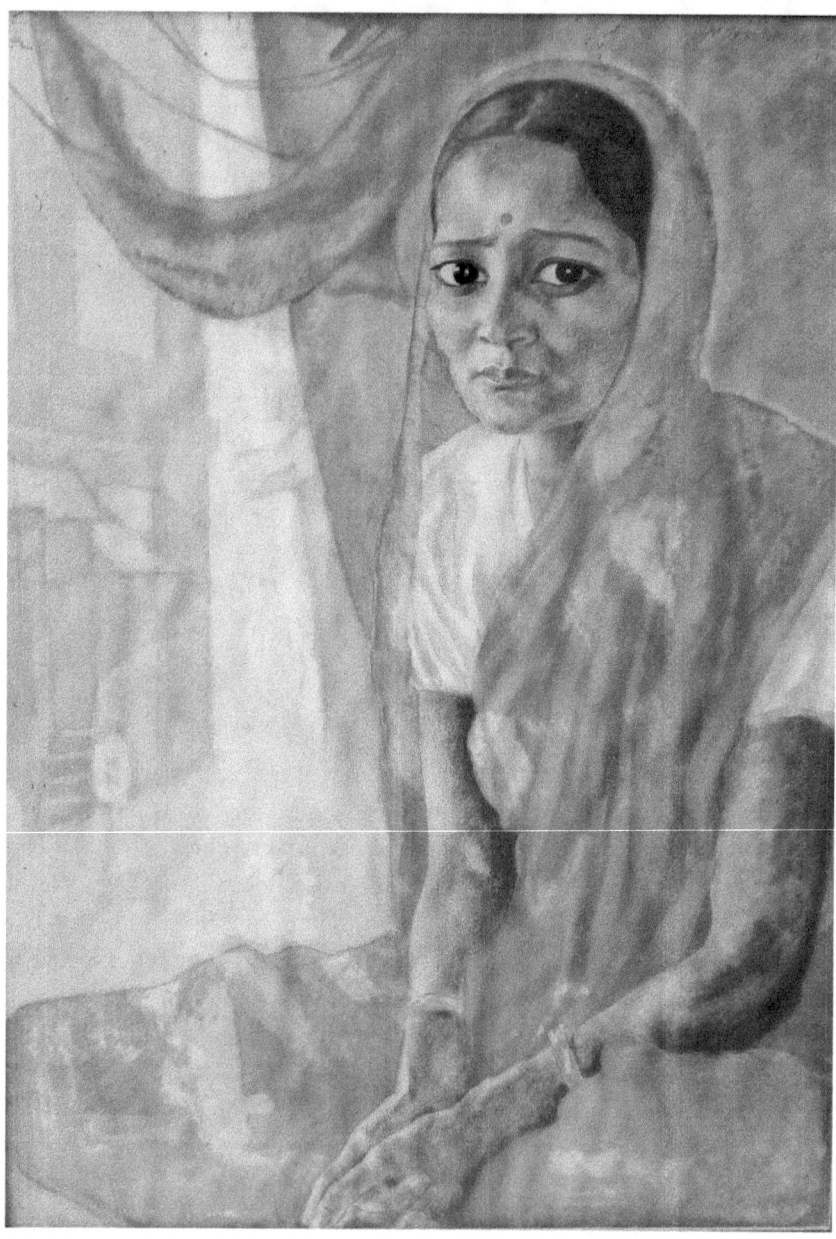

Figure 45. Magda Nachman. *Portrait of a Maharashtrian Woman* (*courtesy of Brian and Darryl D'Monte*).

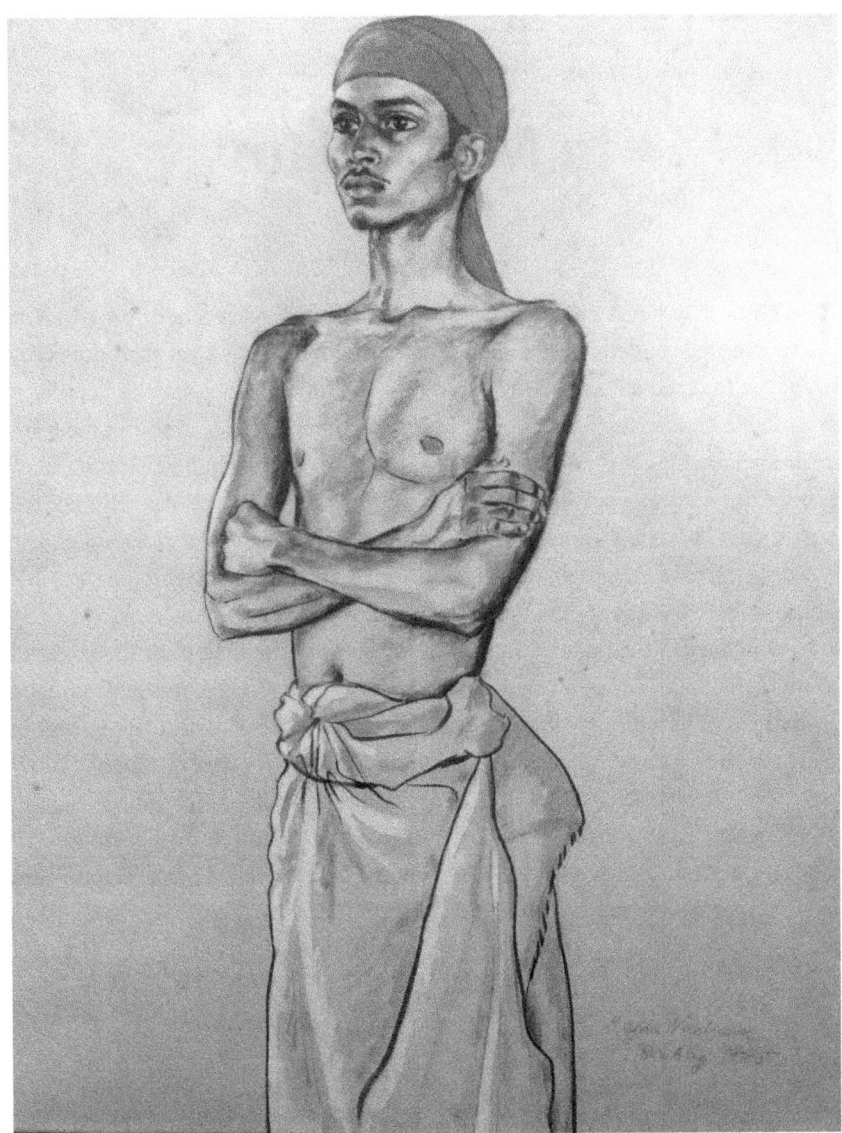

Figure 46. Magda Nachman. *Portrait of a Young Man*, Bombay, 1945.

CHAPTER 17

In Memoriam

Li Gotami was not the only one who mourned Magda on her death. Magda the refugee ended her life far away from her native land, yet surrounded by friends who cared about her and loved her. As Hilde Holger put it in her obituary, Magda "had many great friends who adored her as I did." Another memoirist, Irene Pohrille, who calls Magda the "little stout lady with the charming face," echoes this sentiment: "She used to help struggling young artists who adored her. Magda had many friends who were devoted to her."[1] And so although she was driven from her homeland, she ended up in a place that she could have called home. For what is home, after all, if not a place of caring and loving friends?

On Magda's death, an outpouring of memories spilled over the pages of newspapers and journals. "Quiet, almost shy," thus Goetz, she had touched many lives. The obituaries were a tribute to her "sincerity and her hatred of ostentation and humbug, her innate kindness and her sense of humor and fun."[2] "Mr. Oscar Brown, the Chief Presidency Magistrate of Bombay, declaring her posthumous exhibition open, paid a tribute to the artist's courage, her versatile faculties, and uncanny gift of deep human insight." He called her a "magnificent lady."[3] In the same issue of the *Times of India*, Rudi von Leyden wrote:

> The great little lady of the Bombay art world is no more. As an artist she died in harness. All those who take one of her pictures home from this exhibition will take with them a small part of this friendly, generous, and tragic figure that was Magda Nachman. One of Europe's countless persecuted, she instinctively understood those who stand by the road-side when life passes by and she painted them not so much with pity but with a feeling for the tragic condition and dignity of the simple and the poor. Her sympathy with human nature made her a good observer of type and a portraitist of a very special human kind.

---

1   *Aesthetics* 5, no. 1 (January–March 1951), 18.
2   H. Kohn. "Memories of Magda Nachman," *Aesthetics* 5, no. 1 (1951): 14–15.
3   "Artist Dies 4 Hours Before Opening of Exhibition. Tribute to Magda Nachman," *Times of India*, February 13, 1951.

The younger generation of artists in Bombay had in her a faithful friend and understanding critic. Although conservative in her own style of work, she welcomed and encouraged those who went in search of horizons new. They will remember her for her gentleness and for the strength with which she lived through a life that was all but kind to her. And these two qualities, gentleness and strength, speak to us from every painting in this exhibition, which is a fitting memorial to her life's work.[4]

The *Free Press Bulletin of Bombay* declared that the "great old lady of the Bombay art world, who had been a faithful friend and understanding critic of the young artists, had been gathered by the great beyond." Her life, the bulletin went on, "was a continuously brave fight against adversities which would have broken a weaker character or hardened a less noble mind."[5] Her contemporaries addressed Magda with terms of endearment and respect in public media even during her life. The leading art journal of the time, *MARG*, in an overview of the exhibitions in the first quarter of 1950, reported on a one-woman show: "Magda Nachman, the Grand Old Lady of Bombay, had her usual show at the I. F. L. Hall. There was the usual gentleness in her colors and humanness in her themes."[6] In its tribute to Magda after her death, *MARG* expressed a hope that "Her art, which was stamped with the lyrical bent of her own personality, will always be remembered."[7]

A melancholy feeling sweeps over me when I think that "the younger generation of artists" of Bombay, who did remember her, are also no more. Many of them became prominent artists whose paintings found their way to art museums all over the world. What could they have told me about Magda? Sometimes, I think I see Magda's sensibility in some of their paintings. The eyes that look at me from Ara's portraits or his nudes drawn in one swoop of the brush seem to me to originate with Magda.

The obituaries offer some glimpses of Magda's European life and some particulars of her life in Bombay. Lama Anagarika Govinda had first heard about Magda from a German friend who had come from Berlin, who reported that he had met a refugee artist there: "'The Russian lady is a painter who specializes

---

4   Ibid.
5   "Magda Nachman Truly Interpreted India," *The Free Press Bulletin of Bombay*, February 14, 1951. The review is signed P. K. S.
6   *MARG* 4, no. 2 (1950): 60. "Grand Little Lady" or "Great Little Lady" are Magda's epithets often repeated whenever she is mentioned in the press.
7   *MARG* 5, no. 1 (1951): 66.

in animal studies. It is wonderful how she has caught the characteristics of animals." And he described how she went day by day to the Berlin zoo, spending endless hours in the company of animals, patiently producing hundreds of sketches, until she was acquainted with every form and movement of the model. Thus Lama Govinda had long known of Magda and Acharya when, in Bombay, he found his way to

> a small, old-fashioned house on Walkeshwar Road, which next to the huge concrete blocks of modern flats on the opposite side of the road, looked like a frightened child that lost its way in the weeds.

Inside, he found Acharya, Magda, and their cats:

> The cats seemed to be equally at home here as the paintings, among and on which they walked and sat nonchalantly, as if to say that after all *they* were the masters of the house.

That was the place I had found on Walkeshwar. But there were no cats. Cats are rare in Bombay. I saw a cat with her kittens once, on top of Malabar Hill. I wondered whether they were descendants of Magda's cats. Govinda continued:

> Magda Nachman's love for animals was apparently shared by her husband, who with a lively sense of humor related the story of their wanderings in Europe: how they left Russia after the Revolution, the hard times through which they went there and in Berlin, their travels in Germany, France and Switzerland, and their final decision to settle down in India.[8]

What wouldn't I have given to have been present at the telling of that tale! I have been gathering the crumbs of the Acharyas' lives left behind in an occasional letter, a snapshot, a rumor. Did Lama Govinda write a more detailed account of his first meeting with the Acharyas? Maybe someday I will come across it.

Still, even crumbs can be assembled into a mosaic. Acharya's "sense of humor," emphasized by Govinda, I know of from his account of his "heroic deeds," which Acharya puts in quotation marks, even though historians consider them heroic without the scare quotes. His personality shines through his writing as Magda's does through her painting. And there are Magda's words as

---

8   *Aesthetics* 5, no. 1 (January–March 1951).

reported by the obituary writers: "Every struggle and every emotional experience that lifts us out of the rut of daily life, makes our soul richer, less self-centered, more open to the nonegoistical side of life" (Govinda). Perhaps those were not her exact words, but I trust that they express what she meant to say. Li Gotami recorded Magda's voice distinctly: "Death and life are *both* illusions, anyway." In her youth, Magda studied anthroposophy. Now in India, Hinduism and Buddhism would have been congenial with her youthful faith and study of Rudolf Steiner. In his article in the *Illustrated Weekly* that accompanies three pictures by Magda,[9] Lama Govinda writes of her exceptional knowledge of Indian philosophical and religious literature.

Yet another memoirist, a Miss H. Kohn, kindly quotes from postcards that she received from Magda:

> These days the cats love me very much and want all to sleep with me and three cats together are as hot as a furnace. If I get up, they follow me, if I sneak into bed again, thinking I have got rid of them, they all come back at once. One should really not keep cats in a hot country. Now all cats are on the table before me and it is difficult to write.

And:

> The heat is frightful, and I feel flat and uninspired. I wish I could go to Matheran for two months and paint there in peace. But no chance.

And:

> It is now three weeks I sent the designs to … and they have not even acknowledged receipt. But after all, my life is always like this. I can only believe in miracles and they generally happen.

And:

> We are still miraculously alive. In the neutral way of things we should be dead years and years ago. Somehow I cannot stand the heat at all. I need badly a rest in a cooler climate, but this is denied me.[10]

9   "Magda Nachman: The Artist and Her Work," *Illustrated Weekly*, December 3, 1950.
10   Ibid., 14–15.

The complaints of heat came not long before Magda suffered the stroke that killed her. Her health had been compromised since her youth, and the Indian climate was far from ideal for her condition. Despite the hostile climate and constant lack of money, she not only stayed "miraculously alive," but made life worth living. Her contemporaries in their reminiscences say as much. Here is Mrs. Gertrude Murray Correa:

> Even in our bravest and brightest moments, few of us are able to do anything than fling a veil of shimmering pretense over the ugliness, the grimness of the present day world. Magda Nachman not only faced it, and without shrinking—she proved to us that there is still nobility, courage, endurance and love around us everywhere, to rejoice and uplift the hearts of all who remember our common humanity.[11]

A day after the opening of her exhibition, "her husband and her friends stood in the cemetery broken-hearted to watch her being buried" (Irene Pohrille).[12] I tried to find Magda's grave. In her time, there was only one Christian cemetery in the city: half for Catholics and half for all other Christians. The cemetery officials could not find Magda's name in the registry. Which does not mean she is not there. Indians are not big on keeping accurate records, as I discovered. On the other hand, Magda's Lutheran baptism sixty-one years ago might have meant very little to her after having been considered Jewish under Nazi law and later coming in close contact with various Asian belief systems and philosophies. What was her faith by that time? What cemetery might have been mentioned in an obituary? I am still looking.

The first task at hand for Acharya after Magda's death was to preserve and promote her work. He wrote to Shivaram Karanth that he wanted to keep their flat as Magda's memorial gallery. He also wrote that he was trying to write his autobiography as Magda wished him to do.[13] Acharya asked an anarchist friend in London, Albert Meltzer, to find a gallery to exhibit paintings left behind by his wife. And he wrote to Hem Day, a prominent Belgian anarchist:

---

11 Ibid., 17.
12 Aesthetics 5, no. 1 (January–March 1951), 18.
13 Quoted in Subramanyam, *M. P. T. Acharya*, 146. Kota Shivaram Karanth (October 10, 1902– December 9, 1997) was a Kannada writer, social activist, and journalist.

I have been ill for the last three years and postponed writing a large number of friends abroad. Recently my wife and breadwinner also died and I feel like a baby without anyone to take care of me. I am now 65 years old.[14]

Unfortunately, Acharya's years were numbered too. He died on March 20, 1954.

---

14 Letter to Hem Day, May 15, 1951, Centre d'archives de la Fédération Wallonie, Brussels, Mandyam Acharya, révolutionnaire agitateur indou (200280). Hem Day is the pseudonym of Marcel Dieu (1902–1969), Belgian libertarian, journalist, and anti-militarist, whom Acharya befriended in Europe and with whom he continued to correspond.

Epilogue

In late May 2016, I flew to St. Petersburg to attend the opening of an exhibition in the Russian Museum, *The Circle of Petrov-Vodkin*, which featured works by students of Kuzma Petrov-Vodkin, who in 1910 had taken over the direction of the Zvantseva Academy following Bakst's departure for Paris. The exhibition featured pictures taken from the storerooms of the Russian Museum that had rarely if ever been exhibited before and from other museums as well,[1] but also from private collections. The exhibition began with pictures by Nadezhda Lermontova, Julia Obolenskaya, and Vera Zhukova, all students first and foremost of Bakst. There was also a picture by Magda. The work of younger artists who joined the academy after Bakst's departure and studied under Petrov-Vodkin followed, among them Raisa Kotovich-Borisyak, who had become a close friend of Julia and Magda. For the first time I saw original paintings by artists with whom I had been living for the past six years; I had read their private correspondence and through it had become their intimate acquaintance. I was saying hello to familiar names as if to old friends.

Magda's picture *Peasant Woman*, which is so different from her Indian works, overwhelmed me (figure 23). Magda painted this picture around 1916. It was exhibited in a Moscow art show and bought by an art collector, as Julia reported in her 1926 talk on the Zvantseva Academy. In 1920, it became part of the collection of the Museum of Fine Arts of Tatarstan, in Kazan. Its fate at the time was typical of many works that were being sent off to museums far and wide with the idea of acquainting the working classes, to whom it now belonged, with high art. The painting hung in the Kazan museum until 1946, when along with many other works of art it was condemned by the authorities as a product of formalism, and therefore alien to the Soviet people and to the goals of socialist realism. It was ordered to be destroyed.

---

1   Other contributing museums: State Museum of the History of St. Petersburg, Moscow Museum of Contemporary Art, Research Museum of the Russian Academy of Arts, Nizhny Tagil Museum of Fine Arts, St. Petersburg Museum of Theater and Musical Arts, State Museum of Fine Arts of the Republic of Tatarstan.

One of the museum's curators, Sagadat Ishmuratova, risking her freedom, took several condemned canvases—Magda's among them—out of their frames, rolled them up, and hid them in various obscure corners of the museum. In the 1960s, shortly before her death, she revealed what she had done to a curator who had just joined the museum's staff and had expressed interest in art beyond the confines of socialist realism. At the first opportunity, the young man took the canvases home and kept them hidden until the 1990s, when the danger of harboring forbidden art had passed. They are now back in the museum's collection.[2]

Unfortunately, Magda's picture arrived at the Russian Museum too late to be included in the show's catalogue. For me, of course, Magda's picture was the star of the show. For I had given Magda Nachman back to the world from which she had vanished sixty-five years before. And in the process, Magda had worked a miracle of her own. Through her invigorated presence on the internet, I had been contacted not only by the Swiss/British branch of the family, descendants of Magda's sister Adele, but by Magda's great-grandniece Natalia Mikaberidze, who lives in Moscow, descended from another older sister, Eleanor. Through email, I introduced the British and Russian cousins, who had not known of each other's existence. And then Natalia found the descendants of yet another older sister, Erna, the sister with whom Magda had stayed in Likino during the civil war. That branch of the family lives near the Siberian city of Krasnoyarsk.

Although the forebears of UK great-grandnieces Sophie and Margret had had their share of hardship in the 1920s through 1940s in Switzerland, nothing can compare with the tragic fate of Natalia's family and that of her relatives from Krasnoyarsk. In 1899, Eleanor Nachman married James Schmidt, curator of the Hermitage picture galleries.[3] They had four children, some of whom Magda tutored on occasion at home in St. Petersburg and during summer vacations in Finland. Two of the boys died during the time of the civil war: one drowned; the other died of typhus. Eleanor's daughter, little Magda, was arrested in 1924 on trumped-up charges and sent to the formidable Solovki prison camp, located in the remote Solovetsky Islands, in the White Sea. After a few years, following heroic efforts by her parents to free her, she was allowed to settle in the Vladimir region, northwest of Moscow. She was forbidden to live in a large city and thus could not return to Leningrad, where her parents and one surviving brother still lived. During the late 1920s and early 1930s, despite his efforts to prevent

---

2   See Natal'ia Gerasimova, "Magda Nachman i sud'ba ee kartiny," in *Kuz'ma Petrov-Vodkin i ego shkola*, ed. Il'dar Galeev (Moscow: Galeev-Gallery, 2015), vol. 1, 200–203.

3   On Schmidt, see *Bibliografika*. https://bioslovhist.spbu.ru/person/950-shmidt-dzhems-alfredovich.html.

it, James Schmidt witnessed the sale of many of his beloved Hermitage paintings by the Soviets for hard currency. He died in 1933, by which time, according to his great-granddaughter, he had already been dismissed from his post.

Eleanor's last remaining son became an officer in the merchant marine. When his ship returned to Leningrad from Spain in 1938, where it had delivered a cargo of arms in support of the Republican forces in the Spanish Civil War, he was arrested and shot. His wife was sent to Siberia. His two small daughters were rescued by relatives, and they eventually were taken in by their grandmother. Sometime in the 1930s, little Magda was allowed to return to her mother in Leningrad.

On August 21, 1941, as the German army was approaching Leningrad, a decree was issued "On the Deportation of Socially Dangerous Persons from Leningrad and Its Environs." Among the undesirables were thousands of ethnic Germans, who, following the beginning of the Siege of Leningrad in September 1941, were accused of espionage and treason, and deported to various camps. By the end of the year, that campaign had somewhat subsided, but by February 1942, a new wave of arrests and deportations began on a much wider scale.

Eleanor died early that year, leaving her daughter Magda in charge of her two granddaughters, Ingrid and Erna, aged six and eight. Magda decided that the three of them would take their lives rather than undergo deportation. On her fortieth birthday, March 22, 1942, she prepared three draughts of poison, and as an example showed the girls how to drink it quickly. The girls refused to follow their aunt, and after her death found themselves alone in besieged Leningrad. One of those girls, Erna, would become Natalia Mikaberidze's mother.

Magda knew about the deaths of her two nephews, who had died before her departure in 1922. She wrote to Julia about those tragedies. She probably heard about her niece's arrest in 1924, since there is evidence that she was corresponding with her family for at least a few more years. In all likelihood, her correspondence with her family ceased sometime in the 1930s.

Magda's second older sister, Erna Knorre, did not fare much better. Of her three children, two died in labor camps: one son at the Belomorkanal camp, the other in a penal colony at a Siberian mine. Erna and her husband helped to bring up their grandchildren, who now live in Krasnoyarsk.

Sophie and I flew to Krasnoyarsk to meet her cousin, Erna's eighty-five-year-old granddaughter Oksana. She had become a mathematics teacher in a village school. Although she has lived all her life among the peasantry, she still retains a certain grace and refinement of language that had been passed on to her by the previous generation. Oksana recalled the family's one-room house with a Russian stove, built by her grandfather, in a village to which they had been forced to move from Likino. It contained beautiful furniture that they had brought with them: a fine wooden desk and chest, a washstand with a mirror, and her grandmother's trunk full of mysterious objects—an ostrich feather, long white kid gloves, and dresses trimmed with lace. When on occasion the trunk was opened, the children would gather around to marvel at the treasures, but no one ever explained to them the vanished world from which those strange remnants of a bygone era had come, nor why they had to be hidden.

There was also a rolled-up canvas. Oksana might have known that it was her grandmother's portrait painted by some vanished relative. But on the parts of the picture of which she managed to get a glimpse, she could not make out any human features—it seemed to be just some random brushstrokes. In the summer of 1918, Magda wrote to Julia that she was painting Erna's portrait. Her sister had sprained her ankle and so, forced into immobility, was willing to pose. And there it was, but there was no story to go with it. There were no stories at all about life before the revolution. It would have been dangerous for the children to know whence they had come from and who their family was.

Oksana also showed us family photographs, about which she knew nothing. In the 1960s, Erna's husband had set fire to most of them: piles of photographs, albums, and handwritten notes, all of it incriminating evidence of the family's background and of having relatives who lived abroad and were therefore a possible subversive influence. And who needed it now, that past life, those people dead and gone and fading from memory, or dispersed to the ends of the earth? Life had become a matter of just getting by. Oksana had a few photographs that had survived her grandfather's bonfire. She showed Sophie a picture of a young woman with two little girls. We could see by their dress that it must have been taken early in the twentieth century. Oksana had no idea who they were. But Sophie knew, and she could date the picture to within a year. The young woman was Sophie's grandmother, Adele, posing with two of her daughters, Klara and Stella, aged about one and three, the older of whom would become Sophie's mother. The third daughter, Irene, had not yet been born. So it must have been taken around 1916 or 1917. But from a letter written in Russian that Theo had sent me, I knew even more. I knew that in 1916, the photograph had been sent to Erna in Likino from Lausanne by her younger sister Adele.

Sophie was in tears. For her, it was a miracle to have encountered, in a far-off Siberian village, a picture of her mother that she had never seen before. Then

Oksana brought out some objects passed down from her grandmother—some linens and napkins that Erna had embroidered, a few silver spoons with her monogram (Sophie has identical spoons with her grandmother's monogram in her London house), a small jam pot, and a silver spoon rest—treasures from her grandmother's trunk that must have seemed as though from another world to a family that had lived a simple peasant life, growing their own vegetables, sawing and splitting their own wood for fuel, and using an outhouse because there was no indoor plumbing. Erna cooked on the Russian stove and sewed clothes for the whole family out of old remnants and cast-off clothing.

Erna's grandson Alexei, whose father had died in the gulag, learned from his grandfather to hunt, fish, and garden. He followed his grandfather and father and became a forester. For many years he was the director of the Stolby Nature Sanctuary, near Krasnoyarsk. He is retired now.

He, too, showed me some family photographs. Who were those people? Some were known, but the identities of many were a mystery. The generation who would have written that this was Uncle Boris or that was Auntie Katya had missed their chance. There was now an unbridgeable gulf between the culture in which the grandparents had been raised and that in which their grandchildren had to live.

Today, a century after the Russian Revolution and the destruction of "bourgeois" culture, some of the forgotten Russian twentieth century is being reclaimed. The school of Russian modernism to which Magda belonged that had been eclipsed first by the Russian avant-garde in the first decades of the twentieth century and then by socialist realism is experiencing a revival similar to that experienced by the Russian avant-garde a few decades ago. Kuzma Petrov-Vodkin, although not shown much during the Soviet period, made his first comeback in the mid-1960s with a major exhibition. But it would be another half-century before artists associated with the Zvantseva school would begin to be properly appreciated. The exhibition *The Circle of Petrov-Vodkin* that opened in the Russian Museum in St. Petersburg in June 2016 was only one among several recent shows devoted to works by those painters whose work had been all but lost. Some of them had died during the Russian Civil War; others had disappeared in the gulag, emigrated, perished in World War II, or had given in to the Soviet regime by changing their style or finding a different creative niche (some became art restoration specialists or worked in theater wardrobe rooms). Their paintings began to surface in the storage rooms of major museums, in private collections, and in the small provincial museums where the Soviet authorities had sent them in the 1920s in a short-lived program of popularizing art.

One of the first among Magda's schoolmates at Zvantseva's academy whose works were recovered from the dustbin of history to which the Soviets had consigned the works of "formalism" was Sergei Kalmykov, an eccentric who left Petersburg soon after the revolution and returned to his native Orenburg, in the southern Urals, a thousand miles to the southeast, and then to Almaty, in Kazakhstan, yet another 1,500 miles southeast. He survived in both cities by playing the village idiot, dressing like a clown, with tin cans attached to his shoulders, and painting openly in the streets for all to see his "crazy" output. Kalmykov died in 1967, and in the 1990s, over a thousand of his paintings were "discovered" in Almaty. Since then, he has had several posthumous solo exhibitions, for which catalogues were issued.

Another solo show that would have been very close to Magda's heart was mounted in spring 2016 in the Grabar All-Russian Art, Scientific and Restoration Center in Moscow. The title of the show was "Returning Forgotten Names: Graphic Works by Julia Obolenskaya." This is how it came about. In 1953, thirty-three works in various media by Obolenskaya were de-accessioned from the archive of the State Literary Museum and given to the Restoration Center to be used as scrap material for testing chemicals used in art restoration. Someone at the center noticed the extraordinary artistic value of that work destined for destruction and stuffed it in a drawer, where it remained in limbo for fifty-six years. Then one day, the center's staff met and decided that the time had come to restore Obolenskaya's work, mount a public exhibition, and then return the restored works of art to the Literary Museum. The show was widely advertised, and the curators were even interviewed on television.

When I came to Moscow in June 2016, Obolenskaya's show had already been taken down and put aside to be packed for transfer. In a controlled-temperature storage room, the young curators showed me the restored pictures, sheet by sheet. They had undertaken a great work of love in giving Julia Obolenskaya her first solo exhibition, seventy-one years after her death.

That spring, there was yet another exhibition of students of Petrov-Vodkin—*The School of Kuzma Petrov-Vodkin*—this time in the Gallery-Galeev, in Moscow. Furthermore, two different major exhibitions of the Zvantseva Academy's founding teacher, Léon Bakst, took place in 2016, the first in the Russian Museum, in St. Petersburg, and another in the Pushkin Museum of Fine Arts, in Moscow. Both exhibitions commemorated the 150th anniversary of Bakst's birth and were the first major shows of this great Russian artist mounted in Russia since the October Revolution.

And finally, as I was completing my book in spring 2018—exactly a hundred years since Natalia Grekova had written to Julia Obolenskaya that Nadezhda Lermontova "need[ed] to organize an exhibition; there [were] many pictures, and all together, they define[d] her as an artist,"[4] an exhibition of works by Lermontova was underway in Moscow. Not much has been preserved: many of her works were lost or destroyed during the Siege of Leningrad. But there is enough to see what a great artist she was.

On June 2, 2016, at the opening of the exhibition in the Russian Museum, descendants of Magda's three sisters stood in front of *Peasant Woman* for a family photograph. There was something poignant and admirable that these people had journeyed from distant places to acknowledge a relative from their common past and that the occasion that brought them together was the rediscovery of an indomitable painter and her art.

But where is Magda's work now? I had roamed the globe in search of her paintings. Out of her large oeuvre I have located only a handful of original works. By all accounts, she exhibited widely. Exhibitions in Russia in which she participated list many titles of her paintings. She had at least one solo exhibition in Berlin, and Nabokov in his review mentioned several titles. Catalogues and reviews of Magda's shows in India mention many titles, and her last show in Bombay exhibited a large number of paintings. Yet I have been able to locate only a handful of pictures in Russia, thirteen pictures in India, two in Israel, seventeen paintings and sketches in Great Britain, and three in the United States.

Magda, where are you?

---

4   August 6/19, 1918 (old and new styles), RGALI, f. 2080, op. 1, no. 24, 96.

Bibliography

ARCHIVAL MATERIAL

Archive of the Tata Institute for Fundamental Research, Mumbai, India.

Archives Nationales, Paris, Institut Français d'Histoire Sociale, E. Armand papers. 14AS/211/1.

Centre d'archives de la Fédération Wallonie, Brussels, Mandyam Acharya, révolutionnaire agitateur indou (200–280).

GLM—State Literature Museum, manuscript division, Collection of Julia Obolenskaya, fond 348.

GTG—State Tretyakov Gallery, manuscript division, Collection of Julia Obolenskaya, fond 5.

Houghton Library, Harvard University, collections of Leon Trotskii and Ruth Fischer, Cambridge, USA.

IOR—India Office Records (includes some War Office records), British Library, UK.

IRLI—Institute of Russian Literature (Pushkin House), Collection of Maximilian Voloshin, 562.

New York Public Library, Berg Collection, Vladimir Nabokov, USA.

The Newberry Library (Chicago). Nicolaas Steelink Collection. Chief Correspondence from 1922 to 1953.

Politisches Archiv, Auswärtiges Amt, vol. R 287476: Abteilung III, Indien Privata, Germany.

Pskov regional archive, Velikie Luki.

RGALI—Russian State Archive of Literature and Art, Collection of Julia Obolenskaya, fond 2080; Collection of Konstantin Kandaurov, fond 769; Collection of E. Ya. Efron, fond 2962.

RGASPI—Russian State Archive of Social and Political History, Collection of Third Communist International (The COMINTERN, fond 495).

Russian Museum, Manuscript Division, Collection of Sofia Dymshits-Tolstaya, fond 100, no. 249.

PUBLICATIONS

Acharya, M. P. T. *Reminiscences of an Indian Revolutionary*. Edited by Bishamber Dayal Yadav. New Delhi: Anmol Publications, 1991.

Acharya, M. P. T. *We Are Anarchists: Essays on Anarchism, Pacifism, and the Indian Independence Movement, 1923–1953*. Edited by Ole Birk Laursen. San Francisco: AK Press, 1996.

Aesthetics 5 (no. 1), 1951. Bombay: Youths' Art and Culture Circle.

Alekseeva, Larisa. *Tsvet vinograda. Iuliia Obolenskaia. Konstantin Kandaurov*. Moscow: AST, 2017.

Ashton, Leigh, ed. *The Art of India and Pakistan*. New York: Coward-McCann Inc., 1947.

Avrich, Paul. *Anarchist Portraits*. New Jersey: Princeton University Press, 1988.

Barooah, Nirode K. *Chatto: The Life and Times of an Indian Anti-Imperialist in Europe*. Oxford: Oxford University Press, 2004.

Bailey, F. M. *Mission to Tashkent*. Oxford: Oxford University Press, 1992.

Bakst, Lev. "Puti klassitsizma v iskusstve." *Apollon* 2 (1909): 63–72 (part 1) and 3 (1909): 46–61 (part 2).

———. "Vystavka v redaktsii Apollona." *Apollon* 8 (1910): 44–45.

———. "Ob iskusstve segodniashnego dnia," *Stolitsa i usad'ba* 8 (1914).

Becker, Seymour. "The 'Great Game': The History of an Evocative Phrase." *Asian Affairs* 43, no. 1 (2012): 61–80.

———. *Russia's Protectorates in Central Asia: Bukara and Khiva, 1865–1924*. London: Routledge Curzon, 2004.

Benua, Aleksandr. "L. S. Bakst. E. E. Lansere." In *Istoriia russkoi zhivopisi v XIX veke*. Moscow: "Respublika," 1999, 410–413.

Bernstein, Lina. "'Umerla v priiute Seriozhina doch' Irina'—Tekst i kontekst." *Toronto Slavic Quarterly* 56 (2016). http://sites.utoronto.ca/tsq/56/Bernstein56.pdf.

Bernstein, Lina and Elena Nekludova. "Kursivnyi shrift epokhi." *Nashe Nasledie* 121–122 (2017): 60–77, 106–131.

Bhabha, Jamshed, ed. *Homi Bhabha as Artist: A Selection of His Paintings, Drawings and Sketches*. Bombay: Marg Publication, 1968.

Bird, Alice (pen name of Agnes Smedley). "The Baltic Sea a British Lake." *Modern Review*, December 1921, 710.

Blank, Stephen. "Soviet Reconquest of Central Asia." In *Central Asia: Its Strategic Importance and Future Prospects*, edited by Hafeez Malik, 39–64. New York: St. Martin's Press, 1994.

Bombay Art Society: Diamond Jubilee, 1888–1948. Bombay: Bombay Art Society Diamond Jubilee Committee, 1949.

Bombay Chronicle, 1947–c. 1954.

Bowlt, John E. *Moscow & St. Peterburg, 1900–1920: Art, Life & Culture*. New York: Vendome Press, 2008.

Boyd, Brian. *Vladimir Nabokov. The Russian Years*. New Jersey: Princeton University Press, 1990.

Budnitskii, Oleg, and Aleksandra Polian. *Russko–evreiskii Berlin, 1920–1941*. Moscow: NLO, 1913.

Chabrier, Edith. "Les délégués au Premier Congrès des peuples d'Orient." *Cahiers du monde russe et soviétique* 26, no. 1 (1985): 21–42.

Chatterji, R. "The Art of Magda Nachman." *Bharat Jyoti*, February 22, 1947.

Chowdhury, Indira. "The Laboratory and Its Double: The Making of the Scientist–Citizen at TIFR." Center for the Advanced Study of India, University of Pennsylvania, Casi Working Paper Series, Number 12–01, June 2012.

Chukovskii, Kornei. *Sobranie sochinenii v 15-ti tomakh*. Vol. 11. Moscow: TERRA–Book Club, 2006.

Clark, Katerina. *Petersburg: Crucible of Cultural Revolution*. Harvard, MA: Harvard University Press, 1995.

Cooper, Homee. *The Chetana Leaflet*. Undated.

Dalmia, Yashodhara. *The Making of Modern Indian Art: The Progressives*. New Delhi: Oxford University Press, 2000.

Dearborn, Mary. *Mistress of Modernism: The Life of Peggy Guggenheim*. Boston: Houghton Mifflin, 2004.

Dobuzhinskii, Mstislav. *Vospominaniia*. Moscow: Nauka, 1987.

Field, Andrew. *Nabokov: His Life in Part*. London: Hamish Hamilton, 1977.

Franz, Margit. "Jewish Representer of the Indian Soul." In *Jews and the Indian National Project*, edited by Kenneth X. Robbins and Marvin Tokayer, 177–192. New Delhi: Niyogi Books, 2015.

Free Press Bulletin, February 14, 1951.

Freidenberg, Ol'ga. "Fragmenty iz memuarov. God 17." *Voprosy literatury* 5 (2017). Publication and annotations by N. Kostenko.

Gandhy, Kekoo, "The Beginnings of the Art Movement." http://www.india-seminar.com/2003/528/528%20kekoo%20gandhy.htm.

Gerasimova, Natal'ia "Magda Nachman i sud'ba ee kartiny." In *Kuzma Petrov-Vodkin i ego shkola*, edited by Ildar Galeev. Moscow: Galeev-Gallery, 2015.

Goldman, Emma. *My Disillusionment in Russia*. New York: Doubleday, Page & Company, 1923.

Goetz, Hermann. "Magda Nachman: A Russian Interpreter of India." *Bulletin of the Baroda Museum and Picture Gallery* 5 (1947–1948): 79–83.

Harrison, Marguerite. *Marooned in Moscow: The Story of an American Woman Imprisoned in Russia*. London: Thornton Butterworth Limited, 1921.

Hopkirk, Peter. *Setting the East Ablaze: Lenin's Dream of an Empire in Asia*. London: John Murray, 1984.

Internationalist (pseudonym of Albert Meltzer). "M. P. T. Acharya." *Freedom* 15, August 14, 1954: 3.

Ivanov, Vladislav. *Russkie sezony teatra Gabima*. Moscow: Akter, rezhisser, teatr, 1999.

Ivanov, Viacheslav, "Legion i Sobornost'." In *Sobranie sochinenii v 4 tomakh*, vol. 3: *Stat'i*. Brussels: Foyer Oriental Chrétien, 1979, 253–261.

Kapur, Geeta. *When Was Modernism: Essays on Contemporary Cultural Practice in India*. New Delhi: Tulika Books, 2000.

Karanth K. S. *Ten Faces of a Crazy Mind. Autobiography*, translated by Sri H. Y. Sharada Prasad. Bombay: Bhatatia Vidya Bhavan, 1993.

Khodasevich, Vladislav. "Knizhnaia palata." In *Literaturnye stat'i i vospominania*, 333–344. New York: Chekhov Publishing House, 1954.

———. "Vtorogo noiabria." In *Sobranie sochinenii*, vol. 1. Moscow: AO "Soglasie," 1996.

Lenin, Vladimir. "Draft Theses on National and Colonial Questions for the Second Congress of the Communist International." In *Collected Works*, vol. 31, translated by Julius Katzer. Moscow: Progress Publishers, 1965.

Lim, Susanna Soojung. *China and Japan in the Russian Imagination, 1685–1922: To the Ends of the Orient*. New York: Routledge, 2015.

Livshits, Benedikt. *Polutoraglazyi strelets*. Leningrad: Sovetskyi pisatel', 1989.

Lukomskii, G. K. (George). "Mir iskusstva." *Zhar-Ptitsa* 1 (1921): 17–18.

Malevich, Kazimir. Editor's note. *Vestnik ispolkoma moskovskikh vysshikh gosudarstvennykh khudozhestvennykh masterskikh* 1 (1920): 1–3.

Maksimovskaia, Liudmila. *Ust'-Dolysskie istorii*. St. Petersburg: Nestor-Istoriia, 2009.

———, ed. "Nevel' v kontse 10-kh–nachale 20-kh gg. XX veka." *Nevel'skii sbornik* 12 (2007): 207–240.

Meltzer, Albert. *I Couldn't Paint Golden Angels: Sixty Years of Commonplace Life and Anarchist Agitation*. San Francisco: AK Press, 1996.

Mitter, Partha. *The Triumph of Modernism: Indian Artists and the Avant-garde 1922–1947*. London: Reaktion Books, 2007.

Molot (twice-weekly newspaper of the Nevel soviet), 1918–1920.

Nabokov, Nicholas. *Bagázh: Memoirs of a Russian Cosmopolitan*. New York: Atheneum, 1975.

Nabokov, Vladimir. *Glory*. New York: McGraw-Hill International, Inc., 1971.

———. *Letters to Véra*. New York: Alfred A. Knopf, 2015.

———. "Vystavka M. Nakhman-Achariia. Galereia Kaspar." *Rul'*, November 1, 1928, 4.

Naipaul, V. S. *India: A Million Mutinies Now*. New York: Viking, 1991.

Nazhivin, I. F. *Zapiski o revoliutsii*. Moscow: Kuchkovo pole, 2016.

Nazarov, Paul. *Hunted through Central Asia*. Oxford: Oxford University Press, 1993.

Obolenskaia, Iuliia. "V shkole Zvantsovoi pod rukovodstvom L. Baksta i M. Dobuzhinskogo." *Toronto Slavic Quarterly* 37 (2011): 209–242. Edited and with a commentary and annotation by Lina Bernstein and Elena Nekludova.

Oesterheld, Joachim. "British Policy towards German-Speaking Emigrants in India, 1939–1945." In *Jewish Exile in India, 1933–1945*, edited by Anil Bhatti and Johannes H. Voigt, 25–44. New Delhi: MANOHAR in association with Max Mueller Bhavan, 1999.

Overstreet, Gene D., and Marshall Windmitter. *Communism in India*. Bombay: Perennial Press, 1960.

Owen, Nicholas. *The British Left and India: Metropolitan Anti-Imperialism, 1885–1947*. New York: Oxford University Press, 2008.

Persits, M. A. *Revoliutsionery Indii v strane Sovetov*. Moscow: Progress, 1983.

Poole, Ernest. *The Village: Russian Impressions*. New York: Macmillan and Co., Limited, 1919.

Prakash, G. *Mumbai Fables*. New Jersey: Princeton University Press, 2010.

Price, Ruth. *The Lives of Agnes Smedley*. Oxford: Oxford University Press, 2005.

Pruzhan, Irina. *Lev Samoilovich Bakst*. Leningrad: Iskusstvo, 1975.

Ramnath, Maia. *Decolonizing Anarchism*. San Francisco: AK Press and the Institute for Anarchist Studies, 2011.

Roy, M. N. *M. N. Roy's Memoirs*. Delhi: Ajanta Publications, 1984.

Repin, Il'ia. "Ob Aleksandre Benua, Obere i prochikh. …" *Birzhevye vedomosti*, November 19, 1911.

———. "Pis'ma Repina Zvantsevoi." In *Mir iskusstv. Almanakh*, vol. 4. St. Petersburg: Dmitrii Bulanin, 2001.

Romanov, A. S. "Inostrannye korrespondenty v Moskve: Otchety gidov-perevodchikov NKID. 1920 g." *Istoricheskii arkhiv* 2 (2009): 119–147.

Rostislavov, Alexander. "Trudoliubie vmesto khudozhestva." *Mir Iskusstva*, no. 1 (1901).

Sabashnikova, Margarita. *Zelenaia zmeia*. Moscow: ENIGMA, 1993.

Schiff, Stacy. *Véra (Mrs. Vladimir Nabokov)*. New York: Random House, 1999.

Shirma, V. G. "Organy upravleniia teatral'nymi organizatsiiami Vitebskoi gubernii v 1917–1924." *Uchenye zapiski* (Vitebsk University) 10 (2010): 109–114.

Schurer, H. "Karl Moor—German Agent and Friend of Lenin." *Journal of Contemporary History* 5, no. 2 (1970): 131–152.

Sheppard, Samuel T. "Bombay City Gazetteer." In *Bombay Place Names and Street Names*. Bombay: The Time Press, 1917.

Shklovskii, Victor. *Sentimental'noe puteshestvie. Vospominaniia 1917–1922*. Moscow: Gelikon, 1923.

Shlegel', Karl. *Berlin, Vostochnyi vokzal.* Moscow: NLO, 2004.

Somov, Konstantin, *Pis'ma E. N. Zvantsevoi.* http://konstantinsomov.ru/let.

Subramanyam, C. S. M. P. T. *ACHARYA: His Life and Times: Revolutionary Trends in the Early Anti-Imperialist Movements in South India and Abroad.* Chennai: Institute of South Indian Studies, 1995.

Terkel', E. (ed.). "Pis'ma I. E. Repina E. N. Zvantsevoi." In *Mir iskusstv. Almanakh*, vol. 4. St. Petersburg: Dmitrii Bulanin, 2001.

Tikhonov, Iurii. *Afghanskaia voina Stalina: Bitva za Tsentral'nuiu Aziiu.* Moscow: Iauza, 2008.

Troianovskii, Konstantin. *Vostok i revoliutsiia (Vostok pri svete revoliutsii).* Moscow: Izdatel'stvo vserossiiskogo tsentral'nogo ispolnitel'nogo komiteta sovetov R., S., K. i K. deputatov, 1918.

Trotskii, Lev. *Problemy kul'tury. Kul'tura perekhodnogo perioda.* Moscow: T8RUGRAM, 2018.

Tsvetaeva, Anastasiia. "Marinin dom." In *Neischerpaemoe*, edited by Stanislav Aidinian. Moscow: Otechestvo, 1992.

Tsvetaeva, Marina. *Neizdannoe. Sem'ia: Istoriia v pis'makh.* Moscow: Ellis Lak, 2012.

———. "Zhivoe o zhivom (Voloshin)." In *Sochineniia. Proza*, vol. 2, 190–254. Moscow: Khudozhestvennaia literatura, 1980.

Tugenkhol'd, Iakov. "V zheleznom tupike," *Severnye zapiski* 7–8 (1915).

Tuli, Nevielle. *The Flamed Mosaic: Indian Contemporary Painting.* New Delhi: HEART and Mapin Publishing, 1997.

Usmani, Shaukat. *Historic Trip of a Revolutionary (Sojourn in the Soviet Union).* New Delhi: Sterling Publishing Private Limited, 1977.

Varlamov, A. N. *Andrei Platonov.* Moscow: Molodaia gvardiia, 2011.

Volin (V. M. Eikhenbaum). "Pis'ma o perezhitom." *Anarkhicheskii Vestnik*, no. 1 (1923): 30–39.

Voloshin, Maximilian. *Sobranie sochinenii*, vol. 12: *Pis'ma 1918–1924.* Moscow: Ellis Lak, 2013.

Williams, Robert C. *Culture in Exile.* Ithaca: Cornell University Press, 1972.

Wullschlager, Jackie. *Chagall: A Biography.* New York: Alfred A. Knopf, 2008.

Zagorodnikova, Tatiana, and P. M. Wastitko, eds. *Russko-indiiskie sviazi, 1900–1917.* Moscow: Russian Academy of Science, 1999.

Index

Patel, Gieve, 209

Patel, Shared, xii, 231

Pavlovsk, 20

People (Indian), 181, 185

Perm, 57

Pestel, Vera, 94–95

Petit, Rutty, (Rati), 237–238, see also
    Gotami, Li

Petras, Charles, 2–3, 239

Petrograd, 75–76, 78, 83, 87–88, 101, 106,
    111, 114, 126, 128–129, 153, 155, see
    also St. Petersburg & Leningrad

Petrov-Vodkin, Kuzma, 32, 51, 63–64,
    73, 78, 90, 251, 255–256

Pets, Maria, 54

Pevsner, Antoine, 188

Plato, 56

Platonov, Andrei, 93–94
    Foundation Pit, The, 94

Plotinus, 56

Pohrille, Irene, 1, 244, 248

Poland, 105

Polenov, Vasily Dmitrievich, 74

Polunin, Vladimir, 7

Pontovich, Eduard, 101

Poole, Ernest, 83, 109n8

Portugal, 144

Post-Impressionism, 32

Potekhin, A., 118
    Ill–Gotten, Ill–Spent, 118

Pound, Ezra, 51

Pra, 71, 73, 77, see also Kirienko-
    Voloshina, Elena

Prague, 2, 194, 203

Prakash, Gyan, 205

Prakhov, Adrian, 43

Pravda, 167

Presnyakov, Valentin I., 115, 138

Price, Ruth, 153, 157n30

Progressive Artists' Group (Bombay),
    16–17, 209, 216

Progressive Writers' Association (India),
    208

Proudhon, Pierre–Joseph, 210

Prüfer, Curt Max, 179, 181, 197

Pumpyansky, Lev, 112

Pundole Art Gallery (Mumbai),
    228–229

Pune, 14n2, 236

Puni, Ivan, 188

Pushkin, A., 67, 118, 123, 128,
    165n14
    Angelo, 118
    Bridegroom, The, 118
    Queen of Spades, 118

Pushkin Museum of Fine Arts
    (Moscow), 256

Rabb Barq, Abdur, 148, 156

Radetsky, F. K., 162n5

Raiba, Abdul Aziz, 18

Rao, Raja, 221

Rao, Shrimati Shanta, 221, 230–231

Raza, H. S., 2n3, 14–15, 18

Red Army, 99, 111, 113, 147, 149–150,
    158, 193

Rech, 48

Reisner, Igor, 157n31, 171, 174, 176,
    181, 187

Rembrandt van Rijn, 37

Repin, Ilya, 31, 45, 48

Reul de, P., 190

Reynolds, Graham, 219

Riga, 2, 20–22, 101, 188

Rimsky-Korsakov, Nikolai, 44
    Scheherezade, 44

Roeder, Klara Emilia Maria von, 20, 165,
    see also Nachman, Klara

Rogozinsky, Vladimir, 69n6, 76

Rostislavov, Alexander, 29, 43, 48

Row, Rampart, 221

Roy, Jamini, 2n2, 206, 219, 232

www.ingramcontent.com/pod-product-compliance
Lightning Source LLC
Chambersburg PA
CBHW071520180526
45171CB00002B/323